Who Was the *Toshav*?

JORAM MAYSHAR
msjoram@huji.ac.il
The Hebrew University, Jerusalem 91905, Israel

The term תושב (*tôšāb*; toshav) appears in the Bible fourteen times, mostly in passages associated with the Holiness Code (H). It is typically interpreted as referring to an alien who resides in a foreign country on a long-term basis. I propose, instead, that it had an economic meaning, referring to "a rent-paying (farming) tenant," that is, someone who cultivates land that he does not own and pays rent to the landlord. In the course of supporting this interpretation, I offer a framework for understanding the social structure envisioned by H and for appreciating H's innovative social aspirations.

The term תושב (*tôšāb*; toshav) appears in the Bible fourteen times, of which ten are in passages associated with the Holiness Code (H), including seven times in Leviticus 25.[1] Yet the question that constitutes the title of this article continues to perplex commentators.[2] The term תושב is often translated by words that

---

[1] Following Israel Knohl (*The Sanctuary of Silence: The Priestly Torah and the Holiness School* [Minneapolis: Fortress, 1995]) and Jacob Milgrom (*Leviticus 23–27: A New Translation with Introduction and Commentary* [AB 3C; New York: Doubleday, 2001]), I associate Exod 12:45 and Num 35:15 with H.

[2] As expressed by Alfred Bertholet, "What the actual difference between *toshav* and *ger* was, is an extraordinarily difficult question. Every scholar has his own idea about it and none is convincing" (*Die Stellung der Israeliten und Juden zu den Fremden* [Freiburg i.B.: J. C. B. Mohr, 1896], 157; my translation). Recent scholars who tackled this issue include Jan Joosten, *People and Land in the Holiness Code: An Exegetical Study of the Ideational Framework of the Law in Leviticus 17–26* (VTSup 67; Leiden: Brill, 1996); Rolf Rendtorff, "The *Gēr* in the Priestly Laws of the Pentateuch," in *Ethnicity and the Bible* (ed. Mark G. Brett; Biblical Interpretation Series 19; Leiden: Brill, 1996); Milgrom, *Leviticus 23–27*; Jean-François Lefebvre, *Le jubilé biblique: Lv 25, Exégèse et Théologie* (OBO 194; Göttingen: Vandenhoeck & Ruprecht, 2003); and several contributors to the volume *The Foreigner and the Law: Perspectives from the Hebrew Bible and the Ancient Near East* (ed. Reinhard Achenbach et al.; Beihefte zur ZABR 16; Wiesbaden: Harrassowitz, 2011). The latter include Achenbach, "*gēr – nåkhrî – tôshāv – zār*: Legal and Sacral Distinctions regarding Foreigners in the Pentateuch," 29–52; Rainer Albertz, "From Aliens to Proselytes: Non-Priestly and Priestly Legislation Concerning Strangers," 53–70; and Christophe Nihan, "Resident Aliens and Natives in the Holiness Legislation," 111–34.

225

emphasize foreignness, such as "foreigner," "stranger," "guest," "alien," or "immigrant"; by words that connote a form of residency, such as "resident," "settler," "dweller," or "lodger"; and mostly by a term that combines these two interpretations: "sojourner." I propose that, at least in H, תושב did not have an ethnic connotation but rather had an *economic* meaning, referring to "a rent-paying (farming) tenant"—someone who cultivates land that he does not own and pays rent to the landlord.³

My arguments in support of this proposal will be (a) exegetical: the proposed interpretation explaining the text better than the existing interpretations (sections II–III); (b) contextual: the extensive incidence of land tenancy in the neighboring countries and the comparability of the social distinctions that are made by H to those prevailing elsewhere in antiquity (section IV); and (c) philological: employing extrabiblical evidence (section V).

I. Preliminary Observations

Apart from the unique, and possibly earliest, case of 1 Kgs 17:1, the term תושב is always paired with another term. Nine times it is paired with גֵּר (*gēr*): Gen 23:4; Lev 25:23, 35, 40, 47, 48; Num 35:15; Ps 39:13; 1 Chr 29:15; and four times with שָׂכִיר (*śākîr*): Exod 12:45; Lev 22:10; 25:6, 40. The word pair גר ותושב has been widely recognized as an instance of hendiadys referring to a single person.⁴ I do not contest this interpretation, but I argue against its standard translation as "resident alien," where תושב is understood as "resident."⁵

---

³ As noted below, 1 Kgs 17:1 and Gen 23:4 are exceptions to this interpretation. Theophile James Meek translated תושב as "serf"—a person defined by his servitude and his inability to leave the land ("The Translation of Ger in the Hexateuch and Its Bearing on the Documentary Hypothesis," *JBL* 49 [1930]: 172–80). Accordingly, Meek presented the תושב's status as inferior to that of the free hireling—in contrast to my interpretation. The term תושב was rendered as "tenant" in at least three English translations: JPS of Lev 22:10; NRSV of Lev 25:23; and NASB of 1 Chr 29:15. Norman C. Habel adopted the NRSV translation of Lev 25:23 (*The Land Is Mine: Six Biblical Land Ideologies* [OBT; Minneapolis: Fortress, 1995], 98). Robert North extended it to Lev 25:35, 40 (but not to vv. 6, 47, 48) (*The Biblical Jubilee ... After Fifty Years* [AnBib 145: Rome: Pontifical Biblical Institute, 2000], 87–91; see below). The term תושב is usually translated in German as *Beisass* or *Halbbürger*, implying a secondary form of residency. Erhard S. Gerstenberger used the term *Pächter* ("tenant") in translating Lev 25:23, 35, 47, but not in the remaining verses of Leviticus (*Leviticus: A Commentary* [trans. Douglas W. Stott; OTL; Louisville: Westminster John Knox, 1996]). He interprets גר ותושב as referring to two individuals—the alien and/or the tenant, rather than as hendiadys.

⁴ In the rabbinic literature גר תושב (without the conjunction) acquired the new meaning of a Gentile who upholds the seven Noahide laws, unlike the convert to Judaism (the גר צדק).

⁵ Joosten does not consider גר ותושב to be hendiadys, proposing that גר "is a juridical term," defining the rights of a free resident alien, while תושב describes a weak and dependent "social

The first difficulty with this standard interpretation is that the term גר in itself refers to a free alien who resides on a long-term basis away from his native country. The גר is thereby distinguished from the foreigner (נָכְרִי [*nokrî*] or בֶּן נֵכָר [*ben nēkār*]), who is also a free alien, but who is perceived to be away from his homeland only temporarily. Indeed, the terms comparable to גר in Akkadian (*ubāru*) and in Greek (μέτοικος) are customarily translated as "resident alien." That is, the long-term residency of the גר away from his ancestral home is an integral element of this designation. This implies that the standard interpretation of גר ותושב as a hendiadys that means resident alien is suspect, since גר on its own already has this exact meaning. This makes the conjunct term תושב redundant rather than a qualifying adjective, as is expected in hendiadys. And if תושב does not qualify גר, why was it incorporated in these nine biblical verses? According to my alternative proposal, גר ותושב is a proper hendiadys that means "alien tenant." Hence, the term תושב in this word pair does describe the גר.[6] In particular, it properly qualifies the גר by excluding the alien hireling.[7]

A second general difficulty is posed by the four cases in which תושב is paired with שכיר. Ezra Zion Melamed suggested that the word pair שכיר ותושב was a hendiadys as well. Jacob Milgrom concurs and argues that the term תושב by itself "is a nonexistent socio-economic entity."[8] Milgrom translates שכיר ותושב as

---

condition: a 'sojourner', one who immigrated from another locality and who must attach himself to a free citizen in order to assume his livelihood" (*People and Land*, 74). Lefebvre suggests that גר ותושב is an immigrant who is a stable resident of a community, living independently but subject to corvée (*Le jubilé biblique*, 244).

[6] In references to an individual who is both a tenant and an alien, it is not evident how to identify the subordinate term. One may as well consider גר to modify תושב, thus excluding the Israelite tenant. Yitzhak Avishur demonstrates that in the Hebrew Bible the order of the terms in a hendiadys can vary and does not establish which one is primary (*Stylistic Studies of Word-Pairs in Biblical and Ancient Semitic Literatures* [AOAT 210; Neukirchen-Vluyn: Neukirchener Verlag, 1984]).

[7] Along with Joosten (*People and Land*, 64), I assume that the meaning of the term גר as designating a resident alien remained unchanged in the various layers of the Torah. In contrast, Achenbach ("*gêr – nåkhrî – tôshav – zâr*"), Albertz ("From Aliens to Proselytes"), and Nihan ("Resident Aliens") posit that the term acquired a more elevated meaning in H. These scholars suggest that the term גר ותושב was designed by H to designate an alien resident with a *lower* status than the גר. Following Bertholet (*Die Stellung der Israeliten und Juden*, 174), Achenbach argues that H perceived the גרים as almost "fully integrated members of the religious community," while the תושבים did not have similar religious rights and obligations (pp. 41, 47–48). Albertz (p. 58) and Nihan (pp. 117–19) posit that the תושב represents a poor and dependent resident alien, while the גר is an economically independent person who might be wealthy. Albertz (p. 58 n. 21) even presumes that, according to H, the גר was entitled to own land.

[8] Melamed, "Two That Are One (En Δia Δyoin) in the Bible" (in Hebrew), *Tarbiz* 16 (1945): 173–89; and Milgrom "The Resident Hireling," in *A Light for Jacob: Studies in the Bible and the Dead Sea Scrolls in Memory of Jacob Shalom Licht* (ed. Yair Hoffman and Frank H. Polak; Jerusalem: Mosad Byalik, 1997); the quotation is from Milgrom, *Leviticus 23–27*, 2187.

"resident hireling" and interprets it as referring to a long-term employee who lives on the landowner's land—like "the California migrant farm worker who receives room and board from his employer"—as distinguished from the day laborer.[9] Even though this interpretation is not widely shared, the customary interpretation that this word pair refers to two types of individuals, a hired hand and an alien sojourner, is also suspect. Since these two categories are simply incompatible, their conjunction makes little sense.

According to my proposed interpretation, the phrase שכיר ותושב refers to two categories of farmers. Both cultivate land that they do not own, and both are the landlord's dependents and may be expected to reside in the landlord's estate. However, the שכיר receives wages, follows instructions, and is typically supervised, whereas the תושב is an unsupervised, independent farmer whose lease contract enables him to cultivate the landlord's land, in return for paying the agreed-upon rent. While the שכיר is servile, the תושב is, in effect, the landlord's partner.[10] Thus, I propose that the word pair שכיר ותושב is in fact a merismus, intended to refer to all free and but economically dependent residents.[11]

The following diagram attempts to encapsulate H's perception of Israelite civil society as a whole. As discussed in section IV below, this conception is essentially similar to that which prevailed in Mesopotamian and Greek societies. It consists of four exclusive broad categories of people, represented by the shaded cells.[12] The free, native Israelite, who is considered a full-fledged citizen (אֶזְרָח [ʾezrāḥ]) is at the top of the hierarchy.[13] At the bottom is the slave, who might be either of Israelite

---

[9] Milgrom, *Leviticus 23–27*, 2221.

[10] Baruch A. Levine translates תושב in Lev 22:10; 25:6, 40 (and only there) as "bound laborer" (*Leviticus* ויקרא: *The Traditional Hebrew Text with the New JPS Translation* [JPS Torah Commentary; Philadelphia: Jewish Publication Society, 1989], 149, 170, 179). He argues that the term is subject to "varying interpretations, according to context," but that it "often designates a foreign 'resident,' a merchant or laborer" (p. 170). He explains that the reference to "bound laborer" may reflect a Mesopotamian form of indenture, indicating "one who was seized in default of debt and then compelled to 'reside' in the home of the creditor until he worked off his obligation" (p. 170; see also 149, 171, 211). Levine thus interprets the שכיר and the תושב as two separate individuals but places the indentured תושב below the hired laborer. Gerstenberger (*Leviticus*, 321, 370, 371) applies Levine's translation of the term תושב in these three verses.

[11] I thank a *JBL* reviewer for pointing this out to me. Thus, the two conjunctions differ: גר ותושב refers to the intersection of the two categories—one who is both גר and תושב; תושב ושכיר refers to the union of the two groups—one who is either a תושב or a שכיר.

[12] This scheme ignores class distinctions among the citizens and conflates three types of distinctions: legal (between free people and slaves), economic (between independent and dependent people), and ethnic-residential (between the native, the foreigner, and the resident alien).

[13] The term אזרח is often translated as "native" or "home-born" (see Joosten, *People and Land*, 35). Following Milgrom (*Leviticus 23–27*, 1949, 2051) and others, I translate it as "citizen." To realize why אזרח could not have been synonymous with native-born, one should note that

or of foreign ethnicity. The foreigner, who is but a temporary resident among the Israelites and is expected to adhere to the ancestral deities, is placed outside the domestic society. But the resident alien (גר), who resides among the Israelites on a long-term basis, is placed within the domestic hierarchy. The resident alien—a status bequeathed from father to offspring—was free but was not a full-fledged citizen. In particular, he was denied the privilege of owning land in perpetuity, a right that was reserved to citizens only. Therefore, a farming resident alien was necessarily dependent on the Israelite landowner and probably lived on his patron's estate.

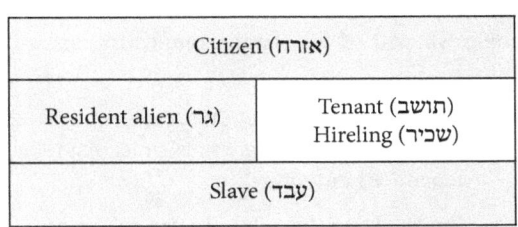

As depicted in the diagram, the גר category (at least those who were employed in farming) naturally subdivides into two exclusive and exhaustive *economic* classes: the rent-paying tenant (תושב) and the wage-receiving hireling (שכיר).[14] I posit that the social status of the hireling was perceived to be inferior to that of the tenant. I presume that H considered all the nonslave Israelites to be "citizens" but recognized that dispossessed Israelite farmers could be tenants or employees, along with the resident aliens. Moreover, given that most resident aliens employed in agriculture were probably tenants rather than hirelings (see section III) and that most tenants were of foreign ethnicity, the close association between the categories of גר and תושב may have led to the use of this word pair as a hendiadys.[15]

Leviticus 25 implies that a native Israelite could be enslaved by a resident alien—in which case he would (apparently) lose his citizenship status. Moreover, the home-born גר could clearly not become an אזרח, while a Jewish returnee from Babylon was considered automatically a citizen.

[14] This might have excluded the urban artisan גר, but it is more likely that the conjunction of שכיר and תושב, when applied to aliens, was indeed a merismus, intending to refer to all the aliens by specifying their two main categories of agricultural employment.

[15] Compare the discussion in section IV of the evolved meaning of the term πάροικος.

II. The Textual Evidence

To test this proposed interpretation against the standard interpretations, I posit a number of criteria. I distinguish between (a) verses pertaining to תושב and שכיר, and (b) verses pertaining to תושב and גר.

(a) Verses with תושב and שכיר

Three criteria distinguish my proposed interpretation from the alternatives that view the word pair תושב and שכיר either as a hendiadys or as pertaining to two people, where the תושב is interpreted noneconomically as a resident, sojourner, or the like.

- (a1) The conjunction תושב ושכיר refers to two different persons and is not a hendiadys; rather, it is a merismus that refers to all free but economically dependent individuals.

- (a2) The שכיר and the תושב are two exhaustive economic categories of farming dependents who are not slaves. When applied to aliens, the conjunction of these two categories is thus a synonym for the generic resident alien (גר).

- (a3) The תושב was perceived to have a superior social status to the שכיר.

For my later analysis of גר ותושב, I will also seek to establish consistency with:

- (a4) An Israelite could be a תושב or a שכיר.

Lev 25:6 provides support for the first three criteria. It instructs landowners on eating the produce of the fallowed land in the sabbatical year:[16]

והיתה שבת הארץ לכם לאכלה לך ולעבדך ולאמתך ולשכירך ולתושבך הגרים עמך.

> And the Sabbath of the land shall be for you to eat—to you, and to your male slave, and to your female slave; and to your employee and to your tenant who reside with you.

The structure of the verse suggests that, just as the male and female slaves are two distinct persons, so are the שכיר and the תושב. The usage of the verb "who reside" (הגרים), which typically describes alien residency, implies that the שכיר and the תושב that are referred to here are aliens. Moreover, since the slave is not referred to as a "resident," the plural form of this verb implies that the שכיר and the תושב

---

[16] All the translations below incorporate my proposed interpretation of תושב.

are two distinct categories of dependents (a1). The placing of the hireling next to the slave fits the hierarchy criterion (a3). Since this directive is evidently not intended to exclude any poor dependent (compare Exod 23:11), one may deduce that these two categories were intended to include *all* the resident aliens (a2).

Exodus 12:43–50 concerns participation by non-Israelites in eating the Passover sacrifice. The foreigner is not allowed to participate in eating this sacrifice (v. 43). An alien slave who is owned by an Israelite should be circumcised and can then participate in the sacrifice (v. 44). The next verse, however, seems to treat the תושב ושכיר just like the foreigner and to forbid them from participation (v. 45):

תושב ושכיר לא יאכל בו.

    The tenant and the employee shall not eat in it.

On the other hand, v. 48 tells us that an alien who resides among the Israelites could participate in the Passover sacrifice, just like the citizen, provided that he is circumcised. This jumble of instructions has perplexed scholars.

Exodus 12:45 is typically interpreted as categorically denying participation of the תושב and the שכיר and, thus, distinguishing them unconditionally from the גר.[17] Yet this makes little sense. I contend that vv. 45 and 48 were intended to complement each other. That is, both verses refer to the entire group of resident aliens, in accordance with criterion (a2). The set of directives in 12:43–50 finds a simple interpretation as referring to the four categories of people in the diagram above: (i) an Israelite (אזרח) has to participate in the Passover sacrifice; (ii) the (foreign) slave of an Israelite has to be circumcised and is then obliged to participate; (iii) foreigners are not entitled to participate; (iv) resident aliens as a rule will not participate (v. 45), but they are entitled to participate if they are circumcised (v. 48). Unlike the slave, the resident alien is not *obliged* to be circumcised; but, unlike the foreigner, he is *entitled* to participate in the Passover sacrifice, conditionally. The interpretation of the conjunction תושב ושכיר in 12:45 as synonymous with גר thus supplies much sense to the entire passage (a2).[18] The listing of the תושב ahead of the שכיר accords also with criterion (a3).

Leviticus 22:10–16 deals with a similar issue of who among the priest's

---

[17] Thus, for example, Christiana van Houten suggests that the גר, the תושב, and the שכיר were three mutually exclusive categories (*The Alien in Israelite Law* [JSOTSup 107; Sheffield: JSOT Press, 1986], 126, 162–63). Nihan discusses others with a similar view ("Resident Aliens," 115–16).

[18] Cornelis Houtman considers תושב ושכיר to be a hendiadys that refers to a single person: "resident alien hired worker" (*Exodus* [4 vols.; Historical Commentary on the Old Testament; Kampen: Kok, 1993–2002], 2:207). But he argues, as I do, that Exod 12:45 "does not embody an absolute ordinance. On condition of circumcision, the hired worker, like any alien, can hold the meal."

dependents is entitled to share in eating the portion of sacrifices that the priest obtains for his own household. Leviticus 22:10 stipulates:

וכל זר לא יאכל קדש תושב כהן ושכיר לא יאכל קדש.

> And all laymen shall not eat the sanctified offering; the priest's tenant and employee shall not eat the sanctified offering.

Leviticus 22:11 explains that in this case, too, the slave is considered to be a member of the immediate household and is entitled to eat the sanctified food, provided that he is circumcised. But all other dependents of the priest are barred from participation. According to Lev 22:12, this includes even the priest's daughter, if she has married a זר—presumably an Israelite layman.[19] That is, this passage denies a share in the sanctified food to *all* of the priest's dependents who are not an integral part of his immediate household. In contrast to Exod 12:43–50, even a circumcised resident alien would not be able to share in consuming the sanctified offering.

The parallelism within Lev 22:10 suggests that the term "all laymen" in v. 10a is comparable to the phrase "the priest's tenant and employee" in v. 10b. This implies that v. 10b refers to more than one person.[20] Moreover, the inclusive appeal to "all laymen" in v. 10a suggests that in referring to the תושב and the שכיר in v. 10b the intention was to include *all* the potential free and dependent laymen in the priest's estate—(a1). Since Israelites (like the priest's son-in-law) are evidently included in the reference to "all laymen" in v. 10a, the terms תושב and שכיר in v. 10b should be interpreted as potentially referring to Israelites as well—(a4). Finally, in accordance with (a3), it is the tenant who is mentioned here first, alongside the priest.

The potential presence of the two types of farming agents in the priest's estate makes economic sense. The priest would be expected to spend time in the temple, from where he obtains the sacrificial food, and would not be expected to work the fields himself. Now, unlike the wage-receiving agricultural worker, who is typically not bound to a particular plot of land, the tenant is under a contractual obligation to cultivate a particular plot of land, at least for the season from sowing to reaping.

---

[19] The word זר (*zār*) appears three times in Lev 22:10–16. Given the reference to the priest's married daughter and other parallels (Exod 29:33; 30:33; Num 1:52; 3:10, 38; 18:4, 7), this term is best interpreted here as referring to any layman, and in Num 17:5 explicitly to one who does not descend from Aaron. There is therefore no basis for Achenbach's assertion that the term זר in H referred to "foreigners, who are not unwillingly integrated as *gerim* into the social-religious community of Israel" ("gēr – nākhrî – tôshav – zār," 45).

[20] The placement of the word "priest" between the two categories strengthens this conclusion. Milgrom states that the compound תושב כהן ושכיר "has bedeviled commentators over the ages" (*Leviticus 17–22: A New Translation with Introduction and Commentary* [AB 3B; New York: Doubleday, 2000], 1861). Adhering to his claim that תושב ושכיר is a hendiadys, he translates this phrase as: "a priest's resident hireling." But this phrase is but a standard case of a combined construct state, where "priest" serves as the genitive for both תושב and שכיר.

This observation can explain why Lev 22:10b refers to the tenant specifically as attached to the priest: "the priest's tenant."[21]

The fourth case that mentions תושב and שכיר is Lev 25:39–40:

39וכי ימוך אחיך עמך ונמכר לך לא תעבד בו עבדת עבד: 40כשכיר כתושב יהיה עמך ...

> And if your brother will be impoverished with you, and was sold to you—do not work him the work of a slave. Like an employee or like a tenant he shall be with you....

The Israelite is instructed to treat a fellow Israelite whom he has purchased for a slave (apparently due to defaulting a debt) as a שכיר or as a תושב—that is, as a legally *free* dependent individual.[22] This verse clearly implies that Israelites could be considered as belonging to these two economic categories (a4).[23] The hired employee is mentioned here first, since the reference point is the slave—in accordance with (a3). Once the hendiadys interpretation is ruled out, the placement of the תושב in tandem with the שכיר confirms that these should be compatible categories: if the שכיר is an economic rather than a civil designation, so must be the תושב—(a2).

(b) Verses with גר and תושב

Three additional criteria are offered to test the interpretation of גר ותושב:

(b1) גר ותושב is a proper hendiadys that refers to a single person: the alien tenant. In particular, תושב qualifies the noun גר by excluding the alien hireling.

---

[21] Joosten notes that in H (unlike in D) the word גר never occurs with a genitive, but that תושב does, as in this case. This suggests to him that the תושב must have been attached "to a free citizen in order to assure his livelihood" (*People and Land*, 74). My somewhat similar interpretation is analogous to the practice in Athens, where the metic (μέτοικος) was perceived to be attached to a particular estate (οἶκος) and to a particular citizen-patron (προστάτης).

[22] I assume that this means that the indentured Israelite has still to repay his debt through unpaid work, but that his legal rights as free person are retained (implying, presumably, that he could not be beaten or sold and would be able to sue his master). North translates Lev 25:40 similarly (*Biblical Jubilee*, 90).

[23] The interrelation between vv. 39–40 and vv. 47–54 is instructive. The latter passage directs Israelites to redeem a brother who was enslaved by an alien tenant. Some commentators interpret this as proof of intended discrimination against the alien slave owner. Yet, since the redeemer had to compensate the alien slave owner in full, Lev 25:47–54 did not infringe much on the slave owner's property rights. In particular, the alien was not denied the right to treat the Israelite slave as his property, unlike the Israelite slave owner (Lev 25:39–40). And yet, while the intention was that the Israelite slave would, in effect, lose the legal status of a slave, slavery among aliens is explicitly permitted.

(b2) As a lease holder, the tenant has ample uses for a slave, and, unlike the hireling, if prosperous, he might be able to afford one. On the other hand, unlike the hireling, the tenant also has contractual obligations to pay the rent and possibly also to pay off loans. If unfortunate, the תושב could thus be indentured, if he failed to meet his obligations.

(b3) The תושב's lease to cultivate the land was temporary, conditional, and revocable.

In analogy to Lev 25:39–40, which was just examined, 25:35 stipulates:

וכי ימוך אחיך ומטה ידו עמך והחזקת בו גר ותושב וחי עמך.

And if your brother shall be impoverished, and stretched his hand to you—you should sustain him as an alien tenant, so that he shall live with you.

Milgrom describes this verse as representing the second of three stages of impoverishment.[24] In the first stage, a distressed Israelite still possesses some real estate. In the second stage, no property is left for sale, but the Israelite is still free and not evidently in debt. In the third stage, examined above (Lev 25:39–40), the Israelite has defaulted already and had become enslaved.

In the second stage, fellow Israelites are called on to help their impoverished brother economically.[25] Commentators who understand גר ותושב as "resident alien" have often been vexed by v. 35: in what way can it be virtuous to treat an impoverished Israelite as a resident alien, and what does it entail altogether? The problem is compounded by noting that in the more dire third stage of impoverishment the destitute Israelite is to be treated "like a שכיר and like a תושב" (v. 40), with no mention of foreign ethnicity. Is it then possible that in the second stage the Israelite is to be treated as a resident alien? The attempts to resolve these problems are many, and rather inadequate.[26]

According to my interpretation of v. 35, the Israelites are called on to offer their propertyless brother employment as a tenant farmer—quite likely on his own

---

[24] Milgrom, *Leviticus 23–27*, 2191–93, 2204–12.

[25] Commentators debate the meaning of the verb והחזקת, which could literally mean "seize him." Adapting Baruch A. Levine, "On the Semantics of Land Tenure in Biblical Literature," in *The Tablet and the Scroll: Near Eastern Studies in Honor of William W. Hallo* (ed. Mark E. Cohen et al.; Bethesda, MD: CDL, 1993), I interpret this verb as a call for taking responsibility, in analogy to its use in reference to individuals who assumed responsibility for repairing segments of Jerusalem's wall in Nehemiah 3.

[26] These difficulties led to a harmonization of the verse in the Syriac by the addition of a negative: "do not hold him as a resident alien." The KJV applies a different solution: "thou shalt relieve him: yea, though he be a stranger," thus extending the clause to impoverished aliens. Following his identification of גר as a juridical term, Joosten suggests that the intention of v. 35 is that the impoverished Israelite "really becomes a *ger*." He explains, "The Israelite who sells his own heritage and leaves it in order to settle elsewhere in the land becomes a *ger* in relation to his 'brother'" (*People and Land*, 71).

seized land.²⁷ This interpretation is in line with the next two verses (vv. 36–37), where the Israelites are told to provide their impoverished brother with interest-free loans. Consistent with criteria (a3) and (b1), whereas in the third stage of destitution the enslaved Israelite is to be elevated to the status of a hired employee or a tenant (v. 40), in this more benign stage, the Israelite is compared *only* to the higher ranked tenant—with no mention of the employee. This interpretation does not explain, though, why the גר was mentioned here to begin with. As noted earlier, given the strong practical correspondence between alien residents and tenants, I propose that the phrase גר ותושב in v. 35 was employed here by H as a generic reference to a farming tenant, without any intended slight (as is verified by Lev 25:23).

The terms גר and תושב are mentioned three times in Lev 25:45, 47:

וגם מבני התושבים הגרים עמכם מהם תקנו וממשפחתם אשר עמכם אשר הולידו בארצכם והיו לכם לאחזה.

And also from among the alien tenants who reside with you; from them you can purchase, and from their families that are with you to which they gave birth in your country; and they shall be to you permanent slaves (Lev 25:45)

וכי תשיג יד גר ותושב עמך ומך אחיך עמו ונמכר לגר תושב עמך ...

And if an alien tenant with you will prosper, and if your brother was impoverished with him, and was sold to an alien tenant with you ... (Lev 25:47)²⁸

These verses concern two cases of enslavement: of an alien tenant to an Israelite (v. 45), and of an Israelite to an alien tenant (v. 47).

Why do these verses consider only the alien tenant and thus, in effect, exclude the alien hireling from being either a potential slave or a potential slave owner? This is explained, I contend, by considerations (b1) and (b2). The tenant, if successful, had a need for a slave and could afford to purchase one (v. 47). The wage earner, in contrast, was not expected either to need a slave or to afford one. At the other end of fortune, the tenant might need loans and had a contractual obligation to pay the rent (in the case of a fixed-rent tenancy). Thus, unlike the wage-earning alien resident, if unfortunate, he could find himself unable to meet his legal obligations and, as a result, could become enslaved (v. 45).

Leviticus 25:23 will be discussed in the next section. The remaining verse of H is Num 35:15:

---

²⁷ Milgrom's interpretation is similar: "Presumably, [an Israelite who forfeited his land] continues to work on his land, not as its owner—he sold it—but as a tenant" (*Leviticus 23–27*, 2207–8). See also North, *Biblical Jubilee*, 11.

²⁸ The noun גר is not explicit in Lev 25:45 but is implied (as in Lev 25:6) by the use of the plural form of the verb גור. The retention of the conjunction between גר and תושב in the LXX, the Samaritan Pentateuch, and the Syriac witnesses indicates that its absence in Lev 25:47b may be due to a late scribal error.

לבני ישראל ולגר ולתושב בתוכם תהיינה שש הערים האלה למקלט.

> To the children of Israel and to the alien tenant amongst them, these six towns shall be for refuge.

According to my interpretation, the alien tenant is granted the right to find refuge in the designated towns, but this right is denied to the low-ranking alien hireling. It is not clear what could have motivated this exclusion, but the possibility that this was intentional is supported by the fact that also the slave was not entitled to find refuge in these towns.[29]

The four remaining attestations of the term תושב are all outside H. Psalm 39:13 and 1 Chr 29:15 adopt the terminology of H (and in particular Lev 25:23).[30] These verses depict the Israelites as alien tenants in order to emphasize their vulnerable hold on the land. The other two cases probably antecede H. In 1 Kgs 17:1, Elijah is described as an inhabitant of a place in the Gilead (אליהו התשבי מתשבי גלעד). This may be the earliest of the fourteen verses. The affinity between מִתֹּשָׁבֵי and Elijah's description as הַתִּשְׁבִּי is perplexing. But it is apparent that תושב was applied here to mean some form of residency, with no economic or ethnic significance.[31]

In Gen 23:4, Abraham appeals to the Hebronites about purchasing a burial plot, describing himself as גר ותושב אנכי עמכם. The episode is usually ascribed to P, which I presume to antecede H. It makes little sense that the author intended to depict Abraham as a farming tenant. The intention was apparently to describe Abraham as a landless alien whose residency depends on a landlord-patron, in conformity with the Akkadian term for a housing tenant (see section IV below).

III. H's Social Vision in Leviticus 25:23

The most significant verse by H that employs the term תושב is Lev 25:23. It purports to provide the rationale for much of H's social-economic legislation:

והארץ לא תמכר לְצְמִתֻת כי לי הארץ כי גרים ותושבים אתם עמדי.

> And the land shall not be sold in perpetuity—for the land is mine; for you are alien tenants with me.

---

[29] Significantly, in Josh 20:9 the city of refuge is described as designed for every alien who resides among the Israelites, without the qualifying adjective about the תושב.

[30] Meir Paran, *Forms of the Priestly Style in the Pentateuch* (in Hebrew; Jerusalem: Magnes, 1989), 244.

[31] Based on the LXX, some commentators suggest that מתשבי refers to Elijah's birthplace and became a variant of תושב as the result of a later corruption (Bertholet, *Die Stellung der Israeliten und Juden*, 156 n. 4).

The identification of the Israelites as tenants (v. 23b) is presented here as a consequence of the land belonging to God (v. 23a).[32] Indeed, the explicit recognition of Israel as Yhwh's (alien) *tenants* reinforces the often recognized idea that this verse envisions a patron–client relation between Yhwh and Israel.[33]

Inasmuch as the Israelites are God's tenants, their hold on the land is thus perceived as fleeting and conditional—like that of the alien tenant. The alternative of viewing תושב in this verse as synonymous with either "alien" or "resident" evidently fails to convey this essential legal-economic aspect of the Israelite's lack of permanent title to their land.

This interpretation of the term תושב in Lev 25:23 enhances our understanding of H's overarching vision of the tripartite interrelation between God, Israel, and the promised land. In particular, it implies that, as aliens, the Israelites could never acquire unconditional title to the land that Yhwh granted them. The conditionality of the Israelites' right to the land is the major theme of Leviticus 26. If the Israelite tenants violated the landlord's instructions, their tenancy grant would be revoked: they would be exiled, and their land would become desolate—though, significantly, it would not be granted to anyone else (26:33).

As God's tenants, the Israelites are also obliged to pay rent. This, indeed, is how many commentators interpret the justification provided in Lev 27:30 for the tithe to the priests and Levites. Significantly, God is perceived to own the entire land *directly*—neither via the king nor via the temple—and to have granted land parcels directly to patrimonial households.[34] Thus, unlike the case of temple land in the neighboring nations, the priests and Levites are perceived only as the landlord's collection agents, without possessing any authority on how the land is to be managed.

This landlord–tenant relationship provides also the rational for additional contractual obligations that the landlord imposes on his tenants: (a) to fallow *his* land in the seventh year (25:2–7); (b) to observe the jubilee law (25:8–17), under which land assignments revert to those who were granted the land initially (25:2); and (c) to enable land redemption in the interim period (25:24–34).

---

[32] Others have already employed the term "tenant" in translating this verse. The NRSV translates, "with me you are but aliens and tenants" (v. 23b). Van Houten (*Alien in Israelite Law*, 124) quotes the NRSV translation but discards its interpretation of who the תושב is. North (*Biblical Jubilee*) provides two alternative translations. In one, v. 23b reads, "and you are but residents (*gerim*) who have become my tenants (*tošabim*)" (p. 33), and in the other: "and ye are tenants and migrant-workers with me" (p. 88).

[33] Habel (*Land Is Mine*, ch. 6) offers the most extensive analysis along this line. This interpretation clearly conforms to criterion (b3). The exclusion of the dependent hireling is also sensible in this case (b1).

[34] This fits H's two-faceted ideology of holiness (see Knohl, *Sanctuary of Silence*, 180–96): *all* the land of Israel is holy, not only the temple precinct; and *all* the people of Israel are holy, not only the priests.

This interpretation of Lev 25:23 carries some further insights concerning the dual terminology employed by H.³⁵ The people described as "aliens tenants" in 25:23 are the Israelites. They are "aliens" and "tenants" in their own promised land only in a virtual sense. Those whom H addresses as alien tenants elsewhere in ch. 25 are actually landless tenants. By employing this terminology, H seeks to put the actual and the virtual alien tenant on equal footing. This conforms to another of H's overarching principles: the civil-law equality of the אזרח and the גר.³⁶

IV. The Social-Economic Context

My presumption is that the pertinent legislation by H was composed in the restoration period and was conceived according to the land tenure system and the related social structure that prevailed in Yehud at the time.³⁷ It is thus imperative to examine that structure in more detail. The evidence about the Israelite economy and society in the restoration period is, however, very sparse. The patrimonial land tenure system that prevailed in the preexilic period is believed to have been disrupted by the exile, and possibly even before that.³⁸ The most pertinent source

---

³⁵ H employs a dual terminology also in the second principle of Leviticus 25, which provides a rationale why Israelites should not be enslaved: "For it is to me that the Israelites are servant-slaves" (25:55). All the Israelites are characterized as God's servant-slaves; but, unlike the real slaves discussed elsewhere in ch. 25, they are only virtual slaves.

³⁶ Significantly, in the motivation for this equality in Lev 19:34, the Israelites are described as having been resident aliens in Egypt, rather than slaves, as in the comparable admonitions in Deuteronomy (5:13–14; 10:19; 16:11–12; 24:21–22).

³⁷ Milgrom (*Leviticus 23–27*) and Joosten (*People and Land*) argue for a preexilic date for H. I adopt the dating suggested by, among others, Christophe Nihan, *From Priestly Torah to Pentateuch: A Study in the Composition of the Book of Leviticus* (FAT 2/25; Tübingen: Mohr Siebeck, 2007). The presumption that the verses that mention תושב and אזרח in H originated in the redaction phase of the Torah may explain why these terms are unique to these passages and to later sources.

³⁸ It is often claimed that the patrimonial land tenure system started to fall apart already in the late monarchic period, with the formation of large estates owned by absentee landlords. Robert North (*Sociology of the Biblical Jubilee* [AnBib 4; Rome: Pontifical Biblical Institute, 1954], 46–55) and Jeffrey A. Fager (*Land Tenure and the Biblical Jubilee: Uncovering Hebrew Ethics through the Sociology of Knowledge* [JSOTSup 155; Sheffield: JSOT Press, 1993]) survey the evidence on the emergence of "latifundisms" and consider whether this may have prompted the composition of Leviticus 25. Walter J. Houston argues that this phenomenon may have been restricted in the preexilic period to the immediate surroundings of Jerusalem and Samaria ("Exit the Oppressed Peasant? Rethinking the Background of Social Criticism in the Prophets," in *Prophecy and Prophets in Ancient Israel: Proceedings of the Oxford Old Testament Seminar* [ed. John Day; Library of Hebrew Bible/Old Testament Studies 531; New York: T&T Clark, 2010], 101–16). H. G. M. Williamson examines the limited evidence on the shifting role of kinship in the postexilic period

on the actual (as distinct from idealized) agrarian situation in Yehud is Neh 5:1–13. According to this dramatic passage, smallholders protested to Nehemiah that they had to pledge their family members and their land in order to obtain food (on credit), and to borrow money to pay taxes.[39]

Given the lack of more detailed documentation on actual land-tenure practices in Yehud, I plan to examine the evidence from Mesopotamia. As well as providing a pertinent perspective for Yehud, Mesopotamia's long-standing economic and social institutions may have served as a model for H. The more relevant region of Mesopotamia for this purpose is the rain-fed north, rather than the river-irrigated southern alluvium. However, our textual evidence about agrarian practices in northern Mesopotamia is mostly from Nuzi in the fifteenth–fourteenth centuries B.C.E., while the evidence from the mid-first millennium B.C.E. comes almost exclusively from lower Mesopotamia. Nuzi's society was divided into three broad classes: the upper class consisted of the nobility and aligned state and temple professionals, all of whom were exempt from state duties; the middle class consisted of free people who were subject to army and state duties; and at the bottom were slaves.[40] The middle class was subdivided into four categories, the lowest of which (below the land-owning peasantry) was named *aššābu*. This category is described by Eva Von Dassow in terms equivalent to my proposed interpretation of the biblical תושב: "This term literally means 'resident' or 'tenant' and the class so denoted apparently comprised people who were indeed residents or tenants on property owned by others, property that they cultivated on behalf of their landlords.... Members of the class designated *aššābu* may have had their own land in the past, but lost it in consequence of debt."[41]

In southern Mesopotamia of the mid-first millennium B.C.E., most of the arable land was owned by institutions (including the temples, the king, and his

---

("The Family in Persian Period Judah: Some Textual Reflections," in *Symbiosis, Symbolism and the Power of the Past: Canaan, Ancient Israel, and Their Neighbors from the Late Bronze Age through Roman Palaestina. Proceedings of the Centennial Symposium, W. F. Albright Institute of Archaeological Research and American Schools of Oriental Research, Jerusalem, May 29–May 31, 2000* [ed. William G. Dever and Seymour Gitin; Winona Lake, IN: Eisenbrauns, 2003], 469–85).

[39] See, most recently, Bob Becking, "Social Consciousness in the Persian Period: The Case of Nehemiah 5," in idem, *Ezra, Nehemiah and the Construction of Early Jewish Identity* (FAT 80; Tübingen: Mohr Siebeck, 2011), 74–84.

[40] This roughly corresponds to the three classes in the Code of Hammurabi: the citizen (*awilum*), the free commoner (*muškēnum*), and the slave (*wardum*).

[41] Von Dassow (*State and Society in the Late Bronze Age: Alalaḫ under the Mittani Empire* [Studies on the Civilization and Culture of Nuzi and the Hurrians 17; Bethesda, MD: CDL, 2008], 354. See also Carlo Zaccagnini, "Proprietà fondiaria e dipendenza rurale nella Mesopotamia settentrionale (XV–XIV secolo A.C.)," *Studi Storici* 3 (1984): 707–9.

beneficiaries) or by major private landlords.⁴² The cities enjoyed a large measure of autonomy and the land of each city's temple was controlled by a popular assembly of free citizens who shared in its income.⁴³ The land of all these large absentee landlords was cultivated by dependent farmers. Aliens constituted a major part of these farmers, ever since the Neo-Assyrian mass deportations into Mesopotamia. Their status was hereditary by the male line; they were free but were not allowed to own land.⁴⁴

Slaves were employed in Mesopotamia mostly as household servants or as craftsmen, and not in agriculture. This is typically explained by the inherent difficulty of supervising farm work.⁴⁵ For the same reason, also wage-earning hired workers were not typically employed in agriculture.⁴⁶ Michael Jursa summarizes, "The urban upper class tended to lease their land to free tenants rather than farm it themselves or with slaves."⁴⁷ This was often done through intermediaries (such as the Murašu or the Egibi families) who subleased the land of the major absentee landlords to lower level lessees. The latter typically subleased it further to the actual cultivators, creating a multilayered system of lease contracts.⁴⁸ Tenant cultivators, thus, played a predominant role in Mesopotamia in the Neo-Babylonian period, as indeed, they had ever since the days of Sumer.⁴⁹ The main Akkadian term for these

⁴² See Michael Jursa, *Aspects of the Economic History of Babylonia in the First Millennium BC: Economic Geography, Economic Mentalities, Agriculture, the Use of Money and the Problem of Economic Growth* (AOAT 377; Münster: Ugarit, 2010) 27, 55–57.

⁴³ Gojko Barjamovic, "Civic Institutions and Self-Government in Southern Mesopotamia in the Mid-First Millennium BC," in *Assyria and Beyond: Studies Presented to Mogens Trolle Larsen* (ed. Jan Gerrit Dercksen; Uitgaven van het Nederlands Instituut voor het Nabije Oosten te Leiden 100; Leiden: Nederlands Instituut voor het Nabije Oosten, 1994). Muhammad A. Dandamaev describes the citizens as potential shareholders ("Babylonian Popular Assemblies in the First Millennium B.C.," *Bulletin of the Canadian Society for Mesopotamian Studies* 30 [1995]: 23–29).

⁴⁴ Muhammad A. Dandamaev, *Slavery in Babylonia: From Nabopolassar to Alexander the Great (626–331 BC)* (trans. Victoria A. Powell; DeKalb: Northern Illinois University Press, 1984), 643–46. Elsewhere Dandamaev summarizes: "Aliens enjoyed no civil rights since they did not possess land within the city's common fund and therefore could not become members of the people's assembly" ("Neo-Babylonian Society and Economy," *CAH* 3.2 [2nd ed.], 257).

⁴⁵ Dandamaev concludes that "slave labor did not play a decisive role in agriculture in Babylonia, … it was used to a very limited extent compared to the labor provided by small landholders and free tenants … slave labor was not able to compete successfully with free labor and proved to be unprofitable" (*Slavery in Babylonia*, 277).

⁴⁶ However, large temple estates were often cultivated by teams of temple personnel and hired farm workers who were recruited mostly from among long-term resident aliens (Dandamaev, *Slavery in Babylonia*, 121–31; Jursa, *Aspects of the Economic History*, 187–89).

⁴⁷ Jursa, *Aspects of the Economic History*, 31. Dandamaev summarizes similarly: "the temples, the king and other large landholders leased out either all or most of their land" (*Slavery in Babylonia*, 50).

⁴⁸ Jursa, *Aspects of the Economic History*, 397.

⁴⁹ Piotr Steinkeller, "The Renting of Fields in Early Mesopotamia and the Development of the Concept of 'Interest' in Sumerian," *JESHO* 24 (1981): 113–45.

farming tenants, *errēšu*, pertained particularly to sharecroppers, whose rent was a fraction of the crop.⁵⁰ Many of the exiled Judeans in Babylon were engaged as such free tenant farmers.⁵¹

In order to widen the perspective, I will briefly consider also evidence from ancient Athens, which, like Israel and northern Mesopotamia, relied on dry farming.⁵² The social structure of Athens in the sixth to the fourth centuries B.C.E. consisted of three broad classes. Full-fledged citizens (πολίτας) were the only ones entitled to own real estate and to participate in the peoples' assembly. At the bottom of the social hierarchy were slaves, mostly captured foreigners but also those indentured for failing to repay debts. In between was a mixed class of people who were not citizens but were nevertheless free. They consisted of freed slaves and, mostly, of resident aliens (μέτοικοι) from neighboring city-states. As in Mesopotamia, the status of the metics was hereditary by the male line, and they were denied the right to own real estate.⁵³

Most land in Athens was privately owned. In the Archaic period, it was usually cultivated by the landowners, often with the help of a few slaves. Owner-operated farms were still common after Solon's reforms, but large estates proliferated. These were typically cultivated by tenant farmers, rather than by hired workers.⁵⁴

The evidence from ancient Mesopotamia and from ancient Greece thus conforms in general to the social structure that was posited in the diagram on p. 229. More specifically: (a) the upper social stratum consisted of free citizens who were the only ones eligible to own land in perpetuity; (b) the lowest strata consisted of slaves, who were typically employed in domestic service or in manufacturing and not in farming; (c) in the middle were mostly free resident aliens, who cultivated land that they did not have the right to own; (d) much land was owned by absentee

---

⁵⁰ See *CAD* 4:304–6; Michael Jursa, "Pacht: C. Neubabylonische Bodenpacht," in *RlA* 10.3/4:172–83; idem, *Neo-Babylonian Legal and Administrative Documents: Typology, Contents, and Archives* (Guides to the Mesopotamian Textual Record 1; Münster: Ugarit, 2005), 25–27.

⁵¹ According to Ran Zadok, "most of the Jews in the Nippur rural area were engaged in agriculture as holders and tenants of small and middle-sized fiefs" (*The Jews in Babylonia during the Chaldean and Achaemenian Periods according to the Babylonian Sources* [Studies in the History of the Jewish People and the Land of Israel 3; Haifa: University of Haifa, 1979], 87–88).

⁵² Given that Egypt's agriculture was based on flood irrigation, its situation was quite different. The land in Egypt belonged, at least in principle, either to the realm or to temple foundations. It was cultivated almost exclusively by tenant-serfs.

⁵³ Moses I. Finley, *The Ancient Economy* (updated ed.; Sather Classical Lectures 43; Berkeley: University of California Press, 1999), 48; and David Whitehead, *The Ideology of the Athenian Metic* (Cambridge: Cambridge Philological Society, 1977). The foreigner (ξένος) was outside this domestic social structure.

⁵⁴ Finley, *Ancient Economy*, 65–67, 73–74. He claims, "Enterprises hiring free men on even a semi-permanent basis are simply not found in the sources" (p. 74). Robin Osborne concludes, "Property leasing is found to be going on a very large scale, involving significant proportions of the total agricultural land in a city" ("Social and Economic Implications of the Leasing of Land and Property in Classical and Hellenistic Greece," *Chiron* 18 [1988]: 323).

landlords and was cultivated predominantly by tenants rather than by slaves or hired workers.

It stands to reason that this was also the social structure in Israel. In particular, the preponderance of farm tenancy throughout the ancient Near East suggests that this form of land tenure was prevalent also in Yehud in the restoration period.[55] Given the clear economic distinction between the rent-paying tenant and the wage-receiving hired worker, it would be highly unlikely that in H's economic legislation the שכיר would have been mentioned repeatedly and the farming tenant ignored altogether.

V. Philological Evidence from Extrabiblical Sources

As noted above, the farming tenant in Nuzi in the mid-second millennium B.C.E. was referred to by the term *aššabu*. This Akkadian term derives from the verb *ašābu* meaning "to sit down" or "to reside"—the cognate of the Hebrew ישב, from which תושב stems—and apparently originated in northern Mesopotamia.[56] Diverse sources from southern Mesopotamia from the Neo-Babylonian period employ the noun *aššābu* [or (w)*aššābu(m)*] to denote a "housing tenant" or a "resident," typically in an urban location.[57] There is thus ample evidence for the use of the Akkadian *aššabu* as an economic term designating a rent-paying lessee.[58]

The extensive evidence from Nuzi on the more specific usage of *aššabu* to denote a farming tenant precedes the presumed date of H by almost a millennium.[59] There is, however, one clear attestation for this specific usage of the term

[55] John S. Kloppenborg provides evidence for such a state of affairs from the Hellenistic period ("The Growth and Impact of Agricultural Tenancy in Jewish Palestine [III BCE–I CE]," *JESHO* 51 [2008]: 31–66).

[56] See *AHw* 3:1480–84, 1488; and Jeremy A. Black, Andrew George, and Nicholas Postgate, *A Concise Dictionary of Akkadian* (2nd corrected printing; SANTAG 5; Wiesbaden: Harrassowitz, 2000), 435–36; hereafter *CDA*.

[57] *CDA* identifies the principal meaning of (w)*aššābu(m)* as "tenant." See also *CAD* A/2:460–61. In one Neo-Babylonian source (*CAD* A/2:462) the term *aššābu* was used for dependent people in the countryside. This reference may have been to tenant farmers who resided in a house provided by the landlord.

[58] Michael Jursa (private communication) concludes that in an urban context *aššābu* refers to "lessees of houses," and in a rural context to "non-landowning strata of the population working on institutional estates."

[59] Earlier scholars relied uncritically on parallels between the social customs in Nuzi and those in the patriarchal narrative in order to date the latter to the mid-second millennium B.C.E. In rejecting this dating methodology, John Van Seters argued that these parallels can be explained in that social customs persisted from the second millennium to the first (*Abraham in History and Tradition* [New Haven: Yale University Press, 1975]). This persistence of social customs implies that one should not reject the possibility that some terminology in Nuzi was adopted by H. Indeed,

from the Neo-Babylonian period. Significantly, while this document (MB 74439) comes from the Sippar temple of Ebabbar (in Babylon), it was recently identified by Jursa as pertaining to the temple's estate by the Ḫābūr river in *northern* Mesopotamia.⁶⁰ In conjunction with the sources from Nuzi, this source indicates that the term *aššabu* for a farming tenant continued to be used in the Neo-Babylonian period and may have been specific to northern Mesopotamia. I conjecture that this term pertained in northern Mesopotamia to a *fixed-rent* tenant, and hence its adoption in southern Mesopotamia for the housing tenant—whose rent is always of the fixed type.⁶¹

Further support for the economic interpretation of תושב as tenant (of a house) is provided by a late-fifth-century B.C.E. usage of the Aramaic term תותב in the Ahiqar document from Elephantine. The pertinent proverb is translated by James M. Lindenberger: "I have carried straw and lifted bran, but there is nothing more lightly than a *totav*."⁶² Following the standard biblical interpretation, Lindenberger translates the term תותב as "foreigner," while A. E. Cowley and others translate it as "sojourner" or "stranger."⁶³ Lindenberger notes that in a Syriac version of

---

the strong affinity of the evidence from Nuzi (and northern Mesopotamia in general) to the Bible may reflect the fundamental similarity between Israel and that (mostly) rain-fed region. The specific institutional affinities that are relevant for this study include landless temples, the predominance of owner-cultivated farming, the perception that land belonged to the king and was granted to patronymic families in return for services to the realm, legal restrictions on the alienation of ancestral land, and periodic proclamation of דרור (*děrôr*; Lev 25:10).

⁶⁰ See Michael Jursa and K. Wagensonner, "The Estates of Šamaš on the Ḫābūr," in *Festschrift for Matthew W. Stolper* (ed. W. Henkelman et al., forthcoming); and Jursa, *Die Landwirtschaft in Sippar in Neubabylonischer Zeit* (AfO 25; Vienna: Institut für Orientalisk der Universität Wien, 1995), 133–34.

⁶¹ According to Bojana Janković, in southern Mesopotamia, an *errēšu* was a sharecropper while an *ikkaru* was a farming tenant with a fixed rental ("Between a Rock and a Hard Place: An Aspect of the Manpower Problem in the Agricultural Sector of Eanna," in *Approaching the Babylonian Economy: Proceedings of the START Project Symposium Held in Vienna, 1–3 July 2004* [ed. Heather D. Baker and Michael Jursa; AOAT 330; Münster: Ugarit, 2005], 174). These two terms repeat in the same meaning in the Mishnah. It distinguishes between the sharecropper אָרִיס (*ʾārîs*, from Akkadian *errēšu*) and the fixed-rent farming tenant חוֹכֵר (*ḥôkēr*). The latter term relates to *Akkār*, which is attested in the Sassanid and early Islamic periods and derives from the Akkadian *ikkaru*. See Michael G. Morony, "Landholding in Seventh-Century Iraq: Late Sasanian and Early Islamic Patterns," in *The Islamic Middle East, 700–1900: Studies in Economic and Social History* (ed. Abraham L. Udovitch; Princeton Studies on the Near East; Princeton: Darwin, 1981), 163.

⁶² Lindenberger, *The Aramaic Proverbs of Ahiqar* (JHNES; Baltimore: Johns Hopkins University Press, 1983), 98–99, 245–346.

⁶³ Cowley, *Aramaic Papyri of the Fifth Century B.C.* (Oxford: Clarendon, 1923), 216 line 112, 223. The paired proverb (line 111 in Cowley) is missing the last word, which presumably corresponded to תותב. But this paired proverb has a close parallel in Prov 27:3 (cf. Sir 22:14–15, *b. B. Bat.* 98b), where that missing word refers to "a fool."

Ahiqar, the ending of the proverb refers to "a man who settles in the house of his father-in-law." He concludes that the intention of the Elephantine proverb was to refer derogatorily to someone of despised status like the resident alien. But, given that the Syriac version refers to a son-in-law, and given that it employs the verb (though not the noun) יתב, which establishes affinity to the Aramaic version, it seems best to posit that תותב in the Aramaic proverb was intended to refer to a freeloading tenant-lodger. The presumed Mesopotamian origin of the story of Ahiqar, and of its Syriac version, suggest that the Aramaic תותב was indeed the equivalent of the Akkadian aššābu, and that it had the meaning of a lessee. Given that the Aramaic תותב is the cognate of the Hebrew תושב, this supports both the proposed Akkadian etymology of the biblical term and its economic interpretation.

The Akkadian and Aramaic evidence therefore suggests that the term תושב had an economic meaning that was unrelated to alien ethnicity, and that it conveyed economic dependence in some form of tenancy. I presume that this is how the term was employed in Genesis 23, and that the subsequent legislation by H in the restoration period adapted the terminology of Genesis 23 and applied it more specifically to farm tenancy, employing the term's meaning in northern Mesopotamia.[64] However, it is quite likely that this Hebrew term was employed in reference to tenancy only in literary circles. Its economic meaning may thus have been lost by the time of the Septuagint translation of the Pentateuch in Alexandria, when economic activity switched entirely to Aramaic or Greek.

The LXX translators typically rendered the biblical תושב with the term πάροικος.[65] The contention that they no longer understood the intended meaning

---

[64] Jursa's identification of the error in the common presumption that there was a canal named Ḫābūr by Sippar implies that the prophet Ezekiel resided probably in northern Mesopotamia ("Estates"). Given the apparent dependence of H on Ezekiel, this may provide a possible clue to why H adopted such northern terminology.

[65] Genesis 23:4 and Ps 39:12 provide the two exceptions. In these verses, where the subjects are Abraham and David, respectively, the translators employed the term παρεπίδημος (someone attached to the δῆμος, an immigrant) and used πάροικος (instead of προσήλυτος) to translate גר, so as to avoid identifying either Abraham or David as a convert. Interestingly, the term πάροικος appears once in the book of Judith. The KJV translates Jdt 4:10: "Both they, and their wives, and their children, and their cattle, and every stranger [πάροικοι] and hireling, and their servants bought with money, put sackcloth upon their loins." The list of dependents in this verse is highly reminiscent of the biblical verses examined above. In his attempt to reconstruct the original Hebrew text, Yehoshua M. Grintz renders the beginning of this verse as: הם ונשיהם וטפם, ובהמתם וכל תושב ושכיר ועבד מקנת כסף ... (Sefer Yehudith [in Hebrew; 1957; repr., Jerusalem: Bialik Institute, 1986]). If correct, this would provide another example where my proposed economic interpretation of the תושב makes better sense than the KJV alternative. The economic dependents—the tenant, the hireling, and the slave—are listed here according to my proposed social hierarchy. This reconstruction would be pertinent if Judith was indeed composed originally in Hebrew, as several scholars maintain, and if its author still understood the economic meaning of the term. The latter presupposition would gain standing if one accepts the opinion of Grintz and

of this biblical term is but a variant of a well-recognized claim that is well illustrated by the mistranslations of the related terms גר and זר. Even though the term גר was used in the Hebrew Bible consistently for resident aliens, the LXX translated it mostly as referring to a convert (προσήλυτος). Similarly, even in places where זר was evidently intended for an Israelite laymen (Exod 29:33; Lev 22:10–13), the LXX translated it as equivalent to a foreigner (compare Exod 12:43; Lev 22:35).

The term πάροικος, which the LXX employed to translate תושב was applied in Greek sources of the late Hellenistic period to the resident alien, instead of the previous term μέτοικος, which fell into disuse.[66] At that stage, the term πάροικος seems to have had only an ethnic dimension, without any economic meaning. As a highly pertinent postscript on the vicissitude of terminology, it is instructive to note that in the late Byzantine period (in the tenth century C.E.), this term resurfaced as a synonym for the tenant farmer, having lost entirely its older ethnic dimension.[67] In analogy to my interpretation of Lev 25:35, one may speculate that this happened because at some intermediate stage there was a high correspondence between farm tenancy and alien ethnicity; after many generations that blurred internal ethnic distinctions, the term ended up referring solely to farm tenants.

VI. Conclusion

My proposed economic interpretation of the term תושב in the legal writings associated with H is supported by diverse considerations and resolves several important textual difficulties. In pursuing this objective, I offered a framework for understanding H's social perceptions as based on the social structure that prevailed in (northern) Mesopotamia. However, it is evident that H did not seek to reproduce the Mesopotamian social structure but was meticulously bent on reforming it—in line with Israel Knohl's proposal that H "offers a comprehensive social reform."[68]

The present analysis clarifies key components of the social reform that was envisioned by H. Thus, according to Lev 25:39, an indentured Israelite is to be treated like an employee or a tenant, retaining his legal status as free person. The perception of the Israelites as tenants in Lev 25:23 is designed to secure equality in the long run, by prohibiting the distress sale of land in perpetuity, beyond the jubilee year. Moreover, it is apparent that the Holiness School aimed to integrate the resident aliens. Beyond the repeated calls for equating the legal status of the גר

---

a minority of scholars that Judith dates to the late Persian period, instead of the prevailing consensus of a second-century B.C.E. provenance.

[66] H. Schaefer, "Paroikoi," PW 18.4:1695–1707.

[67] Paul Lemerle, *The Agrarian History of Byzantium from the Origins to the Twelfth Century: The Sources and Problems* (trans. Gearóid Mac Nincaill; Galway: Galway University Press, 1979).

[68] Knohl, *Sanctuary of Silence*, 217.

and the citizen (אזרח), the proposed interpretation of Exod 12:43–49 reveals that H sought to integrate the גר religiously—foreshadowing the subsequently developed institution of conversion. Thus, on the condition of voluntary circumcision, the גר is provided with the option to participate in the Israelite religious festivals.

These legal reforms may seem wanting from a modern humanitarian perspective. But they amount to a radical advance in that direction from the norms that prevailed in the ancient world, and even from the relatively benign norms in the Deuteronomic social legislation.

Two Clearings of Goats (1 Kings 20:27): An Interpretation Supported by an Akkadian Parallel

AMITAI BARUCHI-UNNA
abaruchi@huji.ac.il
The Hebrew University of Jerusalem, Jerusalem 91905, Israel

Supported by an Akkadian parallel, a new rendering of 1 Kgs 20:27b is suggested: "The Israelites encamped opposite them (covering) an area of the size of two clearings of goats, while Aram filled the land."

Context leaves little doubt that the Hebrew כשני חשפי עזים, "like two ḥśps of goats" (1 Kgs 20:27), describing the camp of the sons of Israel as opposed to "Aram filled the land," means to illustrate the meager size of the Israelite army. A question does arise, however, concerning the literal meaning of the noun חשיף, which occurs in its construct plural form in this phrase. The root חשף is documented in the Hebrew Bible in eleven verbal and two nominal occurrences and can be confidently understood as meaning "exposure, bareness."[1] The nouns of the pattern *qatīl* can be "adjectives used substantively with a passive meaning to denote duration in state."[2] Hence, the expected meaning of the word חשיף may be "something that had been exposed." The construction with the noun "goats" may therefore mean "something that had been exposed by goats," probably a piece of land.

This reading was adopted by Yehuda Kiel, who interpreted the whole phrase

---

I would like to thank Professor Mordechai Cogan for his helpful comments on a draft of this article and Dr. Eran Viezel, with whom I discussed its realistic aspects.

[1] See already Menaḥem Ibn Saruq, *Maḥberet Menaḥem* (in Hebrew; London: Ḥevrat Meʿorere Nirdamim, 1854), 96; and also BDB, 362, s.v. חשׂף. Taking חשׂפי as equivalent of Arabic حشف (ḥšf) "to contract (the eyelids)" (hence: חשיף is "handful, little flock"; see *HALOT* 1:359) requires a further emendation of the Hebrew into חשפי. For this emendation, cf. James A. Montgomery, *A Critical and Exegetical Commentary on the Books of Kings* (ed. Henry Snyder Gehman; ICC; Edinburgh: T&T Clark, 1951), 329.

[2] GKC §84l; Joüon §88Eb. See also Joshua Fox, *Semitic Noun Patterns* (HSS 52; Winona Lake, IN: Eisenbrauns, 2003), 192–94. For example: נשיא (a chief, one lifted up) from נשא (*qal*: "to lift"); חליל (a pipe) from חלל (*qal*: "to pierce").

as an imprecise measure of land: "the land that two flocks of goat may 'expose' (= uncover), that is: 'lick' (cf. Num 22:4), within one day."³ He supported this reading by pointing to a similar imprecise measure of land: "within a half of an area, which a yoke of oxen might plow (in a day?)" (כבחצי מענה צמד שדה; 1 Sam 14:14).

This interpretative direction should, however, be fine-tuned in accord with the behavior of goats in reality. Goats tend to be dispersed in the pasture, typically leaving no clearings behind. An area exposed by goats that can be used as an imprecise measure of land would therefore probably relate to the bare area left when a temporary goat enclosure built by herders was moved away. Intensively trampled and covered with a coat of dung, such a piece of land remained cleared of vegetation for a significant period and was surely a part of the pastoral landscape.

A similar understanding seems to be behind the Aramaic translation of 1 Kgs 20:27, כתרי גזרי עזין, with the noun גזרא understood as derived either from the word גדר ("fence")—hence "sheepfolds,"⁴ which is poorly documented—or from the root גזר ("to cut"), whose existence in Aramaic is better documented.⁵ If one accepts the latter, the Aramaic translation can be rendered "something that is cut by goats," probably the grass covering a piece of land.

Other translations, such as "younger goat," which is supported by the Septuagint,⁶ and the most common "little flock,"⁷ have no satisfying etymology. While the translation "exposed (flocks of) goats"⁸ is in accord with the meaning of the root חשׂף, it nevertheless contrasts the unprotected Israelites to the numerous Arameans, which seems to miss the main feature of opposition of the two parties.

Indicating the extent of an area and emphasizing its unexpected smallness by means of equating it with an area that suffices for goats is found also in Akkadian literature. A central motif in "The Legend of Etana" is the eagle carrying the hero to heaven. Their elevation from the land is illustrated by descriptions of the reduction in size of certain components of the landscape, introduced by means of a dialogue between Etana and the eagle. According to one of the later versions,

---

[3] Kiel, *Sefer Melachim* (in Hebrew; Daʿat Miqra; Jerusalem: Mossad Harav Kook, 1989), 404.

[4] See Qimḥi on 1 Kgs 20:27; and also Jastrow, 232, s.v. גזרא, גיזרא I.

[5] Jastrow, 232, s.v. גזרא, גיזרא II.

[6] E.g., NEB: "They seemed no better than a pair of new-born kids." See Montgomery, *Critical and Exegetical Commentary*, 328–29; Joseph Robinson, *First Book of Kings* (CBC; Cambridge: Cambridge University Press, 1972), 230.

[7] See, e.g., BDB, 362; *HALOT* 1:359; *DCH* 3:325 ("little flock"); NIV; NRSV; KJV ("little flocks of kids"); (N)JB ("herd"); Karl Friedrich Keil and Franz Delitzsch, *Commentary on the Old Testament*, vol. 3, *I & II Kings, I & II Chronicles, Ezra, Nehemiah* (trans. James Martin; Grand Rapids: Eerdmans, 1973), 265 ("two little separate flocks of goats"); Paul R. House, *1, 2 Kings* (NAC; Nashville: Broadman & Holman, 1995), 227; Jerome T. Walsh, *1 Kings* (Berit Olam; Collegeville, MN: Liturgical Press, 1996), 305; Simon J. De Vries, *1 Kings* (WBC 12; Waco: Word, 1985), 242 ("little bunch").

[8] Mordechai Cogan, *I Kings: A New Translation with Introduction and Commentary* (AB 10; New York: Doubleday, 2004), 461, 467.

following an elevation of one *bēru* (ca. 10,800 meters), the bird asked the hero what the land looked like, and the man answered that the land had become a fifth, and that "the wide sea is as (small as) an animal enclosure" (*tâmtu rapaštu mala tarbaṣi*).⁹ Obviously, this object was chosen to illustrate the smallness of the sea when looked at from above, as opposed to the description of its wideness in the first part of the sentence. Similarly, in 1 Kgs 20:27, "an area of two pieces of land that goats expose" is in contrast to the following phrase according to which "Aram filled the land." The Akkadian parallel adds support for Kiel's overlooked interpretation. My suggested translation, then, is, "The Israelites encamped opposite them (covering) an area of the size of two clearings of goats, while Aram filled the land."

⁹See J. V. Kinnier Wilson, *The Legend of Etana* (Warminster: Aris & Phillips, 1985), 116 IV/C 33; Claudio Sapporetti, *Etana* (Palermo: Sellerio, 1990), 110 ("stazzo"); Michael Haul, *Das Etana-Epos: Ein Mythos von der Himmelfahrt des Königs von Kiš* (Göttinger Arbeitshefte zur altorientalischen Literatur 1; Göttingen: Seminar für Keilschriftforschung, 2000), 196 ("Viehhürde"). See also *CAD* T, 220, s.v. *tarbaṣu* 1a3´c´; *AHw*, 1327–28, s.v. *tarba/āṣu*.

SBL New and Recent Titles

THE KING JAMES VERSION AT 400
Assessing Its Genius as Bible Translation and Its Literary Influence
David G. Burke, John F. Kutsko, and Philip H. Towner, editors
Paper $61.95, 978-1-58983-798-0   580 pages, 2013   Code: 061126
Hardcover $81.95, 978-1-58983-800-0   E-book $61.95, 978-1-58983-799-7
Biblical Scholarship in North America 26

A USER'S GUIDE TO THE NESTLE-ALAND 28 GREEK NEW TESTAMENT
David Trobisch
Paper $12.95, 978-1-58983-934-2   80 pages, 2013   Code: 069205
Hardcover $25.95, 978-1-58983-936-6   E-book $12.95, 978-1-58983-935-9
Text-Critical Studies 9

THE BIBLE AS CHRISTIAN SCRIPTURE
The Work of Brevard S. Childs
Christopher R. Seitz, editor
Paper $41.95, 978-1-58983-713-3   348 pages, 2013   Code: 061125
Hardcover $56.95, 978-1-58983-884-0   E-book $41.95, 978-1-58983-714-0
Biblical Scholarship in North America 25

THE KINGDOMS OF ISRAEL AND JUDAH IN THE EIGHTH AND SEVENTH CENTURIES B.C.E.
Antoon Schoors, Translated by Michael Lesley
Paper $35.95, 978-1-58983-264-0   316 pages, 2013   Code: 063205P
Hardcover $50.95, 978-1-58983-764-5   E-book $35.95, 978-1-58983-671-6
Biblical Encyclopedia 5

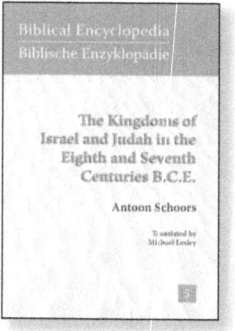

TEXTUAL HISTORY AND THE RECEPTION OF SCRIPTURE IN EARLY CHRISTIANITY
TEXTGESCHICHTE UND SCHRIFTREZEPTION IM FRÜHEN CHRISTENTUM
Johannes de Vries and Martin Karrer, editors
Paper $54.95, 978-1-58983-904-5   448 pages, 2013   Code: 060460
Hardcover $74.95, 978-1-58983-906-9   E-book $54.95, 978-1-58983-905-2
Septuagint and Cognate Studies 60

Society of Biblical Literature • P.O. Box 2243 • Williston, VT 05495-2243
Phone: 877-725-3334 (toll-free) or 802-864-6185 • Fax: 802-864-7626
Order online at www.sbl-site.org

Satan, Yhwh's Executioner

RYAN E. STOKES
rstokes@swbts.edu
Southwestern Baptist Theological Seminary, Fort Worth, TX 76122

In recent decades, scholars have taken great care not to assume that "the śāṭān" of Job 1–2 and of Zechariah 3 is supposed to be the archenemy of God and the opponent of good, as is Satan in later Jewish and Christian literature. Nevertheless, scholars have yet to eliminate anachronistic assumptions from their discussions of this figure as he is presented in the Hebrew Scriptures, maintaining that the śāṭān in Job and Zechariah holds the office of heavenly "prosecuting attorney" or "accuser." After surveying the uses of the noun שָׂטָן and the verb שָׂטַן in the Hebrew Scriptures, this article argues that these words never denote "accusation" in this literature but refer exclusively to physical "attack." This article further contends that in legal contexts the noun שָׂטָן can refer specifically to an "executioner" and that "the Executioner" is the proper understanding of הַשָּׂטָן in Zechariah and Job.

Then I heard a loud voice in heaven, proclaiming, "Now have come the salvation and the power and the kingdom of our God and the authority of his Messiah, for the accuser of our comrades has been thrown down, who accuses them day and night before our God. (Rev 12:10)[1]

Who is Satan? What does Satan do? According to popular imagination and centuries of Christian theology, Satan is the archenemy of God, the opponent of all that is good; Satan does evil. Bible scholars, to their credit, now recognize that the biblical authors conceived of the nature and activity of this figure somewhat differently from later theologians. According to the present scholarly consensus, the early literature portrays Satan (or *the śāṭān*, הַשָּׂטָן, as he is referred to in the Hebrew Scriptures) as "the Adversary," or, more specifically, "the Accuser."[2] He serves God

---

[1] English translations of the Bible in this article will follow the NRSV, except that the noun שָׂטָן will occasionally be transliterated as śāṭān rather than translated, and הַשָּׂטָן will be rendered "the śāṭān." Any other deviations from the NRSV will be noted as they occur.

[2] See, e.g., Gerhard von Rad and Werner Foerster, "διαβάλλω, διάβολος," TDNT 2:73–75 (von Rad); T. H. Gaster, "Satan," IDB 4:224–25; Peggy L. Day, *An Adversary in Heaven: śāṭān in the Hebrew Bible* (HSM 43; Atlanta: Scholars Press, 1988), 25–43; Victor P. Hamilton, "Satan," ABD 5:985–86; Bruce Baloian, "שָׂטַן," NIDOTTE 3:1231; C. Breytenbach and P. L. Day, "Satan שטן

as a sort of prosecuting attorney in the heavenly court. This conception of the early *śāṭān* tradition is based on an understanding of the Hebrew root שׂטן, which appears both in the nominal form שָׂטָן and as the verb שָׂטַן.³ The noun שָׂטָן is typically taken to mean "adversary" or "accuser." The verb שָׂטַן likewise is understood to refer to acts of "opposition" or "accusation."⁴ If the standard translations of these words are correct, then so is the scholarly consensus that the *śāṭān* of the Hebrew Scriptures is the Adversary or the Accuser.

In this article, however, I contend that scholars have misunderstood the words שָׂטָן and שָׂטַן. Although near the end of the first century C.E. John would speak of Satan as "the Accuser [ὁ κατήγωρ] of our comrades" (Rev 12:10), there is virtually no evidence that either שָׂטָן or שָׂטַן ever refers to accusation in the Bible. Instead, these words denote physical attack. The noun שָׂטָן should be translated "attacker," and in some legal contexts "executioner." The title הַשָּׂטָן in the Hebrew Scriptures, therefore, should be understood as "the Attacker" or, more likely, "the Executioner."

This study consists of four main parts. (1) I will begin by establishing the semantic range of the noun שָׂטָן as it is used in narrative texts, since the literary contexts provided by these narratives leave little room for doubt as to what the word denotes. (2) Next, I will look at both the noun שָׂטָן and the verb שָׂטַן in the book of Psalms, where their meaning, though not entirely unclear, is slightly more elusive than in the narratives. Psalm 109, which contains four occurrences of the root שׂטן and is often cited in conjunction with Zechariah 3, will require special attention. (3) In light of the preceding semantic analysis, I will examine the nature and activity of "the *śāṭān*" in Zechariah 3. (4) Finally, "the *śāṭān*" of Job 1–2 will be considered. Some brief concluding remarks and a short excursus dealing with the noun שִׂטְנָה will bring the article to a close.⁵

Σατάν, Σατανᾶς," *DDD* (2nd ed.), 726–32; J. H. Walton, "Satan," *Dictionary of the Old Testament: Wisdom, Poetry and Writings* (ed. Tremper Longman III and Peter Enns; Downers Grove, IL: IVP Academic, 2008), 714–15; Chad T. Pierce, "Satan and Related Figures," *The Eerdmans Dictionary of Early Judaism* (ed. John J. Collins and Daniel C. Harlow; Grand Rapids: Eerdmans, 2010), 1196–97. Exceptional is the viewpoint articulated by Friedrich Horst, that the idea of Satan as "the Accuser" does not appear in the Hebrew Scriptures but arises in the postbiblical period (*Hiob* [BKAT 16; Neukirchen-Vluyn: Neukirchener Verlag, 1968], 1:13–14). See also G. Wanke, who says that שָׂטָן does not refer to "accusers" but merely to "opponents in legal matters" ("שָׂטָן *śāṭān* adversary," *TLOT* 3:1268–69). Similarly, although Nielsen acknowledges that שָׂטָן can denote a specifically legal kind of opposition, she stops short of saying that the word can mean "accuser" ("שָׂטָן *śāṭān*; שָׂטַן *śāṭan*; שָׂטַם *śāṭam*," *TDOT* 14:73–77).

³ In this article, I employ the Hebrew script שָׂטָן when speaking of the word itself but make use of the transliteration *śāṭān* to designate the figure to whom the word refers.

⁴ In addition to the works cited in n. 2, see, e.g., *HALOT*, 1316–17, s.vv. שׂטן, שָׂטָן.

⁵ The root שׂטם, although it will not be dealt with in this article, is also sometimes discussed in conjunction with שׂטן. The root שׂטם can be seen in the verb שָׂטַם (Gen 27:41; 49:23; 50:15; Job 16:9; 30:21; Ps 55:4 [3]) and in the noun מַשְׂטֵמָה (Hos 9:7, 8), which *HALOT* defines in terms of "enmity," "hostility," or "persecution" (pp. 640–41, 1316).

I. שָׂטָן IN NARRATIVE TEXTS

שָׂטָן in Biblical Hebrew can be used with reference either to a human or to a superhuman being, and its particular nuance can vary depending on the context in which it occurs. Generally speaking, the translation of שָׂטָן as "adversary" or "opponent" is not altogether incorrect. This translation does, however, lack precision. שָׂטָן in the Hebrew Scriptures denotes not opposition or adversity generically, but specifically violent, physical attack. This attack is at times of a military kind and is often, if not exclusively, supposed to be lethal. This meaning can be observed in 1 Sam 29:4.

> But the commanders of the Philistines were angry with him; and the commanders of the Philistines said to him, "Send the man back, so that he may return to the place that you have assigned to him; he shall not go down with us to battle, or else he may become a śāṭān to us in the battle. For how could this fellow reconcile himself to his lord? Would it not be with the heads of the men here?

In this passage, the Philistines with whom David has aligned himself express fear that the famed Israelite warrior might turn on them in the midst of battle and become a śāṭān to them, slaying the Philistine soldiers in order to ingratiate himself with Saul. A similar use of שָׂטָן is found in 1 Kgs 5:18 [Eng. 5:4], which describes the early part of Solomon's reign as a period of peace in which there was "neither śāṭān nor misfortune." David was unable to build the temple because his reign was occupied with securing the land. Solomon, on the other hand, unthreatened militarily by any śāṭān, is in a position to build the temple. Later on in Solomon's reign, on account of the king's involvement with the worship of foreign gods, Yhwh raises up Hadad the Edomite and a marauder by the name of Rezon as "śāṭāns," foreigners who attack Solomon and Israel.[6]

A technical, legal usage of the noun שָׂטָן can be observed in 2 Sam 19:22–24 [Eng. 21–23]. As David is returning to Jerusalem following Absalom's failed coup, he encounters the Benjaminite Shimei. At their previous meeting, as David was fleeing Jerusalem on account of Absalom's revolt, Shimei cursed David and hurled stones at him. Fearful for his life now that David is being restored to the throne, Shimei hurries to meet the soon-to-be-reinstated king and to beg him for mercy. But Abishai, one of David's commanders, is not swayed by Shimei's plea for pardon. Abishai calls for the Benjaminite's life: "Shall not Shimei be put to death for this, because he cursed the Lord's anointed" (19:22)? David responds to Abishai's demand for Shimei's execution as follows: "What have I to do with you, you sons of Zeruiah, that you should today become my śāṭān? Shall anyone be put to death in Israel this day" (2 Sam 19:23)?[7] This passage is consistent with the others we have

---

[6] See 1 Kgs 11:14, 23, 25. Gerhard von Rad's argument that Hadad and Rezon are "accusers" of Israel is not persuasive ("διαβάλλω, διάβολος: The OT View of Satan," *TDNT* 2:73).

[7] The words "that you should today become my śāṭān" in this verse translate the Hebrew

considered up to this point, in that שָׂטָן seems to refer to physical attack. Given the context, in which Shimei's crime would justify his being put to death, "executioner" would be an appropriate translation of שָׂטָן in this verse.[8]

Conversely, Peggy Day contends that שָׂטָן in 2 Sam 19:23 is used in a forensic sense, meaning "accuser."[9] "Accuser," however, is far less compelling as a translation of שָׂטָן in 2 Samuel 19 than is "attacker" or "executioner" for several reasons:

1. Abishai is not, correctly speaking, an "accuser" in this passage, but is one who would execute Shimei for his treason. Shimei's guilt is not in question, so no prosecution is necessary for establishing his guilt. What is in question, given Shimei's guilt, is whether he will die for his crime. Abishai calls for Shimei to be put to death. David responds to Abishai's suggestion with two related rhetorical questions: "What have I to do with you, you sons of Zeruiah, that you should today become my śāṭān?" and "Shall anyone be put to death in Israel this day?" David then assures Shimei of the answer to these questions; Shimei will not die. Abishai's speech in this passage should be understood in light of his speech at an earllier point in the narrative, when David first encountered Shimei, who cursed and threw stones at the deposed king. At that time, Abishai offered David his services as executioner, "Why should this dead dog curse my lord the king? Let me go over and take off his head" (2 Sam 16:9). As in the earlier meeting of David and Shimei, Abishai is not so much an accuser as a willing executioner.

2. This understanding of Abishai's role in this passage and of the label śāṭān is further supported by the fact that David rebukes not Abishai alone but the "sons of Zeruiah." Abishai's brother Joab does not "accuse" Shimei in this passage. In fact, Joab is not said to be involved in the discussion of Shimei's fate at all. David's rebuke of the "sons of Zeruiah" is comprehensible, however, when read within the larger narrative context of Samuel–Kings. Joab distinguishes himself repeatedly as one whose zeal for protecting David's interests leads him to eliminate political rebels capitally, even though such action is clearly against the king's more magnanimous wishes (2 Sam 3:17–39; 18:5–33; 20:4–10; 1 Kgs 2:5–6). Abishai, too, on multiple occasions demonstrates his eagerness to execute David's enemies. In addition to the two encounters between David and Shimei when Abishai offers his services as

---

כי תהיו־לי היום לשטן. The NRSV renders this phrase, "that you should today become an adversary to me." Day, whose work will be considered more fully below, correctly argues that ל in this verse does not indicate that Abishai would be acting "against" David, but "on behalf of" David ("Abishai the śāṭān in 2 Sam 19:17–24," CBQ 49 [1987]: 545). (See Judg 6:31 for another example of ל in the sense of "on behalf of.") Abishai is suggesting not that he attack David but that he attack Shimei for David.

[8] The adjective "legal," as employed in the paragraph above and throughout the article, does not necessarily imply that a formal trial or courtroom procedure is involved, but simply that the attack on a person's life is justified by that person's guilt, as is the case Numbers 22 and 2 Samuel 19.

[9] Day, "Abishai the śāṭān in 2 Sam 19:17–24," 543–47.

an executioner, Abishai also volunteers to take the life of Saul on David's behalf (1 Sam 26:7-11). On each of these occasions, David, true to form, denied Abishai permission to take the life of his enemy. David's words to the sons of Zeruiah in this pericope are situated within a larger narrative in which Abishai's and Joab's zeal for execution time and time again earns David's ire. It is this violent activity on the part of the sons of Zeruiah that merits David's rebuke and the label śāṭān.

3. That שָׂטָן refers to Abishai in his proposed role of attacker or executioner on David's behalf is consistent with the other uses of this noun that we have considered up to this point, all of which refer to physical acts of violence. The translation "accuser" requires that one posit a usage of שָׂטָן that we have not hitherto observed.

Furthermore, "executioner" seems to be the meaning of שָׂטָן in other passages. This meaning is attested in Numbers 22, which contains the comical account of Balaam's journey by donkey to assist Balak king of Moab against the Israelites. It displeases Yhwh that Balaam has set out on this mission against God's people, so the angel of Yhwh, sword in hand, stands in Balaam's path as his śāṭān (Num 22:22). Fortunately for Balaam, his donkey perceives the danger and three times takes steps to evade the angel and avert Balaam's swift demise. Each time the donkey does this, however, Balaam, who is oblivious to the threat to his life, beats his donkey for what the seer mistakes for insubordination. Once Balaam becomes aware of the armed messenger, the angel of Yhwh says to him, "Why have you struck your donkey these three times? I have come out as a śāṭān, because your way is perverse before me. The donkey saw me, and turned away from me these three times. If it had not turned away from me, surely just now I would have killed you and let it live" (Num 22:32b-33). Had the donkey not protected Balaam, the angel of Yhwh would have fulfilled his role as a śāṭān by executing Balaam.[10]

Having surveyed the narrative passages in which the noun שָׂטָן occurs, one observes that this noun does not refer to an adversary generically but to an "attacker" who intends to harm physically or kill another person. In some passages, this attacker is of a military kind (1 Sam 29:4; 1 Kgs 5:18). שָׂטָן can also carry a more specific nuance in certain legal contexts, but this meaning is not "accuser" as is widely held. Rather, the attacker in this legal sense is an "executioner" of the guilty (Num 22:22, 32; 2 Sam 19:23). There is no evidence whatsoever in these narrative passages that שָׂטָן ever means "accuser."

---

[10] The notion of śāṭān as executioner may also lie behind what is the most debated passage referring to a śāṭān in the Hebrew Scriptures, 1 Chr 21:1. I have argued elsewhere that the śāṭān of 1 Chr 21:1 is a punishing emissary of God and is probably to be identified with the sword-wielding angel of Yhwh who appears in vv. 12-30 of the same chapter ("The Devil Made David Do It ... Or *Did* He? The Nature, Identity, and Literary Origins of the *Satan* in 1 Chronicles 21," *JBL* 128 [2009]: 91-106). According to the Chronicler's narrative, this śāṭān is responsible for the deaths of seventy thousand Israelites.

II. שָׂטַן AND שָׂטָן IN THE BOOK OF PSALMS

When it comes to ascertaining the meaning of a word, the book of Psalms poses a different sort of challenge from that posed by the narrative books of the Hebrew Scriptures. The poetry of the Psalms seldom offers the kinds of explicit and concrete details afforded by historical narrative. One must often make do with historically unspecific language and imprecise poetic parallelism in an effort to triangulate the meaning of an unknown lexeme. The very characteristics that give the Psalms their universal appeal can frustrate the lexicographer. The case of שׂטן is no exception to this rule. Limited though one's data may be, the evidence of the Psalms suggests a meaning for this root that is consistent with what one observes in the narrative books. In the three Psalms in which it occurs, the root שׂטן refers not to "accusation" but to physical attack.

The first instance of שָׂטַן in the book of Psalms is found in Ps 38:21 [Eng. 20]. "Those who render me evil for good are my *adversaries* [יִשְׂטְנוּנִי] because I follow after good." The verb שָׂטַן in this verse is treated variously by commentators and translators. It has been translated as "to be an adversary" (Craigie, RSV, NRSV, NKJV), "to oppose" (NASB), and "to harass" (NJPS).[11] It has also been rendered more specifically as "to accuse" (Kraus, ESV, NAB rev. ed.), "to lodge accusations" (NIV), and "to slander" (Dahood).[12] Although שָׂטַן in this verse clearly refers to an action that would bring someone harm (רָעָה), it is difficult to be more specific about the nature of the action. The meaning "attack" (Goldingay, HCSB [Holman Christian Standard Bible]), however, would certainly fit the historical context of Psalm 38.[13] Psalm 38 begins with the suppliant seeking divine healing from illness, but he also asks God for protection from enemies who seek his life: "Those who seek my life lay their snares; those who seek to hurt me speak of ruin, and meditate treachery all day long" (38:13 [Eng. 12]). While certainty about the specific

---

[11] Peter C. Craigie, *Psalms 1–50* (WBC 19; Waco: Word, 1983), 301.

[12] Mitchell Dahood, *Psalms: A New Translation with Introduction and Commentary* (3 vols.; AB 16, 17, 17A; Garden City, NY: Doubleday, 1966–70), 1:234, 237; Hans-Joachim Kraus, *Psalms 1–59: A Continental Commentary* (trans. Hilton C. Oswald; Minneapolis: Fortress, 1993), 410. Kraus translates שָׂטַן as "sein gram" (*Psalmen I* [BKAT; Neukirchen-Vluyn: Neukirchener Verlag, 1961], 294). Dahood bases his translation "to slander" in part on his translation of גדל in 38:17 as "to calumniate" and in part on the uses of שׂטן in Psalms 71 and 109. As for the meaning of גדל, Dahood's translation is dubious and has not been accepted by any other commentators, to my knowledge. The *hiphil* of גדל, as one finds in Ps 38:17, is typically translated as "to magnify [oneself]" or "to boast." Further, while Dahood is correct to compare the use of שָׂטַן in this psalm with its uses in Psalms 71 and 109, he is incorrect, as will be shown below, to understand שָׂטַן in these passages as "to slander."

[13] John Goldingay, *Psalms* (3 vols.; Baker Commentary on the Old Testament Wisdom and Psalms; Grand Rapids: Baker Academic, 2006–8), 1:537.

meaning of שָׂטַן in this psalm is impossible, it is reasonable to suppose that the root שׂטן refers to physical "attack." Not only is it the case that the root שׂטן elsewhere denotes a physical act of attacking and killing a person, but this is also precisely the situation about which the suppliant requests divine assistance. Nothing in this passage suggests that the word means "to accuse" or "to slander." The translation "attack," then, is more likely the intended meaning of שָׂטַן in Psalm 38.

One finds a very similar state of affairs in Ps 71:13, which the NRSV renders, "Let my *accusers* [שֹׂטְנֵי נַפְשִׁי] be put to shame and consumed; let those who seek to hurt me be covered with scorn and disgrace." As with 38:21, translations proffered for the participial form of שָׂטַן in this verse include "adversaries" (Tate, Hossfeld and Zenger ["Widersacher"], NASB, NKJV, HCSB) as well as "accusers" (RSV, NRSV, NIV, ESV, NJPS) and "slanderers" (Dahood).[14] Further, as in Psalm 38, it is the translation "to attack" (Goldingay, NAB rev. ed.) that most probably conveys the sense of שָׂטַן in this verse.[15] The suppliant in Psalm 71 asks God to deliver him from the hand of the wicked (71:4), his enemies who conspire against him and watch for his life (71:10–11).[16] Those who "attack [his] life" (שֹׂטְנֵי נַפְשִׁ[י]) intend to bring him "harm" (רָעָה). Once again, physical attack with intent to kill seems to be the meaning of שָׂטַן, and once again there is no basis for the translation "accusers." Psalm 71 also offers some guidance in the interpretation of the final psalm to be considered, Psalm 109.

Psalm 109 has the potential to contribute much to the present investigation. The verb שָׂטַן occurs three times in this psalm (vv. 4, 20, and 29). Additionally, the noun שָׂטָן occurs once (v. 6). Psalm 109 also contains an intriguing terminological parallel with Zechariah 3. Both passages speak of a *śāṭān* standing to the right (עמד על־ימין) of a person (Ps 109:6; Zech 3:1).[17] For this reason, commentators find Psalm 109 to be determinative for their interpretation of Zechariah 3. Although recent translations and commentaries are virtually unanimous in their rendering of שָׂטָן and שָׂטַן in Psalm 109 in terms of "accusation," there is little in this psalm that actually suggests this meaning.[18] As with the other passages that have been considered up to this point, a much stronger case can be made that "attack with lethal intent" is what these words denote.

---

[14] Marvin E. Tate, *Psalms 51–100* (WBC 20; Dallas: Word, 1990), 208; Frank-Lothar Hossfeld and Erich Zenger, *Psalmen 51–100* (HTKAT; Freiburg: Herder, 2000), 290; Dahood, *Psalms*, 2:170. Kraus translates שָׂטַן as "die nachstellen" (*Psalmen I*, 488).

[15] Goldingay allows that שָׂטַן in this verse may refer to accusation: "The adversaries are people who are attacking (*śāṭan*), perhaps by accusing" (Psalms, 2:372).

[16] Cf. also Ps 35:4; 40:15 [14]; 70:3 [2], which resemble 71:13 very closely, except that שֹׂטְנֵי נַפְשִׁי is replaced by מְבַקְשֵׁי נַפְשִׁי ("those who seek my life").

[17] The parallel between Psalm 109 and Zechariah 3 will be discussed in the next section.

[18] For an example of an interpreter who understands this psalm primarily in terms of accusation, in addition to the commentaries cited below, see Hans Schmidt, *Das Gebet der Angeklagten im Alten Testament* (Giessen: A. Töpelmann, 1928), 40–46.

The opening verses of Psalm 109 describe the harassment that the psalmist receives from his enemies. These verses also contain the psalm's first occurrence of שָׂטָן.

> Do not be silent, O God of my praise.
> For wicked and deceitful mouths are opened against me,
>   speaking against me with lying tongues.
> They beset me with words of hate,
>   and attack me [ילחמוני] without cause.
> In return for my love they *accuse* me [ישטנוני],
>   even while I make prayer for them.
> So they reward me evil [רעה] for good,
>   and hatred [שנאה] for my love. (Ps 109:1–5)

The psalmist claims that his enemies are attacking him without justification. He is receiving hatred for his love and is subjected to harm (רעה) in return for doing good.[19] The psalmist also claims that his enemies are speaking hateful and false words against him (vv. 2–3). The psalmist decries malicious speech in v. 20, as well. With reference to the imprecatory prayer of vv. 6–19, the psalmist says, "May that be the reward of my *accusers* [שטני] from the LORD, of those who speak evil against my life." While it is not impossible that the words spoken by the psalmist's enemies against his life include accusations, this is by no means the only possible interpretation of these lines. False and malicious speech can take a variety of forms, and nothing in Psalm 109 indicates that this hateful speech takes the form of accusation. More likely, the psalmist attributes words to his opponents such as those attributed to the psalmist's opponents in Psalm 71, which was considered above: "For my enemies speak concerning me, and those who watch for my life consult together. They say, 'Pursue and seize that person whom God has forsaken, for there is no one to deliver'" (71:10–11). That the words שָׂטָן and שָׂטָן in Psalm 109 pertain to an attack on the psalmist's life is supported also by the psalmist's use of the word לחם ("to fight," "to make war") in v. 3. Though much about the suppliant's situation is ambiguous, the language he uses to describe his distress is clearly that of physical assault.[20] The third instance of שָׂטָן in Psalm 109 is in v. 29: "May my *accusers* [שטני] be clothed with dishonor; may they be wrapped in their own shame as in a mantle."

---

[19] Cf. the similar statement in Ps 38:21.

[20] Regarding the pair of terms לחם and שָׂטָן in Ps 109:3–4, Goldingay states, "Initially the suppliant's language uses the language of battle, but then it speaks more literally in indicating that the attacks take the form of accusations" (*Psalms*, 3:278). Ironically, so confident is Goldingay that שָׂטָן means "to accuse" that he interprets לחם figuratively so as to accommodate this understanding of שָׂטָן. If one simply recognizes that the root שטן is used in Psalm 109 as it is used elsewhere in the Hebrew Scriptures, to refer to physical attack, then it makes perfect sense that שָׂטָן would be used alongside of לחם. (Pertinently, one should observe, the nouns שָׂטָן and מִלְחָמָה appear together in 1 Sam 29:4.) One need not interpret one of the words in a way that is contrary to its literal sense in order to reconcile them. This is not to deny that the psalmist may employ לחם and

The close resemblance between this verse and Ps 71:13, which also expresses the wish that those who "attack" the psalmist would be ashamed and clothed with dishonor, increases the likelihood that שָׂטַן carries the same meaning in both passages, "to attack."

The final occurrence of the root שׂטן to be considered in this section is in Ps 109:6. For many commentators, this verse uses the noun שָׂטָן unambiguously to refer to an "accuser" or a "prosecuting attorney."[21] In her discussion of the meaning of שָׂטָן, Day states, "There seems to me to be little doubt that śāṭān has a forensic connotation in Ps 109:6."[22] Although a forensic understanding of שָׂטָן in this verse appears reasonable at first glance, more careful analysis reveals that "attacker" is a better translation.

> Appoint a wicked man [רשׁע] against him;
>   let an *accuser* [שׂטן] stand on his right.
> When he is tried [בהשׁפטו], let him be found guilty [יצא רשׁע];
>   let his prayer [תפלתו] be counted as sin [תהיה לחטאה].
> May his days be few;
>   may another seize his position.
> May his children be orphans,
>   and his wife a widow. (Ps 109:6–9)[23]

In order to make her case for a forensic understanding of שָׂטָן in 109:6, Day first argues that one must interpret vv. 6–19 as a discrete unit, apart from its context in Psalm 109.[24] This separation of vv. 6–19 from the rest of the psalm is more conducive to Day's forensic interpretation than reading the psalm as a unity would be,

---

שָׂטָן figuratively, but simply to observe that, in the case of both words, he uses the language of physical assault/combat to describe his situation.

[21] Dahood interprets Ps 109:6–7 as referring to a postmortem judgment and the śāṭān of this passage as Satan, whom he regards as a superhuman prosecutor (*Psalms*, 3:101–2). Though most commentators understand the śāṭān of Ps 109:6 to be a prosecutor, Dahood's interpretation of the figure in this passage as superhuman has won few followers.

[22] Day, *Adversary in Heaven*, 31. More recent interpreters who understand the language of v. 6 forensically include Stephen Egwim, "Determining the Place of vv. 6–19 in Ps 109: A Case Presentation Analysis," *ETL* 80 (2004): 116–18; Frank-Lothar Hossfeld and Erich Zenger, *Psalmen 101–150* (HTKAT; Freiburg: Herder, 2008), 183.

[23] The NRSV supplements v. 6 by adding the words "They say" at the beginning, identifying vv. 6–19 as a quotation of the psalmist's enemies: "They say, 'Appoint a wicked man …'"

[24] Day (*Adversary in Heaven*, 30–31) points to the difference in the number of enemies between vv. 1–5, 20–31 (plural) and 6–19 (singular) as evidence for distinct compositional units. As examples of commentators who make this distinction, she cites Moses Buttenwieser, *The Psalms, Chronologically Treated, with a New Translation* (Chicago: University of Chicago Press, 1939), 742; and Oswald Loretz, *Die Psalmen: Beitr. d. Ugarit-Texte zum Verständnis von Kolometrie u. Textologie d. Psalmen* (AOAT 207; Neukirchen-Vluyn: Neukirchener Verlag, 1979), 2:158–59. She also notes other commentators who regard Psalm 109 as a compositional unity, whose arguments she finds unconvincing.

since, as we have seen, the verb שָׂטַן occurs elsewhere in Psalm 109 with the likely meaning of "to attack." Day then supports her inference that the *śāṭān* of 109:6 is an accuser with the observation that בהשפטו "clearly indicates" that the goal of the *śāṭān* is to bring someone to justice. Day further asserts that the expression "to stand on the right hand" in v. 6 is also "clearly forensic."[25]

The evidence that Ps 109:6–7 speaks of an accusing *śāṭān*, however, is not nearly as clear as Day would have one think. One weakness of Day's interpretation of the passage is that it requires her to divorce vv. 6–7 from the rest of Psalm 109. Although it is possible that vv. 6–19 constitute a distinct compositional unit within the psalm, an interpretation of שָׂטַן that is consistent with its context is still preferable to one that is at odds with its context. Furthermore, there are no grounds for Day's claim that "stand on the right hand" is forensic, let alone "clearly forensic." In support of this claim, Day cites Roland de Vaux's discussion of judicial procedure in ancient Israel. Regarding the location of the accuser during a trial, de Vaux says only, "The accuser was the 'adversary,' the *śāṭān*; he stood on the right of the accused (Ps 109:6; Za 3:1)."[26] Since de Vaux's only evidences for the supposition that an accuser would stand on the right of someone are two passages whose meaning is presently in question, they constitute an insufficient basis for a forensic reading of "stand on the right hand." That an accuser would stand on the right side of the defendant is entirely without support apart from the alleged evidence of Psalm 109 and Zechariah 3.[27] Further, נשפט, which, according to Day, shows that the psalmist wanted his enemy to be brought to justice, rarely, if ever, means "to be judged" or "to be tried," as it is translated in v. 7 by the NRSV.[28] More typically, it means "to enter into dispute" and can even mean simply "to quarrel."[29]

The speaker in Ps 109:6–7, rather than expressing his desire that a criminal trial will result in a verdict of guilty for his enemy, may be voicing his wish simply that an attacker will kill his enemy. Though his opponent may seek justice, the speaker hopes that it will be wickedness that transpires (בהשפטו יצא רשע) and that his enemy's appeal for arbitration, whether to God or to a human authority, will fail to prevent sin from occurring (תפלתו תהיה לחטאה). This understanding of these lines makes better sense of the expression יצא רשע in v. 7, which the NRSV

---

[25] Day, *Adversary in Heaven*, 31.

[26] De Vaux, *Ancient Israel: Its Life and Institutions* (trans. John McHugh; New York: McGraw-Hill, 1961), 156.

[27] On the significance of the *śāṭān* standing to a person's right in Psalm 109, see the discussion below in relation to Zechariah 3.

[28] H. Niehr cites Ps 9:20 [Eng. 19]; Ps 37:33; and Ps 109:7 as passages in which this form can be translated "to be judged" ("שָׁפַט *šāpaṭ*," *TDOT* 15:421). The meaning "to be judged," however, is far from certain in these passages. In Ps 37:32–33, as in Psalm 109, the word refers unambiguously to a wicked person's (רשע) attempt to kill a righteous person.

[29] Ibid. See 1 Sam 12:7; 2 Chr 22:8; Prov 29:9; Isa 43:26; 59:4; 66:16; Jer 2:35; 25:31; Ezek 17:20; 20:35, 36; 38:22; Joel 4:2.

translates "let him be found guilty." A wish for a verdict of guilty does not seem to be the plain meaning of this expression. In 1 Samuel 24, after refusing to take advantage of an opportunity to kill Saul, David assures the king that he does not intend to kill him: "As the ancient proverb says, 'Out of the wicked [מרשעים] comes forth wickedness' [יצא רשע]; but my hand shall not be against you" (1 Sam 24:14 [Eng. 13]). David uses the expression יצא רשע to speak of the murderous activity that one would expect to come from wicked persons (מרשעים). The speaker in 109:6–7 uses these words to articulate his hope that a wicked person (רשע), a śāṭān (שָׂטָן), will kill his enemy.

Even were one to maintain, on the basis of the presence of נשפט or of other supposedly legal terminology, that Psalm 109 depicts a judicial proceeding, there is nothing in this passage that suggests that the śāṭān in such a proceeding would function as an "accuser."[30] Based on the analysis up to this point, one would expect this śāṭān to be an attacker of some sort. In a judicial context, this śāṭān would probably be an executioner, such as Abishai in 2 Samuel 19. Whether it is hoped that the attack will take place in a legal setting or otherwise, the intended outcome of this encounter with a śāṭān is stated unequivocally in vv. 8–9. Regarding his enemy, the speaker says, "May his days be few.... May his children be orphans and his wife a widow" (109:8–9). As elsewhere in the Hebrew Scriptures, שטן in Psalm 109 seems to denote lethal, physical attack.

It would be impossible to prove beyond a doubt that שטן never refers to accusation, particularly in the book of Psalms, where the specifics of the various passages' historical settings are difficult to determine with absolute certainty. If one is willing to assume that שטן refers to accusation, it would be possible to read the psalms in which it occurs with this meaning. Apart from this sort of a priori understanding of the root, however, evidence that these psalms speak of accusation is meager. There is little support in the psalms and in the narratives considered above that שָׂטָן or שָׂטַן ever refers to accusation. In contrast, physical and lethal attack is very clearly the idea behind the use of the noun שָׂטָן in the narrative portions of the Hebrew Scriptures. In addition, this meaning is supported contextually and makes excellent sense in all of the psalms in which the root שטן occurs. That the words refer to lethal, physical attack is especially well supported in Psalm 109.

Having considered all of the occurrences of שָׂטָן and שָׂטַן outside of Zechariah 3 and Job 1–2, one is now in a position to consider their meaning in these two important passages. Zechariah is a natural place to begin, since interpreters often link this passage with Psalm 109.

---

[30] Hossfeld and Zenger offer an insightful analysis of Psalm 109 as a "*Gerechtigkeitspsalm*," citing as evidence for their interpretation an impressive amount of potentially legal language in the psalm (*Psalmen 101–150*, 181–95). Some of the supposed legal terminology they cite, however, is that which we have called into question above. They assume, for instance, that an accuser would "stand on the right" of a defendant and that יצא רשע refers to a guilty verdict.

III. The Śāṭān in Zechariah 3

3:1Then he showed me the high priest Joshua standing before the angel of the LORD, and Satan [הַשָּׂטָן] standing at his right hand to accuse him [לְשִׂטְנוֹ]. 2And the LORD said to Satan [הַשָּׂטָן], "The LORD rebuke you, O Satan [הַשָּׂטָן]! The LORD who has chosen Jerusalem rebuke you! Is not this man a brand plucked from the fire?" 3Now Joshua was dressed with filthy clothes as he stood before the angel. 4The angel said to those who were standing before him, "Take off his filthy clothes." And to him he said, "See, I have taken your guilt [עֲוֺנֶךָ] away from you, and I will clothe you with festal apparel." 5And I said, "Let them put a clean turban on his head." So they put a clean turban on his head and clothed him with the apparel; and the angel of the LORD was standing by. 6Then the angel of the LORD assured Joshua, saying 7"Thus says the LORD of hosts: If you will walk in my ways and keep my requirements, then you shall rule my house and have charge of my courts, and I will give you the right of access among those who are standing here." (Zech 3:1-7 NRSV)

This translation of Zech 3:1–7 represents the scholarly consensus as to how these verses are to be understood with regard to the identity and activity of the śāṭān. Two aspects of this rendering of the passage merit comment. First, the NRSV translates לְשִׂטְנוֹ in 3:1 as "to accuse him." Second, it renders הַשָּׂטָן in 3:1–2 as "Satan." Since this is a semantic study of the root שׂטן, I will not here discuss the grammatical distinction between "Satan" and "the Satan," as one would usually translate a noun with the definite article.[31] One should note, however, that the transliteration of הַשָּׂטָן as Satan is not as interpretively neutral as it might at first appear, since the NRSV and several other translations provide readers with an explanatory note defining this term as "the Accuser."[32] Commentators and translators alike are virtually unanimous that what the śāṭān is doing in this scene is accusing Joshua and that the śāṭān is in fact "the Accuser."[33]

---

[31] Day (*Adversary in Heaven*, 43) suggests that the definite article in הַשָּׂטָן does not point to a particular śāṭān, as in "*the*" śāṭān, but indicates that the figure is "*a certain unspecified*" śāṭān (emphasis mine). The precise nuance of the definite article in these instances is beyond the scope of this study, as is the question of how the definite article relates to the tradition history of "Satan" in the Hebrew Scriptures.

[32] See also, e.g., NIV, ESV, NASB. The NJPS departs from the convention of translating הַשָּׂטָן as Satan, and has "the Accuser" in the body of the translation itself, not relegated to an explanatory note. The NAB rev. ed. translates לְשִׂטְנוֹ as "to accuse him," but has the more generic "the adversary" for הַשָּׂטָן.

[33] E.g., Carol L. Meyers and Eric M. Meyers, *Haggai, Zechariah 1–8: A New Translation with Introduction and Commentary* (AB 25B; New York: Doubleday, 1987), 183–86; Hinckley G. Mitchell, John Merlin Powis Smith, and Julius A. Bewer, *A Critical and Exegetical Commentary on Haggai, Zechariah, Malachi and Jonah* (ICC; Edinburgh: T&T Clark, 1912), 147–49 (Mitchell); David L. Petersen, *Haggai and Zechariah 1–8: A Commentary* (OTL; Philadelphia: Westminster, 1984), 189–90; Dominic Rudman, "Zechariah and the Satan Tradition in the Hebrew Bible," in

What is somewhat surprising, given this scholarly unanimity, is that there is absolutely no evidence in the context of Zechariah 3 itself that accusation is indeed what is happening or that the śāṭān should be understood as the Accuser. Zechariah 3:1 itself says only that the śāṭān stood at Joshua's right to śaṭan him. Granted, the contents of ch. 3 are not obviously incompatible with the supposition that the śāṭān is functioning as an accuser. For example, the śāṭān's activity appears to be connected in some way with the fact that Joshua is wearing filthy clothing (which is associated with the high priest's iniquity). In addition, the śāṭān's activity is assessed negatively, eliciting Yhwh's rebuke (3:2). For these reasons, scholars who have assumed that "accuser" and "to accuse" are possible meanings of שָׂטָן and שָׂטַן have been able to translate and interpret this passage accordingly.

Having surveyed the evidence for such uses of שׂטן outside of Zechariah 3, however, the assumption that this root denotes "accusation" can no longer be sustained. And the contextual clues provided by the passage, though they are not obviously incompatible with this understanding of the śāṭān and his activity, are not enough in and of themselves to warrant the translations "the Accuser" and "accuse" in 3:1–2. Since the evidence supplied by ch. 3 alone is insufficient for determining the meaning of שָׂטָן and שָׂטַן, one's primary guide as to their meaning must be their use elsewhere in the Hebrew Scriptures.[34] One must also look to other

---

Tradition in Transition: Haggai and Zechariah 1–8 in the Trajectory of Hebrew Theology (ed. Mark J. Boda and Michael H. Floyd; Library of Hebrew Bible/Old Testament Studies 475; New York: T&T Clark, 2008), 191; Ralph L. Smith, *Micah–Malachi* (WBC 32; Waco: Word, 1984), 199. Interestingly, the LXX translator did not understand the activity of the śāṭān in this way, but rendered the verb שָׂטַן with ἀντίκειμαι. The verb ἀντίκειμαι can denote adversarial activity of various sorts, often of a military kind (e.g., Exod 23:22; 2 Sam 8:10; Esth 8:11). It does not mean "to accuse."

[34] Attempts to explain שָׂטָן etymologically have been unsuccessful. Knut Tallqvist claims that the root שׂטן occurs in Akkadian with the meaning "to feud" (*Akkadische Götterepitheta: Mit einem Götterverzeichnis und einer Liste der prädikativen Elemente der sumerischen Götternamen* [StudOr 7; Helsinki: Societas orientalis fennica, 1938], 240). KBL also relates the Hebrew שׂטן to this supposed Akkadian root (p. 918). *AHw*, however, identifies the Akkadian root not as *śṭn* but as the Št stem of *etēm/nu(m)* (1:260). So also Day, *Adversary in Heaven*, 23; Wanke, "שָׂטָן *śāṭān* adversary," 1268. N. H. Tur-Sinai argues that שָׂטָן was derived from the root שׁוט ("to roam to and fro") and that a śāṭān was one who would roam around the earth and report any disloyalty to the king that he observed (*The Book of Job: A New Commentary* [rev ed.; Jerusalem: Kiryath Sepher, 1967], 38–45). This etymology, however, has been rightly rejected by Adolphe Lods, "Les origines de la figure de Satan: Ses fonctions à la cour céleste," in *Mélanges Syriens: Offerts à monsieur René Dussaud* (2 vols.; Paris: P. Geuthner, 1939), 2:658–59; Rivkah Schärf Kluger, *Satan in the Old Testament* (trans. Hildegard Nagel; Studies in Jungian Thought; Evanston, IL: Northwestern University Press, 1967), 30–31; Day, *Adversary in Heaven*, 20–22; Nielsen, "שָׂטָן *śāṭān*; שָׂטַן *śaṭan*; שָׂטַם *śāṭam*," 73; Breytenbach and Day, "Satan שׂטן Σατάν, Σατανᾶς," 726. More recently, Manfred Görg has posited a connection between the figure of "the śāṭān" in the Hebrew Scriptures and the Egyptian verb *śdnj* (from *dnj*), arguing that the śāṭān of the Hebrew Scriptures is a superhuman "enforcer" (*Vollstrecker*) ("Der 'Satan' – der 'Vollstrecker' Gottes?" *BN* 82 [1996]: 9–12). It seems unlikely, however, from both a semantic and a phonetic standpoint that there is any etymological

passages that resemble Zechariah 3 formally and conceptually in order to comprehend more completely the context of these words.

In view of the fact that "lethal, physical attack" is the meaning of שָׂטַן and שָׂטָן attested elsewhere in the Hebrew Scriptures, this is also almost certainly the meaning of these words in Zechariah 3. More specifically, it was shown that שָׂטָן is in some instances used with reference to capital punishment (Num 22:22, 32; 2 Sam 19:23). In these passages, the attacker functions as an "executioner." This seems to be the sense of the root שׂטן in Zechariah 3, the first verse of which should be translated as follows:

> Then he showed me the high priest Joshua standing before the angel of YHWH,
> and the Executioner standing on his right to execute him. (Zech 3:1)

That the *śāṭān*'s attack should be understood more precisely as "execution" is strongly suggested by the contents of ch. 3.

Zechariah does not in this passage portray the high priest as an innocent victim of undeserved assault by evildoers, as the suppliant portrays himself in the psalms considered above. Joshua is guilty of some unspecified iniquity, which Zechariah associates with the priest's filthy garments (3:3–4), so the *śāṭān*'s attack on Joshua's life is not without justification.[35] The *śāṭān* in this scene resembles the *śāṭān* whom Balaam encountered on his way to Moab, a superhuman executioner of the guilty. In Zechariah's vision, the angel of YHWH intervenes on behalf of Joshua, protecting him from the *śāṭān*'s attack. When compared with the other passages that speak of a *śāṭān*, the scene in Zechariah 3, in some respects, has its closest parallel in 2 Samuel 19. In the 2 Samuel pericope, Abishai stands ready to serve as David's *śāṭān* and to execute Shimei for his crime, but David rebukes the would-be executioner and shows mercy to Shimei. So also in Zechariah 3 the *śāṭān* is poised to put Joshua to death for his iniquity, but the angel of YHWH rebukes the *śāṭān* and extends pardon to Joshua.

---

relationship between the Egyptian *śdnj* and the Hebrew root שׂטן. Given the tenuous nature of the proposed etymologies for שָׂטַן to date, the Hebrew Scriptures' usage of this word and of its cognate שָׂטָן remains one's primary guide to the meaning of these words.

[35] There may be more at stake in Zechariah 3 than simply the fate of the high priest. Scholars disagree as to whether the Satan's opposition in this passage is directed at Joshua alone or at the community represented by this high priest. Day, for example, finds in this passage a controversy over whether Joshua was fit to be invested as high priest (*Adversary in Heaven*, 118–21). Meyers and Meyers argue that the purpose of this scene is to legitimate an expanded role for the priesthood (*Haggai, Zechariah 1–8*, 180–82). Petersen, on the other hand, contends that the *śāṭān*'s accusations concerned not only the position of the priest but also that of the entire community before God (*Haggai and Zechariah 1–8*, 194–96). He cites Exod 28:36–38 and Num 18:1, which speak of the high priest bearing the guilt of those he represents. Relevant to this discussion is the fact that the *śāṭān* is rebuked in the name of "Yahweh *who has chosen Jerusalem*" (3:2). However, it is not the social and religious realities to which this vision points but the nature of the *śāṭān* within the scene described that is the concern of the present discussion.

The identification of the *śāṭān* as a superhuman executioner garners additional support from a comparison of Zechariah 3 with two other passages from the Hebrew Scriptures, although these two passages do not mention a *śāṭān* figure. Exodus 28 contains instructions concerning the clothing that Aaron and his descendants are to wear when they enter Yhwh's presence. At the conclusion of these instructions, the following warning pertaining to the priestly vestments is given: "Aaron and his sons shall wear them when they go into the tent of meeting, or when they come near the altar to minister in the holy place; or they will bring guilt [עָוֹן] on themselves and die" (Exod 28:43). According to Exodus 28, were a priest to approach Yhwh clothed inappropriately, he would incur guilt and invite death. Zechariah seems to envision a scenario similar to the one warned against in Exodus, as he describes the priest Joshua standing guilty (עָוֹן) before the angel of Yhwh and wearing filthy garments (3:3–4). Joshua's very life is at stake, and the *śāṭān* in this passage is the one who would take Joshua's life were it not for the angel of Yhwh's intervention.

A second passage that sheds light on Zechariah 3 is the familiar account of Isaiah's vision of God and prophetic commission in Isaiah 6. In this passage, when Isaiah beholds God, he immediately recognizes that his life is in danger because of his iniquity. The prophet exclaims, "Woe is me! I am lost, for I am a man of unclean lips, and I live among a people of unclean lips; yet my eyes have seen the King, the Lord of hosts!" (6:5). At that point, one of Yhwh's divine attendants takes action to spare Isaiah's life, taking a burning coal from the altar and touching Isaiah's mouth with it. The seraph then explains to Isaiah, "Behold, this has touched your lips; your guilt [עָוֹן] is taken away, and your sin forgiven" (6:7). Once Isaiah's guilt has been removed, Isaiah receives his commission to prophesy to the people.

Zechariah's vision of Joshua follows the same sequence. Like Isaiah, Joshua stands in the presence of the (angel of) Yhwh. And, like Isaiah, Joshua is in peril for his life on account of his guilt (Zech 3:1–3). Then, as the seraph touches a coal to the prophet Isaiah's unclean lips and declares that his guilt has been removed, so also the divine attendants in Zechariah 3 remove the priest Joshua's filthy clothes and the angel of Yhwh declares that he has taken away Joshua's guilt (3:4). Once his guilt has been removed and the danger eliminated, Joshua receives his commission to serve as high priest (3:7), just as Isaiah received his commission to prophesy. These formal and conceptual parallels between Zechariah 3 and other passages reinforce the conclusion of the semantic analysis above, that a *śāṭān* is one who would take another's life by physical attack. Zechariah 3 describes not just any *śāṭān*, however, but "the *śāṭān*," God's superhuman executioner.

What is to be made of the terminological similarity between Zechariah 3 and Psalm 109 ("stand on the right side") is not as apparent. That Zechariah offers the reader information about the location of the characters in his vision in ch. 3 should likely be understood in light of the fact that such locative descriptors appear, as well, in Zechariah's other visions. In ch. 1, the prophet sees a man "on" (עַל) a horse standing "among" (בין) myrtle trees with other horses "behind" (אחר) him. In ch. 4, Zechariah sees two olive trees "on the right" (על־ימין) and "on the left" (על־שמאול) of a bowl. These olive trees are said to be the two anointed ones who stand "by" (על) the Lord of the whole earth. In ch. 5, Zechariah describes a woman "inside" (בתוך) a basket and mentions two angels who lift up the bowl "between" (בין) heaven and earth. In 6:1, the prophet sees four chariots coming out "from between" (מבין) two mountains. In 3:1, the prophet, as he does elsewhere, describes the location of the various elements of his vision. He may be saying no more than that the Satan was standing next to the high priest.[36]

This would differ from the situation in Ps 109:6, where "on the right" (על־ימין) seems to be used more idiomatically. The psalms frequently speak figuratively of a person's "right side" as a position from which one person would support another (e.g., Pss 16:8; 73:23; 109:31; 110:5; 121:5; 142:5).[37] According to Job 30:12, the right side might also be a position, figuratively, from which one would oppose another. In Ps 109:6, the expression על־ימין parallels the על of the preceding line.

> Appoint a wicked man against him [עליו];
> let a śāṭān stand on his right [על־ימינו].

The idea of a śāṭān standing "on a person's right" in Ps 109:6 should also be understood in contrast with the statement later in the psalm that it is God who stands "at the right hand" (לימין) of the needy (109:31).

Although Psalm 109 and Zechariah 3 both employ the language of a śāṭān "standing to the right" of someone, it is not evident that the situations depicted in these passages are analogous. As argued above, it is possible that Psalm 109 describes a judicial scene in which a śāṭān would serve as an executioner. In that case, both Zech 3:1 and Ps 109:6 would refer to an executioner standing to the right of a guilty individual. Although it is possible that Psalm 109 depicts a legal scene along the lines of Zechariah 3, the ambiguities of the psalm make it difficult to determine with confidence whether it actually does so. Even if Zechariah 3 and Psalm 109 are related, there is no evidence either in Zechariah or in the psalm that a person's right side was a position from which one would issue accusations in a forensic setting.

Of the other passages that mention a śāṭān in the Hebrew Scriptures, Numbers 22 and 2 Samuel 19 are more recognizably analogous to Zechariah 3 than is Psalm 109. These passages, which speak of executioners, assist the interpreter in comprehending the role of the śāṭān in Zechariah 3. The theological and formal correspondence of Exodus 28 and Isaiah 6 to Zechariah 3, though these two texts do not mention a śāṭān, points in the same direction, strengthening the argument that Zechariah's śāṭān is not an accuser but an executioner.

---

[36] So also Mitchell, Smith, and Bewer, *Haggai, Zechariah, Malachi and Jonah*, 149.
[37] See also Isa 41:13; 45:1; and 63:12 for this use of "the right side."

IV. The Śāṭān in Job 1–2

The title הַשָּׂטָן appears twelve times in the first two chapters of Job. When it comes to discerning the meaning of the title, however, Job 1–2, like Zechariah 3, leaves open more than one interpretive possibility. Despite the more elaborate narrative context provided by Job and the frequency of הַשָּׂטָן, the book of Job offers no unambiguous indication of the meaning of the noun שָׂטָן. As a result of this ambiguity, scholars have proffered various readings of Job 1–2 and various translations for הַשָּׂטָן. Some commentators regard the śāṭān in Job as "the Adversary" or "the Opponent."[38] Others understand this figure more specifically as "the Accuser" or "the Prosecutor."[39]

Complicating matters somewhat is the nature of Job's circumstances, which are supposed to be at the same time both exceptional and typical. Job's exemplary virtue, his great wealth, and his extreme suffering are extraordinary. His undeserved suffering and righteousness in the midst of it, on the other hand, are supposed to be meaningful to ordinary readers who find themselves suffering unjustly. Similarly, the portrait of the śāṭān in Job is probably to be regarded as typical in some respects and atypical in others. One must engage in a bit of careful reading between the lines in order to determine what was supposed to have been the śāṭān's business as usual.

Based on the present study's analysis of שָׂטָן up to this point, one would expect "the śāṭān" in Job to be an attacker. Since the word is used exclusively in this way elsewhere, unless there is compelling evidence to the contrary, this is likely to be the way it is used in Job as well. Given that the designation הַשָּׂטָן is identical to that found in Zechariah 3, and given that this figure reports to Yhwh among the "sons of God" in Job (1:6; 2:1), one would expect, more specifically, for this attacker to be, as in Zechariah, a superhuman "executioner." What remains is to determine

---

[38] See, e.g., David J. A. Clines, *Job 1–20* (WBC 17; Dallas: Word, 1989), 19–20; Samuel Rolles Driver and George Buchanan Gray, *A Critical and Exegetical Commentary on the Book of Job* (ICC; New York: Scribner's Sons, 1921), 11.

[39] Scholars who regard the śāṭān as "the Accuser/Prosecutor" include Robert Gordis, *The Book of God and Man: A Study of Job* (Chicago: University of Chicago Press, 1965), 70; Marvin H. Pope, *Job: Introduction, Translation, and Notes* (AB 15; Garden City, NY: Doubleday, 1965; 3rd ed., 1973), 9–11; Tremper Longman III, *Job* (Baker Commentary on the Old Testament Wisdom and Psalms; Grand Rapids: Baker Academic, 2012), 82–83. According to William D. Reyburn, translators have two valid options when it comes to translating הַשָּׂטָן in Job 1–2: (1) transliteration with translation, e.g., "Satan the accuser" or (2) translation only, e.g., "the accuser, the tester" (*A Handbook on the Book of Job* [UBS Handbook Series; New York: United Bible Societies, 1992], 39). Norman C. Habel defines הַשָּׂטָן as "the accuser/adversary/doubter" (*The Book of Job* [OTL; Philadelphia: Westminster, 1985], 89). John E. Hartley defines שָׂטָן as an "opponent at law" (*The Book of Job* [NICOT; Grand Rapids: Eerdmans, 1988], 71).

whether this meaning is further supported by, or at least is compatible with, its context in Job.

The evidence of Job itself, allusive though it may be, also suggests that the *śāṭān* is thought to be a superhuman executioner of the wicked. Several aspects of the narrative indicate that an understanding of the *śāṭān* as God's "attacker" or "executioner," rather than "accuser," lies in the story's background. First, while the *śāṭān* certainly questions the motivation for Job's unwavering fear of God, Job has committed no crime, nor does the *śāṭān* accuse Job of having committed a crime.[40] The *śāṭān* does, however, launch a vicious physical assault on Job, destroying Job's property, killing Job's children, and afflicting Job's body. The meaning "attacker" is quite appropriate for the activity of the *śāṭān* in Job. Second, although Job suffers despite his innocence, the *śāṭān*'s conversation with God assumes that God's normal policy is to protect the righteous but to stretch out the divine hand to strike the wicked. Behind the idea of the *śāṭān* who attacks the upright and blameless Job, presumably, is the notion of a *śāṭān* who has God's tacit authorization to bring this sort of trouble on the wicked. In the case of Job, the *śāṭān* must obtain special permission from YHWH to attack an innocent individual.

Third, one can perhaps detect an underlying understanding of the *śāṭān* as "the Executioner" in YHWH's instructions to him regarding his attack on Job. When the *śāṭān* challenges God to strike Job, God assents, telling the *śāṭān* that all that Job has is in the *śāṭān*'s hand. But each time that God hands Job over to the *śāṭān*, God curtails the *śāṭān*'s authority, instructing him in the first instance not to strike Job's flesh and bones (1:12). In the second instance, God permits the *śāṭān* to attack Job's body but forbids him to take Job's life (2:4–6). These instructions limiting the *śāṭān*'s freedom would have been necessary, given that the use of such physical and lethal force would have normally been within the purview of "the Executioner's" authority.

To be sure, the book of Job, in an effort to address the complex problem of human suffering, describes the *śāṭān*'s activity in a way that moves well beyond the simple meaning of this figure's title. The *śāṭān* certainly does more in this narrative than attack and kill, and Job has much more to say about the nature and activity of the *śāṭān* than can be addressed in the present article. Nevertheless, despite the complexity of the book of Job, it is not difficult to see how the notion of "the Executioner" lies in the background of the story's description of the *śāṭān*. The translation of הַשָּׂטָן as "the Executioner" in Job 1–2, as in Zechariah 3, is supported by the word's usage outside the passage as well as by a contextual analysis of the passage.

---

[40] Although it is not impossible construe the *śāṭān*'s claim in Job 1–2 as an "accusation" in an abstract sense, this is not a straightforward reading of the text. F. Rachel Magdalene, for example, argues that the *śāṭān* accuses Job of "blasphemous intent" (*On the Scales of Righteousness: Neo-Babylonian Trial Law and the Book of Job* [BJS 348; Providence: Brown Judaic Studies, 2007], 106–17). The *śāṭān* does not imply that Job has the "intent" to do evil, but that the motivation for Job's loyalty to God is suspect. This legal interpretation of Job 1–2 also presupposes that the title "the *śāṭān*" means "the Accuser."

V. Conclusion

The tradition of a superhuman *śāṭān*, whether a *śāṭān* as in Numbers 22 and 1 Chronicles 21 or *the śāṭān* as in Zechariah 3 and Job 1–2, is among those traditions in the Hebrew Scriptures that pertain to superhuman agents of death, who visit God's enemies with capital judgment. One example of this sort of figure is the "destroyer" (המשחית) who kills the firstborn children of Egypt on the eve of the exodus (Exod 12:23). The angel of Yhwh also serves as a messenger of death in several passages. We have already noted Numbers 22, where the angel of Yhwh comes out as a *śāṭān* to kill Balaam. It is also the angel of Yhwh who, in response to the prayer of Hezekiah, strikes down 185,000 Assyrians who have marched on Judah (2 Kgs 19:35//Isa 37:36).[41] It is the angel of Yhwh, as well, who kills seventy thousand Israelites as a result of David's unwise census in 2 Samuel 24. It should be no surprise that the Chronicler's retelling of this story attributes this census and the death that ensues to the activity of a *śāṭān*, an executioner from Yhwh (1 Chr 21:1).

There is much more to be said about the *śāṭān* tradition and its varied manifestations in Zechariah and Job and in later literature. My forthcoming book on Satan in biblical and early Jewish literature (Eerdmans) addresses the history of the tradition more fully.[42] My arguments in this article are simply the following: (1) There is insufficient basis for the scholarly consensus that שָׂטָן means "accuser" and that שָׂטַן means "to accuse"; (2) a better case can be made that these words refer to lethal, physical "attack" and that שָׂטָן can in some instances be translated as "executioner"; (3) "executioner" and "execute" are very likely the proper understandings of שָׂטָן and שָׂטַן in Zechariah 3 and Job 1–2.

---

[41] Cf. the parallel account in 2 Chronicles 32, where the figure who kills the Assyrians is not the "angel of Yhwh," but simply an angel sent by Yhwh.

[42] One question that is raised but not answered by this study is the following: If שָׂטָן does not mean "accuser" in the Hebrew Scriptures, then how and when did the *śāṭān* become "the Accuser [ὁ κατήγωρ] of our comrades" (Rev 12:10)? To deal with this question fully would take one further into exegesis and tradition history than is within the scope of this semantic study. A very brief answer to the question, however, is that this development probably took place among Greek-speaking theologians. The LXX most often renders שָׂטָן and שָׂטַן with *διαβαλλ-: διαβολή (Num 22:32); διάβολος (1 Chr 21:1; Job 1:6, 7, 9, 12; 2:1, 2, 3, 4, 6, 7; Ps 108:6 [MT 109:6]; Zech 3:1, 2); ἐνδιαβάλλω (Num 22:22; Ps 37:21 [MT 38:21; Eng 38:20]; 70:13 [MT 71:13]; 108:4, 20, 29 [MT 109:4, 20, 29]). It also uses ἐπίβουλος (1 Sam 29:4; 2 Sam 19:23 [Eng. 22]; 1 Kgs 5:18 [Eng. 5:4]), ἀντίκειμαι (Zech 3:1) and the transliteration σαταν (1 Kgs 11:14, 23, 25]). The noun διάβολος and its cognates can refer to adversaries and various kinds of opposition. Although διάβολος can at times mean "accuser," according to W. Foerster, "accuser" is not the word's primary meaning ("διαβάλλω, διάβολος," *TDNT* 2:71–73). The same can be said of the root *διαβαλλ- in general. It is very unlikely, for instance, that διαβολή and ἐνδιαβάλλω in Num 22:22, 32 are supposed to refer to accusation. Given the semantic range of διάβολος, however, whatever the intent of the LXX translators, their use of this word opened the door for later interpreters to view the *śāṭān* (LXX ὁ διάβολος) as "the Accuser."

Excursus: The Meaning of שִׂטְנָה

The noun שִׂטְנָה occurs twice in the Hebrew Scriptures, though never together with שָׂטָן or שָׂטַן. In Gen 26:21, שִׂטְנָה is the name given to a well, because the herdsmen of Isaac and the herdsmen of Gerar "quarrel" (רִיב) over it.[43] The second passage in which שִׂטְנָה appears is Ezra 4:6, which says that during the reign of Xerxes the people of the land write a שִׂטְנָה that is intended to hinder Judah's reconstruction efforts. Although שִׂטְנָה in this passage is often translated as "accusation" (e.g., NRSV, NAB rev. ed., NIV, NJPS, ESV), we know none of the specifics of this letter. It was clearly a document of "opposition" of some sort.[44] The way in which this document was supposed to impede Judah's reconstruction efforts, however, is not specified.

Translators' choice of "accusation" for the word can only be based on the presumption that the root שׂטן carries this connotation, not on information as to the letter's contents found in Ezra 4:6 itself. A mistaken conflation of the שִׂטְנָה letter of 4:6 with a later letter described in Ezra 4:7–16 may also contribute to the (mis)understanding of שִׂטְנָה as an "accusation."[45] The later letter, which was written during the reign of Artaxerxes, suggests to Persian authorities that Jerusalem's rebuilding will lead to revolt. This letter, however, is not called a שִׂטְנָה. The contents of the earlier document, which *is* called a שִׂטְנָה, are unknown. Even were the later letter to be called a שִׂטְנָה, it would not be clear whether the word itself denoted accusation or simply meant "opposition." Judging from the two instances of this word in the Hebrew Scriptures, שִׂטְנָה does not appear to be identical in meaning to its cognates שָׂטָן and שָׂטַן. Nor, based on these two occurrences, can שִׂטְנָה be said to denote accusation.

---

[43] Cf. Gen 26:20, where another well is named עֵשֶׂק under similar circumstances. A verb based on the root עשק occurs in the same verse and is a *hapax legomenon*.

[44] So Horst, *Hiob*, 1:14.

[45] See, e.g., Nielsen, "שָׂטָן *śāṭān*," 75.

Jehoiakim's Dehumanizing Interment as a Ritual Act of Reclassification

SAUL M. OLYAN
Saul_Olyan@brown.edu
Brown University, Providence, RI 02912

Though scholars rarely comment on the beastly nature of Jehoiakim's predicted interment in Jer 22:18–19 ("[With] the burial of an ass he shall be buried, / Dragged and cast outside the gates of Jerusalem"), it is significant and worthy of careful explication, for it suggests a ritual act of reclassification: the king is to be punished by being dehumanized through the burial of his corpse, presumably in order to increase his shame. That ritual reclassification with animals represents a loss of rank for a king is made explicit in the narrative of Nebuchadnezzar's dream in Dan 3:31–4:34 and is implicit in various cuneiform descriptions of dehumanizing punitive rites imposed on living captive enemy rulers by Neo-Assyrian monarchs. Such ritual reclassification of a king represents a potentially efficacious assault on his own royal, hegemonic claims to honor, elite rank, exalted status, and, in some instances, even divinity. Far from being great, the reclassified Jehoiakim, like Nebuchadnezzar and the captive enemies of the kings of Assyria, is, according to Jer 22:18–19, nothing more than a beast with no claim whatsoever to royal honor or privilege.

In an article published in 2005, I noted in passing that the burial of Jehoiakim envisioned by Jer 22:18–19 was but one biblical example of dishonorably disposing of a corpse by casting it (שׁלך, hiphil/hophal) into an undesirable burial place or into an open area such as a field or square where it might remain exposed.[1] Clearly a

---

I am indebted to Jamie Novotny, Tracy Lemos, Stanley Stowers, Jordan Rosenblum, Michael Fox, Matthew Neujahr, and the journal's two anonymous reviewers for their helpful critical comments on an earlier draft of this article. Any errors of fact or judgment that remain are, however, my responsibility alone.

[1] Olyan, "Some Neglected Aspects of Israelite Interment Ideology," *JBL* 124 (2005): 601–16, specifically 606–7. Other examples of the ritual casting of a corpse (שׁלך, hiphil/hophal) include 2 Sam 18:17, in which Absalom's corpse is thrown into a pit in the woods, after which it is covered by a pile of stones; Josh 8:29, in which the corpse of the king of Ai is cast at the opening of the city gate, where it is piled over with stones; Jer 26:23, in which Uriah the prophet's corpse is cast into "the tombs of the people" after his execution by Jehoiakim; and 2 Kgs 9:25–26, in which Jehu

punitive ritual act, and one of profound disrespect and disregard,[2] the casting of the remains of the dead is paralleled in a number of cuneiform texts, including Hammurapi's Laws, *Enuma elish*, and Ashurbanipal's annals.[3] It is characteristic of the handling of vanquished foes, executed adversaries, and others thought to deserve particularly contemptuous treatment, according to extant biblical and cuneiform texts.[4] Yet the casting of Jehoiakim's corpse is but one component in a

---

orders his assistant to cast King Jehoram's corpse onto Naboth's plot of land. See also Josh 10:26–27; Jer 36:30; and 41:9, among other examples of corpse casting, as well as 2 Sam 20:21–22, in which the severed head of the rebel Sheba is cast over the wall of Abel Beth-maacah, and Isa 14:19, in which the remains of the "king of Babylon" will be cast out from his tomb (והשלכת מקברך ואתה). For a defense of this reading of Isa 14:19, see Saul M. Olyan, "Was the 'King of Babylon' Buried before His Corpse Was Exposed? Some Thoughts on Isa 14,19," *ZAW* 118 (2006): 423–26. Jeremiah 22:19 mentions both the dragging and the casting of the corpse as ritual acts of contempt. Though Morton Cogan is probably correct that the use of שלך hiphil/hophal for living persons in passages such as Ezek 16:5; Gen 21:15; and Jer 38:6, 9 likely means "abandon" rather than "cast," such cannot be the case in texts such as Isa 14:19 (והשלכת מקברך ואתה, "As for you, you shall be cast from your tomb …"), 2 Sam 20:21 (ראשו משלך אליך בעד החומה, "His head shall be cast over the wall to you") and 2 Kgs 9:25 (שא השלכהו בחלקת שדה, "Lift [him] and cast him on the property …") in which it is clear that the corpse or a part of it is cast. Though some of the other texts using שלך hiphil/hophal to describe the manipulation of a corpse might lend themselves to Cogan's interpretation (e.g., Jer 36:30), I believe most do not. For Cogan's argument, see "A Technical Term for Exposure," *JNES* 27 (1968): 133–35. He does not make reference to corpses in his article.

[2] That the casting of a corpse is a ritual act of dishonor and hostility is apparent when it is contrasted with normal, honorable biblical burial rites such as lamentation, a funeral procession with a bier, and the placement of the corpse in the family tomb by family members (see, e.g., Judg 16:31; 2 Sam 2:32; 3:31–32 and the discussion in Olyan, "Israelite Interment Ideology," 603–6). That these normal ritual acts honor the dead (כבד) is clearly stated in texts such as 2 Sam 10:3; Isa 14:18; and 2 Chr 32:33. The disrespect and disregard associated with corpse casting are made explicit in Isa 14:19, which compares the corpse cast out of its tomb to a "despised shoot" (נצר נתעב) and a "trampled corpse" (פגר מובס).

[3] See Hammurapi's Epilogue, in which Ishtar is called upon to cast up a heap of the corpses of soldiers serving a future ruler who slights Hammurapi (51:12–16; Rykle Borger, *Babylonisch-Assyrische Lesestücke* [2nd ed.; 2 vols.; AnOr 54; Rome: Pontificium Institutum Biblicum, 1979], 1:48); *Enuma elish* iv 104, in which Marduk casts down Tiamat's corpse and stands upon it (Philippe Talon, *The Standard Babylonian Creation Myth Enūma Eliš* [SAA Cuneiform Texts 4; Helsinki: Neo-Assyrian Text Corpus Project, 2005], 54); Ashurbanipal's narrative in which King Ahsheri of Mannea's corpse is said to be cast in the street of his city (Prism A III 9 and B III 85; Rykle Borger, *Beiträge zum Inschriftenwerk Assurbanipals: Die Prismenklassen A, B, C = K, D, E, F, G, H, J und T sowie andere Inschriften* [Wiesbaden: Harrassowitz, 1996], 35); and Ashurbanipal's notation that the bones of dead Babylonians were cast outside the cities of Babylon, Kutha, and Sippar, after the dogs and pigs were through with them (Prism A IV 77–85; Borger, *Beiträge zum Inschriftenwerk*, 45). The Akkadian verb used is *nadû*. For other examples of its usage, see *CAD* 11:73–74.

[4] I note that these are literary representations of punitive rites and that they ought to be treated as such by scholars. That means that we cannot know the extent to which corpse casting

constellation of ritual actions said by the text to constitute "the burial of an ass" (קבורת חמור), a domesticated animal.[5] Though scholars rarely comment on the beastly nature of Jehoiakim's predicted interment, it is significant and worthy of careful explication, for it suggests a ritual act of reclassification: the king is to be punished by being dehumanized through the burial of his corpse, presumably in order to increase his shame.[6] That ritual reclassification with animals represents a loss of rank for a king is made explicit in the narrative of Nebuchadnezzar's dream in Dan 3:31–4:34 and is implicit in various cuneiform descriptions of dehumanizing punitive rites imposed on living captive enemy rulers by Neo-Assyrian monarchs. Like the interment of Jehoiakim, such reclassification is most likely intended to shame the victim, even if no explicit rhetoric of humiliation is employed.

---

and other manifestations of ritual violence were actually practiced in any particular place and time, though the literary representations of such acts must have resonated with intended audiences to some degree at least. See further the astute remarks of Seth Richardson concerning the propagandistic nature of both literary and pictorial representations of Neo-Assyrian acts of violence against enemies, including the dead ("Death and Dismemberment in Mesopotamia: Discorporation between the Body and Body Politic," in *Performing Death: Social Analyses of Funerary Traditions in the Ancient Near East and Mediterranean* [ed. Nicola Laneri; Oriental Institute Seminars 3; Chicago: Oriental Institute of the University of Chicago, 2007], 198). Richardson raises the possibility that the Neo-Assyrian narratives are intended less to document practice and more to "persuade and assure Assyrian (rather than terrorize subject) audiences."

[5] On ritualization and ritualized acts, see Catherine M. Bell, *Ritual Theory, Ritual Practice* (New York: Oxford University Press, 1992), 88–93. For a general survey of animal comparisons in the Hebrew Bible, of which Jer 22:19 is an implicit example, see Eckart Schwab, "Die Tierbilder und Tiervergleiche des Alten Testaments: Material und Problemanzeigen," *BN* 59 (1991): 37–43. Though Schwab lists Jer 22:19 among his examples, he says nothing about it.

[6] On classification, see Bruce Lincoln, *Discourse and the Construction of Society: Comparative Studies of Myth, Ritual, and Classification* (New York: Oxford University Press, 1989), 7–8, 131–74. Lincoln speaks not only of hegemonic taxonomies/classifications and those who are invested in them, but of "countertaxonomic discourses" (= "counterclassification") "that mobilize novel social formations" and their purveyors (e.g., pp. 7–8, 174). That social rank and privilege are a result of classification is emphasized by Lincoln (e.g., pp. 7–8). What I am calling reclassification is roughly the equivalent of Lincoln's "counterclassification," though I note that agents of reclassification not only challenge hegemonic classifications but may be hegemons themselves in certain contexts (e.g., the Neo-Assyrian examples discussed ahead, in which victorious Assyrian kings ritually reclassify vanquished captive enemy rulers as domesticated animals). In still other settings, hegemony is not the focus of ritual reclassification. Examples of this include the separation rites of the Nazirite in Num 6:1–8 (abstention from the products of viticulture, shaving, and corpse contact) and those connected to the dedication of the Levites in Num 8:5–7 (purification sprinkling, shaving the entire body, washing garments, among others). On classification in religions, see also Jonathan Z. Smith, "Classification," in *Guide to the Study of Religion* (ed. Willi Braun and Russell T. McCutcheon; London: Cassell, 2000), 35–43. For reflections on classification as a human activity, see Brian K. Smith, *Classifying the Universe: The Ancient Indian Varna System and the Origins of Caste* (New York: Oxford University Press, 1994), 3–5, brought to my attention by J. Z. Smith ("Classification," 38).

The physical disposition of Jehoiakim's corpse is one of two aspects of the king's interment on which Jer 22:18–19 focuses, the other being the denial of lamentation:

> Therefore, thus says Yhwh to Jehoiakim son of Josiah, king of Judah:
> "They shall not lament [ספד] for him,
>   'Alas my brother, alas sister';
> They shall not lament for him,
>   'Alas lord, alas his majesty.'
> (With) the burial of an ass [קבורת חמור] he shall be buried,
>   dragged [סחב] and cast [שלך] outside the gates of Jerusalem."

Many scholars have commented on the withholding of lamentation for the dead king, though few have had anything to say about the physical acts that characterize the burial, and the relationship between the dragging and casting of the king's corpse and the denial of lamentation for him remains in the main unexplored.[7] Yet the passage suggests that the withholding of lamentation, the acts of dragging and casting the corpse, and the abandonment of the corpse in the open outside the city gates are all components of a single ritual constellation: the burial of an ass.[8] These actions must be considered as an ensemble if the text is to be interpreted with any kind of cogency. Thus, my analysis, in contrast to that of most scholars, will consider all aspects of Jehoiakim's anticipated animal burial.

Needless to say, the predicted interment of Jehoiakim is highly unusual in a number of respects. According to the Deuteronomists, the kings of Judah are typically buried in royal tombs inside the City of David (e.g., 1 Kgs 2:10; 11:43; 14:31; 2 Kgs 12:22; 14:20; 15:7; 16:20). This is true of kings who are killed elsewhere and

---

[7] See, e.g., Wilhelm Rudolph, *Jeremia* (2nd rev. ed.; HAT 12; Tübingen: Mohr Siebeck, 1958), 129–31; Artur Weiser, *Das Buch des Propheten Jeremia: Kapitel 1–25,14* (4th rev. ed.; ATD 20; Göttingen: Vandenhoeck & Ruprecht, 1960), 191; John Bright, *Jeremiah: A New Translation with Introduction and Commentary* (AB 21; Garden City, NY: Doubleday, 1965), 142; William McKane, *A Critical and Exegetical Commentary on Jeremiah* (2 vols.; ICC; Edinburgh: T&T Clark, 1986), 1:532–33; Robert P. Carroll, *Jeremiah: A Commentary* (OTL; Philadelphia: Westminster, 1986), 432; William L. Holladay, *Jeremiah 1: A Commentary on the Book of the Prophet Jeremiah, Chapters 1–25* (Hermeneia; Philadelphia: Fortress, 1986), 597–98; Ronald E. Clements, *Jeremiah* (IBC; Atlanta: John Knox, 1988), 134; Wolfgang Werner, *Das Buch Jeremia*, vol. 1, *Kapitel 1–25* (Neuer Stuttgarter Kommentar, Altes Testament 19; Stuttgart: Katholisches Bibelwerk, 1997), 196. Jack R. Lundbom spends some time discussing the actions of v. 19 and notes their indignity but does not relate them to the withholding of lamentation (*Jeremiah 21–36: A New Translation with Introduction and Commentary* [AB 21B; New York: Doubleday, 2004], 144–46). See similarly Georg Fischer, *Jeremia 1–25* (HTKAT; Freiburg: Herder, 2005), 664. Many commentators note that 2 Kgs 24:6, which states that Jehoiakim "lay down with his ancestors," a normal idiom for a natural death and burial in the family tomb (Lundbom, *Jeremiah 21–36*, 144), stands in tension with the anticipated interment of Jer 22:18–19.

[8] In contrast to most commentators, Benjamin A. Foreman recognizes that the lack of lamentation is part of what constitutes "the burial of an ass" (*Animal Metaphors and the People of Israel in the Book of Jeremiah* [FRLANT 238; Göttingen: Vandenhoeck & Ruprecht, 2011], 111 n. 15).

brought back to Jerusalem for burial, for example, Amaziah (2 Kgs 14:20).⁹ Even Manasseh is said to be buried in his tomb in the garden of Uzzah, presumably a locus within the city (2 Kgs 21:26). Though typically unmentioned in Deuteronomistic royal entombment notices, the narrative of Abner's funeral (2 Sam 3:31–35) suggests a number of ritual acts that might be components of an honorable interment process. These include a funeral procession with a bier, the tearing of garments, girding on sackcloth, weeping, fasting, and lamentation by mourners (ספד). The installation of the corpse in a tomb, preferably that of the family, is represented as the ideal interment in any number of biblical texts.¹⁰

Yet none of these ritual acts characterizes Jehoiakim's predicted interment. The statement that Jehoiakim will not be lamented, an obvious reversal of a ritual norm, is probably intended to suggest that other ritual acts honoring the deceased (e.g., weeping and tearing garments) will also be denied him.¹¹ The disposition of Jehoiakim's body outside the city of Jerusalem is an inversion of the royal norm according to the burial notations of the Deuteronomistic History cited above.¹² That Jehoiakim's body is to be dragged (סחב), cast (שלך), and left in the open contrasts sharply with the handling of the corpse typical of an honorable burial (e.g., procession with a bier, as in 2 Sam 3:31, and installation in a tomb).¹³ As mentioned, the withholding of lamentation (and, implicitly, other mourning rites), the dragging of the corpse, and its casting and abandonment outside the city gates together constitute what the text describes as "the burial of an ass" (קבורת חמור), a ritual procedure wholly unlike the norm for human interment as it is represented in biblical materials.¹⁴ It is noteworthy that mourning rites are not associated with an animal's death or burial in surviving biblical texts, and this might explain in part the emphasis on the denial of lamentation in Jer 22:18. It may also be the case that

---

⁹ Josiah also is brought back to Jerusalem for burial "in his tomb" (2 Kgs 23:30).

¹⁰ See n. 2 for texts that speak explicitly of such acts constituting an honorable burial. On the range of routine mourning behaviors, see, e.g., Gary A. Anderson, *A Time to Mourn, A Time to Dance: The Expression of Grief and Joy in Israelite Religion* (University Park: Pennsylvania State University Press, 1991), 49, 60–67; and Saul M. Olyan, *Biblical Mourning: Ritual and Social Dimensions* (Oxford: Oxford University Press, 2004), 29–34. On interment in the family tomb as the ideal, see further my discussion in "Israelite Interment Ideology," 603–4, 607–10.

¹¹ Most biblical texts that mention mourning the dead refer to one or two mourning rites only; these likely function as synecdoche for a larger combination of rites that constitute mourning. On this point, see my discussion in *Biblical Mourning*, 29 and n. 5.

¹² Also noted by Lundbom, *Jeremiah 21–36*, 146. Fischer observes that such a burial is not usual for a king, citing the example of Solomon (*Jeremia 1–25*, 664).

¹³ As I have noted elsewhere, the verb "to drag" (סחב) is also used of the behavior of dogs toward abandoned corpses in Jer 15:3. In contrast, an honorably buried corpse is "set to rest" (נוח) in a tomb ("Israelite Interment Ideology," 607 and n. 18). Fischer also mentions Jer 15:3 in his comments on the passage (*Jeremia 1–25*, 664).

¹⁴ As noted in n. 8, Foreman, unlike most commentators, recognizes that the lack of lamentation together with the acts described in v. 19 constitute what is meant by "the burial of an ass" (*Animal Metaphors*, 111 n. 15).

the withholding of elegiac words acknowledging the honor of the dead king (e.g., הדה, אדון) is intended to underscore his diminishment.[15] In any case, the fact that the king is to receive a domesticated animal's burial suggests that he is to be ritually reclassified as such an animal, presumably in order to diminish him and magnify his shame beyond what a single act of corpse abuse (e.g., simple abandonment of his corpse in the city) might accomplish.[16] Several biblical and cuneiform texts offer parallels to such ritual reclassification and diminishment of a king.

Daniel 3:31–4:34 narrates a dream of Nebuchadnezzar.[17] In this dream, the king is condemned to lose his reason and become in effect an animal on account of his transgressions, with the text drawing on both the imagery of domesticated animals and that of wild beasts and birds to describe the king's transformation. He receives the "mind of a beast" (לבב חיוה), according to 4:13. Driven away from humans, he is to reside with animals. He is to be fed grass as are cattle; covered with dew because he has no shelter, his hair grows like eagles' feathers and his nails grow to be like the claws of birds (4:22, 29, 30).[18] The mention of Nebuchadnezzar being driven away from humans and fed grass as if he were a domesticated bovine (4:22, 29) suggests that there are ritual dimensions to his transformation and that these are distinct from his receiving an animal's mind from Yhwh and losing his reason as a result.[19] The ritual actions of driving Nebuchadnezzar and feeding him grass, in combination with his loss of reason, result in his effective transformation. In short, there are both ritual and miraculous dimensions to Nebuchadnezzar's dehumanization.[20] When Nebuchadnezzar recognizes Yhwh's power and agency,

---

[15] Cf. Fischer, who suggests that the lack of mourning is to be explained by the happiness resulting from the end of a tyranny (*Jeremia 1–25*, 664).

[16] Fischer understands "the burial of an ass" to mean that the king's corpse is to be handled in the manner of an animal's carcass and speaks in passing of Jehoiakim ending up as an animal ("*Weit außerhalb der Gemeinschaft und wie ein Tier* endet ein Mensch und auch ein König"; *Jeremia 1–25*, 664 [italics in the original]).

[17] All verse citations for the pericope are from the MT unless otherwise indicated. On the complex relationship of the MT and the OG of this passage, see the helpful, succinct discussion of John J. Collins, *Daniel: A Commentary on the Book of Daniel* (Hermeneia; Minneapolis: Fortress, 1993), 219–21.

[18] According to the OG of v. 30b, Nebuchadnezzar's nails become like the claws of a lion rather than like those of a bird, as in the MT, and his hair becomes like an eagle's wings. For the text-critical issues raised by these alternative readings, see Collins, *Daniel*, 212. Christopher B. Hays argues that the bird and animal imagery used in v. 30 has a direct relationship to the dead, the underworld, and demonic aggression, and that its use suggests Nebuchadnezzar's "extreme affliction" ("Chirps from the Dust: The Affliction of Nebuchadnezzar in Daniel 4:30 in Its Ancient Near Eastern Context," *JBL* 126 [2007]: 305–25). Though this may be the case, Hays too readily plays down Nebuchadnezzar's loss of reason, another aspect of his dehumanization and a paramount focus of the passage.

[19] That a loss of reason is assumed by Nebuchadnezzar's receiving the mind of a beast is made clear in v. 33, which states that his reason was eventually restored to him. I note that Dan 4:30 states that Nebuchadnezzar "ate grass like cattle," in contrast to 4:22, 29, where he is fed.

[20] My thanks to Tracy Lemos for help with sharpening this argument.

his reason (מנדעא) is restored, as are his majesty and position as king (4:33). The narrative ends with Nebuchadnezzar's acknowledgment that his own arrogance led to his humbling by Yhwh: God "is able to bring low [להשפלה] those who walk in pride." In other words, Yhwh diminishes Nebuchadnezzar by effectively dehumanizing him and rewards him by restoring him to his previous state once Nebuchadnezzar recognizes Yhwh's power and agency. That Nebuchadnezzar's reclassification constitutes a loss of rank is made explicit by the statement that Yhwh "is able to bring low [להשפלה] those who walk in pride." That such debasement results in humiliation is very likely assumed by the narrative, even if not stated explicitly, given that Nebuchadnezzar loses his "majesty" (הדר) and "radiance" (זיו), and his kingdom loses its "honor" (יקר), all of which are eventually restored, according to 4:33.[21]

A number of cuneiform texts describe the diminishment of captive enemy kings through their ritual reclassification as domesticated animals. In Sennacherib's Nebi Yunus inscription, the king of Assyria ties up Shuzubu, the captive king of Babylon, at Nineveh's citadel gate "with a bear" (*da-bu-ú-iš*).[22] Ashurbanipal makes an example of the Arabian rebel Uaite son of Hazael by putting a collar on him and making him guard the citadel gate of Nineveh along with two fierce, though domesticated, beasts: "with a bear and a dog I tied him up" (*it-ti a-si* UR-GI$_7$ *ar-ku-us-šú*).[23] Ammuladi of Qidri is treated similarly, put on guard duty with dogs.[24] These literary examples and others[25] suggest what may well be a Neo-Assyrian royal topos: the ritual dehumanization of a living, captive king in order to punish him, shame him, and demonstrate the power of Assyria's gods and, by extension, their chosen

---

[21] Daniel 5:20, recapping the events of 3:31–4:34, states that Nebuchadnezzar himself had his honor taken away from him. The root שפל has associations with humiliation and self-abasement in a number of Semitic languages, including Aramaic, Hebrew, and Akkadian. On this, see the brief survey in K. Engelken, "שפל *šāpēl*," *TDOT* 15:442–43, with citations.

[22] A. Kirk Grayson and Jamie Novotny, *The Royal Inscriptions of Sennacherib, King of Assyria (704–681 BC), Part 1* (Royal Inscriptions of the Neo-Assyrian Period 3/1; Winona Lake, IN: Eisenbrauns, 2012), 223 (text 34, lines 33b–36a). See, similarly, 230 (text 35, lines 13′b–15′). My thanks to Jamie Novotny for making this edition available to me for citation before publication.

[23] Borger, *Beiträge zum Inschriftenwerk*, 62 (Prism A VIII 8–14). That the bear on guard duty has been domesticated is suggested by its role as a guard and its urban locus. Even if the bear and dog are aggressive and threatening, they are nonetheless under the control of the authorities, in contrast to wild beasts, and so are domesticated (see *Oxford English Dictionary*, s.v. "domesticate": "to accustom [an animal] to live under the care and near the habitations of man; to tame *or bring under control*" [www.oed.com/view/Entry/56668; my emphasis]).

[24] Borger, *Beiträge zum Inschriftenwerk*, 62 (Prism A VIII 15–29, esp. 27–29).

[25] Richardson ("Death and Dismemberment," 197 and n. 39) observes that "animal similes" are commonplace in these narratives, citing several additional texts that I have not mentioned here. In addition, see Esarhaddon's statements concerning Asuhili of Arza in Erle Leichty, *The Royal Inscriptions of Esarhaddon, King of Assyria (680–669 BC)* (Royal Inscriptions of the Neo-Assyrian Period 4; Winona Lake, IN: Eisenbrauns, 2011), 17–18 (text 1 III 39–42); 29 (text 2 I 57–63); 37 (text 3 II 10′–14′). My thanks to Jamie Novotny for providing the examples from Esarhaddon's accounts.

monarch, the king of Assyria.²⁶ The punitive dimension of the act is explicit in Ashurbanipal's description of Uaite's fate as a "severe punishment."²⁷ The humiliation is implicit in the captive king's thorough and very public debasement at the citadel gate.²⁸ The power and agency of the Assyrian gods and their chosen ruler are brought into relief through the public demonstration of the utter powerlessness of the victims of such abuse, as Ashurbanipal himself suggests.²⁹

How does Jer 22:18–19 compare to Dan 3:31–4:34 and the various cuneiform texts I have discussed? In each case, a king is the victim, though only in the Neo-Assyrian examples is the perpetrator also a king; in the biblical examples, it is Yhwh who is the agent of Nebuchadnezzar's and Jehoiakim's dehumanization. Furthermore, in the Neo-Assyrian texts, the captive king who is ritually reclassified as an animal is living, and his association is with domesticated animals, albeit aggressive ones, and their assigned tasks (e.g., dogs and bears guarding a city gate). Like the captive kings of the Neo-Assyrian examples, Nebuchadnezzar of Dan 3:31–4:34 is living and is ritually reclassified with domesticated animals, though of a more docile nature (cattle); unlike the kings, he lives in the field for the period of his punishment, not in the city, loses his reason through a divine intervention, and also takes on aspects of the appearance of wild birds and beasts.³⁰ In contrast to all of the other examples I have discussed, Jehoiakim is dead, and Jer 22:19 forecasts the dishonorable ritual disposition of his corpse in the manner of that of

---

²⁶ For a comparable Neo-Assyrian visual representation, see *ANEP*, 447, an inscribed stela from Zinjirli portraying Esarhaddon towering over two leashed captive kings. Tallay Ornan compares the similar imagery of the Broken Obelisk from Nineveh and notes the antiquity of the motif of the king's leashed captives in Egypt ("Who Is Holding the Lead Rope? The Relief of the Broken Obelisk," *Iraq* 69 [2007]: 62, 64–65 and 65 n. 10, citing *ANEP*, 323, 325, 326).

²⁷ Borger, *Beiträge zum Inschriftenwerk*, 62 (Prism A VIII 10: *an-nu kab-tu*).

²⁸ Note the public locus of each rite of reclassification: the citadel gate of Nineveh and the lock (*ši-ga-ru*) of the gate. Jamie Novotny has pointed out to me that the citadel gate would have been the most prominent and visible locus in Nineveh and that the humiliation of captive kings would have been witnessed by visiting foreign dignitaries as well as Nineveh's inhabitants (oral communication).

²⁹ E.g., Borger, *Beiträge zum Inschriftenwerk*, 62 (Prism A VIII 8–9). Although David Marcus mentions several of the examples discussed above in his study of Neo-Assyrian animal similes, he does not explore their implications ("Animal Similes in Assyrian Royal Inscriptions," *Or* 46 [1977]: 88, 92).

³⁰ While cattle are domesticated, eagles and lions in the wild are obviously not. It is unclear what kind of birds the MT of Dan 4:30 refers to. Daniel 3:31–4:34 mixes imagery of both domesticated animals and wild beasts and birds in its portrayal of Nebuchadnezzar's transformation, perhaps to underscore its extremity and, therefore, Yhwh's power as agent to remake Nebuchadnezzar and to undo the transformation. Nevertheless, the mixing of imagery in this text is perplexing, given that wild animals such as the lion and wild birds such as the eagle often have positive cultural resonances and are not emblems of submission, in contrast to domesticated beasts (e.g., 2 Sam 1:23; Ezek 17:3; Amos 3:8). See further Marcus, "Animal Similes," 87 (on the lion and wild bull in cuneiform literature) and 94–95 (on the eagle).

an ass, a docile domesticated animal most closely comparable to the cattle that keep Nebuchadnezzar company. The association of the dehumanized king with domesticated animals in these texts may be no accident, given that domesticated animals, even if they are fierce and not docile, are subject to the authority and control of human masters, in contrast to animals in the wild.[31] Thus, ritual reclassification with domesticated animals may have been thought to be especially dishonoring for a king, as it brings into relief his submission to the authority of the reclassifying agent, whether a fellow king or a deity.[32]

In Jer 22:18–19 and the other examples I have treated, kings living or dead are dehumanized through rites that reclassify them as domesticated animals: the treatment of the king's corpse as if it were an ass's carcass; collaring, chaining, or putting captive kings on a leash as if they were domesticated guard animals and assigning animal roles to them; kings placed in the company of animals rather than humans; a king driven and fed grass as if he were a domesticated bovine. In all of these cases, the king, whether dead or alive, is separated from humans, human activity, human roles, and human loci, in effect becoming an animal, to his evident shame. It may be that Jer 22:18–19 and the other texts that I have discussed here are evidence of a pan–West Asian literary and visual topos of the dehumanized king, whether living or dead, who is condemned to severe, humiliating punishment through his ritual reclassification with domesticated animals.[33] At all events, such ritual reclassification of a king represents a potentially efficacious assault on his own royal, hegemonic claims to honor, elite rank, exalted status (e.g., הדה, אדון), and, in some instances, even divinity.[34] Far from being great, the reclassified Jehoiakim, like Nebuchadnezzar and the captive enemies of the kings of Assyria, is, according to Jer 22:18–19, nothing more than a beast with no claim whatsoever to royal honor or privilege. Thus, ritual reclassification with domesticated animals, is, potentially, an effective tool to diminish the enemy, the rebel, the offender, even if he is a king. In the case of Jer 22:18–19, it ought to be recognized as yet another tactic in the larger prophetic project of countering kings and their claims.[35]

---

[31] Domesticated animals are not infrequently portrayed as docile in biblical and cuneiform literatures. See, e.g., Num 22:21–35; Isa 1:3; 11:6–7; Prov 7:22, among many biblical examples. The use of domesticated animals as examples of submission and docility in Neo-Assyrian literary imagery is explored by Marcus, "Animal Similes," 91–94. On the positive cultural associations of wild animals, see the texts cited in the preceding note.

[32] It may be that reclassifiation with docile domesticated animals was viewed as more humiliating than reclassification with aggressive domesticated animals, though here I speculate.

[33] I hope to explore this possibility further in another publication.

[34] Texts suggesting the divinity of Davidic monarchs include 2 Sam 7:14; Isa 9:5; Ps 2:7; 89:26. On reclassification or counterclassification as a challenge to hegemonic taxonomies, see my discussion of Bruce Lincoln's work in n. 6 above.

[35] On this particular prophetic role, see, e.g., Frank Moore Cross, *Canaanite Myth and Hebrew Epic: Essays in the History of the Religion of Israel* (Cambridge, MA: Harvard University Press, 1973), 223–29.

New and Recent Titles

THE FORGOTTEN KINGDOM
The Archaeology and History of Northern Israel
Israel Finkelstein

The French edition of this volume, *Le royaume biblique oublié* (Odile Jacob. 2013), received the "Prix Delalande-Guérineau" of the Académie des Inscriptions et Belles-Lettres.
Digital open-access, 978-1-58983-911-3   210 pages, 2013   Code: 062805
Paper $24.95, 978-1-58983-910-6   Hardcover $39.95, 978-1-58983-912-0
Ancient Near East Monographs 5

TEL DAN IN ITS NORTHERN CULTIC CONTEXT
Andrew R. Davis

This book provides a detailed description of the temple complex at Tel Dan in northern Israel during the Iron Age and develops a portrait of Iron Age worship at the temple.
Paper $32.95, 978-1-58983-928-1   226 pages, 2013   Code: 061720
Hardcover $47.95, 978-1-58983-930-4   E-book $32.95, 978-1-58983-929-8
Archaeology and Biblical Studies 20

GODS IN DWELLINGS
Temples and Divine Presence in the Ancient Near East
Michael B. Hundley

Gods In Dwellings examines the major temples and the gods who inhabit them in ancient Egypt, Mesopotamia, Hittite Anatolia, and Syria-Palestine.
Paper $58.95, 978-1-58983-918-2   452 pages, 2013   Code: 064703
Hardcover $78.95, 978-1-58983-920-5   E-book $58.95, 978-1-58983-919-9
Writings from the Ancient World Supplements 3

ROYAL HITTITE INSTRUCTIONS AND RELATED ADMINISTRATIVE TEXTS
Jared L. Miller

The entire corpus of Hittite Instruction texts, newly translated, with introductory essays, references, and indices.
Paper $53.95, 978-1-58983-656-3   474 pages, 2013   Code: 061531
Hardcover $73.95, 978-1-58983-769-0   E-book $53.95, 978-1-58983-657-0
Writings from the Ancient World 31

Society of Biblical Literature • P.O. Box 2243 • Williston, VT 05495-2243
Phone: 877-725-3334 (toll-free) or 802-864-6185 • Fax: 802-864-7626
Order online at www.sbl-site.org

Is Amos (Still) among the Wise?

JOHN L. MCLAUGHLIN
johnl.mclaughlin@utoronto.ca
University of St. Michael's College, Toronto, ON M5S 1J4, Canada

The book of Amos and the prophet himself continue to be interpreted in light of the Israelite wisdom tradition on the basis of proposed links to wisdom forms, vocabulary, and ideas, plus geographical factors. Although some studies have considered individual suggestions of wisdom influence in Amos, they reach different conclusions. In addition to this lack of consensus, to date no one has considered all the arguments for wisdom influence in Amos together. This article fills that gap by presenting a detailed analysis of all such claims, demonstrating that even in the few cases where there is a superficial similarity between Amos and wisdom forms, terms, or ideas, such features have a function or nuance in the book of Amos that is very different from their use in the wisdom tradition. Thus, Amos should no longer be interpreted in light of the Israelite wisdom tradition.

Although some scholars had previously noted points of contact between Amos and the wisdom literature, the first concentrated effort to demonstrate wisdom influence in the book of Amos was Samuel Terrien's 1962 essay, in which he proposed eight specific correlations (plus other general ones) between the prophet and the biblical wisdom literature.[1] Two years later Hans Walter Wolff published a brief monograph that expanded and supplemented Terrien's arguments and argued that Amos was a clan elder.[2] Many, but not all, of their claims have been evaluated separately by James L. Crenshaw and J. Alberto Soggin, and to lesser extents in other surveys of wisdom influence in general.[3] However, no one has considered all

[1] Terrien, "Amos and Wisdom," in *Israel's Prophetic Heritage: Essays in Honor of James Muilenburg* (ed. Bernhard W. Anderson and Walter J. Harrelson; New York: Harper & Bros., 1962), 108–15.

[2] Wolff, *Amos' geistige Heimat* (WMANT 18; Neukirchen-Vluyn: Neukirchener Verlag, 1964), translated as *Amos the Prophet: The Man and His Background* (trans. Foster R. McCurley; ed. John Reumann; Philadelphia: Fortress, 1973); see also idem, *Joel and Amos: A Commentary on the Books of the Prophets Joel and Amos* (trans. Waldemar Janzen, S. Dean McBride, Jr., and Charles A. Muenchow; Hermeneia; Philadelphia: Fortress, 1977), passim.

[3] Crenshaw, "The Influence of the Wise on Amos: The 'Doxologies of Amos' and Job 5, 9–16; 9, 5–10," *ZAW* 79 (1967): 42–52; Soggin, "Amos and Wisdom," in *Wisdom in Ancient Israel: Essays*

the arguments for wisdom influence in Amos together, while Crenshaw added another that has not received the same evaluation as those of Terrien and Wolff. Moreover, each interpreter reached different conclusions as to the extent of wisdom influence in Amos, accepting some proposals rejected by others, and vice versa. In addition, commentators continue to identify various amounts of wisdom material in Amos.[4] Some even go beyond just linking individual parts of the book with wisdom to interpret the prophet himself against that background, which has implications for understanding the book as a whole.[5] Moreover, if Amos does display wisdom connections, that would factor into determining the extent of wisdom influence in the First Testament beyond the traditional wisdom books (Job, Proverbs, Qoheleth). As such, although Terrien's and Wolff's treatments are now some fifty years old, the issue remains relevant for contemporary scholarship. But since there is no comprehensive examination of possible wisdom influence in Amos and the existing limited treatments have not produced any consensus, it is necessary to analyze all proposed evidence in order to determine whether interpreting Amos in light of the Israelite wisdom tradition is valid.

Previous evaluations of possible wisdom influence beyond the acknowledged Israelite wisdom literature have looked for examples of wisdom forms, wisdom vocabulary, and wisdom ideas.[6] However, individual points of similarity to wisdom

---

in Honour of J. A. Emerton (ed. John Day, Robert P. Gordon, and H. G. M. Williamson; Cambridge: Cambridge University Press, 1995), 119–23; see also Hans-Jürgen Hermisson, *Studien zur israelitischen Spruchweisheit* (WMANT 28; Neukirchen-Vluyn: Neukirchener Verlag, 1968), 88–92; Hans Heinrich Schmid, "Amos: Zur Frage nach der 'Geistigen Heimat' des Propheten," *WD* 10 (1969): 85–103, esp. 92–96; R. N. Whybray, *The Intellectual Tradition in the Old Testament* (BZAW 135; Berlin: de Gruyter, 1974), 73, 119, 131, 140–42; Ronald E. Clements, *Prophecy and Tradition* (Growing Points in Theology; Oxford: Blackwell, 1975), 76–79; Donn F. Morgan, *Wisdom in the Old Testament Traditions* (Oxford: Blackwell, 1981), 66–72; R. N. Whybray, "Prophecy and Wisdom," in *Israel's Prophetic Tradition: Essays in Honour of Peter R. Ackroyd* (ed. Richard Coggins, Anthony Phillip, and Michael Knibb; Cambridge: Cambridge University Press, 1982), 188–90.

[4] E.g., James Limburg, *Hosea—Micah* (IBC; Louisville: John Knox, 1988), 82; Francis I. Andersen and David Noel Freedman, *Amos: A New Translation with Introduction and Commentary* (AB 24A; New York: Doubleday, 1989), passim, esp. 13, 147, 384–85, 468, 519, 520; Shalom M. Paul, *Amos: A Commentary on the Book of Amos* (Hermeneia; Minneapolis: Fortress, 1991), 4, 104–5, 161 n. 27; Jörg Jeremias, *The Book of Amos: A Commentary* (trans. Douglas W. Stott; OTL; Louisville: Westminster John Knox, 1998), 22, 51 n. 13; Richard J. Coggins, *Joel and Amos* (NCB Commentary; Sheffield: Sheffield Academic Press, 2000), 85, 108, 137; Daniel J. Simundson, *Hosea, Joel, Amos, Obadiah, Jonah, Micah* (AOTC; Nashville: Abingdon, 2005), 151, 152, 161, 162, 166, 182; R. Reed Lessing, *Amos* (Concordia Commentary; St. Louis: Concordia, 2009), 208, 214–15, 290, 324–25. See also Victor H. Matthews, *Social World of the Hebrew Prophets* (Peabody, MA: Hendrickson, 2001), 70.

[5] Paul, *Amos*, 105; Limburg, *Hosea—Micah*, 82; Simundson, *Hosea, Joel, Amos, Obadiah, Jonah, Micah*, 152, but contrast his p. 162. Granted, none is as extensive in this regard as Wolff, *Amos the Prophet*.

[6] See the discussions in James L. Crenshaw, "Method in Determining Wisdom Influence on 'Historical' Literature," *JBL* 88 (1969): 129–42; Whybray, *Intellectual Tradition*, 71–76; Morgan,

forms, vocabulary, or ideas by themselves are not necessarily evidence of wisdom influence. Since wisdom draws on experience, it is not unreasonable to expect some commonality among different types of literature.[7] Moreover, a speaker or author may appropriate a form or motif that is characteristic of one type of literature and adapt it to his or her own purposes, but that does not make that person a member of the group that generated and/or preserved the form or motif.[8] Therefore, both "life setting" and nuance are important: is a wisdom form or term being used in the same way as it would have been used by the sages? If not, the possibility of wisdom influence in any given case is significantly weakened, if not destroyed.[9] Finally, single points of contact may simply be coincidental, so it is also important to consider the cumulative weight of various arguments when taken together.[10]

With these points in mind, I turn now to a reevaluation of Terrien's and Wolff's arguments for wisdom influence in Amos, and specifically for the wisdom tradition as a major social context for the prophet and his message. Their arguments fall into the three categories mentioned above, namely, wisdom forms, wisdom vocabulary, and wisdom ideas, plus a fourth: geographical links. I will consider each category in turn, starting with the last one, after which I will discuss the additional proposal by Crenshaw.

I. Geographical Links

Both Terrien and Wolff propose a wisdom context for Amos on the basis of geographic connections. Terrien notes that in the prophetic literature Beer-sheba is mentioned only in Amos 5:5; 8:14 and that the name Isaac stands for the nation of Israel only in Amos 7:9, 16. Since Isaac was the father of Jacob (Israel) and Esau (Edom), and Amos's home in Tekoa was close to both Beer-sheba and Edom,

---

Wisdom in the Old Testament Traditions, 13–29; Roland E. Murphy, *The Tree of Life: An Exploration of Biblical Wisdom Literature* (3rd ed.; Grand Rapids: Eerdmans, 2002), 98–102.

[7] Crenshaw, "Influence of the Wise," 44; idem, "Method in Determining Wisdom Influence," 132–33; Schmid, "Amos," 99, 101–2; J. William Whedbee, *Isaiah and Wisdom* (Nashville: Abingdon, 1971) 24; Whybray, *Intellectual Tradition*, 75, 119, 122; Soggin, "Amos and Wisdom," 120; Murphy, *The Tree of Life*, 100.

[8] In fact, a person can use a group's forms, terms, and content against that very group, either as a critique of the group or as a challenge to it to live up to what it professes. For a discussion of the prophets using wisdom traditions to critique the wise, see William McKane, *Prophets and Wise Men* (SBT 44; London: SCM, 1965), 65–112. For Isaiah in particular, see Joseph Jensen, O.S.B., *The Use of tôrâ by Isaiah: His Debate with the Wisdom Tradition* (CBQMS 3; Washington, DC: Catholic Biblical Association of America, 1973); J. Fichtner, "Isaiah among the Wise," in *Studies in Ancient Israelite Wisdom* (ed. James L. Crenshaw; Library of Biblical Studies; New York: Ktav, 1976), 432–37.

[9] Crenshaw, "Method in Determining Wisdom Influence," 133–34; Whybray, *Intellectual Tradition*, 74, 75.

[10] Murphy, *Tree of Life*, 101.

Terrien posits that Amos could have interacted with Edomites, who are noted for their wisdom in Jer 49:7 (cf. 1 Kgs 5:11 [Eng. 4:30–31]; Obad 8).[11] However, various names are used for the nation in the book of Amos, all more frequently than Isaac. The most common is Israel itself, which occurs twenty-five times (including in parallel with both instances of Isaac) plus once in the book's superscription, but we also find Jacob six times (3:13; 6:8; 7:2, 5; 8:7; 9:8) and Joseph three times (5:6, 15; 6:6). The latter two point to a northern emphasis over a southern one and, together with "Israel," demonstrate an overwhelming preference for names other than Isaac to refer to the nation. This indicates that Isaac was not an important term for Amos after all.[12] Certainly, if the name pointed to Edomite wisdom as a significant influence on the prophet, we would expect to find it more than twice. As for Beer-sheba, both references to the city are in sequence with places of worship, indicating that the prophet is concerned with it as a cultic site, not for any putative wisdom connections. Moreover, since there are no indications in the book of Amos of any contacts between Beer-sheba, Tekoa, or Amos himself and Edom, such speculation is a thin thread upon which to hang wisdom influence in Amos.[13]

Wolff also thinks that Amos, as a native of Tekoa, would have encountered Edomites while pasturing his flocks and notes as well the skilled oratory of a "wise woman" from Tekoa (2 Samuel 14).[14] With respect to the first point, I need only echo his own "great caution" about such claims with respect to the use of Isaac and Beer-sheba.[15] As for the wise woman of Tekoa, she received her words from Joab (2 Sam 14:3), which makes her a poor exemplar of wisdom.[16] But in any case, the fact that one woman from Tekoa was called "wise" does not mean that everyone from there was wise, or was influenced by the wise, anymore than the fact that there were priests in Jerusalem meant that all its residents were priests.

II. Wisdom Forms

A. *The Graduated Numerical Saying (Amos 1:3–2:6)*

Both Terrien and Wolff point to the graduated numerical sayings in the Oracles against the Nations as evidence of wisdom influence in Amos.[17] There is

---

[11] Terrien, "Amos and Wisdom," 113–14. On Edom and wisdom, see Robert H. Pfeiffer, "Edomitic Wisdom," *ZAW* 64 (1926): 13–25.

[12] Christo Lombaard thinks that the name was added after 722 B.C.E. to appeal to a southern audience ("What Is Isaac Doing in Amos 7?" *OTE* 17 [2004]: 435–42).

[13] Cf. Wolff, *Amos the Prophet*, 78–80. He cites Terrien's claim approvingly but adds, "Only with great caution may one have recourse to such conjectures as hypotheses" (p. 80). See also Soggin, who simply notes that Terrien's view is "far-fetched" ("Amos and Wisdom," 123).

[14] Wolff, *Amos the Prophet*, 77–78.

[15] See n. 13 above.

[16] Crenshaw, "Influence of the Wise," 45.

[17] Terrien, "Amos and Wisdom," 109–10; Wolff, *Amos the Prophet*, 34–44; idem, *Joel and*

no doubt that the x / x + 1 formula appears more frequently in the wisdom literature than anywhere else, but it is not exclusive to that corpus; it is found also in Jer 36:23; Mic 5:5; and Hos 6:2.[18] However, the wisdom usage is distinct from those three biblical texts as well as from the Amos passages, in that the wisdom texts enumerate the individual elements of the x / x + 1 formula up to the higher number. This reflects the didactic nature of the wisdom usage, which is to correlate the various items listed. Moreover, the final item is often climactic, involving a surprising twist. Proverbs 30:18-19 exemplifies this, with the final line challenging the reader to make a connection between the previously listed "way" of a bird, a serpent, and a ship, with the "way" of a man and a woman.[19] In contrast, with the exception of the oracle against Israel (which lists more than four offenses), there is only one thing mentioned in each Amos text. Although this may reflect the climactic role of the final element in the wisdom form, without the preceding three items indicated in the repeated phrase, "for three sins of [X] and for four," the emphatic function of the fourth element is lost.[20] Moreover, the content in Amos is radically different

---

Amos, 95-96, 138; they were anticipated by Johannes Lindblom, "Wisdom in the Old Testament Prophets," in *Wisdom in Israel and in the Ancient Near East: Presented to Professor Harold Henry Rowley by the Society for Old Testament Study in Association with the Editorial Board of Vetus Testamentum* (ed. Martin Noth and D. Winton Thomas; VTSup 3; Leiden: Brill, 1955), 202-3, and are followed by Crenshaw, "Influence of the Wise," 49; Jeremias, *Book of Amos*, 22; Simundson, *Hosea, Joel, Amos, Obadiah, Jonah, Micah*, 161; Lessing, *Amos*, 290. While some of the oracles may be later additions to Amos, at least some are authentic; for example, Wolff himself considers Amos 1:9, 11; 2:4 to be secondary (*Joel and Amos*, 139-41). For detailed discussions of the redactional issues, compare the treatments in Paul, *Amos*, 16-27, and Dirk U. Rottzoll, *Studien zur Redaktion und Komposition des Amosbuchs* (BZAW 243; Berlin: de Gruyter, 1996), 22-50.

[18] It also occurs outside the Bible at *KTU* 1.17.II.26-46 and Ahiqar vi 72. The full form is found in wisdom texts in Job 5:17-27; Prov 6:16-19; 30:15-16, 18-19, 21-23, 24-28, 29-31; Sir 25:7-11; 26:5-6, 28-29; 50:25-26. On the form itself, see Wolfgang M. W. Roth, "The Numerical Sequence X/X+1 in the Old Testament," *VT* 12 (1962): 300-311; idem, *Numerical Sayings in the Old Testament: A Form Critical Study* (VTSup 13; Leiden: Brill, 1965), passim; Georg Sauer, *Die Sprüche Agurs: Untersuchungen zur Herkunft, Verbreitung und Bedeutung einer biblischen Stilform unter besonderer Berücksichtigung von Proverbia c. 30* (BWANT 5.4; Stuttgart: Kohlhammer, 1963); Meir Weiss, "The Pattern of Numerical Sequence in Amos 1-2: A Re-Examination," *JBL* 86 (1967): 416-23.

[19] This emphatic aspect of the final item is present to varying degrees in the other wisdom texts, most explicitly in Prov 6:19; 30:29-31; Sir 25:7-11; 26:6-9, 28-29; 50:26. The Sirach texts in particular expound on the final item to varying lengths.

[20] Contra Morgan, *Wisdom in the Old Testament Traditions*, 68. Weiss proposes that in Amos the numbers should be added to achieve 7, indicating each nation's "complete sin" ("Pattern of Numerical Sequence," 419-20; see, more recently, Karl Möller, *A Prophet in Debate: The Rhetoric of Persuasion in the Book of Amos* [JSOTSup 372; Sheffield: Sheffield Academic Press, 2003], 183-84). This would support my argument that Amos departs from wisdom usage, but note the scholarly criticism of Weiss summarized in Paul, *Amos*, 28. Rather than provide the actual numbers, Soggin renders the phrase as "innumerable crimes," which also makes my point (*The Prophet Amos: A Translation and Commentary* [trans. John Bowden; London: SCM, 1987], 32;

from the content of the wisdom texts. Whereas the wisdom tradition in general and the numerical sayings in particular gain insight into human experiences by reflection on nature and everyday human affairs, Amos 1:3–2:3 consists of divinely revealed ("Thus says Yhwh") condemnations of excesses in war, with 2:4–5 also appealing to "the law of Yhwh." With respect to the former, however frequent warfare was in the ancient world, neither the crimes that Amos denounces nor the source of his message was the normal, everyday human experience that constitutes the primary basis for wisdom insights. Thus, the prophet's use of the graduated numerical form's introductory words independently of the wisdom usage of the form itself suggests that he may have had only a passing familiarity with the opening formula without any insight into its function as a wisdom form. In any case, it has been adapted to the proclamation of the message he received from God and integrated into the Oracle against the Nations form so much that it cannot be used to establish a wisdom background for Amos.[21]

B. Didactic/Rhetorical Questions
(Amos 3:3–6, 8; 5:20, 25; 6:2, 12; 9:7)

Terrien points to the series of cause-and-effect questions in Amos 3:3–6, 8 as well as other questions in 5:25; 6:2, 12; and 9:7 as evidence of a didactic approach taken from the wisdom tradition.[22] Wolff adds 5:20 to the list and argues not only that all these questions are comparisons rooted in common experiences of nature and humankind but also that 3:3–6a, 8a in particular constitute the logical basis for the conclusions in vv. 6b and 8b.[23] However, as Terrien himself admits, "The use of the interrogative maxim is so widespread in the Old Testament in general that it cannot be presented as an argument tending to show points of contact between the wise and Amos."[24] An obvious example is the entrance liturgies found in Pss 15:1–5;

---

idem, "Amos and Wisdom," 121); cf. Terrien's reference to "an implication of indefiniteness" ("Amos and Wisdom," 110).

[21] A point acknowledged by Wolff: "The 'graded numerical saying' is never employed by Amos himself in the way that clan instruction is fond of using it" (*Joel and Amos*, 96). Roth considered the formula in Amos too divergent to be an example of the form at all (*Numerical Sayings*, 63 n. 3).

[22] Terrien, "Amos and Wisdom," 11–12; see already Walter Baumgartner, "The Wisdom Literature," in *The Old Testament and Modern Study: A Generation of Discovery and Research* (ed. H. H. Rowley; Oxford: Clarendon, 1951), 211; Lindblom, "Wisdom in the Old Testament Prophets," 201, 203.

[23] Wolff, *Amos the Prophet*, 6–16; idem, *Joel and Amos*, 93–94; cf. Morgan, *Wisdom in the Old Testament Traditions*, 69–70. Many recent commentators also consider Amos 3:3–6, 8 to be evidence of wisdom influence: Andersen and Freedman, *Amos*, 33, 147, 384–85; Paul, *Amos*, 104–5; Jeremias, *Book of Amos*, 51; Simundson, *Hosea, Joel, Amos, Obadiah, Jonah, Micah*, 182; Lessing, *Amos*, 214.

[24] Terrien, "Amos and Wisdom," 112. This is echoed by Crenshaw, "Influence of the Wise," 46–47; Soggin, "Amos and Wisdom," 121–22; contrast Soggin, *Prophet Amos*, 58.

24:3-6; and Mic 6:6-8 (cf. Isa 33:14-16). Wolff disputes the liturgies' relevance, arguing that the questions in Amos are rooted in common experience, especially of nature, and not the cult, but many of them are in fact linked to Israel's religious traditions.[25] While the questions in Amos 3:2-5 and 8a are based in nature, v. 6a moves into the more specialized realm of warfare, while vv. 6b and 8b refer to Yhwh, thus invoking Israel's specific religious beliefs. Moreover, v. 8b asks about the compulsion to prophesy on behalf of Yhwh, once again removing the verse from the realm of common human experience. At the same time, the questions about nature do not provide the basis for the conclusions in vv. 6b and 8b, as Wolff claims. There is nothing in the initial questions that would lead one to the specifically Israelite beliefs in 3:6b and 8b. Rather, they are separate questions to which the speaker expects affirmative responses.[26] Since each is self-contained and does not lead necessarily to the next, it is incorrect to speak of this as a "didactic" passage and, on that basis, to conclude that it demonstrates wisdom influence in Amos.

The other so-called didactic questions in Amos do not require a wisdom background or approach either. Even though Amos 5:20 asks about the Day of the Lord, another concept firmly rooted in Israel's religious and cultic traditions, Wolff points to the double comparison in 5:19 as indicative of wisdom's didactic approach.[27] But that verse does not reflect on common experience, as in the wisdom tradition; rather, it presents unusually extreme scenarios to illustrate that the people's understanding of the Day of the Lord is wrong. Similarly, the question about sacrifice in 5:25 requires knowledge of Israel's cultic laws and its wilderness traditions. Nor is 6:2 a matter of common human experience, but instead requires knowledge of the specific history of the foreign cities named.[28] On the other hand, 6:12 is better

---

[25] Wolff, *Amos the Prophet*, 12-13; contrast Crenshaw, "Influence of the Wise," 47. Crenshaw (his n. 21) also points to Jer 2:5-15 as another example of non-wisdom use of questions in a prophet; the passage includes questions, comparison with other nations (v. 10; cf. Amos 6:2; 9:7), and a reference to lions (v. 15; cf. Amos 3:4 and 8). Similarly, note the "trial" passages of Second Isaiah that repeatedly ask whose power or knowledge can compare with Yhwh's (e.g., Isa 41:26; 43:9; 44:7; 45:21; 46:5; etc.).

[26] See Soggin, *Prophet Amos*, 59; idem, "Amos and Wisdom," 122.

[27] Wolff, *Amos the Prophet*, 15-16. See also Andersen and Freedman, *Amos*, 519, 520, 601, 604.

[28] The precise historical reference is disputed, but if the point of comparison is a warning, the cities would have been defeated, which suggests some time after Shalmaneser III's claims of victory over Calneh (Kullani) in 858 b.c.e. and Hamath in 853 b.c.e., plus Gath's defeat by Hazael ca. 815 b.c.e. (2 Kgs 12:18) or its destruction by Uzziah of Judah ca. 760 b.c.e. (2 Chr 26:6); thus, e.g., Paul, *Amos*, 202-4; see also Andersen and Freedman, *Amos*, 558-59. If the point is Samaria's superiority, that would require that the cities were still independent, which would mean a period before Tiglath-pileser III's conquest of Calneh and Hamath in 738 b.c.e., plus Philistia, and thus Gath, in 734 b.c.e.; for this view see, e.g., William Rainey Harper, *A Critical and Exegetical Commentary on the Books of Amos and Hosea* (ICC 18; Edinburgh: T&T Clark, 1912), 144-46; Rottzoll, *Studien zur Redaktion*, 155-56.

classified as an "impossible saying," which is related to the riddle.[29] According to Crenshaw, wisdom is only one of a number of contexts in which riddles were used, so the presence of a derivative form in 6:12 is hardly probative.[30] Finally, 9:7 comprises comparative questions that rely on the revelation of Yhwh's universal rule and involvement with the surrounding nations, as well as the concrete history of those nations and Israel's own specific exodus tradition. In other words, the verse is not based on common experience or observation, as is the case in the wisdom tradition.

In sum, the questions Terrien and Wolff cite do not require a wisdom context and, for the most part, contradict it. This raises the question whether "didactic" is the best designation for Amos's questions, inasmuch as it prejudges their intent as educational, thereby predisposing one to think of the wisdom tradition. "Rhetorical" questions, in the sense that no answer is given because the answer can be assumed, is a better term: it is more semantically neutral than "didactic" but able to encompass that nuance as well.

C. Woe Oracles (Amos 5:18–20; 6:1–7)[31]

Wolff situates the prophetic woe oracles within the realm of clan wisdom, a position first suggested by Erhard S. Gerstenberger.[32] Gerstenberger starts from the woes' nature as "general and timeless indictments of historically unspecified evildoers."[33] To this he adds a common interest in both justice and intoxication in the

---

[29] On the relationship between the two, see James L. Crenshaw, "Impossible Questions, Sayings, and Tasks," *Semeia* 17 (1980): 19–34; idem, "Riddles," *ABD* 5:722–23; on riddles in general, see Crenshaw, "Wisdom," in *Old Testament Form Criticism* (ed. John H. Hayes; Trinity University Monograph Series in Religion 2; San Antonio: Trinity University Press, 1974), 239–45; idem, "Riddles," 721–23, and the bibliographies in both.

[30] "The life setting of the riddle was diverse, ranging from initiation ceremonies to courtship and marriage, as well as the political contests between kings and their courtiers, ritual questions in catechetical form, banquets …, children at play, and in the schools" (Crenshaw, "Wisdom," 241). The only example of a full riddle in the First Testament occurs during the celebration of Samson's marriage to an unnamed Philistine woman (Judg 10:14–18).

[31] Although הוי is best translated as "alas" rather than "woe" (see n. 37 below), I retain the traditional terminology for the sake of convenience.

[32] Gerstenberger, "The Woe-Oracles of the Prophets," *JBL* 81 (1962): 249–63; Wolff, *Amos the Prophet*, 17–34; idem, *Joel and Amos*, 94, 243–45. They are followed by Ronald E. Clements, "The Form and Character of Prophetic Woe Oracles," *Semitics* 8 (1982): 24–25. Crenshaw admits that this might be a case of "indirect" influence; Soggin dismisses Wolff's proposal as "obviously untenable" without further comment; and Morgan says that "it is not one of the more convincing arguments for wisdom influence in Amos" (Crenshaw, "Influence of the Wise," 49, but cf. his pp. 47–48; Soggin, "Amos and Wisdom," 120; Morgan, *Wisdom in the Old Testament Traditions*, 69).

[33] Gerstenberger, "Woe-Oracles," 252; see also Wolff, *Joel and Amos*, 94; James G. Williams, "The Alas-Oracles of the Eighth Century Prophets," *HUCA* 38 (1967): 82 n. 19.

woe oracles as well as the wisdom literature.³⁴ In addition, Gerstenberger considers הוי ("alas") the counterpoint to אשרי ("happy"), a common wisdom term.³⁵ He argues that those whose deeds and attitudes were deemed valuable would be pronounced אשרי while הוי was addressed to those whose actions or thoughts were unacceptable. Building on the wisdom recognition that different actions had either positive or negative results, the prophetic הוי announced that those who did negative things would experience "woe."

Unfortunately, neither הוי and אשרי nor הוי and wisdom in general are ever linked in the First Testament: except for 1 Kgs 13:30, הוי occurs only in the prophetic books. Moreover, Gerstenberger finds "happy" and "woe" together only twice, and those instances only through emendation.³⁶ But even then the opposite of אשרי is not even הוי, but אוי, which Günther Wanke has shown is syntactically, and therefore semantically, distinct from הוי.³⁷ As for Gerstenberger's other points, although we today might find the woes "timeless" and "historically unspecified," the prophet's audience would not have.³⁸ Even without a regnal year attached to each woe, Amos's contemporaries would know who "those who desire the Day of the Lord" (5:18) or "the confident on Mount Samaria" (6:1) were, especially with the definite article plus participles in the woes serving as vocatives.³⁹ Finally, social

---

³⁴ Gerstenberger, "Woe-Oracles," 254–58; Wolff, *Joel and Amos*, 244, 245.

³⁵ Gerstenberger, "Woe-Oracles," 260–61; Wolff, *Amos the Prophet*, 25–29. But contrast Whybray, *Intellectual Tradition*, 125–26.

³⁶ From אָמְרוּ to אַשְׁרֵי in Isa 3:10–11 and from אִי to אוֹי in Qoh 10:16–17; see Gerstenberger, "Woe-Oracles," 261.

³⁷ Wanke, "אוי und הוי," *ZAW* 78 (1966): 215–16. אוי is found twenty-five times, twenty-two times with the preposition ל, nineteen times with a personal pronoun or suffix. In contrast, in thirty-one of its fifty-one instances, הוי precedes a group or individual described negatively, usually with a participle. It is followed by an individual introduced by a preposition four times only, is followed twice by a name, serves as an interjection eight times (half with a negative connotation and half as a call for attention) and occurs six times in a funerary lament. Cf. Christof Hardmeier's statistics on הוי as presented in Wolff, *Joel and Amos*, 242–43 n. 108, and Wolff's own breakdown on p. 242. As a result, אוי is best translated as "woe to me/you/him [because] ..." while הוי should be rendered as "Alas!" (J. G. Williams, "Alas-Oracles," 75). Wolff recognized the difference between the two Hebrew words, which led him into some contradictory statements. For instance, he acknowledges that "a clear distinction can be recognized between הוי ('woe, alas') utterances and אוי ('woe, ah') utterances ...," but two pages later he proceeds "to draw the latter into our considerations" (Wolff, *Joel and Amos*, 242, 244).

³⁸ See also Waldemar Janzen's criticism (*Mourning Cry and Woe Oracle* [BZAW 125; Berlin: de Gruyter, 1972] 21, 41 n. 3) that Gerstenberger's characterization of the woe oracle is valid only by excluding over half the word's occurrences from consideration.

³⁹ For a participle with the definite article functioning as a vocative, see GKC, §126e–f; *IBHS*, §13.5.2; Ronald J. Williams, *Williams' Hebrew Syntax* (3rd ed.; revised and expanded by John C. Beckman; Toronto: University of Toronto Press, 2007), §89. For this usage in Amos 6:1, see Janzen, *Mourning Cry*, 22–23; Delbert R. Hillers, "*Hôy* and *Hôy*-Oracles: A Neglected Syntactical Aspect," in *The Word of the Lord Shall Go Forth: Essays in Honor of David Noel Freedman in Celebration of His Sixtieth Birthday* (ed. Carol L. Meyers and M. O'Connor; Winona Lake, IN: Eisenbrauns,

justice and drunkenness need not be traced specifically to a wisdom setting. Such concerns were part of a shared social ethos and were not linked to any single group or tradition.[40]

Rather than a wisdom context, the prophetic woe oracles are derived from funerals. In its sole occurrence outside the prophetic literature, the word הוי is part of a lament over the deceased "man of God" from Judah (1 Kgs 13:30). Similarly, in Jer 22:18 the prophet says that King Jehoiakim will be buried without the customary lamentations (הוי occurs four times), while in Jer 34:5 mourners will pronounce הוי ("Alas lord") over King Zedekiah. Since the verb ספד ("lament") is found in all three verses from Jeremiah, funerals, not clan wisdom, were clearly the original *Sitz im Leben* for pronouncing הוי.[41] Despite this, Wolff associates funeral laments with clan wisdom through extended families as well as the reference to mourners as "wise [women]" (החכמות) in Jer 9:16.[42] But most village members, "wise" or not, would join in a family's mourning.[43] Jeremiah, on the other hand, spoke in the capital, Jerusalem, and used the root חכם in Jer 9:16 of professional skill or expertise, not common wisdom traditions. If the terms "wisdom" or "wise" alone indicate the wisdom tradition, then artisans (Exod 35:31–36:1), tailors (Exod 28:3), scribes (Jer 8:8), sailors (Ps 107:27), shipbuilders (Ezek 27:8–9) and practitioners of warfare (Prov 21:22; Isa 10:13), commerce (Ezek 28:4–5), and sorcery (Isa 47:9–13; cf. the Babylonian magicians in Daniel)—that is, virtually everyone—are part of it. Wolff's proposition expands the definition of "wisdom" so widely that it becomes meaningless. Regardless, Wolff acknowledges that "the הוי of Amos

---

1983), 185–88; J. J. M. Roberts, "Amos 6:1–7," in *Understanding the Word: Essays in Honor of Bernhard W. Anderson* (ed. James T. Butler, Edgar W. Conrad, and Ben C. Ollenburger; JSOTSup 37; Sheffield: JSOT Press, 1985), 156, 163 n. 8; Andersen and Freedman, *Amos*, 556.

[40] Issues of justice, for instance, obviously belong to the judiciary, although Jean-Paul Audet derives law and wisdom from a common background ("Origines comparées de la double tradition de la loi et de la sagesse dans le Proche-Orient ancien," in *25th International Congress of Orientalists (Moscow, 1960)* (ed. B. G. Gafurova; 5 vols.; Moscow: Izd. vostochnoĭ literatury, 1962–63), 1:352–57; see also Erhard S. Gerstenberger, *Wesen und Herkunft des 'apodiktischen Rechts'* (WMANT 28; Neukirchen-Vluyn: Neukirchener Verlag, 1965). See too Crenshaw's concerns about a too-inclusive search for wisdom influence ("Method in Determining Wisdom Influence," 129–42); cf. Janzen, *Mourning Cry*, 24. See further below concerning social justice.

[41] First proposed separately by Richard J. Clifford, "The Use of HÔY in the Prophets," *CBQ* 28 (1966): 458–64; Wanke, "אוי und הוי," 215–18. See also Hans-Joachim Kraus, "הוי als prophetische Leichenklage über das eigene Volk im 8. Jahrhundert," *ZAW* 85 (1973): 15–46; H.-J. Zobel, "הוי *hôy*," *TDOT* 3:361–62; and especially the detailed treatment of the idea in Israel as well as the surrounding nations in Janzen, *Mourning Cry*, 3–19; and Jacques Vermeylen, *Du prophète Isaïe à l'apocalyptique: Isaïe I–XXXV, miroir d'un demi-millénaire d'expérience religieuse en Israël* (EBib; Paris: Gabalda, 1978), 2:503–52. Cf. the double funerary cry of הו in Amos 5:16–17, right before the הוי of 5:18.

[42] Wolff, *Joel and Amos*, 243.

[43] Kraus, "הוי als prophetische Leichenklage," 19.

resonates much more strongly with the unnerving tone of the cry of funerary lamentation than is the case in our *postulated* pedagogical wisdom sayings."[44] Therefore, it does not indicate wisdom influence on Amos.

D. Exhortation Speech (Amos 4:4–5; 5:4–6, 14–15)

The final possible wisdom form in the book of Amos is the exhortation speech. Wolff points to the use of antithetical parallelism and the cause-and-effect nature of what will happen if the prophet's admonition is not followed, both of which he considers characteristic of wisdom.[45] Soggin simply dismisses the similarities as the result of a shared cultural background, which is likely true.[46] But more important for our discussion, the Amos texts that Wolff cites differ in both form and content from his wisdom parallels. Most commentators, including Wolff, acknowledge the form-critical similarities between the exhortations in Amos and priestly calls to worship.[47] Wolff tries to draw a distinction on the basis of the consequence clause in the Amos texts, which is absent from the priestly form, but there is no consequence in Amos 4:4–5. Wolff argues that the reference to transgressions in v. 4 fills this function, but it is actually part of the exhortation itself. Thus, the transitional word "therefore" (לְמַעַן) that Wolff considers part of the wisdom form is not present because the verse states what the prophet calls them to *do* at Bethel, not the *consequence* of going there. Moreover, the passage uses synonymous parallelism, not the antithetical parallelism that, for Wolff, indicates wisdom influence. On the other hand, while consequences are stated in Amos 5:4–6 and 14–15, this can easily be explained in terms of the prophetic judgment oracle, in which an indictment establishes the basis for the concluding announcement of divine judgment.[48] It is more likely that Amos has combined elements of the priestly worship formula and the prophetic judgment oracle into the existing exhortations than that they are the result of wisdom influence.

[44] Wolff, *Joel and Amos*, 245 (emphasis added).

[45] Wolff, *Amos the Prophet*, 44–53; he builds on Gerstenberger, *Wesen und Herkunft*, 43–45.

[46] Soggin, "Amos and Wisdom," 120; see also Morgan, *Wisdom in the Old Testament Traditions*, 69; Crenshaw does not discuss this point. See also n. 7 above for discussions of commonality across genres and literary traditions.

[47] Wolff, *Amos the Prophet*, 49; idem, *Joel and Amos*, 211–12, 232, 234 (in the latter Wolff considers Amos 5:14–15 to be a secondary insertion); see also, more recently, Jeremias, *Book of Amos*, 67–68. The exhortations are actually parodies of priestly calls to worship. Note especially Amos 5:21–24, where Amos uses the priestly "acceptance of sacrifice" formula to state the exact opposite, although no one thinks this indicates that Amos was a priest (thus James Luther Mays, *Amos: A Commentary* [OTL; Philadelphia: Westminster, 1969], 106; Wolff, *Joel and Amos*, 261; Paul, *Amos*, 188–89; Jeremias, *Book of Amos*, 101–3).

[48] Claus Westermann, *Basic Forms of Prophetic Speech* (trans. Hugh Clayton White, with a foreword by Gene M. Tucker; Philadelphia: Westminster, 1967; repr., Cambridge: Lutterworth; Louisville: Westminster John Knox, 1991), 129–89.

The last two exhortations can be further distinguished from the wisdom tradition on the basis of their content. Amos 5:4–6 and 14–15 encourage the hearer to engage in an activity that will bring life, which Wolff correctly identifies as "the final goal of all wisdom teaching."[49] However, in most of the wisdom texts that Wolff cites, life comes from the pursuit of wisdom itself (e.g., Prov 4:4; 7:2; 9:6; 13:20; 15:4; 19:20), whereas in Amos 5:4 and 6 life results from seeking Yhwh. Once again, this specification of the God of Israel is in contrast to the reflection on common human experiences that is at the heart of the wisdom tradition. Similarly, the basis for life in Amos 5:14–15 is doing good rather than evil. Wolff compares this with the approbation of righteousness in Prov 11:19, 23; 12:28, but the Amos text is different. In Proverbs, it is righteousness and the righteous in general that lead to life, whereas in Amos it is specific actions, namely, seeking good and avoiding evil (5:14a and 15a), which are further defined in 5:15a as establishing justice in the gate, thus indicating the legal system. Moreover, in Proverbs the exact nature of the "life" that results from righteousness is not specified, but in Amos it is linked to blessings by Yhwh, the God of Israel. At the same time, in Amos 5:15b this is presented as only a possibility, which is quite different from the certitude offered in the wisdom tradition in general, and the texts that Wolff cites in particular.

Thus, the connections proposed between the exhortation texts in Amos and putative wisdom forms are, upon closer examination, not as precise as Wolff suggests. Both the form and the content of the passages in Amos show significant differences from the wisdom texts that are offered as parallels. The few points of contact are too general to require that the prophet explicitly knew and used the wisdom tradition in formulating his message.

III. Wisdom Terminology

A. סוד

"Surely the Lord Yhwh does nothing, without revealing his secret
[גלה סודו] to his servants the prophets." (Amos 3:7)

Terrien notes that, although the word סוד appears with different nuances in a variety of biblical writings, "in the sense of 'intimate secret,' however, the word appears to be typical of the wisdom literature.... We may say that the word sôd is par excellence a sapiential term."[50] Crenshaw and Soggin both dismiss the verse as a later addition, and in this they are almost certainly correct.[51] Not only is the

---

[49] Wolff, *Amos the Prophet*, 47.

[50] Terrien, "Amos and Wisdom," 112. He lists Job 15:8, 17 (but the term is not there); 19:19; 29:4; Prov 3:32; 11:13; 15:22; 20:19; 25:9; Sir 8:17; 9:4, 14; 42:12 plus ten instances elsewhere (he omits Jer 6:11; 15:17, for a total of twelve nonwisdom instances). Lessing also links this verse to wisdom influence (*Amos*, 208).

[51] Crenshaw, "Influence of the Wise," 44; Soggin, "Amos and Wisdom," 122; idem, *Prophet Amos*, 58.

statement intrusive, breaking up a series of questions, but the phrase "his servants the prophets" is characteristic of Deuteronomistic language.[52] I consider it here for the sake of completeness but note that the term's nuance in Amos 3:7 is very different from that in the wisdom literature. Of the thirteen occurrences in wisdom texts, סוד is the object of the verb גלה ("reveal"), as in Amos 3:7, only in Prov 11:13; 20:19; and 25:9. All three Proverbs texts have a negative sense of betraying another's secret, whereas Amos 3:7 refers to God confiding secrets.[53] Job 15:8 is closer to the latter, linking wisdom with hearing what was said in "the council [סוד] of God," which in turn is reminiscent of Jer 23:18, 22a, where admission to "the council [סוד] of YHWH" is the mark of a true prophet. This is the sense of גלה סודו in Amos 3:7, namely, that God confides divine secrets to his trusted servants, as opposed to the wisdom idiom of גלה plus סוד in Prov 11:13; 20:19; and 25:9, in which humans betray the confidence of other humans.

B. נכחה

"They do not know how to do right [נכחה]." (Amos 3:10)

Terrien claims that the word נכחה in Amos 3:10 is unique among the preexilic prophets, but that "undoubtedly it is a favorite term of wisdom."[54] Although the word is used in Isa 30:10 by that prophet's opponents ("Prophesy not to us what is right" [נכחה]), Terrien considers them to be sages in the royal court.[55] However, there is no evidence of that in the verse, and in any case the term is associated with what the prophet would be expected to prophesy, not with courtly wisdom. Thus, the term is not as "unique" to Amos among the preexilic prophets as Terrien suggests.

Terrien's claim that נכחה "is a favorite term of wisdom" is also open to challenge. The word occurs a total of eight times, of which only three are from the wisdom literature, and one of those is even from the much later book of Sirach.[56]

---

[52] See 2 Kgs 17:13, 23; 21:10; 24:2; cf. Jer 7:25; 26:5; 35:15; 44:4. Amos 3:7 is considered secondary by, among others, Mays, *Amos*, 61; Wolff, *Amos the Prophet*, 7 n. 26; idem, *Joel and Amos*, 181; Rottzoll, *Studien zur Redaktion*, 118–22; Jeremias, *Book of Amos*, 54; and, more recently, Tchavdar S. Hadjiev, *The Composition and Redaction of the Book of Amos* (BZAW 393; Berlin: de Gruyter, 2009), 28–29. But contrast, e.g., Paul, *Amos*, 112–13; Möller, *Prophet in Debate*, 226; and Jason Radine, *The Book of Amos in Emergent Judah* (FAT 2/45; Tübingen: Mohr Siebeck, 2010), 24–25.

[53] The negative nuance occurs also in Sir 8:17; 9:4, but these occurrences should be used with caution, since they are about 550 years after the time Amos himself. Although it has a different verb, Job 19:19 is similar, with its reference to Job's rejection by his "intimate friends" (literally, "men of my secret"; מתי סודי).

[54] Terrien, "Amos and Wisdom," 112; he is followed by Wolff, *Amos the Prophet*, 56–59; idem, *Joel and Amos*, 193. Crenshaw allows that it may indicate "indirect" wisdom influence ("Influence of the Wise," 46).

[55] Terrien, "Amos and Wisdom," 112.

[56] Proverbs 8:9; 24:26; Sir 11:21; Terrien also lists Prov 26:28, but the word does not occur

Three instances of a word, constituting barely one-third (or one-quarter, if we exclude Sir 11:21) of the total number, do not make it a "favorite term" of wisdom, especially since the preexilic prophetic uses in Amos 3:10 and Isa 30:10 also constitute one-quarter of the total occurrences. But, more importantly, the term has a very different nuance in Amos 3:10 than in Prov 8:9 and 24:26. The latter two verses clearly deal with speech, whereas Amos 3:10 deals with action. Sirach 11:21 is the only wisdom text where the word is connected with action, but the chronology would indicate influence from Amos on Sirach. 2 Samuel 15:3 is closer to the nuance in Amos: Absalom says to legal claimants, "See, your claims are good and right [נכחים], but there is no one deputed by the king to hear you." Terrien and Wolff link this to royal wisdom circles, but the context indicates a matter for the law courts.[57] In short, not only is Terrien's very identification of נכחה as a wisdom term questionable, but the word has a completely different nuance in Amos 3:10 from that in the wisdom literature.

C. ויטרף לעד אפו

"His anger tore perpetually." (Amos 1:11)

Terrien notes that אף occurs with the verb טרף only here and in Job 16:9 and 18:4, and so he designates the combination a "sapiential idiom."[58] Both Crenshaw and Soggin dismiss the verse as secondary, with Soggin also noting that the verb is often emended to וַיִּטֹּר ("he kept [his anger]") with the Syriac and the Vulgate.[59] In addition to these points I would also question whether two instances are sufficient to constitute an "idiom"; one would expect an idiom to be found more frequently. Moreover, the combination of terms has different nuances in each Joban text, which are themselves distinct from the nuance in Amos 1:11. In Job 16:9, Job complains that God's anger tears at him, while in Job 18:4 Bildad says that Job tears at himself with his anger. In the former, divine anger is the subject of the verb and is directed at a human being, whereas in the latter, human anger is the means of tearing at

---

there. In addition to Amos 3:10 and Isa 30:10, the other instances of the word are 2 Sam 15:3; Isa 26:10; 57:2; 59:14.

[57] Terrien, "Amos and Wisdom," 112; Wolff, *Amos the Prophet*, 59; contrast Soggin, "Amos and Wisdom," 122. See also Whybray, who argues that Absalom would be unlikely to use a supposedly specialized wisdom term when speaking to people who were not part of the royal court (*Intellectual Tradition*, 141).

[58] Terrien, "Amos and Wisdom," 113.

[59] Crenshaw, "Influence of the Wise," 44; Soggin, "Amos and Wisdom," 122. On the authenticity of the verse, see, e.g., Mays, *Amos*, 36; Rottzoll, *Studien zur Redaktion*, 32–35; Jeremias, *Book of Amos*, 23. For the emendation, contrast the views of Wolff and Barthélemy with that of Paul (Wolff, *Joel and Amos*, 130; Dominique Barthélemy, *Critique textuelle de l'Ancien Testament*, vol. 3, *Ezéchiel, Daniel et les Douze Prophètes* [OBO 50.3; Fribourg: Editions Universitaires; Göttingen: Vandenhoeck & Ruprecht, 1992], 642; Paul, *Amos*, 66).

oneself. In contrast to both, in the MT of Amos 1:11 one nation's anger is directed against another. In short, even if we accept the verse as authentic to Amos and do not emend the verb, the supposed analogies in Job 16:9 and 18:4 are neither common enough nor consistent enough with each other to constitute an "idiom," while the usage in Amos 1:11 is significantly different from both.

D. משכיל

"Therefore the prudent [המשכיל] will keep silent in that time." (Amos 5:15a)

This term is mentioned neither by Terrien nor by Wolff, but rather by Soggin, who nonetheless dismisses the verse as a later addition.[60] Regardless, although the term is a wisdom one, it is not exclusive to the wisdom tradition and can be used differently.[61] That is certainly the case here. Rather than insightful reflection on general human experiences, in Amos 5:13 the word connotes a judicious reaction to an extreme situation; thus, it is rendered as "prudent" in all modern English translations.

IV. Wisdom Ideas

A. Sheol

"Though they dig into Sheol / From there shall my hand take them." (Amos 9:2)

Terrien claims that, apart from Amos 9:2, the idea that Yhwh interacts with the underworld is found only in wisdom texts (Prov 15:11; Job 26:61) and in Ps 139:7, which he considers a wisdom Psalm. Since Amos simply assumes that God can enter into Sheol in order to exact judgment, Terrien asserts that the wisdom texts have influenced Amos rather than the reverse.[62] Soggin rejects Terrien's claim in favor of seeing all of Amos 9:1–4 as rhetorical exaggeration, which is especially evident in the second half of v. 2, since heaven would be an unlikely place to hide from God.[63] More importantly, contrary to Terrien's assertion, the idea that Yhwh can reach into the underworld is not exclusive to the wisdom tradition. First of all, Psalm 139 is not usually considered a wisdom psalm, which reduces the supposedly wisdom provenance of the idea.[64] Second, God sends people or things to Sheol (or the Pit) in Deut 32:22; 1 Sam 2:6; Ezek 26:20; 31:16; 88:6 and takes them from there

---

[60] Soggin, "Amos and Wisdom," 123.
[61] Whybray, *Intellectual Tradition*, 137–38.
[62] Terrien, "Amos and Wisdom," 110–11.
[63] Soggin, "Amos and Wisdom," 121. Crenshaw does not consider the matter.
[64] Crenshaw surveys eight scholars who have proposed lists of wisdom psalms, only one of whom includes Psalm 139 (*The Psalms: An Introduction* [Grand Rapids: Eerdmans, 2001], 87–95).

in 1 Sam 2:6; Hos 13:14; Jonah 2:3, 7; Pss 30:3; 49:16; 86:13 (cf. also Pss 18:5 and 16; 56:13; 103:4; 116:3 and 8).[65] In short, the idea was far more widespread than Terrien indicates, and its presence in Amos need not be attributed to any wisdom influence on the prophet or his ideas.

B. Social Justice (Amos, passim)

Wolff links Amos's calls for social justice to his supposed wisdom background. In particular, he considers Amos's concern for unjust scales and opposition to an extravagant lifestyle to be characteristic of wisdom literature, and he also notes that the terms "justice" (משפט) and "righteousness" (צדקה) occur in parallel frequently in both Amos and wisdom literature, as do the terms for the "helpless" (דל), the "poor" (אביון), and the "oppressed" (עני/ענו).[66] However, concern for justice is found throughout the ancient Near East in general and most parts of the First Testament in particular.[67] It is especially prevalent in the prophets, so if advocating justice constitutes wisdom influence, then virtually all the biblical prophets have been influenced by that tradition.[68] In the First Testament this is exemplified by special concern for the weaker members of society, such as orphans, widows, and foreigners, three groups who normally did not have a male Israelite to defend their

---

[65] See also Walther Eichrodt, *Theology of the Old Testament* (trans. J. A. Baker; 2 vols.; OTL; Philadelphia: Westminster, 1967), 2:221–23.

[66] See Wolff, *Amos the Prophet*, 59–67, 70–76, for references and discussion. He also points out that two of the three instances of "justice" and "righteousness" together and the sole instance of "justice" alone in Amos appear in so-called wisdom forms (Amos 5:7, 15; 6:12), and that even though the other instance of both terms together (5:24) occurs within a cultic formula, there Amos uses the formula against that tradition, the verse uses comparisons, and it is followed by "didactic" questions (*Amos the Prophet*, 61). However, I have already demonstrated a nonwisdom provenance for all these features.

[67] See Bruce C. Birch, *What Does the Lord Require? The Old Testament Call to Social Witness* (Philadelphia: Westminster, 1985); Waldemar Janzen, *Old Testament Ethics: A Paradigmatic Approach* (Louisville: Westminster John Knox, 1994); Pietro Bovati, *Re-establishing Justice: Legal Terms, Concepts and Procedures in the Hebrew Bible* (trans. Michael J. Smith; JSOTSup 105; Sheffield: JSOT Press, 1994); Moshe Weinfeld, *Social Justice in Ancient Israel and in the Ancient Near East* (Jerusalem: Magnes; Minneapolis: Fortress, 1995); Bruce V. Malchow, *Social Justice in the Hebrew Bible: What Is New and What Is Old* (Collegeville, MN: Liturgical Press, 1996); John Barton, *Ethics and the Old Testament* (London: SCM, 1998); Enrique Nardoni, *Rise up, O Judge: A Study of Justice in the Biblical World* (trans. Seán Charles Martin; Peabody, MA: Hendrickson, 2004). An even longer list of works treating justice in the different types of biblical literature and individual books could be provided.

[68] For justice in the prophets in general, see Carol Dempsey, *Hope Amid the Ruins: The Ethics of Israel's Prophets* (St. Louis: Chalice, 2000); Joseph Jensen, *Ethical Dimensions of the Prophets* (Collegeville, MN: Liturgical Press, 2006); John L. McLaughlin, *Justice in the Balance: Learning from the Prophets* (Toronto: Novalis, 2008). Here too, a lengthy bibliography dealing with justice in individual prophets could be produced.

rights and so were commended to the protection of all. Concern for these three groups is found also in various types of biblical literature, and the legal material in particular links it to the exodus, not wisdom teaching.[69]

As for Wolff's specific "wisdom" topics, despite his assertion that weights are mentioned in the Pentateuch only in Leviticus 19, which he links to clan traditions, honest weights are a concern in Deut 25:13–15 as well, indicating that the topic is equally at home in the legal tradition.[70] This subject is also addressed in Hos 12:7; Mic 6:10, 11; and Ezek 45:10, so the prophet's concern about it in Amos 8:5 need not be attributed to wisdom influence. At the same time, in Amos 4:1 and 6:4–6 (cf. 2:8 and 5:11), the prophet does not oppose a lavish lifestyle in and of itself, but because "they are not grieved over the ruin of Joseph" (Amos 6:6), that is, because it results from injustice. But to argue that his concern about the injustice that enables their luxury indicates wisdom influence because his concern for justice derives from the wisdom tradition is circular reasoning.

Nor are Wolff's lexical links to the wisdom tradition in this regard secure. For instance, "justice" and "righteousness" are established word pairs that occur in virtually all types of literature in the Hebrew Bible, so their combination in wisdom literature does not make the formulation a wisdom one.[71] In fact, of the forty-nine times the words occur together, only four (less than 8 percent) are in wisdom texts: Job 37:23; Prov 8:20; 16:8; 21:3. Moreover, although "justice" and "righteousness" always appear in that order in Amos (5:7, 24; 6:12), they do so in only one wisdom text (Job 37:23); instead, the sequence "righteousness" and then "justice" is the dominant order in the wisdom tradition (Prov 8:20; 16:8; 21:3).[72] In sum, the fact

---

[69] Concern for one or more of these groups is found in legal (e.g., Deut 16:11, 14; 26:12–13; etc.), sapiential (Job 6:27; 22:9; 24:3, 9; etc.), psalmic (Pss 10:14, 18; 68:5; etc.), and prophetic (Isa 1:17, 23; Jer 5:28; 7:6; 22:3; Ezek 22:7; Zech 7:10; Mal 3:5) texts. It is explicitly contrasted with Israel's slavery in Egypt in Exod 22:21; 23:9; Lev 19:34; Deut 10:18; 24:17–18, 21–22. Note also the distribution indicated in the title of F. Charles Fensham's study: "Widow, Orphan and the Poor in Ancient Near East Legal and Wisdom Literature," *JNES* 21 (1962): 129–39.

[70] Schmid, "Amos," 94.

[71] In addition to wisdom texts and Amos, the two words appear together in historical (2 Sam 8:15//1 Chr 18:14; 1 Kgs 10:9//2 Chr 9:8), legal (Lev 19:15; Deut 16:18–20), prophetic (Isa 1:27; 5:7, 16; 9:6; etc.; Jer 4:2; 9:23; 22:3, 15; etc.; Ezek 18:5, 19, 21, 27; 33:4, 16; etc.; Mic 7:9), and psalmic texts (Pss 72:1–2; 99:4; 106:3; etc.). S. Holm-Nielsen links both terms to the covenant tradition, rather than wisdom ("Der Socialkritik der Propheten," in *Denkender Glaube: Festschrift Carl Heinz Ratschow zur Vollendung seines 65. Lebensjahres am 22. Juli 1976 gewidmet von Kollegen, Schülern u. Freunden* [ed. Otto Kaiser; Berlin: de Gruyter, 1976], 20–22).

[72] Ahuva Ho argues for a different nuance depending on the order of the two terms (*Ṣedeq and Ṣedaqah in the Hebrew Bible* [American University Studies: Series 7, Theology and Religion 78; New York: P. Lang, 1991], 147). If we include משפט combined with the related but different term צדק ("right"), the wisdom distribution is closer: they occur together thirty-one times in the First Testament, with צדק coming first in three wisdom texts (Job 29:14; Prov 1:3; 2:9) and second in four (Job 8:3; 35:2; Qoh 3:16; 5:7). However, a main point of Ho's monograph is that צדק and צדקה have distinct nuances, which lessens the relevance of צדק to our point.

that the words are parallel in Amos is not indicative of wisdom influence, and, in fact, their occurrence in the reverse order to most wisdom instances of the pair argues for the opposite.

There are similar problems when it comes to the terms for the marginalized. Wolff claims that "in wisdom the references to those in want employ the terms in pairs throughout—precisely as in Amos."[73] However, neither part of that statement is correct; the terms דל, אביון, and עני/ענו appear alone twenty times in wisdom texts and three times in Amos 3.[74] Moreover, combining any of the terms is not distinctively characteristic of the wisdom literature: although two of the terms do appear together eight times in wisdom texts, they are linked thirty-six times (including four times in Amos) in other contexts.[75] In fact, since sixteen of those instances are in the Psalms and twelve are in prophetic texts other than Amos, it would be more accurate to say that linking the terms is a greater concern to either the Psalms or the prophets than to the wisdom tradition. At the very least, since two of the three words occur together in twelve prophetic texts outside Amos, it is neither necessary nor appropriate to appeal to the wisdom literature to explain their combination in Amos.

C. Universalism (Amos 1:3–2:3; 6:2; 9:7)

Both Terrien and Wolff point to Amos's knowledge of the surrounding nations and their affairs, his assumption of a common morality and fate for them and Israel, and the view that YHWH exercised lordship over them, as indicative of a universalistic worldview derived from the wisdom tradition.[76] On a general level, this presumes that only the wisdom tradition would hold such views, which is hardly tenable. Members of the royal court and those engaged in international commerce,

---

[73] Wolff, *Amos the Prophet*, 71.

[74] The word דל occurs alone in Job 5:16; 20:10, 19; 31:16; 34:19; Prov 10:15; 19:4, 17; 21:13; 22:16; 28:3, 8, 11; 29:7, 14; אביון appears without either of the other terms in Job 29:16; and ענו/עני is found alone in Job 36:15; Prov 3:34; 14:21; 16:19. In Amos 2:6, אביון is parallel to צדיק ("the righteous"), and the singular form and content of the verse indicate that it is not directly parallel to the plural דלים and ענוים in Amos 2:7. Similarly, although דל appears at the beginning of Amos 5:11 and אביון at the end of v. 12, this is not a case of distant parallelism: there are eight cola between the two terms, the first word is singular and the second plural, and the latter is parallel to "the righteous" (צדיק) in v. 12.

[75] דל and אביון appear together in Prov 14:31 and 1 Sam 2:8; Isa 14:30; 25:4; Amos 4:1; 8:6; Pss 72:13; 82:4; 113:7; דל and עני/ענו are combined in Job 34:28; Prov 22:22 and Ps 82:3; Isa 10:2; 11:4; 26:6; Amos 2:7; Zeph 3:12; and אביון is linked with עני/ענו in Job 24:2, 14; Prov 30:14; 31:9, 20 and Deut 15:11; 24:14; Pss 9:19; 12:16; 35:10; 37:14; 40:18; 70:6; 72:4, 12; 86:1; 109:16, 22; 140:13; Isa 29:19; 32:7; 41:17; Jer 22:16; Ezek 16:49; 18:12; 22:29; Amos 8:4. When these listings are combined with the thirty times one of the terms appears alone in wisdom texts and the three times in Amos (see n. 74), it is problematic to call their appearance together characteristic of either.

[76] Terrien, "Amos and Wisdom," 114; Wolff, *Amos the Prophet*, 54–56.

for instance, would also be cognizant of other nations. As a landowner and sheep breeder, Amos may have had economic dealings with the surrounding nations and thus become acquainted with their history and activities; at the very least he would have had some degree of leisure in which to learn about such things.[77]

More specifically, the individual texts that Terrien and Wolff cite do not support their view. For instance, Amos 1:2–2:3 consists of Oracles against the Nations, a form found in every prophetic book except Hosea.[78] The point of such oracles is to invoke disaster on Israel's enemies, with the implied correlative being that Israel will be blessed.[79] Any shared morality is used as the basis for announcing disaster for those nations, not as an expression of international solidarity. Nor do the Oracles against the Nations actually express YHWH's concrete rule over those nations: there is nothing to indicate that YHWH had previously communicated how they should interact with one another or that he was able to influence their actions in advance. The passage simply announces that he will punish them after the fact for their actions. Furthermore, the Oracles against the Nations in Amos establish a dual basis for the oracle against Israel in 2:6–16.[80] Amos 1:3–2:3 condemns Israel's neighbors for offenses that are not specifically forbidden by divinely revealed law. Today these would be called "war crimes" or "crimes against humanity," and most people in Amos's day would be shocked at such excesses, not just those influenced by the wisdom tradition. This is followed by the oracle against Judah (2:4–5), which condemns the addressees for failing to follow YHWH's law. The oracle against Israel then denounces the people both for offenses that are explicitly forbidden in Israelite law and for others that are not. Thus, any common morality (which again, would not be exclusive to the wisdom tradition) in the Oracles against the Nations is used in the service of the main purpose in Amos 1–2, which is to hold Israel accountable for its own offenses.

The other two texts suggested by Terrien and Wolff were discussed earlier under "didactic questions." Amos 6:2 does not indicate either a common morality

---

[77] For a discussion of Amos's occupation, see Richard C. Steiner, *Stockmen from Tekoa, Sycomores from Sheba: A Study of Amos' Occupations* (CBQMS 36; Washington, DC: Catholic Biblical Association of America, 2003).

[78] The largest concentrations are Isaiah 13–23, Jeremiah 46–51, Ezekiel 25–32, and Amos 1:3–2:5. On the form in general, see Yair Hoffman, *The Prophecies against Foreign Nations in the Bible* (in Hebrew; Tel Aviv: Tel Aviv University, 1977); Duane L. Christensen, *Prophecy and War in Ancient Israel: Studies in the Oracles against the Nations in Old Testament Prophecy* (BIBAL Monograph Series 3; Berkeley: BIBAL, 1989). For Amos in particular, see John Barton, *Amos' Oracles against the Nations: A Study of Amos 1:3—2:5* (SOTSMS 6; Cambridge: Cambridge University Press, 1980).

[79] John H. Hayes, "The Usage of Oracles against Foreign Nations in Ancient Israel," *JBL* 87 (1968): 81–92, esp. 81–89; Barton, *Amos 1:3–2:5*, 8–15; Christensen, *Prophecy and War*, 18–55.

[80] Barton, *Amos 1:3–2:5*, 3–6, 36–38; Jeremias, *Book of Amos*, 20–21; Jonathan A. Partlow, "Amos's Use of Rhetorical Entrapment as a Means for Climatic [sic] Preaching in Amos 1:3–2:16," *ResQ* 49 (2007): 28–29. This is true even if some are omitted as later additions (see n. 17 above).

or Yhwh's rule over the city-states listed; it simply invokes them as a point of comparison for Israel, and this does not require or even imply wisdom influence. That leaves only Amos 9:7, which does not deal with morality, shared or otherwise. It does assume knowledge of the Ethiopians, Philistines, and Arameans, but once again that would not be exclusive to the sages. Moreover, those groups' movements are presented as analogous to Israel's exodus from Egypt, which lessens any universalism in the text.

In short, the only true element of universalism found in Amos is in 9:7 with respect to Yhwh's involvement with three foreign nations, and that is only in a limited way. It is hardly sufficient to counter the statements elsewhere in the book that Israel is "my people" (7:8; 8:2; 9:10) and Yhwh is "their/your God" (2:8; 4:12),[81] as well as the statement of Yhwh's exclusive relationship with Israel in 3:2. Thus, the attempt to find universalism in Amos as evidence of wisdom influence rests solely on one aspect of a single verse, and as such is not convincing.

D. Other Wisdom Ideas

Both Terrien and Wolff advance other minor points of contact between Amos and the wisdom tradition, but none constitutes a strong argument and so each can be dealt with briefly. Terrien suggests that Amos's interest in astronomy and lack of concern for idolatry derived from wisdom influence.[82] The former is evident only in the reference to the Pleiades and Orion in 5:8a, which is usually considered secondary.[83] Moreover, the constellations are mentioned in Amos not as a matter of wisdom reflection on the nature of the cosmos but in relation to Yhwh, who, as the creator, is also able to punish injustice in Israel. On the other hand, rather than attribute Amos's lack of concern over "idolatry" to a wisdom stance, recent scholarship on the history of ancient Israelite religion indicates that this is more likely because at that time mainstream Yahwism was polytheistic, such that "idolatry" was not an issue at all.[84]

Wolff considers Amos's use of antithetical word pairs to be rooted in clan wisdom, but antithetical constructions are far too common in human communication to be attributed to any single tradition, especially in light of parallelism,

---

[81] Crenshaw, "Influence of the Wise," 45; see also 46.

[82] Terrien, "Amos and Wisdom," 114.

[83] Thus Crenshaw, "Influence of the Wise," 44; Morgan, *Wisdom in the Old Testament Traditions*, 70. Soggin does not address the point. Amos 5:8 is considered secondary by, e.g., Wolff, *Joel and Amos*, 229, 232; Rottzoll, *Studien zur Redaktion*, 242–50; Jeremias, *Book of Amos*, 82.

[84] See, e.g., John Day, *Yahweh and the Gods and Goddesses of Canaan* (JSOTSup 265; Sheffield: Sheffield Academic Press, 2000); Mark S. Smith, *The Origins of Biblical Monotheism: Israel's Polytheistic Background and the Ugaritic Texts* (Oxford: Oxford University Press, 2001); idem, *The Early History of God: Yahweh and the Other Deities of Canaan* (2nd ed.; Grand Rapids: Eerdmans, 2002); David Penchansky, *Twilight of the Gods: Polytheism in the Hebrew Bible* (Louisville: Westminster John Knox, 2005); André Lemaire, *The Birth of Monotheism: The Rise and Disappearance of Yahwism* (Washington, DC: Biblical Archaeology Society, 2007).

including antithetical parallelism, as a feature of Hebrew poetry.[85] In addition, he explains supposed similarities between Amos and Isaiah as the result of Isaiah's direct dependence on the wisdom tradition rather than on Amos (contra Reinhard Fey) but argues that this confirms wisdom influence in the comparable Amos material.[86] A full discussion of Isaiah's use of either the wisdom tradition or Amos cannot be undertaken here. For my purpose it is sufficient simply to note that Wolff makes the point primarily on the basis of the woe form in Amos 5:18–20; 6:1–7; Isa 5:8–24; 10:1–4 and their shared concern for justice, both of which I have demonstrated are not evidence of wisdom influence in Amos.

V. Crenshaw: Theophanies

One other link between Amos and wisdom was proposed by Crenshaw, who saw a "kinship" between the doxologies in Amos and those in Job 5:9–16; 9:5–10 on the basis of the following parallels:[87]

Amos		Job	
5:4, 6	Seek the Lord	5:8	I would seek God
4:13; 5:8	Who makes (עֹשֶׂה)	5:9	Who does (עֹשֶׂה)
5:8b; 9:6b	Who calls for the waters	5:10	He gives rain upon the earth, and sends waters upon the fields
5:8	He turns darkness (צַלְמוּת) to morning, and darkens day to night	5:14	They meet with darkness (חשך) in the daytime, and grope at noonday as in the night
		9:7	Who commands the sun and it does not rise, who seals up the stars
5:10	They hate him who reproves in the gate	5:17	Happy is the man whom God reproves
4:13	He who forms mountains	9:5	He who removes mountains
9:5	He touches the earth and it melts	9:6	Who shakes the earth out of its place, and its pillars tremble
4:13	Who treads upon the heights of the earth	9:8	Who trampled the waves of the sea
5:8	He who makes Pleiades and Orion	9:9	Who made the Bear and Orion, Pleiades and chambers of the south

---

[85] Wolff, *Amos the Prophet*, 67–70; contrast Crenshaw, "Influence of the Wise," 44.

[86] Wolff, *Amos the Prophet*, 80–85; see Fey, *Amos und Jesaja: Abhängigkeit und Eigenständigkeit des Jesaja* (WMANT 12; Neukirchen-Vluyn: Neukirchener Verlag, 1963).

[87] Crenshaw, "Influence of the Wise," 49–51. Pfeiffer had earlier linked Amos 4:13; 5:8–9 and 9:5–6 to "the introduction of Edomitic wisdom literature" and derived the names of the constellations in Amos 5:8 from Job 9:9; 38:31 ("Edomitic Wisdom," 24, esp. n. 2).

There are a number of problems with Crenshaw's proposal, however. First of all, he himself notes that "the Doxologies of Amos come from a subsequent stage textually and historically."[88] Second, he never specifies the extent of the Amos doxologies, but some of the texts he cites are not doxological: "Seek Yahweh and live" (Amos 5:4, 6) is an exhortation and "They hate the one who reproves in the gate" (Amos 5:10) is a statement about a human attitude toward others. Third, the content of many parallels is either too general or too different to be convincing. Examples of the former include the references to seeking the Lord/God in Amos 5:4, 6 and Job 5:8, and the participle עֹשֶׂה in Amos 4:13; 5:8; and Job 5:9; the verb עשה in particular is far too common to be a wisdom term, and in any case has a different nuance in the two books. Other supposed parallels are actually quite different from each other. For instance, in Amos 4:13 God forms the mountains but removes them in Job 9:5, God treads "on the heights of the mountains" in Amos 4:13 but tramples "the waves of the sea" in Job 9:8, and humans hate another human for reproving their injustice in Amos 5:10, but a human is pleased with God's reproof in Job 5:17. Fourth, some parallels use synonyms rather than the same word, such as צלמות for darkness in Amos 5:8 but חשך in Job 5:14, weakening the connection.

In addition to these parallels, Crenshaw lists three terms from the Amos doxologies as indicative of their "wisdom character": שחו, צלמות, and המבליג (Amos 4:13; 5:8, 9, respectively), but in each case the Joban parallels are not from doxologies.[89] Moreover, two of these words have different nuances in Amos and Job. In Amos 4:13, שחו refers to God's "thoughts" that are revealed to humans, whereas in Job (and Prov 23:28) the root שיח always refers to negative human thoughts (rendered "complaint" in the NRSV). Similarly, Amos 5:9 mentions "He who flashes out [המבליג] destruction," but in Job 9:27 and 10:20 the root has a positive connotation.[90] In light of the textual difficulties with המבליג in Amos we may actually be dealing with two different words,[91] but at the very least שחו and המבליג have very different nuances in Amos and Job and so cannot be used to demonstrate wisdom influence.

---

[88] Crenshaw, "Influence of the Wise," 49.

[89] Ibid., 50. The root שיח occurs in Job 7:11, 13; 9:27; 10:1; 21:4; 23:2; בלג is found in Job 9:27; 10:20; and צלמות occurs in Job 3:5; 10:21; 12:22; 16:16; 24:17 (2x); 28:3; 34:22; 38:17.

[90] The NRSV translates the word as "be of good cheer" and "find comfort" respectively in the Job texts; cf. "smile" in Ps 39:13, the only other instance of the root. Crenshaw initially considered Psalm 39 a wisdom psalm, although he later questioned "the very category of wisdom psalms" (compare Crenshaw's "Influence of the Wise," 48, and *Old Testament Wisdom: An Introduction* [rev. and enl. ed.; Louisville: Westminster John Knox, 1998] 172, with his *Psalms*, 94).

[91] The root's basic meaning is "gleam" (BDB, 114), from which the unique NRSV translation in Amos 5:9 could derive. The LXX has ὁ διαιρῶν ("the one who distributes"), leading Wolff to read הַמַּבְדִּיל, with the sense "set apart, appoint" (*Joel and Amos*, 229–30). Other versions also had difficulty with the word, rendering it in Amos 5:9 as "strengthens" (Tg.), "laughs" (Vulg.), "smiles" (Aquila) or "makes ridiculous" (Symmachus). BHS suggests emending to either המפליג ("the one who divides") or הַמַּפִּיל ("the one who brings down"). See further the discussion in Paul, *Amos*, 169.

Thus, Crenshaw's attempt to find wisdom influence in Amos on the basis of the doxologies there and in Job is not convincing, but even if it were, that would still be evidence only of "later redactors among the sages" rather than of Amos's own context.[92]

VI. Conclusion

The preceding analysis demonstrates that there is no evidence of influence from wisdom circles on Amos: the various proposals in this regard do not withstand careful examination. The suggested geographical links are too weak to support a connection; and not only are most of the supposedly distinctive wisdom forms, terms, and ideas not actually characteristic of the wisdom tradition but, when they do appear there, Amos uses them very differently. Similarly, Crenshaw's proposed connections between the theophanies in Job and Amos are either too general, are used differently in the two books, or both. This leaves only the graduated numerical sayings in Amos 1–2, but the form is used so differently from the wisdom tradition that its presence in Amos is probably the result of the author's general awareness of the form without any insight into its actual wisdom usage. Thus, there is no evidence of any greater wisdom influence on Amos than there would have been on most people in that place at that time, both in Israel and in the surrounding nations. This is not to say that Amos cannot be from a rural background and may reflect some aspects of clan socialization, but since this would be common to all rural people, some general similarities would not be surprising. But that is not the same as specifically *wisdom* usage of forms, terms, and ideas. As a result, Amos should no longer be included among the wise, and henceforth commentators should not interpret the prophet, the book, or individual passages in light of the wisdom tradition, nor should the book be included when considering the extent of wisdom influence beyond the books of Job, Proverbs, and Qoheleth. Doing so imports an external background that is not reflected in the book of Amos.

---

[92] Crenshaw, "Influence of the Wise," 49.

SBL New and Recent Titles

IMPRINTS, VOICEPRINTS, AND FOOTPRINTS OF MEMORY
Collected Essays of Werner H. Kelber
Werner H. Kelber
Paper $59.95, 978-1-58983-892-5   526 pages, 2013   Code: 060374
Hardcover $79.95, 978-1-58983-894-9   E-book $59.95, 978-1-58983-893-2
Resources for Biblical Study 74

FRAGILE DIGNITY
Intercontextual Conversations on Scriptures, Family, and Violence
L. Juliana Claassens and Klaas Spronk, editors
Paper $36.95, 978-1-58983-895-6   348 pages, 2013   Code: 060672
Hardcover $51.95, 978-1-58983-897-0   E-book $36.95, 978-1-58983-896-3
Semeia Studies 72

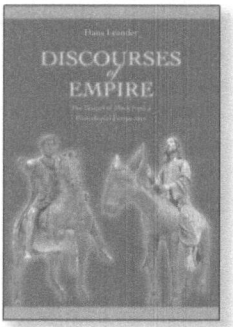

DISCOURSES OF EMPIRE
The Gospel of Mark from a Postcolonial Perspective
Hans Leander
Paper $47.95, 978-1-58983-889-5   404 pages, 2013   Code: 060671
Hardcover $62.95, 978-1-58983-891-8   E-book $47.95, 978-1-58983-890-1
Semeia Studies 71

BEAUTY AND THE BIBLE
Richard J. Bautch and Jean-François Racine, editors
Paper $24.95, 978-1-58983-907-6   136 pages, 2013   Code: 060673
Hardcover $39.95, 978-1-58983-909-0   E-book $24.95, 978-1-58983-908-3
Semeia Studies 73

4QINSTRUCTION
Matthew J. Goff
Paper $45.95, 978-1-58983-782-9   388 pages, 2013   Code: 065502
Hardcover $60.95, 978-1-58983-784-3   E-book $45.95, 978-1-58983-783-6
Wisdom Literature from the Ancient World 2

Society of Biblical Literature • P.O. Box 2243 • Williston, VT 05495-2243
Phone: 877-725-3334 (toll-free) or 802-864-6185 • Fax: 802-864-7626
Order online at www.sbl-site.org

A Note on the Creation Formula in Zechariah 12:1–8; Isaiah 42:5–6; and Old Persian Inscriptions

CHRISTINE MITCHELL
christine.mitchell@usask.ca
St. Andrew's College, University of Saskatchewan, Saskatoon, SK S7N 0W3, Canada

This note explores whether the influence of the Old Persian creation formula as well as its underlying theology can be seen in biblical texts. The particular focus is on Zech 12:1–8 and Isa 42:5–6. While both of these texts use creation language found elsewhere in the Hebrew Bible corpus, the particular content and structure of these texts have strong resonances with the Old Persian texts.

One of the most frequently attested formulas in the corpus of Achaemenid royal inscriptions is the creation formula. In its Old Persian stereotypical form it reads as follows:

baga vazạrka Auramazdā	A great god is Ahuramazda
haya imām būmim adā	Who established this earth
haya avam asmānam adā	Who established that sky
haya martiyam adā	Who established humanity
haya šiyātim adā martiyahạyā	Who established peace for humanity
haya Dārayavaum xšāyaθiyam akunauš	Who made Darius king
aivam parūvnām xšāyaθiyam	One king of many
aivam parūvnām framātāram	One commander of many
	(DNa 1–8; my translation)

The text is found, with minor variations, from the reigns of Darius I, Xerxes I, Artaxerxes I, Artaxerxes II, and Artaxerxes III, from a variety of sites: Persepolis, Susa, Suez, Elvend, Van, Hamadan, and Naqsh-i Rustam.[1] The sequence deity,

---

[1] DNa, DSe, DSf, DSt (without the final two phrases), DZc (with sky before earth and without the final two phrases), DE, XPa, XPb, XPc, XPd, XPf, XPh, XE, XV, A$_1$Pa, A$_2$Hc, A$_3$Pa. For the texts, see Roland G. Kent, *Old Persian Grammar, Texts, Lexicon* (2nd rev. ed.; AOS 33; New Haven: American Oriental Society, 1953); Rüdiger Schmitt, *Die altpersischen Inschriften der Achaemeniden: Editio minor mit deutscher Übersetzung* (Wiesbaden: Reichert, 2009).

creation of earth and sky, creation of humanity, and creation of *šiyāti* for humanity, is intimately linked with the appointment of the Achaemenid king as custodian of the creation and humanity. The king is not a deity, but enjoys particular favor as the deity's instrument.[2]

Beyond the creation of earth, heavens, and humanity, Ahuramazda created *šiyāti* for humanity. This word, often translated as "peace" or "happiness,"[3] has broad cosmic overtones: it is the state of order and wholeness, opposed to the state of chaos elsewhere in the Old Persian inscriptions described as "the Lie" (*drauga*).[4] It shares much of the semantic field of the Hebrew שלום.

The beginning of the second משא (oracle/burden) of Zechariah, Zech 12:1–6, contains an oracle foreseeing Judah's position as Yhwh's favored nation and the defeat of the peoples round about. The Davidic line's prominent role is emphasized in the oracle's continuation in 12:7–8. The oracle begins as follows (12:1; my translation):

The word of Yhwh concerning Israel	דבר־יהוה על ישראל
Utterance of Yhwh	נאם יהוה
Who spreads out heavens	נטה שמים
And establishes earth	ויסד ארץ
And shapes the breath-of-humanity in its core	ויצר רוח אדם בקרבו

In the Old Persian creation formula, the creation of humanity by Ahuramazda is followed immediately by the creation of *šiyāti* for humanity. A reader versed in the Old Persian texts would expect Yhwh, after creating humanity, to create שלום for humanity and to make Darius (or some other Achaemenid) king. It is at this point that Zech 12:1–8 diverges from the sequence found in the Old Persian texts. Instead of order, Yhwh creates (שים) disorder by making Jerusalem a tottering threshold (סף רעל) and a heavy stone (אבן מעמסה) for the nations who gather to besiege it in v. 2. After the creation of disorder and the defeat of the nations in vv. 2–6, *then* Yhwh proclaims that Jerusalem will dwell again in שלום. Finally, in vv. 7–8, the house of David is mentioned for the first time in the book of Zechariah; the house of David will be "like God" (כאלהים).

In its divergence from the Old Persian creation formula, the text of Zech 12:2–6 contests the cosmology/theology behind that formula. In Achaemenid theology, by creating disorder instead of order, Yhwh and his followers are the Lie and

---

[2] The seminal analysis was done by Clarisse Herrenschmidt, "Les créations d'Ahuramazda," *Studia Iranica* 6 (1977): 17–58. See further Bruce Lincoln, *"Happiness for Mankind": Achaemenian Religion and the Imperial Project* (Acta Iranica 53; Leuven: Peeters, 2012), 446–61.

[3] So Kent, *Old Persian*, 210.

[4] Clarisse Herrenschmidt, "Vieux-Perse *šiyāti*," in *La religion iranienne à l'époque achéménide: Actes du colloque de Liège, 11 décembre 1987* (ed. Jean Kellens; Iranica Antiqua Supplement 5; Ghent: Iranica Antiqua, 1991), 13–21; P. O. Skærvø, "The Achaemenids and the *Avesta*," in *Birth of the Persian Empire* (ed. Vesta Sarkhosh Curtis and Sarah Stewart; Idea of Iran 1; London: I. B. Tauris, 2005), 52–84; Lincoln, *Happiness*, 258–68.

should be destroyed by the Achaemenid king. The Achaemenids, rulers of many peoples, would bring their multiethnic army to bear on Jerusalem—particularly their cavalry, which was the basis of Persian might (cf. DNa, DNb)—and so it happens in Zech 12:4. However, in Zechariah, it is out of this battle that Jerusalem's salvation would come, not her destruction as the Achaemenids would have it; a play on the root שלם in Jerusalem may also be read here. The role of the house of David on that day would be comparable to the role of the Achaemenid king in the Old Persian creation texts.

The text of Zech 12:1 uses creation vocabulary similar to a number of other biblical texts (Isa 42:5–6; 44:24; 45:11–12; 51:13, 16; Jer 10:12–16 = 51:15–19; Psalm 104; Job 38:4–5). The strongest linguistic parallel between Zech 12:1 and another biblical text—namely, the use of all three verbs נטה, יסד, and יצר—is with Psalm 104 (vv. 2, 5, 8, 26). Of all of the creation texts with similar vocabulary, only Isa 42:5–6 has the same sequence of heaven–earth–humanity as Zech 12:1:[5]

Thus says the god YHWH	כה אמר האל יהוה
Who creates the heavens and stretches them out	בורא השמים ונוטיהם
Spreads out the earth and its offspring	רקע הארץ וצאצאיה
Gives inhalation to the people upon it	נתן נשמה לעם עליה
And breath to those who walk on it	ורוח להלכים בה
I, YHWH, have named you in righteousness	אני יהוה קראתיך בצדק
And I have grasped you by the hand	ואחזק בידך
And I have shaped you and given you	ואצרך ואתנך
As the people's covenant, the nations' light	לברית עם לאור גוים

(Isa 42:5–6; my translation)

Unlike Zech 12:2–8, which continues after the creation formula to emphasize the disorder before YHWH's ultimate victory, Isa 42:6–9 continues the sequence of heaven–earth–humanity by creating a human figure, the "you" of "I have named you ... grasped you by the hand ... shaped you and given you" (v. 6). This human figure, usually understood to be the servant of 42:1–4, is the one charged with control over the entire earth. Isaiah 42:5–6 maintains the sequence of the Old

---

[5] Carol L. Meyers and Eric M. Meyers see Isa 51:13–16 as the key text, along with Isa 42:5; 44:24; 45:12; Jer 10:12; 51:15; Amos 4:13; 5:8; 9:6; Pss 18:10; 104:2; and Job 9:8; they see Zech 12:1 as alluding to Genesis 2 in its order of creation (*Zechariah 9–14: A New Translation with Introduction and Commentary* [AB 25C; New York: Doubleday, 1993], 311–13). See also Marvin A. Sweeney, *The Twelve Prophets* (2 vols.; Berit Olam; Collegeville, MN: Liturgical Press, 2000], 2:683–84; and Risto Nurmela, "The Growth of the Book of Isaiah Illustrated by Allusions in Zechariah," in *Bringing Out the Treasure: Inner Biblical Allusion in Zechariah 9–14* (ed. Mark J. Boda and Michael H. Floyd; JSOTSup 370; Sheffield: Sheffield Academic Press, 2003), 245–59. Michael H. Floyd sees allusions to Genesis 2 but also to Genesis 1 (*Minor Prophets, Part 2* [FOTL 22; Grand Rapids: Eerdmans, 2000], 495–96). Julia M. O'Brien sees Jeremiah 10 and 51 as the linking texts, highlighting the theme of punishment of the nations (*Nahum, Habakkuk, Zephaniah, Haggai, Zechariah, Malachi* (AOTC; Nashville: Abingdon, 2004], 258).

Persian creation formula and even has as its hero the Persian king Cyrus (so 45:1).[6] The use or adaptation of the Old Persian creation formula would be entirely consistent with the pro-Persian slant of Isaiah 40–48, and even if the author of chs. 40–48 did not know the Old Persian formula, the same order of heaven–earth–humanity–ruler is evident.[7] The omission of the ruler from the list of Yhwh's creative acts in Zech 12:1 is even more striking.

The ideology/theology of the Achaemenids is contested in Zech 12:1–8. Yhwh is posited as the creator (over against Ahuramazda) and the one who will ultimately prevail over Ahuramazda's Order (*arta*) as enforced by the Achaemenid king. Unlike the static paradisal universe promulgated by the Achaemenids, where chaos has already been defeated and the present is an unending order, Zech 12:1–8 as the beginning of chs. 12–14 envisions the Achaemenid order ending "on that day," followed by the new order of Yhwh. Many recent studies of Persian-period Yehud have made use of our increasing knowledge of Persian administration and history to posit Yehud's relation to the Achaemenid heartland. Further work on the relation between the Old Persian texts and Haggai–Zechariah should be done to test these results.

---

[6] Of the recent commentators, only Rex Mason and David L. Petersen have seen Isa 42:5 as the key text for Zech 12:1, making the link largely on the basis of vocabulary, but noting the common structure; they use the language of "doxology" to describe both texts. Petersen notes that these two texts serve as an introduction to the following verses in each case, and that "the appeal to primordial creative acts provides the reason that those who are addressed should believe the prophet" (Mason, "The Use of Earlier Biblical Material in Zechariah 9–14: A Study in Inner Biblical Exegesis" [Ph.D. diss., University of London, 1973], 192; Petersen, *Zechariah 9–14 and Malachi: A Commentary* [OTL; Louisville: Westminster John Knox, 1995], 110–11). However, the focus in Zechariah 12–14 is on the chaos and destruction brought about by Yhwh "on that day," while Isaiah 40–48 has as its emphasis Yhwh's new creation. Joseph Blenkinsopp suggests that the language of Isa 42:1–9 "fits what we know of the early Persian period" (*Isaiah 40–55: A New Translation with Introduction and Commentary* [AB 19A; New York: Doubleday, 2002], 210).

[7] It is important to note that the standard Old Persian order is earth and then heaven (the only exception is DZc); Ahuramazda is not Yhwh, who creates heaven and then earth. See Herrenschmidt, "Les créations," 18.

Intertextual Density, Quantifying Imitation

KRISTIAN LARSSON
kristian.larsson@outlook.com
Lagerlöfsgatan 42, 75426 Uppsala, Sweden

Hypertextual imitation means that a hypotext serves as a model for a hypertext in substantial, both qualitative and quantitative, ways: text A in a sense generates text B with regard to motifs, plot, and/or characterization. Hypertextuality may range from surface-text copying to deep-level emulation. Identifying the latter holds considerable analytical and interpretational problems.

The present article places under scrutiny Dennis R. MacDonald's model of imitation and his thesis that the Gospel of Mark is emulating the Homeric epics. MacDonald presents an impressive number and range of parallels, but his hermeneutic concept of "bulk density" does not adequately address the critical quantitative issues at hand. Synoptic presentations of parallels should be used critically by weighing in quantitative parameters. An argument for imitation should not rely on a decontextualized bulk density.

The article examines the parameter of intertextual density within a quantitative and qualitative framework. Some suggestions are offered on how to deal with textual similarities and differences in a systematic fashion. It is argued that "relative density" is a key component in determining imitation (hypertextuality) on the textual mid- and macrolevel.

The present article examines the quantitative parameter of intertextual density as a way of determining hypertextual imitation. The article reflects on the thesis put forward by NT scholar Dennis R. MacDonald, namely, that the Gospel of Mark stands in a relationship of imitation with Homer's *Odyssey* and *Iliad*.[1] Specifically, he argues that passages in Mark 4–6, 8–9, 11, and 13–14 primarily imitate *Odyssey* 3, 4, 6–7, 10, 16, and 19.[2] Furthermore, he claims that passages in Mark 15–16

I would like to thank the anonymous *JBL* reviewers for their helpful comments on this article. Joacim Jonsson, Uppsala, offered valuable feedback at different stages of the writing process. The present article was made possible through a grant from the Faculty of Languages at Uppsala University.

[1] MacDonald, *The Homeric Epics and the Gospel of Mark* (New Haven: Yale University Press, 2000).

[2] Ibid., 174–84.

primarily imitate *Iliad* 22 and 24.[3] MacDonald's argument is that text B (Mark) uses text A (*Odyssey/Iliad*) as the primary model when it comes to story elements, plot (the linking of events in a meaningful way), and characterization (the way literary characters are described and communicated to the reader). MacDonald is using a concept of "bulk density" that is not well defined and relies heavily on hermeneutics rather than on a method of quantitative measurement.[4]

Systematic studies of intertextual density are still lacking in the scholarly discussion of imitation and hypertextuality. In a recent contribution, biblical scholars Serge Frolov and Allen Wright draw on MacDonald's model in their discussion of the intertextual relationship between the account of David's victory over Goliath in 1 Samuel 17 and *The Epic of Gilgamesh* together with *The Story of Sinuhe*.[5] They state that "the density of parallels" is "very substantial."[6] They have found "four major and six minor parallels" and "at least two and possibly three distinctive details."[7] From their presentation it is not clear why the "bulky" parallels, forming textual clusters of sorts, are in the final analysis accounted for separately from the distinctive details, and what exactly constitutes major and minor parallels respectively.[8] Finally, the authors state that the density is particularly impressive since "the biblical fragment," that is, the hypertext, "is relatively short."[9] Here, a notion of relative density, expressed as volume of parallels over total volume of text, is hinted at but not explicated further.

Although the focus in the following will be on density, I will attempt to review it in a framework of both qualitative and quantitative parameters. Since it would be impossible to do justice to the whole of MacDonald's complex argument, I will give particular attention to the episode of the Gerasene demoniac in Mark 5:1–20 and its supposed imitation of the story of the Cyclops in *Odyssey* 9. This is, in MacDonald's view, one of the most convincing instances of imitation, not least due to the sheer density, volume, of the parallels. The case revolves around fifteen parallels, in conjunction with one motif from the story of Circe in *Odyssey* 10.

I. Copying versus Imitation

The consensus on Markan priority among the Synoptic Gospels is shared by MacDonald. Biblical source criticism has paid some statistical attention to "verbal

---

[3] Ibid., 185–86.
[4] Ibid., 8.
[5] Frolov and Wright, "Homeric and Ancient Near Eastern Intertextuality in 1 Samuel 17," *JBL* 130 (2011): 451–71. For the discussion on density, see 456–58 and 463–66.
[6] Ibid., 466.
[7] Ibid., 471.
[8] Ibid., 463.
[9] Ibid., 466.

agreement," that is, word-for-word parallels between the Synoptic Gospels.[10] A recent statistical model on conditional probability of the relations of verbal agreement safely places Luke last in the chain of direct influence, whereas some statistical doubt remains as to whether Mark or Matthew came first.[11]

It should be obvious that one can use statistical methods and quantitative data to determine intertextual relationships of direct influence when it comes to surface text, and even more so if a verbal agreement is understood to be words appearing in the same grammatical form. Intertextual relations that constitute or come close to surface text copying eliminate a number of subjective factors in the analytical process, although weighing in contextual information on different possible scenarios and premises remains important.

An exact quotation or allusion may function as an indicator of imitation. For such instances, MacDonald provides the original Greek expression in his presentation. But MacDonald's focus lies on more imaginative, innovative imitation of story, plot, and characters rather than discourse. His argument revolves around emulation and "*Kontrastimitationen*," such as biblical scholars have identified in early Christian literature written later than the NT, using pagan literature as contrastive models for their Christian belief and value systems.[12] Such deep-level imitation will be more difficult to identify than a straightforward copying of surface text. The critical response to MacDonald has mainly focused on the issue of "transvaluation," since it has been identified as the core of the argument.[13]

II. Intertextual Types

Theoretically, MacDonald is drawing on Gérard Genette's typology of intertextual relations, in particular his concept of hypertextuality. It thus seems reasonable to give a brief account of Genette's typology of "transtextuality," which is the

---

[10] The statistical analysis of "verbal agreement" (word-for-word, 1:1 relations) in Mark, Luke, and Matthew performed by A. M. Honoré constitutes ground-breaking work in biblical source criticism ("A Statistical Study of the Synoptic Problem," *NovT* 10 [1968]: 95–147).

[11] For constructive statistical criticism of Honoré and an argument for another model of the intertextual relations, see Andris Abakuks, "A statistical study of the triple-link model in the synoptic problem," *Journal of the Royal Statistical Society* Series A 169 (1) (2006): 49–60. The article is available as open-source text: http://eprints.bbk.ac.uk/133/.

[12] MacDonald, *Homeric Epics and the Gospel of Mark*, 2.

[13] Karl Olav Sandnes argues, "If the key motif [of Jesus 'returning home' to Jerusalem] is so slippery in Mark's Gospel, it is difficult to think that it was part of an intentional imitation" of Odysseus returning home to Penelope "in all the passages mentioned" by MacDonald ("Imitatio Homeri? An Appraisal of Dennis R. MacDonald's 'Mimesis Criticism,'" *JBL* 124 [2005]: 722). Sandnes sums up: "Emulation and transvaluation hardly make sense if they are not recognized" (p. 725).

same as what most scholars intend by the term "intertextuality."[14] In the following, I will use the established term "intertextuality" to designate the overarching concept. This does mean, however, that there is a terminological overlap with one of Genette's subtypes.

Genette identifies five main intertextual subtypes, which he tentatively lists in an order of increasing abstraction, from intertextuality as the most specific and concrete type to architextuality as the most general and abstract type.

1. "Intertextuality" is a co-presence of two or more texts, such as is the case when a text contains a quotation from or an allusion to another text.[15] In the OT, Daniel's vision of one like a son of man, a term that Mark's Jesus uses to mask himself as "merely" a Jewish prophet, reads: "one like a human being coming with the clouds of heaven" (Dan 7:13).[16] Mark's Jesus alludes to Daniel when, in his trial before the Jewish authorities, he is asked directly if he is the Messiah:

> Jesus said, "I am; and 'you will see the Son of Man seated at the right hand of the Power,' and 'coming with the clouds of heaven.'" (Mark 14:62)

If an author unknowingly uses passages from a reference text, one may speak of (unconscious) influence. If an author consciously makes use of a text of reference without clearly or adequately indicating that this is the case, the question of plagiarism in both a legal and an artistic/intellectual sense may arise. Neither of these two cases seems to apply to Mark's Jesus referring to Daniel, even though the allusion is not textually marked.

2. "Paratextuality" involves the relations between the main text and the different layers surrounding it in the web of work, author, recipient, and, for more modern works, publisher.[17] The paratextual delimitation of text and work level(s) may not always be that clear-cut, especially when fictional authors and publishers are being deployed. Genette calls the opening lines of the *Iliad* and the *Odyssey*, which became standard models for the epic opening, "incorporated prefaces": "the invocation of the muse, announcement of the subject (the wrath of Achilles; the wanderings of Odysseus), and establishment of the narrative starting point …)."[18] Mark's opening revolves around what one could call an incorporated epigraph, perhaps a composite quotation from Isa 40:3; Mal 3:1; and Exod 23:20.

---

[14] Genette, *Palimpsests: Literature in the Second Degree* (1982; trans. Channa Newman and Claude Doubinsky; Lincoln: University of Nebraska Press, 1997), 1.

[15] Ibid., 1–2.

[16] Biblical quotations follow the NRSV. This translation also forms the basis for MacDonald's English quotations.

[17] Genette, *Palimpsests*, 3. For his main treatment of this topic, see Gérard Genette, *Paratexts: Thresholds of Interpretation* (1987; trans. Jane E. Lewin; Cambridge: Cambridge University Press, 1997).

[18] Genette, *Paratexts*, 164.

The beginning of the good news of Jesus Christ, the Son of God. As it is written in the prophet Isaiah,[19] "See, I am sending my messenger ahead of you, who will prepare your way; the voice of one crying out in the wilderness: 'Prepare the way of the Lord, make his paths straight,'" John the baptizer appeared in the wilderness, proclaiming a baptism of repentance for the forgiveness of sins. (Mark 1:1–4)

The invocation of the prophet Isaiah, together with a few remarks on John the Baptizer as a preceding sign of the Messiah, Mark clearly views as sufficient introduction to the story.

3. "Metatextuality" means that a text explicitly refers to another text, for example, by commenting on or critiquing the text of reference.[20] Manfred Pfister uses the term "referentiality" to designate the degree to which a text not only makes use of but calls attention to or explicitly refers to the underlying text, thereby becoming a metatext—that is, above the text of reference—that adds new meaning and perspective.[21] When Mark's Jesus prophesies the destruction of Jerusalem to follow after his resurrection, he speaks of a sign, the "desolating sacrilege," and underlines that this is an allusion: "But when you see the desolating sacrilege set up where it ought not to be (let the reader understand), then those in Judea must flee to the mountains" (Mark 13:14). The "reader" will in all likelihood recognize the expression as being used by the prophet Daniel in his apocalyptic visions, presumably to designate the desecration of the temple in Jerusalem through worship of false gods.[22] One should distinguish such metatextual commentaries from a meta-intertextuality. Pfister here speaks of "autoreflexivity," meaning that a text self-reflexively refers to its own intertextuality or to intertextuality in general.[23] Whereas text commentaries form an integral part of classic literature, it is only with modernism/postmodernism that intertextuality in itself becomes an aesthetic expression.

4. "Hypertextuality" Genette defines as the modeling of one text on a text of reference.[24] Thus, "hypotext" A in a sense generates "hypertext" B. This is the case with parodies and travesties but also with the poorly executed and/or trivial (pulp fiction, mass genre literature) as well as the respectful and/or masterly executed

---

[19] Alternatively: "in the prophets."
[20] Genette, *Palimpsests*, 4.
[21] Pfister, "Konzepte der Intertextualität," in *Intertextualität: Formen, Funktionen, anglistische Fallstudien* (ed. Ulrich Broich and Manfred Pfister; Konzepte der Sprach- und Literaturwissenschaft 35; Tübingen: Niemeyer, 1985), 26.
[22] In Dan 9:27 and 12:11: "abomination that desolates"; in Dan 11:31: "abomination that makes desolate."
[23] Pfister, "Konzepte der Intertextualität," 27.
[24] Genette, *Palimpsests*, 5.

imitations and pastiches (classic standard works). All of the mentioned hypertextual cases are very different from the mere intertextual quotation or allusion.

5. "Architextuality" means that a text refers to genre conventions or an ideal(ized), stereotypical notion of the discourses of a particular epoch, class, and so on.[25] In other words, architextuality designates a potentially both literary and nonliterary "system reference" as opposed to a specific "text reference" (these two terms stem from Pfister and Broich).[26] In practice, it is in many instances impossible to distinguish between a specific text reference and a general system reference. An author may, for example, have certain concrete texts in mind but refer to their idealized or stereotypical sum or characteristics. It is possible to view parallels between the Gospel of Mark and Homer's epics as resulting from unconscious rhetorical, literary, discursive, and cultural frameworks and codes. A specific text reference, that is, between text A and B, may not always be possible to distinguish from a general system reference, that is, between text A and a group of texts/discourses X. MacDonald himself recognizes this as a factor to be reckoned with, but in practice he seems in most instances to equate a similarity of culturally established motives from, for example, literature, religion, and philosophy (system references) with specific references.

The NT clearly refers intertextually and metatextually, as a commentary of sorts, to the OT. Hypertextuality, however, concerns imitation of story, plot, and characters. With respect to Mark, it addresses the question of how to make the Gospel captivating to its recipients.

MacDonald adheres to a narrow concept of intertextuality that focuses on the author's intended, conscious, and more or less clearly communicated references. He seeks to avoid merely establishing an influence without asking for its function: Is the reader's recognition of the intertextual reference of importance to the author and for the understanding of the text and, if so, in what way? Is it mere copying, or is it a more creative imitation that involves inverting, adding, and subtracting with regard to the text of reference? If the latter modifications occur, are they to be understood as keys for understanding the text with respect to a contemporary reading audience? As we shall see below, MacDonald's model of imitation also pays more or less equal attention to qualitative and quantitative aspects. This distinguishes him from most literary scholars working on intertextuality.

A central theoretical problem in biblical source criticism lies in accounting for textual inconsistencies—viewing them either as part of the original texts, which may draw on various traditions in oral storytelling, or as ultimately caused by the

---

[25] Ibid., 4. See also Gérard Genette, *The Architext: An Introduction* (1979; trans. Jane E. Lewin; Berkeley: University of California Press, 1992).

[26] Manfred Pfister, "Zur Systemreferenz," in Broich and Pfister, *Intertextualität*, 52–58, and, in the same volume, Ulrich Broich, "Zur Einzeltextreferenz," 48–52. Gérard Genette's term "architextuality" is similar to "system reference."

compilation process of a later redactor (editor). If there are inconsistencies, it may be prudent to speak of a rather unreflecting influence rather than a deliberate imitation. Crucially, in MacDonald's argument on the Homeric epics and the Gospel of Mark, the imitation is intended by the author and communicated to and understood by the audience.

The reason MacDonald is pushing for hypertextuality rather than a delimited "intertextuality" in Genette's sense has to do with the potentially much more significant explanatory value. The Gospel of Mark, MacDonald argues, is purposely designed as a contrastive imitation of the Homeric epics, not least intended to demonstrate the virtues of Jesus in comparison to Odysseus and other Homeric characters. Thus, MacDonald is considering (hyper-)textual similarities as well as contrasts. It might be fruitful to compare MacDonald's operationalization of hypertextual parameters with parameters commonly used when discussing intertextual relations in general. The most advanced model I am aware of is offered by Manfred Pfister together with Ulrich Broich.

III. INTERTEXTUAL PARAMETERS

In 1985, Pfister and Broich introduced a flexible model that, at least in a metaphorical sense, measures or scales the intertextual intensity of a text. Different combinations and degrees of the parameters lead to varying intertextual profiles and intensities. Methodically, Pfister admits, the weighing of different parameters against each other poses a considerable difficulty, and an exact measurement of intertextual intensity may be a futile goal.[27] Pfister lists six parameters that in his understanding are qualitative in nature. In his view, the qualitative dimension is central. For his errand, namely, to create a bridge between the structuralist and poststructuralist approaches to intertextuality, this seems fully reasonable.

Two of Pfister's parameters were already touched upon in the discussion of Genette's intertextual subtypes above: "referentiality," that is, thematization of the reference text, and "autoreflexivity," that is, textual reflection on intertextuality itself, in specific or general ways. These two parameters will not concern us any further here. The remaining four qualitative parameters are "communicability," "structurality," "selectivity," and "dialogicity."[28]

Communicability has both a pragmatic (contextual) and a textual component. The pragmatic one concerns the degree to which there is a mutual understanding between author and recipient, a shared awareness of what the author intends with the intertextual reference. Pfister asserts that mainly canonized works of world

---

[27] Pfister, "Konzepte der Intertextualität," 26.
[28] In the German original, "Kommunikativität," "Strukturalität," "Selektivität," and "Dialogizität" (Pfister, "Konzepte der Intertextualität," 27–29).

literature and current, widely discussed and received works would qualify as reference texts with a high degree of communicability, at least with respect to the most general target audience. The textual and pragmatic dimensions both have bearing on the degree of "marking," which can range from subtle/ambiguous to strong/straightforward.[29] It can also vary with respect to differing subgroups of the target audience. The author may be communicating ironically with the recipient, or simply within a commonly shared interpretational framework that is given by common cultural codes and shared stories, myths, texts, and discourses. The pragmatic understanding of author and recipient may render a strong signaling of intertextuality superfluous and even, for aesthetic and other reasons, counterproductive. The pragmatic dimension of communicability partly overlaps with MacDonald's two contextual parameters "accessibility/availability" and "analogy."

Selectivity has to do with the poignancy of the chosen reference. An exact quotation constitutes a high degree of selectivity as opposed to more abstract and general thematic and motivic references. One should note that a high degree of selectivity does not necessarily mean that the reference is textually marked: the quotation could very well be seamlessly integrated into the rest of the textual surroundings. The parameter of selectivity is closely matched by MacDonald's qualitative parameter "distinctiveness."

Dialogicity means that the intertextual relation is characterized by semantic or ideological tension, by ironic relativization or distancing. Since the parameter is essentially about the dialectics generated by contrasting standpoints and perspectives between texts, a complete negation of the original would, in Pfister's view, constitute a lesser degree of dialogical intensity. Pfister is here making use of Mikhail Bakhtin's concept of a dialogicity that is able to subvert hegemonic, stagnant monologicity in a particular culture. Whereas Bakhtin primarily has intratextual dialogicity in mind, that is, the polyphony within a text and also within a certain epoch, Pfister's parameter focuses on the tension between texts. Dialogicity closely corresponds to MacDonald's parameter "interpretability/intelligibility."

Structurality means the degree to which the text of reference serves as a "structural background," as a source of "syntagmatic integration," for extended parts of the text or even the text as a whole. In other words, the parameter of structurality measures the degree to which the parallels go beyond something merely punctual and are forming a substantial backdrop or subtext, such as is the case with central characters and events in James Joyce's *Ulysses* (1922) with reference to Homer's *Odyssey*.[30] Hypertextuality and imitation would clearly demand a high degree of

---

[29] An important study is Jörg Helbig, *Intertextualität und Markierung: Untersuchungen zur Systematik und Funktion der Signalisierung von Intertextualität* (Beiträge zur neueren Literaturgeschichte 3/141; Heidelberg: Winter, 1996).

[30] Genette views Ulysses as a direct transformation of the action of the *Odyssey* to twentieth-century Dublin, whereas Virgil's *Aeneid* is a more complex and indirect imitation of the generic model that the *Odyssey* provides as well as of the particular style of Homer (*Palimpsests*, 5–6).

structurality, where the text of reference offers a macrostructure that ties a larger number of parallels together, albeit difficult to quantify. This invariably leads to the question of quantitative parameters.

Pfister only in passing mentions two parameters he considers to be quantitative: on the one hand, "frequency and density," and, on the other hand, the number of reference texts.[31] At the same time, Pfister warns against a positivistic or one-sided, quantitative measuring of intertext. This is probably sound advice with regard to most approaches to intertextuality, but not for the case of imitation, where the quantitative dimension plays a key role.

We may now move on to give an overview of MacDonald's model of hypertextual imitation.

IV. Imitation: A Model

In his work on the apocryphal *Acts of Andrew* and their relation to Plato and Homer, MacDonald first defined a set of parameters of hypertextual imitation, or "criteria for establishing intertextual dependence."[32] In his study on the Gospel of Mark this set was then modified, mainly by adding the central parameter of distinctiveness, thus arriving at six parameters. In the following, I tentatively ordered these into three groups. A contextual group holds parameters (1) "accessibility/availability" and (2) "analogy." A qualitative group (with respect to single parallels) comprises parameters (3) "distinctiveness" and (4) "interpretability/intelligibility."[33] A quantitative group holds parameters (5) "order" and (6) "density."

The first two parameters are nontextual and concern the historical context and premises. Parameter 1, accessibility/availability, deals with whether the author of text B has access to or knowledge of text A. Parameter 2, analogy, concerns whether the author of text B knows of other authors' texts having been modeled after text A. MacDonald writes,

> Few scholars know Homeric epics as well as the average ancient Greek reader. Not only were the epics the primary—in some cases the sole—texts used in schools, not only did they serve as a cultural encyclopedia nearly everywhere Greek was spoken, they were favorite models for literary imitation, generating hundreds of ancient tales. Expansions on Homeric tales appear in ancient epics,

---

[31] Pfister, "Konzepte der Intertextualität," 30.
[32] Dennis R. MacDonald, *Christianizing Homer: The Odyssey, Plato, and the Acts of Andrew* (New York: Oxford University Press, 1994), 301. MacDonald here lists the criteria (1) "density and order," (2) "explanatory value," that is, interpretability/intelligibility, (3) "accessibility," (4) "analogy," and (5) the imitating author's "motivation," which is closely linked to parameter 2 (p. 302).
[33] With respect to single parallels, distinctiveness is qualitative in nature. However, a chain of trivial, generic parallels may together form a unique/distinctive composite parallel, that is, distinctive on quantitative grounds.

tragedies, and prose. Ancient authors could expect their readers to draw connections with Homer that are invisible to us.[34]

Establishing that the historical and contextual premises are not implausible should, generally speaking, suffice with respect to the mentioned nontextual parameters.[35] The rest is up to the textual indicators. The meager and/or faulty knowledge of the geography and culture of Galilee demonstrated by Mark—either he has not done his research or he is intentionally misleading his audience—gives at least some support to MacDonald's argument with respect to contextual and historical parameters.

The next two parameters are qualitative with respect to single parallels. They concern imitation (similarity) and contrastive imitation (difference/opposition), respectively. Both depend on the attitude, vision, and understanding that guide the author when creating text B, using text A as a model. The parameters are, of necessity, qualitative in nature with respect to single parallels; that is, one can measure the degree of qualitative distinctiveness of each separate parallel. However, a chain of generic, trivial parallels may also be unique and distinctive taken as a whole. In this case, it is rather the quantitative dimension that determines the degree of distinctiveness of the parallel chains.

Parameter 3 constitutes a distinctive similarity between two texts. The question of distinctiveness is fundamental for determining text parallels. MacDonald writes, "Occasionally two texts contain distinguishing characteristics, such as peculiar characterizations, or a sudden, unexpected change of venue, or an unusual word or phrase."[36] This means that a distinctive similarity may be based on surface text, when, for example, an unusual phrasing is imitated. But surface text distinctiveness is far from necessary. For instance, MacDonald claims that a phrase parallel exists between the Cyclops and the Gerasene: "my name is Noman [Nobody]" versus "My name is Legion." There is a formal similarity involving identification through a quantifier. A functional element of the parallel may consist in masking, not revealing, one's identity. Furthermore, Odysseus's presentation of himself as "Nobody" may in the original Greek also be taken to mean "cunning." His full statement to the Cyclops Polyphemus ("famous") is: "My name is Noman; Noman is what my mother and father call me; so likewise all my friends."[37] His reputation and character live on, even if he himself must remain anonymous. In fact, the cunning play with words contributes to Odysseus's escape from the Cyclops. The

---

[34] MacDonald, *Homeric Epics and the Gospel of Mark*, 171.

[35] One may, however, agree with Sandnes's remark on the fragmentary knowledge of Homer among average students: "Knowledge of ancient education certainly substantiates the primary role of Homer, but not necessarily of Homer's whole text or plot" ("Imitatio Homeri?" 727).

[36] MacDonald, *Homeric Epics and the Gospel of Mark*, 8.

[37] Homer, *The Odyssey* (trans. Walter Shewring; Oxford: Oxford University Press, 1980), 108, IX.364–444. The reference denotes the book and the line span from which the excerpt is taken, not the exact lines of the quotation.

Gerasene demoniac, the "unclean spirit," presents himself to Jesus with the words "My name is Legion; for we are many" (Mark 5:9). In doing so, the demon is not trying to mask himself so much as emphasize being part of a collective, which Jesus then defeats not with the powers of the mind but through the powers of the divine. To be able to separate specific text references from general system references one needs a high degree of distinctiveness. When arguing for word-for-word or phrase parallels one should check for rhetorical devices and conventions of language being system references. In other words, the distinctiveness of the device of identification through a quantifier and/or masking one's identity can only be measured relative to the extent of its usage in other contemporary texts.

The fourth parameter has to do with whether a contrasting parallel, that is, one that expresses an opposition/difference, makes more sense of the hypertext, and is able to explain ambiguities and contradictions or provide a larger contrastive interpretational framework for the hypertext. If characterizations of figures contrast, it probably becomes more difficult to pinpoint the distinctiveness of the parallels and to delimit a specific text reference from more general archetypes in literary or mythical traditions. While it is Odysseus's cunning hiding of himself and his (surviving) followers under a herd of sheep in the giant's cave that ultimately allows them to escape from the vicious, man-eating Cyclops Polyphemus, it is also true that Odysseus's headstrongness and recklessness—his followers on several occasions caution against undertaking dangerous actions—are responsible for getting him into trouble in the first place. In MacDonald's overarching interpretational framework, Mark is trying to convey the stark contrast between Odysseus's recklessness and helplessness, on the one hand, and the power and wisdom of Jesus, on the other (although Jesus' wisdom is at times arguably contradicted as a result of the emulation).[38] The fact that MacDonald almost exclusively deals with similarities when specifically comparing Gerasenes with Cyclopes may indicate the uncertainty involved with using contrastive parallels. At any rate, one may note that, from the viewpoint of contrastive imitation of the characterizations of the protagonists Odysseus and Jesus, the case of Cyclopes in *Odyssey* 9 and Gerasenes in Mark 5 (see below) might allow for a higher density of parallels than MacDonald is explicitly arguing for—but it would at the same time run the risk of making the parallels appear unnecessarily far-fetched. In a first analytical step, it seems appropriate to establish parallels through density, order, and historical circumstances. The parameters of intelligibility and the question of counterparallels call for interpretation to

---

[38] MacDonald identifies a potential example of this in Mark 4:36–40, where Jesus seemingly for no reason scolds his disciples for waking him up when a storm is closing in on their boat out on the open sea (*Homeric Epics and the Gospel of Mark*, 60). In *Odyssey* 10.1–69, Odysseus's followers without permission open their master's bag of winds (a gift from Aeolus, the god of winds) while out at sea, thus causing a dangerous storm. It is possible that Mark's emulation of the *Odyssey* here unintentionally makes Jesus' scolding of his disciples appear less than motivated.

such an extent that it is advisable to save this step for the very last stage of the analysis (if contrastive parallels are indeed being used).

The last two parameters are quantitative: order and density.

The degree to which a hypotextual sequence of some length matches the order of a hypertextual sequence is potentially an important indicator of imitation. One could plausibly assume that a matching order in combination with a high density, a sufficient quantitative volume, of text parallels would make a convincing case for imitation.

MacDonald writes,

> Density is determined by bulk, not by count; parallels between two texts may be numerous but trivial, such as "he said," "they went," "she replied." Not even a legion of such parallels would demonstrate imitation. On the other hand, as few as two or three weighty similarities may suffice.... The more often two texts share content in the same order, the stronger the case for literary dependence.[39]

It ought to be immensely weighty parallels if as few as two or three of them are to constitute sufficient evidence for imitation. Since MacDonald's analysis contains a great total amount of parallels between Mark, the *Odyssey,* and the *Iliad,* the absolute number of parallels is not in itself a problem for his argument. But his initial statement is worth repeating: "Density is determined by bulk, not by count." In MacDonald's view, it would be pointless to count parallels, since his concept of bulk density is based on "structurality" (Pfister) and deep-level parallels rather than surface text parallels easily counted, for example, in the case of "verbal agreement"[40] (see p. 310 above). But there is a problem here. Obviously, there is no need to count trivial parallels such as "he said," particularly if they do not form a substantial sequence of matching order, in which case they would add up to a nontrivial parallel chain. Theoretically, it should be clear—and here I seem to differ with MacDonald—that nontrivial parallels should be counted. How else is one to measure what MacDonald after all seems to be aiming at in his pseudo-statistical statement above: "the more often..., the stronger..."?

One may infer from MacDonald's analysis that to establish a macrolevel density of parallels—thus taking on a high degree of intertextual structurality—a critical mass is needed on the micro- and mid-level. On the microlevel a distinctive parallel or a small cluster of parallels may revolve around a phrase, such as is the case with "my name is Nobody"/"My name is Legion"; on the mid-level, around an event structure such as sailing, disembarking, reembarking, and sailing away in the Gerasene episode, or a motif such as Odysseus/Jesus waking up to face a storm on the open sea (Mark 4:36–40).[41] A number of MacDonald's most impressive synoptic presentations are located on the mid-level, such as the synopsis he gives of

---

[39] MacDonald, *Homeric Epics and the Gospel of Mark,* 8.
[40] See p. 310 above.
[41] See n. 38 above.

Cyclops/Gerasene.[42] What I mean by mid-level is that a single parallel presented in an idealized form in the synopsis may be "zoomed in" and thus revealed to hold further minor parallels and details.

The strength of an argument for mid-level imitation depends not only on the degree of matching order but also on the density of the parallels. This is particularly true for generic parallels. MacDonald's claim that two or three distinctive parallels may suffice to prove imitation can, at best, apply only to the textual mid-level. The argument that the textual whole, the macrolevel, can be proven to stand in a relationship of imitation through just a few parallel, distinctive events and the like in effect renders the whole enterprise of observing quantitative parameters meaningless and waters down the concept of hypertextual imitation beyond any real scholarly significance.

Figure 1 is an attempt to stylize a hypertextual relationship. Black markers indicate parallels, and gray markers indicate noncorresponding events, motifs, and characterizations. Theoretically, it should be clear that order, that is, the degree to which the lines in the figure do not cross, and density, that is, the ratio between black and gray dots within hyper- and hypotext respectively, are interdependent parameters. Both are crucial for any argument claiming mid- or macrolevel imitation.

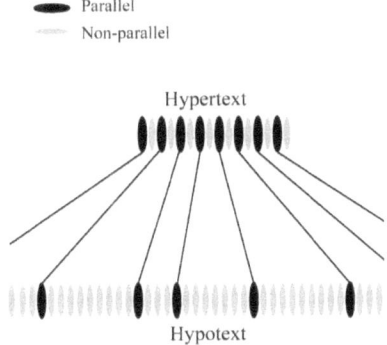

FIGURE 1. RATIO OF PARALLELS/NONPARALLELS IN HYPER- AND HYPOTEXT. (MODEL.)

The fundamental problem of how actually to test MacDonald's thesis remains, as far as I can tell, unsolved.

---

[42] In his main presentation, MacDonald adds the parallel motif of waking up during a storm at sea in the following book 10 of the *Odyssey* and in the previous ch. 4 of Mark, which amounts to a reversal of order and the usage of adjacent text parts (*Homeric Epics and the Gospel of Mark*, 73). While this would probably not be damaging to the argument for imitation, I have for the sake of simplicity left this parallel out. The synopsis in MacDonald's conclusions comprises, with the exception of the Circe motif from *Odyssey* 10, parallels from the same book/chapter in *Odyssey* and Mark (ibid., 175). This is the synopsis discussed in the present article.

V. Order

In MacDonald's view, the story of the exorcism of the Gerasene demoniac in Mark 5 constitutes one of the most convincing instances of imitation, namely, of Homer's story of the Cyclops in *Odyssey* 9 (and a motif from the story of Circe in *Odyssey* 10). The reason for this lies mainly in the "density," that is, the sheer quantitative volume, of the parallels. MacDonald gives a synoptic presentation of the ca. fifteen parallels he identifies (see table 1, in which I have added numbers to MacDonald's original table).[43] A parallel in square brackets means that the order is different between the two texts. For example, in Mark it is only noted toward the end of the story that a large number of swine are grazing about. In the story of the Cyclops, there are a great number of goats and sheep, but MacDonald here also draws on *Odyssey* 10, where the goddess Circe turns many of Odysseus's followers into swine (a situation that is resolved only through the advice of the trickster-god Hermes). The one parallel in parentheses below indicates the usage of nontextual information, namely, that the Cyclops Polyphemus was usually depicted naked. This, in MacDonald's view, corresponds to the implicitly naked demon in Mark: the reader is at the end of the episode informed that the exorcised Gerasene is now "clothed." Synoptic presentations are the general technique employed by MacDonald to present his findings. What this presentation technique above all lends itself to is a discussion of the distinctiveness, the intelligibility, and the order of the parallels.

As MacDonald remarks, Mark's Jesus has an entire fleet of ships ("with other boats") at his disposal, and for some reason he is constantly sailing about in his native Middle Eastern desert landscape on the little lake of Chinnereth, which Mark dubs the "Sea of Galilee."[44] The Markan focus on nautical activities may well be unique among the Synoptic Gospels, but the critical question that must be asked for our purposes is, Are these parallels unique to Mark and Homer? In texts where the main characters are sailing about, there will in all likelihood be disembarking and reembarking of boats, and other generic activities that, of necessity, follow in a particular order, just as our everyday world is largely "scripted" in certain ways. For example, Apollonius Rhodius, in his epic poem *Argonautica* (third century B.C.E.) draws on Homer as well as on a—largely perished—corpus of sea narratives.[45] Generic parallels of this nature clearly do not in themselves support the case for imitation, although they do seem to fit well with a modeling of Jesus as a Super-Odysseus. Only a high degree of matching order of such parallels in comparison to other contemporary texts may give weight to an argument for imitation.

---

[43] MacDonald, *Homeric Epics and the Gospel of Mark*, 175.
[44] Ibid., 55–57.
[45] An introduction to sea narratives and adventures in the Western literary canon is given by Robert Foulke, *The Sea Voyage Narrative* (New York: Routledge, 2002).

TABLE 1. SYNOPSIS OF PARALLELS BETWEEN THE STORIES OF THE CYCLOPS
AND THE GERASENE DEMONIAC (according to MacDonald,
Homeric Epics and the Gospel of Mark, 175)

	Odyssey 9:101–565	Mark 5:1–20
1	Odysseus and his crew, in a convoy, arrived at the land of the Cyclopes.	Jesus and his disciples, with "other boats," arrived at the land of the Gerasenes.
2	On the mountains "innumerable goats" grazed.	[On the mountains "about two thousand" swine grazed.]
3	Odysseus and crew disembarked.	Jesus and his disciples disembarked.
4	They encountered a savage, lawless giant who lived in a cave.	They encountered a savage, lawless demoniac who lived among the caves.
5	He asked if Odysseus came to harm him.	He asked Jesus not to torment him.
6	The giant asked Odysseus his name.	Jesus asked the demoniac his name.
7	Odysseus answered, "Nobody."	The demoniac answered, "Legion."
8	Odysseus subdued the giant with violence and trickery. [Circe had turned Odysseus's soldiers into swine.]	Jesus subdued the demons with divine power and sent them into the swine and then into the sea.
9	The shepherd called out to his neighbors.	The swineherds called on their neighbors.
10	The Cyclopes came to the site asking about Polyphemus's sheep and goats.	The Gerasenes came to the site to find out about their swine.
11	(Polyphemus usually was depicted nude.)	The demoniac, once naked, now is clothed.
12	Odysseus and crew reembarked.	Jesus and his disciples reembarked.
13	Odysseus told the giant to proclaim that he had blinded him.	[Jesus told the healed demoniac to proclaim that he had healed him.]
14	The giant asked Odysseus, who was now aboard ship, to come back.	The demoniac asked Jesus, now aboard ship, if he could be with him.
15	Odysseus refused the request.	Jesus refused the request.
16	Odysseus and crew sailed away.	Jesus and disciples sailed away.

Since Odysseus first, with several ships, lands on an island off the coast of the land of the Cyclopes, from where he then reaches land using only his own ship, it is possible to construct two similar chains of parallels in Homer's text alone. The parameter of order becomes weightier when MacDonald ties in more distinctive parallels to the mentioned generic chain of events. After the protagonists have triumphed, Polyphemus and the Gerasenes (the latter as a collective) call on their neighbors. In both stories, the neighbors come to inquire about their livestock. After the protagonists with crews have reembarked, communication continues between the parties Odysseus/Polyphemus and Jesus/exorcised Gerasene.

The Greek reads: Καὶ ἐμβαίνοντος αὐτοῦ εἰς τὸ πλοῖον παρεκάλει αὐτὸν ὁ δαιμονισθεὶς ἵνα μετ' αὐτοῦ ᾖ.[46] The translation in the NRSV is rendered in the imperfect progressive, that is, continuous, tense: "As he was getting into the boat." MacDonald interprets the parallel as follows: "Homer's implausible conversation between Polyphemus and Odysseus already aboard ship finds an analogy in the equally unusual conversation between the cured demoniac, on land, and Jesus, on ship."[47] But if it cannot be established that Jesus is on ship, the conversation in Mark can hardly be described as unusual. The parallel is highly distinctive only if defined as "continued communication *after* completed reembarking." A less distinctive definition of the parallel such as "continued communication in the context of reembarking," that is, a somewhat vague process, would still be able to form a distinctive chain of generic parallel events, for which a large percentage of generic nautical texts no longer provide a match. If one disregards the issue of temporality, just how distinctive is the parallel? Odysseus and Polyphemus are rather shouting at each other over quite some distance. In Mark, the exorcised Gerasene asks Jesus if he can join him, whereas Polyphemus wants Odysseus to come back, obviously intent on killing him. The nonsimilar requests of the counterparts Polyphemus and the Gerasene are denied by the protagonists. In other words, the communication is similar in that the requests are denied, but different in that the counterparts are asking for quite different things: the Gerasene wishes to take on the role of a follower, that is, the function of a helper, whereas Polyphemus remains an antagonist. If one chooses to define the parallel as a "denied request," the distinctiveness is decreased. The more abstractly one defines a parallel, the less distinctive it is. Alternatively, one may view the denied nonsimilar requests as consisting of a parallel (denial of request) and a nonparallel (nonsimilarity of request). The nonparallel should in that case not be seen as trivial.

The preceding discussion renders the following sequence of eight event parallels, in (almost) matching order: Convoy arrives [1] – sailing party disembarks [3] – the antagonists call on their neighbors [9] – the neighbors come to ask about their livestock [10] – sailing party reembarks [12] – communication between protagonist and antagonist continues (although in Mark this takes place *during* the reembarkment) [14] – protagonist refuses the (nonsimilar) request of the antagonist [15] – sailing party sails away [16]. Parallels 14 and 15 pose some interpretational difficulties emanating from the fact that they contain both similar and nonsimilar, distinctive elements.

MacDonald identifies two parallels of nonmatching order. One of them is fairly straightforward, although not very distinctive, namely, the mention of the great numbers of the livestock [2]: innumerable goats in the *Odyssey*, two thousand

---

[46] *Novum Testamentum Graece* (ed. Eberhard Nestle and Kurt Aland; 28th ed.; Stuttgart: Deutsche Bibelgesellschaft, 2012).

[47] MacDonald, *Homeric Epics and the Gospel of Mark*, 73. In an e-mail message to me, MacDonald admits to the continuous tense being more appropriate but does not feel this affects the overall argument.

swine in Mark. The other parallel is, however, problematic. MacDonald's synoptic presentation suggests that both Odysseus and Jesus ask for their identities to be made known to everyone by their antagonists. This is true with regard to Odysseus. In MacDonald's words, "Odysseus told the giant to proclaim that he had blinded him" (see table 1 above, p. 323).[48] But the description of the supposed parallel passage in Mark, "Jesus told the healed demoniac to proclaim that he had healed him," is misleading. The passage reads:

> But Jesus refused, and said to him, "Go home to your friends, and tell them how much the Lord has done for you, and what mercy he has shown you." And he went away and began to proclaim in the Decapolis how much Jesus had done for him; and everyone was amazed. (Mark 5:19–20)

The cured man is instructed to tell his friends of God's mercy. This clearly does not entail proclaiming to the world what miracles Jesus has performed, whose safety after all depends on remaining anonymous. Contrary to the instructions of Jesus, the man then goes off to the Ten Greek Cities—not to his friends—and specifically relates what Jesus has done. So, whereas Odysseus wants the antagonist to let his identity be known, the cured man reveals the identity of Jesus contrary to the instructions. It might still be possible to see this as a parallel within the framework of a contrastive emulation with the purpose of showing the wisdom of Jesus in comparison to the recklessness of Odysseus, but in that case the distinctiveness is much lessened.

Disregarding the parallel that draws on extratextual information [11], one is left with five remaining events of matching order. These, however, seem to call for some interpretation. By nature, both the antagonists are lawless and savage [4], but whereas the Cyclops concretely and specifically lives in a cave, the Gerasene demoniac more vaguely lives among the tombs, which, as MacDonald points out, are merely caves. The Cyclops asks Odysseus [5] if he intends to do him harm (which he at this point is unable to do). In contrast, the demon, being part of the supernatural, recognizes the true identity of Jesus and asks for mercy. This is followed by two parallels where the roles are reversed [6-7], in that the Cyclops asks Odysseus for his name and gets the answer "Nobody," in contrast to Jesus asking the demon for his name, receiving the answer "Legion." One may argue that the distinctiveness of these events and motifs in a sense makes up for the reversal of roles.

Finally, it is possible that Homer himself alludes to Odysseus's soldiers once being turned into swine by Circe, which in the story of the Cyclops is being triumphantly inverted through their being disguised as (or rather hiding underneath) livestock [8]. Mark's fantasy about demons being driven into two thousand swine and then drowned in the sea may be intended as a grandiose illustration of the fact that Jesus, unlike Odysseus, commands the supernatural and will not submit to demonic forces or magic. Without the Circe motif it would still be possible to

---

[48] MacDonald, *Homeric Epics and the Gospel of Mark*, 175.

identify a more general, less distinctive parallel between the victory of Odysseus and Jesus in this episode.

In sum, MacDonald's synopsis appears strict enough with respect to the order of the parallels. Let us now turn to the parameter of density.

VI. Density

Nonparallel events and the like do not in themselves make the argument for imitation implausible. Any competent imitating author will avoid copying as much as possible and instead let the story take on a life of its own. There are, however, quantitative limits to what proportion of a text the nonparallels may hold before rendering any argument of imitation implausible and/or meaningless. There must be a sufficient mass of parallels and sequences of parallels to make an argument for imitation plausible. After Jesus has driven the demons into the swine and drowned them in the sea, the Gerasene neighbors ask him to leave. This is apparently a nonparallel. The Cyclopes collectively do not respond at all to Odysseus's stealing of the sheep and goats. Polyphemus of course wants Odysseus to come back so he can kill him. The reaction of the Gerasenes is to some extent understandable, considering that they have lost their livestock, but, as MacDonald points out, this is still quite an unusual response to someone who has rid the area of a vile demon. So, other than possibly as a projection of the antagonism of Polyphemus toward Odysseus, the neighborly response is a part of the Gerasene story that has no parallel in the Cyclops story. Furthermore, due to the scarce amount of narrative information characterizing the storytelling of Mark, the response of the Gerasenes comes across as a nontrivial story element.

A fundamental problem that MacDonald does not address is that, once the texts of comparison become large enough, it will always be possible to find parallels of some distinctiveness. Particularly, this will be the case if one allows for large chunks of noncorresponding text, that is, nonparallels, between each parallel. With respect to the density of the parallels, one may want to take the following into account.

The hypotext of the Cyclops story consists of some 24,000 characters (or 4,600 words), whereas the hypertext of Gerasene narrative comprises some 2,000 characters (or 460 words). This gives a ratio of 12 for characters (and 10 for words), meaning that the average distance between parallels in the hypotext is twelve times greater than in the hypertext. In his book *Christianizing Homer*, MacDonald identifies fifteen parallels of mostly matching order between Plato's *Phaedo* and Andrew's Passion (the third and final section of the *Acts of Andrew*).[49] Of these, however, MacDonald deems only about ten to be distinct.[50] These stem from Passion 56–58 and *Phaedo* 64c–e, 67a–c, 80d–81b, and 96c. The whole text span of *Phaedo* 64–96

---

[49] MacDonald, *Christianizing Homer*, 307.
[50] Ibid., 268.

consists of circa 15,000 words or 80,000 characters (the text passages themselves comprise only about 1,000 words or 5,400 characters). The text span of Passion 56–58, reconstructed by MacDonald, consists of about 500 words or 3,000 characters.[51] The average distance between parallels in the hypotext is thirty times greater than in the hypertext.

The Cyclops–Gerasene imitation is based on a total of fifteen parallels. The critical empirical question is, Is it possible to find another hypotextual model for the chain of fifteen parallels that MacDonald lists for the Gerasene story under the quantitative constraint of 24,000 characters?

The density in the Cyclops story corresponds to circa 63 parallels per 100,000 characters (some 18,000 words). The density in *Phaedo* corresponds to 13 parallels per 100,000 characters. The critical theoretical question is: Does a comparison of random texts generate fewer parallels than 63 per 100,000 characters or fewer than 15 parallels per 24,000 characters? If random comparisons will generate more parallels of some distinctiveness, then of course MacDonald's argument for a high density weakens considerably.

Finally, comparing the texts side by side may in itself suffice to cast some doubt on the supposed high density of the parallels (see figures 2A and 2B). Scholars have remarked on flaws of the contextual and qualitative dimensions of MacDonald's argument, particularly on the often vague nature of the parallels and the failure to demonstrate authorial intention.[52] After all, "influence" or "literary dependence" is not the same as a conscious "imitation" communicated to a contemporary audience. My own point is the following: Synoptic presentations should be used critically by weighing in quantitative parameters, in particular density as volume of parallels over total text volume. An argument for imitation should not be allowed to rest on decontextualized, unspecified notions of bulk density.

An objective measure of density would have to consider the relative density of parallels per text volume (characters or words). MacDonald's concept of "bulk density" belongs to a more hermeneutical approach. Perhaps distinguishing various discourse types or textual functions would lead to a still more accurate assessment of intertextual density. The chain of parallels identified by MacDonald in Cyclops–Gerasenes mainly comprises story elements. This should come as no surprise given the nature of the Gospel text, which is centered on story elements with a minimum of scenic description. The scarce dialogue is essentially a function of the plot. In the *Odyssey* text, on the other hand, there are substantial digressions from the primary story line.

---

[51] Ibid., 263–68. See also Dennis R. MacDonald, *The Acts of Andrew and The Acts of Andrew and Matthias in the City of the Cannibals* (SBLTT 33; Christian Apocrypha 1; Atlanta: Scholars Press, 1990).

[52] For example, Sandnes recognizes a reader-oriented value of MacDonald's argument ("Imitatio Homeri?" 727).

Meanwhile he drove all the ewes inside, as well as the she-goats that he was going to milk, leaving the males, both rams and he-goats, outside in the yards. Then he rolled a huge stone to the mouth of the cave—so huge that two and twenty strong four-wheeled waggons would not be enough to draw it from its place against the doorway. When he had so done he sat down and milked his ewes and goats, all in due course, and then let each of them have her own young. He curdled half the milk and set it aside in wicker strainers, but the other half he poured into bowls that he might drink it for his supper. When he had got through with all his work, he lit the fire, and then caught sight of us, whereon he said: "Strangers, who are you? Where do sail from? Are you traders, or **do you sail the sea as rovers, with your hands against every man, and every man's hand against you?" [5]** We were frightened out of our senses by his loud voice and monstrous form, but I managed to say, "We are Achaeans on our way home from Troy, but by the will of Jove, and stress of weather, we have been driven far out of our course. We are the people of Agamemnon, son of Atreus, who has won infinite renown throughout the whole world, by sacking so great a city and killing so many people. We therefore humbly pray you to show us some hospitality, and otherwise make us such presents as visitors may reasonably expect. May your excellency fear the wrath of heaven, for we are your suppliants, and Jove takes all respectable travellers under his protection, for he is the avenger of all suppliants and foreigners in distress." To this he gave me but a pitiless answer, "Stranger," said he, "you are a fool, or else you know nothing of this country. Talk to me, indeed, about fearing the gods or shunning their anger? We Cyclopes do not care about Jove or any of your blessed gods, for we are ever so much stronger than they. I shall not spare either yourself or your companions out of any regard for Jove, unless I am in the humour for doing so. And now tell me where you made your ship fast when you came on shore. Was it round the point, or is she lying straight off the land?" He said this to draw me out, but I was too cunning to be caught in that way, so I answered with a lie; "Neptune," said I, "sent my ship on to the rocks at the far end of your country, and wrecked it. We were driven on to them from the open sea, but I and those who are with me escaped the jaws of death." The cruel wretch vouchsafed me not one word of answer, but with a sudden clutch he gripped up two of my men at once and dashed them down upon the ground as though they had been puppies. Their brains were shed upon the ground, and the earth was wet with their blood. Then he tore them limb from limb and supped upon them. He gobbled them up like a lion in the wilderness, flesh, bones, marrow, and entrails, without leaving anything uneaten. As for us, we wept and lifted up our hands to heaven on seeing such a horrid sight, for we did not know what else to do; but when the Cyclops had filled his huge paunch, and had washed down his meal of human flesh with a drink of neat milk, he stretched himself full length upon the ground among his sheep, and went to sleep. I was at first inclined to seize my sword, draw it, and drive it into his vitals, but I reflected that if I did we should all certainly be lost, for we should never be able to shift the stone which the monster had put in front of the door. So we stayed sobbing and sighing where we were till morning came. When the child of morning, rosy-fingered dawn, appeared, he again lit his fire, milked his goats and ewes, all quite rightly, and then let each have her own young one; as soon as he had got through with all his work, he clutched up two more of my men, and began eating them for his morning's meal. Presently, with the utmost ease, he rolled the stone away from the door and drove out his sheep, but he at once put it back again—as easily as though he were merely clapping the lid on to a quiver full of arrows. As soon as he had done so he shouted, and cried 'Shoo, shoo,' after his sheep to drive them on to the mountain; **so I was left to scheme [beginning of parallel 8]** some way of taking my revenge and covering myself with glory. In the end I deemed it would be the best plan to do as follows: The Cyclops had a great club which was lying near one of the sheep pens; it was of green olive wood, and he had cut it intending to use it for a staff as soon as it should be dry. It was so huge that we could only compare it to the mast of a twenty-oared merchant vessel of large burden, and able to venture out into open sea. I went up to this club and cut off about six feet of it; I then gave this piece to the men and told them to fine it evenly off at one end, which they proceeded to do, and lastly I brought it to a point myself, charring the end in the fire to make it harder. When I had done this I hid it under dung, which was lying about all over the cave, and told the men to cast lots which of them should venture along with myself to lift it and bore it into the monster's eye while he was asleep. The lot fell upon the very four whom I should have chosen, and I myself made five. In the evening the wretch came back from shepherding, and drove his flocks into the cave—this time driving them all inside, and not leaving any in the yards; I suppose some fancy must have taken him, or a god must have prompted him to do so. As soon as he had put the stone back to its place against the door, he sat down, milked his ewes and his goats all quite rightly, and then let each have her own young one; when he had got through with all this work, he gripped up two more of my men, and made his supper off them. So I went up to him with an ivy-wood bowl of black wine in my hands: "Look here, Cyclops," said I, "you have been eating a great deal of man's flesh, so take this and drink some wine, that you may see what kind of liquor we had on board my ship. I was bringing it to you as a drink-offering, in the hope that you would take compassion upon me and further me on my way home, whereas all you do is to go on ramping and raving most intolerably. You ought to be ashamed of yourself; how can you expect people to come see you any more if you treat them in this way?" He then took the cup and drank. He was so delighted with the taste of the wine that he begged me for another bowl full. "Be so kind," he said, "as to give me some more, and tell me your name at once. I want to make you a present that you will be glad to have. We have wine even in this country, for our soil grows grapes and the sun ripens them, but this drinks like Nectar and Ambrosia all in one." I then gave him some more; three times did I fill the bowl for him, and three times did he drain it without thought or heed; then, when I saw that the wine had got into his head, I said to him as plausibly as I could: "Cyclops, **you ask my name [6]** and I will tell it you; give me, therefore, the present you promised me; **my name is Noman [7]**; this is what my father and mother and my friends have always called me." But the cruel wretch said, "Then I will eat all Noman's comrades before Noman himself, and will keep Noman for the last. This is the present that I will make him." As he spoke he reeled, and fell sprawling face upwards on the ground. His great neck hung heavily backwards and a deep sleep took hold upon him. Presently he turned sick, and threw up both wine and the gobbets of human flesh on which he had been gorging, for he was very drunk. Then I thrust the beam of wood far into the embers to heat it, and encouraged my men lest any of them should turn faint-hearted. When the wood, green though it was, was about to blaze, I drew it out of the fire glowing with heat, and my men gathered round me, for heaven had filled their hearts with courage. We drove the sharp end of the beam into the monster's eye, and bearing upon it with all my weight I kept turning it round and round as though I were boring a hole in a ship's plank with an auger, which two men with a wheel and strap can keep on turning as long as they choose. Even thus did we bore the red hot beam into his eye, till the boiling blood bubbled all over it as we worked it round and round, so that the steam from the burning eyeball scalded his eyelids and eyebrows, and the roots of the eye sputtered in the fire. As a blacksmith plunges an axe or hatchet into cold water to temper it—for it is this that gives strength to the iron—and it makes a great hiss as he does so, even thus did the Cyclops' eye hiss round the beam of olive wood, and his hideous yells made the cave ring again. We ran away in a fright, but he plucked the beam all besmirched with gore from his eye, and hurled it from him in a frenzy of rage and pain, **shouting as he did so to the other Cyclopes [9]** who lived on the bleak headlands near him; so they gathered from all quarters round his cave when they heard him crying, and **asked what was the matter with him. [10]** "What ails you, Polyphemus," said they, "that you make such a noise, breaking the stillness of the night, and preventing us from being able to sleep? **Surely no man is carrying off your sheep? [10]** Surely no man is trying to kill you either by fraud or by force?" But Polyphemus shouted to them from inside the cave, "Noman is killing me by fraud; no man is killing me by force." "Then," said they, "if no man is attacking you, you must be ill; when Jove makes people ill, there is no help for it, and you had better pray to your father Neptune." Then they went away, and I laughed inwardly at the success of my clever stratagem, but the Cyclops, groaning and in an agony of pain, felt about with his hands till he found the stone and took it from the door; then he sat in the doorway and stretched his hands in front of it to catch anyone going out with the sheep, for he thought I might be foolish enough to attempt this. As for myself I kept on puzzling to think how I could best save my own life and those of my companions; I schemed and schemed, as one who knows that his life depends upon it, for the danger was very great. In the end I deemed that this plan would be the best: the male sheep were well grown, and carried a heavy black fleece, so I bound them noiselessly in threes together, with some of the withies on which the wicked monster used to sleep. **There was to be a man under the middle sheep, and the two on either side were to cover him, so that there were three sheep to each man. [end of parallel 8]** As for myself there was a ram finer than any of the others, so I caught hold of him by the back, esconced myself in the thick wool under his belly, and hung on patiently to his fleece, face upwards, keeping a firm hold on it all the time.

A. Night and day among the tombs and in the hills he would cry out and cut himself with stones. When he saw Jesus from a distance, he ran and fell on his knees in front of him. He shouted at the top of his voice, "What do you want with me, Jesus, Son of the Most High God? **In God's name don't torture me!" [5]**

B. For Jesus had said to him, **"Come out of this man, you impure spirit!" [8]**

C. Then Jesus asked him, **"What is your name?" [6] "My name is Legion," [7]** he replied, "for we are many." And he begged Jesus again and again not to send them out of the area.

E. Those tending the pigs ran off and **reported this in the town and countryside, [9]** and **the people went out to see what had happened. [10]**

F. When they came to Jesus, they saw the man who had been possessed by the legion of demons, sitting there, **dressed [contextual parallel, 11]** and in his right mind; and they were afraid. Those who had seen it told the people what had happened to the demon-possessed man—and told about the pigs as well. Then the people began to plead with Jesus to leave their region.

D. The demons begged Jesus, **"Send us among the pigs; allow us to go into them." He gave them permission, and the impure spirits came out and went into the pigs. The herd, about two thousand in number, rushed down the steep bank into the lake [8]** and were drowned.

FIGURE 2A. DENSITY OF PARALLELS. (EXAMPLE.)

[On the left: *Odyssey* 9, Cyclops, end part, 17,300 characters. On the right: Mark 5:5–21 (except 5:11), 1,900 characters. The text masses in figures 2A and 2B are not intended to be readable. The images serve to illustrate the quantitative relation between the two text masses.]

Thus, then, did we wait in great fear of mind till morning came, but when the child of morning, rosy-fingered Dawn, appeared, the male sheep hurried out to feed, while the ewes remained bleating about the pens waiting to be milked, for their udders were full to bursting; but their master in spite of all his pain felt the backs of all the sheep as they stood upright, without being sharp enough to find out that the men were underneath their bellies. As the ram was going out, last of all, heavy with its fleece and with the weight of my crafty self, Polyphemus laid hold of it and said: "My good ram, what is it that makes you the last to leave my cave this morning? You are not wont to let the ewes go before you, but lead the mob with a run whether to flowery mead or bubbling fountain, and are the first to come home again at night; but now you lag last of all. Is it because you know your master has lost his eye, and are sorry because that wicked Noman and his horrid crew has got him down in his drink and blinded him? But I will have his life yet. If you could understand and talk, you would tell me where the wretch is hiding, and I would dash his brains upon the ground till they flew all over the cave. I should thus have some satisfaction for the harm this no-good Noman has done me."

As he spoke he drove the ram outside, but when we were a little way out from the cave and yards, I first got from under the ram's belly, and then freed my comrades; as for the sheep, which were very fat, by constantly heading them in the right direction we managed to drive them down to the ship. The crew rejoiced greatly at seeing those of us who had escaped death, but wept for the others whom the Cyclops had killed. However, I made signs to them by nodding and frowning that they were to hush their crying, and told them to get all the sheep on board at once and put out to sea; so **they went aboard, [12]** took their places, and smote the grey sea with their oars. Then, when I had got as far out as my voice would reach, I began to jeer at the Cyclops. "Cyclops," said I, "you should have taken better measure of your man before eating up his comrades in your cave. You wretch, eat up your visitors in your own house? You might have known that your sin would find you out, and now Jove and the other gods have punished you." He got more and more furious as he heard me, so he tore the top from off a high mountain, and flung it just in front of my ship so that it was within a little of hitting the end of the rudder. The sea quaked as the rock fell into it, and the wash of the wave it raised carried us back towards the mainland, and forced us towards the shore. But I snatched up a long pole and kept the ship off, making signs to my men by nodding my head, that they must row for their lives, whereon they laid out with a will. When we had got twice as far as we were before, I was for jeering at the Cyclops again, but the men begged and prayed of me to hold my tongue. "Do not," they exclaimed, "be mad enough to provoke this savage creature further; he has thrown one rock at us already which drove us back again to the mainland, and we made sure it had been the death of us; if he had then heard any further sound of voices he would have pounded our heads and our ship's timbers into a jelly with the rugged rocks he would have heaved at us, for he can throw them a long way."

G. **As Jesus was getting into the boat, [12]**

But I would not listen to them, and shouted out to him in my rage, "'Cyclops, **if any one asks you who it was that put your eye out and spoiled your beauty, say it was the valiant warrior Ulysses, son of Laertes, who lives in Ithaca." [13]** On this he groaned, and cried out, "Alas, alas, then the old prophecy about me is coming true. There was a prophet here, at one time, a man both brave and of great stature, Telemus son of Eurymus, who was an excellent seer, and did all the prophesying for the Cyclopes till he grew old; he told me that all this would happen to me some day, and said I should lose my sight by the hand of Ulysses. I have been all along expecting some one of imposing presence and superhuman strength, whereas he turns out to be a little insignificant weakling, who has managed to blind my eye by taking advantage of me in my drink; **come here, then, Ulysses, [14]** that I may make you presents to show my hospitality, and urge Neptune to help you forward on your journey—for Neptune and I are father and son. He, if he so will, shall heal me, which no one else neither god nor man can do." **Then I said, "I wish I could be as sure of killing you outright and sending you down to the house of Hades, as I am that it will take more than Neptune to cure that eye of yours." [15]**

J. but said, "Go home to your own people and **tell them how much the Lord has done for you, and how he has had mercy on you." [13] So the man went away and began to tell in the Decapolis how much Jesus had done for him. And all the people were amazed.**

H. the man who had been demon-possessed **begged to go with him. [14]**

I. **Jesus did not let him. [15]**

On this he lifted up his hands to the firmament of heaven and prayed, saying, "Hear me, great Neptune; if I am indeed your own true begotten son, grant that Ulysses may never reach his home alive; or if he must get back to his friends at last, let him do so late and in sore plight after losing all his men [let him reach his home in another man's ship and find trouble in his house.]" Thus did he pray, and Neptune heard his prayer. Then he picked up a rock much larger than the first, swung it aloft and hurled it with prodigious force. It fell just short of the ship, but was within a little of hitting the end of the rudder. The sea quaked as the rock fell into it, and the wash of the wave it raised drove us onwards on our way towards the shore of the island. When at last we got to the island where we had left the rest of our ships, we found our comrades lamenting us, and anxiously awaiting our return. We ran our vessel upon the sands and got out of her on to the sea shore; we also landed the Cyclops' sheep, and divided them equitably amongst us so that none might have reason to complain. As for the ram, my companions agreed that I should have it as an extra share; so I sacrificed it on the sea shore, and burned its thigh bones to Jove, who is the lord of all. But he heeded not my sacrifice, and only thought how he might destroy both my ships and my comrades.

Thus through the livelong day to the going down of the sun we feasted our fill on meat and drink, but when the sun went down and it came on dark, we camped upon the beach. When the child of morning rosy-fingered Dawn appeared, I bade my men on board and loose the hawsers. Then they took their places and smote the grey sea with their oars; so **we sailed on [16]** with sorrow in our hearts, but glad to have escaped death though we had lost our comrades.

K. When Jesus **had again crossed over by boat [16] to the other side** of the lake, a large crowd gathered around him while he was by the lake.

FIGURE 2B. DENSITY OF PARALLELS. (EXAMPLE, CONTINUED.)

VIII. CONCLUDING REMARKS AND METHODOLOGICAL SUGGESTIONS

With respect to the alleged parallels of the stories of the Gerasenes and the Cyclopes, the parameter of order does not pose any significant problems. The fifteen parallels that rest solely on textual information contain two parallels of nonmatching order, plus one parallel that partly draws on the Circe episode. This means that, at most, 20 percent of the parallels are of nonmatching order. Allowing for a maximum of 20 percent deviation in the order of the parallels seems sensible with respect to "mid-level" analogies such as the Gerasenes–Cyclopes. Macrolevel analogies that meet this criterion would of course be strengthened as a whole.

The parameter of density ought to lend itself to a discussion of the distribution of differences and similarities between texts of comparison. As discussed above, if fifteen parallels can be found between random texts within a constraint of 24,000 characters, this weakens MacDonald's argument for a high density. However, falsifying an argument for imitation would require a systematic methodology enabling an assessment of the qualitative and distinct elements that are accounted for through the parameter of density. The question of quantitative measure ultimately leads back to the qualities of parallels.

The parameter of distinctiveness should be discussed with respect to the distribution of differences and similarities within each parallel, since this is directly linked to its straightforwardness or, inversely, its reliance on interpretation.

The first parallel in MacDonald's synopsis comprises three elements. (i) Odysseus arrived at the land of the Cyclopes; Jesus arrived at the land of the Gerasenes. (ii) Odysseus sails with sailors; Jesus, with his disciples. (iii) The former involves a convoy; the latter, "other boats." The first element, the journey on sea, constitutes the kernel of the parallel. The other two elements are rather satellites, adding to its distinctiveness. The combination of the three elements constitutes a quite distinct parallel, which can ultimately only be measured in relation to its usage in (unfortunately, largely perished) contemporary narratives.

Differences can be (a) factored in as negative distinctiveness, (b) disregarded, or (c) transvaluated. A problematic aspect of MacDonald's methodology is the disregarding or downplaying of actual differences between supposed parallel text passages. Distinctive (qualitative) and substantial (quantitative) differences are difficult to account for if one argues for an intended imitation that is communicated to an audience.

The fourth parallel in MacDonald's synopsis comprises similarities and differences. (i) Odysseus and crew encountered a giant; Jesus and his disciples encountered a demoniac. Thus, meeting a "monster" constitutes the kernel of this parallel. (ii) The giant was savage and lawless from the viewpoint of Odysseus, not from the viewpoint of his own community of Cyclopes. The demoniac, on the other hand, was an outcast and seen as savage and lawless by everybody. (iii) The giant lived *in* a cave, whereas the demoniac lived *among* the tombs, which are merely caves. The setting is thus not a very distinct element of the parallel, and the characteristics of the antagonists differ.

An equally problematic aspect of the methodology in MacDonald's study is the fact that not only similarities but also transvaluated differences in the form of, for example, recharacterization and plot manipulation are considered as potential imitation. This makes it more or less impossible to verify literary dependence. There is also no compelling reason to assume that a contemporary audience of average learning would make use of elaborate text analysis in order to grasp a subtle emulation, that is, a merely implied model of understanding.

The fifth parallel in MacDonald's synopsis is arguably based on the transvaluated motif of (physical) harm and (spiritual) torment as a kernel. The giant asked Odysseus if he came to harm him, whereas the demoniac rather pleaded to Jesus, whom he recognized, not to torment him.

Parallels 6 and 7 entail a reversal of roles. The act of asking the counterpart's name forms the kernel of parallel 6. The giant, that is, the antagonist, asked Odysseus his name, whereas Jesus, the protagonist, asked the demon his name. The role reversal does make the parallel less distinct. The act of pseudo-identifying oneself or not revealing one's identity may be seen as the kernel of parallel 7: Odysseus answered, "Nobody"; the demoniac answered, "Legion." The roles are reversed, which lessens the distinctiveness. The usage of a quantifier as a name, on the other hand, is a very distinct feature.

The purpose of the present article was to examine the quantitative parameter of intertextual density as a way of determining hypertextual imitation. A strictly hermeneutic approach to imitation that considers only "bulk density" and does not entail quantitative constraints on the textual macro-, mid-, and microlevels opens up for ad hoc interpretation. Avoiding ad hoc interpretations requires a methodology for determining text parallels and for dealing with both similarities and differences in a systematic fashion. The qualitative and quantitative dimensions of parallels should be considered in relation to one another.

One needs to check the plausibility of the textual evidence, on the one hand, and the relative weight of the parallels in relation to contemporary and historically available texts (such as the OT), on the other. On top of this, of course, a potential literary model such as the *Odyssey* may (a) be consciously imitated and communicated to an audience, (b) exert direct but rather unconscious influence with no intended analogies being communicated, (c) exert indirect influence through secondary texts, that is, other "imitations," and (d) overlap with generic and conventional patterns of storytelling (system references).

New and Recent Titles

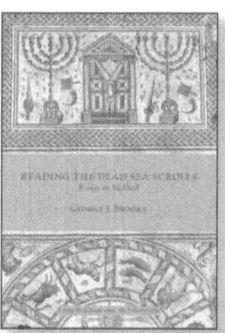

READING THE DEAD SEA SCROLLS
Essays in Method
George J. Brooke, with the assistance of Nathalie LaCoste
Paper $42.95, 978-1-58983-901-4   310 pages, 2013   Code: 063539
Hardcover $57.95, 978-1-58983-903-8   E-book $42.95, 978-1-58983-902-1
Early Judaism and Its Literature 39

ADAM AND EVE IN THE ARMENIAN TRADITIONS, FIFTH THROUGH SEVENTEENTH CENTURIES
Michael E. Stone
Paper $89.95, 978-1-58983-898-7   764 pages, 2013   Code: 063538
Hardcover $109.95, 978-1-58983-900-7   E-book $89.95, 978-1-58983-899-4
Early Judaism and Its Literature 38

FORMATION AND INTERTEXTUALITY IN ISAIAH 24–27
J. Todd Hibbard and Hyun Chul Paul Kim, editors
Paper $31.95, 978-1-58983-886-4   280 pages, 2013   Code: 062617
Hardcover $46.95, 978-1-58983-888-8   E-book $31.95, 978-1-58983-887-1
Ancient Israel and Its Literature 17

ISRAELITE PROPHECY AND THE DEUTERONOMISTIC HISTORY
Portrait, Reality and the Formation of a History
Mignon R. Jacobs and Raymond F. Person Jr., editors
Paper $32.95, 978-1-58983-749-2   254 pages, 2013   Code: 062614
Hardcover $47.95, 978-1-58983-885-7   E-book $32.95, 978-1-58983-750-8
Ancient Israel and Its Literature 14

VALUABLE AND VULNERABLE
Children in the Hebrew Bible, especially the Elisha Cycle
Julie Faith Parker
Cloth $54.95, 978-1-930675-85-8   268 pages, 2013   Code: 140355
E-book $54.95, 978-1-930675-86-5   Brown Judaic Studies 355

Society of Biblical Literature • P.O. Box 2243 • Williston, VT 05495-2243
Phone: 877-725-3334 (toll-free) or 802-864-6185 • Fax: 802-864-7626
Order online at www.sbl-site.org

"I Will Set His Hand to the Sea": Psalm 88:26 LXX and Christology in Mark

J. R. DANIEL KIRK
jrdkirk@gmail.com
Fuller Theological Seminary, Menlo Park, CA 94025

STEPHEN L. YOUNG
Stephen.L.Young@gmail.com
Brown University, Providence, RI 02912

A recent trend in NT scholarship is to see Jesus' participation in actions or attributes allegedly reserved for God as indications that a writer depicts Jesus as divine. One set of texts to which such an argument has been applied is that in which Jesus exercises authority over the seas (Mark 4:35–41; 6:45–52). Our study uses the portrayal of the idealized Davidic king in Ps 88:26 as one whose "hand is set to the sea" to call this specific argument into question. In the psalm, the human king participates in God's rule over the sea without being represented as God. Ancillary support for the plausibility of a human ruling the waters comes from (1) other Judean stories of people exercising control over waters, (2) the coherence of Psalm 88 with the manner in which Jesus is depicted more broadly in Mark, and (3) evidence that other early readers of Judean ("Jewish") Scripture interpreted Psalm 88's language about the Davidic king eschatologically.

καὶ θήσομαι ἐν θαλάσσῃ χεῖρα αὐτοῦ καὶ ἐν ποταμοῖς δεξιὰν αὐτοῦ
(Ps 88:26 [MT 89:25])[1]

Over the past several decades there has been much debate about whether Mark represents Jesus as a human, albeit a specially appointed and empowered human, or as a divine figure.[2] On one end of the spectrum stand scholars such as

---

[1] All translations from Greek sources are our own unless otherwise noted. References to psalm numberings in this article refer to Greek numberings and versification, unless otherwise indicated.

[2] For a recent overview of relevant scholarship, see Daniel Johansson, "The Identity of Jesus in the Gospel of Mark: Past and Present Proposals," *Currents in Biblical Research* 9 (2010): 364–93. In our short article we restrict our focus to Mark for convenience, even though we consider the

James D. G. Dunn, who denies any preexistence for Jesus in Mark and interprets Mark's Christology primarily in terms of Jesus as a divinely appointed eschatological figure.[3] Toward the other end reside scholars such as Daniel Johansson, who affirms "an overlap in the identity between God and Jesus ... which serves to unite God and Jesus.... The exclusive divinity of the God of Israel is maintained, but not to the exclusion of Jesus."[4] A feature claim among scholars arguing for a divine Jesus in Mark is that the Gospel depicts Jesus taking on the roles of God and/or makes claims about him that Judeans[5] of the period would make only about their God.[6]

---

points made below relevant to the kinds of arguments made about Christology in Matthew and Luke as well.

[3] Dunn, *Christology in the Making: A New Testament Inquiry into the Origins of the Doctrine of the Incarnation* (2nd ed.; Grand Rapids: Eerdmans, 1989), 30–31, 46–48, 61–62, 65–97. Johansson lists and summarizes others who hold similar views ("Identity of Jesus in the Gospel of Mark," 371–82).

[4] Johansson, "*Kyrios* in the Gospel of Mark," *JSNT* 33 (2010): 121. Richard Bauckham has pioneered the idea of "divine identity Christology," which seeks to recognize the divinity of Jesus through his participation in actions or attributes that are allegedly reserved for God in early Judean sources (*Jesus and the God of Israel: God Crucified and Other Studies on the New Testament's Christology of Divine Identity* [Grand Rapids: Eerdmans, 2008]). For some other recent occupants of this end of the spectrum, see Johansson, "Identity of Jesus in the Gospel of Mark," 384–88.

[5] To clarify our terminology, we use the label "Judean Scripture" or "Judean sacred writings" for what is conventionally termed the Hebrew Bible. Our goal is to reinscribe in our article's historical description the "ethnic" nature of how these writings would have been recognized by a variety of people in the Hellenistic through early Roman Imperial period Mediterranean. Just as different peoples were often conceived of as having their own ancestral deities and customs, so too would the writings of (what we call) the Hebrew Bible have been thought of as the ancient and sacred books of a people, the Judeans. We also want to avoid the confusion that the label Hebrew Bible could introduce in our article, since we focus on Greek translations of these writings. With "Judean sources" we refer to Judean writings in general from our period of interest, whether writings in our Hebrew Bibles or writings designated by other categorizations such as the Dead Sea Scrolls, the "Old Testament Pseudepigrapha," and so on. On our ethnic emphasis and use of the terminology of "Judean" instead of "Jew," see, e.g., Steve Mason, "Jews, Judaeans, Judaizing, Judaism: Problems of Categorization in Ancient History," *JSJ* 38 (2007): 457–512. For a counterargument, see Seth Schwartz, "How Many Judaisms Were There? A Critique of Neusner and Smith on Definition and Mason and Boyarin on Categorization," *Journal of Ancient Judaism* 2 (2011): 221–38; and for a recent discussion that probes relevant assumptions on both sides of the debate, see Michael Satlow, "Jew or Judaean?" in *"The One Who Sows Bountifully": Essays in Honor of Stanley K. Stowers* (ed. C. Johnson Hodge et al.; BJS 356; Providence, RI: Brown Judaic Studies, 2013), 165–75.

[6] We recognize that, historically speaking, reducing the options to understanding Jesus as human or divine vastly oversimplifies matters. Since, however, the specific argument we address in this study is deployed by scholars arguing for some identity of Jesus with the God of Israel within a framework often designated by labels such as "christological monotheism," we retain this simple binary.

Numerous studies have appeared recently that revolve around this argument or, at least, deploy it in various ways.[7]

One important claim for scholars who advocate a divine Christology comes from Mark's portrayals of Jesus' control over the sea (Mark 4:35–41; 6:45–52). Those who affirm a Christology of divine identity argue that, in these texts, Jesus exercises power and authority reserved for God alone in Judean sources. Thus, Simon J. Gathercole commences his discussion of the relevant passages in Mark as "cases where Jesus seems to be saying or doing something which is a particular prerogative of Yahweh in the OT. Is he acting as one uniquely endowed by God in a *representative* function, or is he in fact acting simply *as* God himself?"[8] Gathercole answers this question with reference to the descriptions of God as the one who stills the storm that threatens God's people in Psalm 106 and as the one who walks on water in Job 9:8.[9] He concludes, "For the moment … the combination of the two passages showing Jesus' mastery of the sea points very strongly to a close identification of him with Yahweh in the OT."[10] Others make similar points about how Jesus' control of the sea in these passages casts him in the role of the God of Israel and/or reflects some kind of identification with the God of Israel.[11] Of particular note for the current study, Joel Marcus argues that the role played by Jesus here is the role played by Yhwh in subduing the forces of chaos in Judean Scripture and thus pushes beyond what is explicable through appeal to the category of Jesus as son of David.[12]

Scholars who assess Jesus' mastery of the sea in Mark as evidence of a divine identity, because Mark thus represents Jesus in ways reserved for the God of Israel in Judean sources, overlook a potentially crucial piece of evidence. In Ps 88:26, God says the following about the royal Davidic figure described in the psalm: "And I will set his hand to the sea and his right hand to the rivers" (καὶ θήσομαι ἐν θαλάσσῃ χεῖρα αὐτοῦ καὶ ἐν ποταμοῖς δεξιὰν αὐτοῦ). Thus, in the very Judean sacred writings that constitute a significant part of Mark's discursive reservoir, we find a figure other

---

[7] E.g., M. Eugene Boring, "Markan Christology: God-Language for Jesus?" *NTS* 45 (1999): 463–70; Daniel Boyarin, *The Jewish Gospels: The Story of the Jewish Christ* (New York: New Press, 2012); Simon J. Gathercole, *The Preexistent Son: Recovering the Christologies of Matthew, Mark, and Luke* (Grand Rapids: Eerdmans, 2006), 57–64; Johansson, "*Kyrios* in the Gospel of Mark," 112, 120; idem, "'Who Can Forgive Sins but God Alone?' Human and Angelic Agents, and Divine Forgiveness in Early Judaism," *JSNT* 33 (2011): 351–74.

[8] Gathercole, *Preexistent Son*, 61 (emphasis original).

[9] Ibid., 62–64.

[10] Ibid., 64.

[11] E.g., Boring, "Markan Christology," 466, 467; Joel Marcus, *The Way of the Lord: Christological Exegesis of the Old Testament in the Gospel of Mark* (Louisville: Westminster John Knox, 1992), 144–45.

[12] Marcus, *Way of the Lord*, 144–45.

than God with authority over the sea.[13] In the context of the psalm, the Davidic king's control over the sea mirrors and is derived from God's own control of the sea highlighted earlier in 88:10.[14] This passage in Judean Scripture therefore attests both the commonly noted specification of Israel's God as the one who controls the sea and the sharing of this authority over the sea with God's royal representative on earth, the king who rules over the sea precisely as a divinely appointed Davidic royal representative. The representation of the Davidic king's authority over the sea in Ps 88:26 thus problematizes standard arguments that Mark 4:35–41 and 6:45–52 indicate a divine identity for Jesus due to their depicting of Jesus in ways reserved for the God of Israel alone in Judean sources.[15]

For the purposes of this short article our goal is not to establish an intertextual presence of Ps 88:26 in the author of Mark's sketches of Jesus but to illustrate how Ps 88:26 necessitates rethinking a common argument for Jesus' divine identity in Mark. Several points further amplify the relevance of Ps 88:26 to this discussion. First, the psalm itself is a plea for the restoration of the Davidic dynasty after the exile, not a celebration of a current-day king or kingship (88:38–45).[16] The depictions of the Davidic king can thus be read as idealized anticipations of what Israel's coming messiah will be and do. Broadly speaking, Mark attempts to answer such biblical anticipations in his story about Jesus the Messiah (Mark 1:1).[17] Second, it has been argued that the overall redaction of the Psalter has brought the reader to a point of exile: lamenting the failure of God to preserve the land, temple, and king.[18] Even if the overall argument is not accepted, the recognition that the lack of

---

[13] From the standpoint of Classical and Hellenistic Greek, the use of ἐν to designate what a royal figure has authority over is surprising. This, however, is the most plausible reading of the passage in context (see 88:10 and comments about it below). The awkward choice of ἐν likely reflects the translators' grappling with the preposition ב in their Hebrew Vorlage. Given this situation, we have chosen to retain the ambiguity and awkwardness in our translation of ἐν, rendering it with "to," while we also explain that readers would understand Ps 88:26 in context as specifying the Davidic figure's authority over the sea and rivers.

[14] In its historical context, these positions in Psalm 88 about Israel's God, the king, and the sea operate within and innovate upon ancient sensitivities about gods' control over the sea and kings as representatives of their gods. See Debra Scoggins Ballentine, *The Conflict Myth and the Biblical Tradition* (New York: Oxford University Press, forthcoming).

[15] Scholars have reached similar conclusions regarding the storm-stilling episodes on different grounds as well. For example, Elizabeth Struthers Malbon (*Mark's Jesus: Characterization as Narrative Christology* [Waco: Baylor University Press, 2009]) argues that "son of David" is a misstatement of how Mark identifies Jesus (e.g., pp. 87–91), but nonetheless reads the storm-stilling passages as indications that Jesus receives his authority from God rather than as indications that Jesus is thereby identified as God (e.g., pp. 140, 141).

[16] See Bernard Gosse, "Le parallélisme synonymique ḥsd ʾmwnh, le Ps 89 et les réponses du quatrième livre du Psautier, Ps 90–106," *ZAW* 122 (2010): 185–98.

[17] See Joel Marcus, *Mark 1–8: A New Translation with Introduction and Commentary* (AB 27; New York: Doubleday, 1999), 145–49.

[18] Robert E. Wallace, "The Narrative Effect of Psalms 84–89," *Journal of Hebrew Scriptures* 11 (2011): 1–15.

kingship itself is a lingering effect of exile underscores that the psalm participates as one thread in the knot of Judean scriptural hopes that God would restore Israel to full participation in the covenant promises (contrast Ps 88:4, 29 with 88:40). Third, for later readers Ps 88:26 not only looks ahead to an idealized future but also potentially links to stories from Israel's past. Both Moses (Exod 14:16, 27) and Joshua (Josh 3:7–4:19) were agents through whom the waters of sea and river (respectively) were controlled.[19] In the case of Moses (whom God had made God [!] to Pharaoh [Exod 7:1]), God tells Moses to do what the text assigns to God himself: "stretch out your hand over the sea and divide it" (Exod 14:16 NRSV), and "the LORD drove the sea back" (14:21). In Joshua, the purpose of the water parting is for Joshua to be established as one with whom the Lord is present as the Lord was present with Moses (Josh 3:7). The fact that only God can control the waters demonstrates, in these texts, that God is at work when a human performs such a task, not that the person has somehow begun to participate in God's identity. Fourth, at least one revolutionary from the first century claimed for himself such God-given authority over the water. Josephus tells of a self-proclaimed agent of God named Theudas, "He stated that he was a prophet and that by a command he would divide [σχίσας] the river" (Josephus, *Ant.* 20.97). A first-century revolutionary claims to be able to control the waters not as a claim to be God but as a claim to be God's agent. We should not, therefore, underestimate the possibility that ancient readers of Judean Scripture could see Ps 88:26 anticipating a human king controlling the waters in a manner seemingly reserved only for God. The God who has this power has already shared it with human agents at earlier points in the biblical narrative. Such a possibility of a God-empowered, water-ruling king might inform the connotations to be drawn from Jesus' control of the seas.

Mark's Gospel has several points of contact with Psalm 88. Verse 27 anticipates that the king will address God, saying, "You are my father." Joachim Jeremias's famous study on Jesus' prayer, ἀββά ὁ πατήρ (Mark 14:36), a prayer found only in Mark, argued that the uniqueness of this form of divine address comes precisely from Jesus addressing God as *my* father.[20] Beyond this address to God, both Mark 14:36 and Ps 88:27 depict God as father being one who has the power (and obligation) to deliver his anointed king. Moreover, in the psalm God says he will

---

[19] The interconnections between Ps 88:26, the Moses/Joshua tradition, and a coming messiah are drawn in the later rabbinic commentary *Pesiqta Rabbati*: "The Holy One, blessed be He, will reply, 'He is the Messiah, and his name is Ephraim, My true Messiah ... And even the seas and rivers will stop flowing,' as it is said (Psalm 89:25 [MT]), 'I will set his hand also on the sea, and his right hand on the rivers'" (*Pesiq. Rab.* 36:1).

[20] Joachim Jeremias, *Abba: Studien zur neutestamentlichen Theologie und Zeitgeschichte* (Göttingen: Vandenhoeck & Ruprecht, 1966), 1–67. Though Jeremias's study is problematic in a number of ways, this point of connection between Mark and the psalm, that an anointed figure addresses God as "my father," is worth noting; even James Barr's famous rejoinder to Jeremias affirms that *ʾabbāʾ* can connote "my father" when used in the vocative ("ʾAbbā Isn't Daddy," *JTS* [1988]: 28–47, esp. 37).

make David his firstborn (Ps 88:28); God speaks twice in Mark, affirming Jesus' sonship in both cases (Mark 1:11; 9:7). In Ps 88:21 the Davidic king is God's δοῦλος; in Mark 10:44–45 the need to become δοῦλος in order to become first is illustrated by the self-giving Son of Man. Finally, the psalm ends not with a vindicated king but with a king who is rejected by God (88:39–40) and who is an object of scorn to his enemies (88:42–46), events that Mark's Jesus endures in ch. 15. The significance of these points of contact is not that Mark intends an extended allusion to Psalm 88 or its particular claims. Rather, the significance is to be found in Mark's having created a discursive world that trades on a set of descriptions of God's coming Messiah similar to those found in the psalm.

Beyond the coherence of Psalm 88's description of the Davidic king with Mark's portrayal of Jesus as God's appointed eschatological representative, we have evidence to suggest that some other literate Christ followers (some of them Judeans) of the early Roman imperial period read Psalm 88 as referring to an eschatological Davidic figure. Several scholars have explored such potential understandings of Psalm 88 in or behind various early Christian writings, including some in the NT.[21] *Testament of Judah* 22 may be particularly relevant for our discussion.[22] In *T. Jud.* 22 we read of a period during which kingship by Judah's descendants will be brought to an end "until the salvation of Israel, until the arrival of the God of righteousness, of Jacob being at rest in peace, and all the nations" (22:2).[23] Then the text describes the eschatological kingship of Judah's line:

Καὶ αὐτὸς φυλάξει κράτος βασιλείας μου ἕως τοῦ αἰῶνος. Ὅρκῳ γὰρ ὤμοσέ μοι Κύριος, μὴ ἐκλείψειν τὸ βασίλειόν μου καὶ τοῦ σπέρματός μου, πάσας τὰς ἡμέρας, ἕως τοῦ αἰῶνος.

And he [God] will preserve the power of my kingdom until eternity. For by oath the Lord swore to me that the royal dwelling of mine and my offspring would not pass away, forever. (*T. Jud.* 22:4)

---

[21] E.g., Donald Juel, *Messianic Exegesis: Christological Interpretation of the Old Testament in Early Christianity* (Philadelphia: Fortress, 1988), 107–10; Douglas A. Campbell has made suggestions about Psalm 88 and Paul's underlying conceptions of Christ; see *The Quest for Paul's Gospel: A Suggested Strategy* (New York: T&T Clark, 2005), 58, 87–89. Of course, none of the earliest extant writings by Christ followers explicitly cites Psalm 88; see Richard B. Hays's comments about both this issue and Juel's discussion of Psalm 88: *The Conversion of the Imagination: Paul as Interpreter of Israel's Scripture* (Grand Rapids: Eerdmans, 2005), 110–11.

[22] Though acknowledging that the author likely worked with existing sources, we treat the *Testament of the Twelve Patriarchs* as a writing by a Christ follower from, perhaps, the second century C.E.; on this, see Marinus de Jonge, *Pseudepigrapha of the Old Testament as Part of Christian Literature: The Case of the Testaments of the Twelve Patriarchs and the Greek Life of Adam and Eve* (SVTP 18; Leiden: Brill, 2003). On this kind of approach to many so-called OT Pseudepigrapha/Apocrypha often claimed to be essentially pre-Christian "Jewish" compositions, see James R. Davila, *The Provenance of the Pseudepigrapha: Jewish, Christian, or Other?* (JSJSup 105; Leiden: Brill, 2005).

[23] The Greek text of the *Testament of Judah* comes from the TLG; translations are our own.

The language here potentially draws from several Davidic texts, including 2 Kgdms 7:16 and Ps 131:11–12.²⁴ However, the eschatological Davidic language of *T. Jud.* 22:4 also seems to work from Ps 88:4–5, 29–30, and 36–37 inasmuch as the psalm shares several lexical choices with *T. Jud.* 22:4 that are lacking in 2 Kgdms 7:16.

First, both Psalm 88 and *T. Jud.* 22:4 use the same verb of God's oath swearing (ὄμνυμι) and specify that God swears to David or to Judah, who stands for the Davidic lineage in the *Testament of Judah*: ὤμοσα Δαυιδ τῷ δούλῳ μου (Ps 88:4); ἅπαξ ὤμοσα ἐν τῷ ἁγίῳ μου εἰ τῷ Δαυιδ (Ps 88:36); "Ορκῳ γὰρ ὤμοσέ μοι [Judah] Κύριος (*T. Jud.* 22:4). Second, both passages deploy the same verb (φυλάσσω) to describe God's maintaining mercy to David forever (εἰς τὸν αἰῶνα φυλάξω αὐτῷ τὸ ἔλεός μου; Ps 88:29), which links to his establishing David's throne forever in 88:30, and God's preserving the power of [Judah's] kingdom forever (φυλάξει κράτος βασιλείας μου ἕως τοῦ αἰῶνος; *T. Jud.* 22:4). Third, just as Psalm 88 specifies that God's actions for David also concern his offspring (τὸ σπέρμα; 88:5, 30, and 37) and their continuing rule, *T. Jud.* 22:4 spells out that Judah's royal dwelling will not ever pass away from him or his offspring (τοῦ σπέρματός μου).²⁵ The parallels between *T. Jud.* 22:4 and Ps 88:4–5 are especially strong, with both stressing that God's swearing an oath (ὄμνυμι) to David involves ensuring the kingship for his offspring (τὸ σπέρμα) forever (ἕως τοῦ αἰῶνος).²⁶ It seems likely, therefore, that Psalm 88's language about the Davidic king factors into the matrix of *T. Jud.* 22:4's outlining of Judahite kingship in the end-time.²⁷ Thus, *T. Jud.* 22:4 provides evidence that an interpreter of Judean Scripture in the early Roman imperial period could read Psalm 88's discourse about the Davidic king as relevant for discussing eschatological Davidic kingship.

---

²⁴ 2 Kingdoms 7:16 speaks of David's kingdom being made sure forever (ἡ βασιλεία αὐτοῦ ἕως αἰῶνος), just as *T. Jud.* 22:4 uses similar language about the power of Judah's kingdom forever (κράτος βασιλείας μου ἕως τοῦ αἰῶνος).

²⁵ ἕως τοῦ αἰῶνος ἑτοιμάσω τὸ σπέρμα σου καὶ οἰκοδομήσω εἰς γενεὰν καὶ γενεὰν τὸν θρόνον σου (Ps 88:5); θήσομαι εἰς τὸν αἰῶνα τοῦ αἰῶνος τὸ σπέρμα αὐτοῦ καὶ τὸν θρόνον αὐτοῦ ὡς τὰς ἡμέρας τοῦ οὐρανοῦ (Ps 88:30); τὸ σπέρμα αὐτοῦ εἰς τὸν αἰῶνα μενεῖ καὶ ὁ θρόνος αὐτοῦ ὡς ὁ ἥλιος ἐναντίον μου (Ps 88:37); μὴ ἐκλείψειν τὸ βασιλεῖόν μου καὶ τοῦ σπέρματός μου, πάσας τὰς ἡμέρας, ἕως τοῦ αἰῶνος (*T. Jud.* 22:4).

²⁶ Though Ps 131:11–12 uses the same two verbs (ὄμνυμι and φυλάσσω) shared by Psalm 88 and *T. Jud.* 22:4 while discussing substantially the same themes, it lacks the specific offspring language (τὸ σπέρμα) and, instead, discusses the royal lineage in terms of David's sons (οἱ υἱοί σου).

²⁷ Psalm 88's language may factor into *T. Jud.* 22:4 with 2 Kgdms 7:16 and Ps 131:11–12 also operating as traditional resources on which the author drew. As is well known, one finds similar interpretive activity across early Judean literature, especially various creative readings capitalizing on similar words or other "hooks" in the text to bring different passages together—generally with some kind of contemporizing focus, whether in relation to ethical, eschatological, or other concerns. For a recent discussion of this kind of interpretive activity for depictions of eschatological figures, though focusing on portrayals involving specifically messianic language, see Matthew V. Novenson, *Christ among the Messiahs: Christ Language in Paul and Messiah Language in Ancient Judaism* (New York: Oxford University Press, 2012), 34–63.

When one combines the future-oriented potential of Psalm 88 itself with the correlation noted here between, on the one hand, how the psalm describes the Davidic king as God's royal son with God's authority and, on the other hand, how some scholars understand Jesus in Mark as God's eschatological Davidic son, and when one adds in *T. Jud.* 22:4's use of Psalm 88, the relevance of Ps 88:26 to the discussion of Mark's Christology increases. We have reason to postulate that a literate Christ follower who draws on Judean Scripture and associated interpretive activity for a representation of Jesus, such as the author of Mark, could plausibly consider God's eschatological Davidic representative to have authority over the sea without necessarily being identified with God himself in the sense that this identification is taken by those arguing for a divine Christology in Mark. Though we thus advance a modest claim, especially as we do not intend to argue here for the presence of Ps 88:26 as an intertextual allusion in Mark 4:35–41 and 6:45–52, we consider it significant for scholarship on the identity of Jesus in Mark. Contrary to the claims of many scholars, Jesus' mastery over the sea in Mark does not necessarily indicate that the author of Mark thus considers Jesus to be divine in the sense of sharing in the identity of Israel's God. While scholars who advance such a position about Jesus in Mark may be correct, this particular argument does not lend the support often claimed for it. Psalm 88:26 and ways that readers of Judean Scripture in the early Roman imperial period handled it illustrate that literate Christ followers could envision a nondivine figure with authority over the sea. In step with Ps 88:26, and in concert with the prior stories of Moses and Joshua, they could well envision that such authority had been granted to an eschatological Davidic figure who was filling the role of God's royal son.

The Biblical Odes and the Text of the Christian Bible: A Reconsideration of the Impact of Liturgical Singing on the Transmission of the Gospel of Luke

JENNIFER KNUST
jknust@bu.edu
Boston University, Boston, MA 02215

TOMMY WASSERMAN
tommy.wasserman@efk.se
Norwegian School of Leadership and Theology, NO-1368 Stabekk, Norway

Sung in Christian liturgies from the earliest period, biblical Odes—a set of songs excerpted from the biblical and apocryphal books—were central to emerging Christian practices and texts, yet their significance as textual witnesses has rarely been studied. Overlooked by text critics and editors, the Odes have largely been omitted from contemporary critical editions of the biblical books, including the very recent twenty-eighth edition of the Nestle-Aland *Novum Testamentum Graece*. This analysis suggests, however, that the liturgical setting of the Odes had a double impact: whereas some of the readings possibly reflect liturgical adaptation, public performance could also set limits on how much these texts could change.

Comparison of the biblical Odes as they appear in the great fifth-century majuscule Codex Alexandrinus, both in their place among the Odes and within their appropriate biblical book, demonstrates that these songs are in fact a valuable textual resource, a conclusion that is further confirmed by an examination of the textual and paratextual features of early Odes manuscripts. A more focused study of the Song of Mary offers additional support to the hypothesis: this song remained remarkably fixed even as Odes traditions and collections remained unsettled. As this study shows, interactions between oral and written forms of transmission are complex, and thus no textual witness can be dismissed solely on the basis of its liturgical setting.

The biblical Odes, a collection of songs excerpted from their biblical and apocryphal contexts and sung during Christian worship from an early period, are an important witness both to the liturgical activities of the earliest Christians and to the transmission of the Bible as it was sung, read, and employed in a number of settings. Still, Odes collections are regularly overlooked by text critics, presumably because liturgical use is often regarded as a source of textual corruption. A closer analysis of the biblical Odes, however, reveals that liturgical singing could sometimes preserve text. Audiences expected the lyrics of well-known songs to remain consistent, and they knew these lyrics well, even in contexts where Greek was no longer the dominant language. It took several centuries for Odes collections to achieve a somewhat stable format—by the early medieval period Odes were circulating as appendixes to the Psalter and most often in collections of nine songs. Nevertheless, a close comparison of the text of the Odes across documentary witnesses, with special attention to the Song of Mary (also known as the Magnificat, in Luke 1:46–55) shows that Odes texts remained remarkably fixed over time. The role of singing in the transmission of the Christian Bible therefore needs to be reconsidered.

I. Early Christian Song

Investigating the activities of the Christians circa 110 C.E., Pliny the Younger reported to the emperor Trajan that the guilt of the Christians involved meeting just before dawn on a fixed day, singing a hymn to Christ, pledging their commitment to virtuous behavior and then gathering later to share a meal:

> They maintained moreover that this was the whole of their guilt or error; that they were accustomed on a certain day to come together before light to sing a hymn to Christ as to a god with each other in turn [*carmenque Christo quasi deo dicere secum invicem*] and to bind themselves by oath—not for any wicked deed—but not to commit thefts or robberies or adulteries, or to break a promise or to deny a deposit when called upon for it. (Pliny the Younger, *Letters* 10.96.7)[1]

Pliny's observation that the Christians "sing a hymn" (*carmenque ... dicere*) would be unlikely to acquit them of the charge of "superstition" (*superstitio*)—the malicious chanting (*cantare* or *incantare*) of songs (*carmina*) was viewed as a dangerous and potent ritual practice in Roman contexts and was therefore explicitly outlawed.[2] Nevertheless, the results of Pliny's investigation accord well with what was claimed by Christians in their own writings, though they surely regarded their

---

[1] Latin text with English translation by John Granger Cook, *Roman Attitudes Toward the Christians* (WUNT 261; Tübingen: Mohr Siebeck, 2010), 148–50.

[2] On the association of chants (*carmina*) with malicious magic, see James Rives, "Magic in the XII Tables Revisited," *Classical Quarterly* 52 (2002): 270–90.

activity as pious (εὐσέβεια) and pleasing to God and not as a form of superstitious chanting. The writer of Colossians, for example, urges Christians to "sing psalms, hymns, and spiritual songs to God" (Col 3:16); Ephesians includes a similar exhortation, urging readers to "sing psalms and hymns and spiritual songs ... singing and making melodies to the Lord in your heart" (Eph 5:19); and the Gospels of Matthew and Mark end the Last Supper account by noting that Jesus and his disciples proceeded to the Mount of Olives "singing hymns" (Matt 26:30; Mark 14:26; cf. Heb 13:15). Singing was clearly an important feature of earliest Christian worship, as it was in religious settings across the Mediterranean world, including in earlier Jewish liturgical practices.[3]

The incorporation of song lyrics within the NT books further confirms the important role of singing in the lives of early Christian assemblies. Though there is no documentary evidence to corroborate it, the songs of praise in the Lukan infancy narrative (1:46b–55, 68–79; 2:14);[4] the "christological hymns" in John

---

[3] On the importance of singing in Roman culture, see Thomas N. Habinek, *The World of Roman Song: From Ritualized Speech to Social Order* (Baltimore: Johns Hopkins University Press, 2005). As Habinek points out, the social and ideological implications of song and performance were quite complex, with *cano*, *canto*, and *carmen* functioning as central aspects of "ritualization" to Roman culture. (For a critique of Habinek's approach, however, see the review by Dennis Feeney and Joshua T. Katz, *JRS* 96 [2006]: 240–42; and that by Nicholas Horsfall, *Herm* 181 [2006]: 252–56). On the importance of singing to the Roman *plebs* in particular, see Nicholas Horsfall, *The Culture of the Roman Plebs* (Bristol: Bristol Classical Press, 2004), esp. 11–19, 31–47. On the importance of songs and singing in classical Greek culture, see Peter Wilson, *The Athenian Institution of the Khoregia: The Chorus, the City and the Stage* (Cambridge: Cambridge University Press, 2000); and the articles in the collection *Music and the Muses: The Culture of 'mousikē' in the Classical Athenian City* (ed. Penelope Murray and Peter Wilson; Oxford: Oxford University Press, 2004). On songs in pre-Christian Jewish contexts, see Hans-Joachim Kraus, *Psalmen* (2 vols.; BKAT 15; Neukirchen-Vluyn: Neukirchener Verlag, 1960–61), esp. 1:xiii–xxxvii, lxi–lxiii. Several copies of psalms, albeit fragmentary, have been found among the Dead Sea Scrolls, attesting to their importance in the practices of the Jews at Qumran. For discussion, see Ulrich Dahmen, *Psalmen- und Psalter-Rezeption im Frühjudentum: Rekonstruktion, Textbestand, Struktur und Pragmatik der Psalmenrolle 11QPs^a aus Qumran* (STDJ 49; Leiden: Brill, 2003); and Peter W. Flint, *The Dead Sea Psalms Scrolls and the Book of Psalms* (STDJ 17; Leiden: Brill, 1997). Matthew E. Gordley has recently considered the didactic character of songs across Greco-Roman antiquity; see his *Teaching through Song in Antiquity: Didactic Hymnody among Greeks, Romans, Jews, and Christians* (WUNT 2/302; Tübingen: Mohr Siebeck, 2011).

[4] The songs incorporated into the Lukan infancy narrative may have had a particularly interesting prehistory. A number of scholars have proposed that these songs were initially composed in some sort of primitive Christian or Second Temple Jewish milieu and were reinterpreted in light of the joy of the arrival of Jesus the Messiah. For further discussion, see François Bovon, *Luke 1: A Commentary on the Gospel of Luke 1:1–9:50* (Hermeneia; Minneapolis: Fortress, 2002), 55–78; Raymond E. Brown, *The Birth of the Messiah: A Commentary on the Infancy Narratives in the Gospels of Matthew and Luke* (2nd ed.; ABRL; New York: Doubleday, 1993), 330–66; Joseph A. Fitzmyer, *The Gospel according to Luke I–IX: Introduction, Translation, and Notes* (AB 28; New York: Doubleday, 1982), 350–57; Birger Olsson, "The Canticle of the Heavenly

(1:1–18), Philippians (2:6–11), Colossians (1:15–20), and 1 Timothy (3:16);[5] and the heavenly songs in Revelation (4:8b, 11; 5:9–10, 12, 13b; 7:10b, 12; 11:15, 17–18; 12:10–12; 15:3b–4; 19:1b–3, 6b–8; 21:3b–4) may have had their origin in early liturgical practices. Even if they did not, they informed later Christian hymns, including the *trisagion*, the hymns by Romanos the Melodist, and the Akathistos hymn to the Virgin Mary.[6] Comments by second- and third-century Christians further demonstrate the centrality of singing to community gatherings: for example, Clement of Alexandria warns that sung praises to God should be temperate even as he assumes that they are central to worship (*Paed.* 2.4), and Tertullian reports that each participant in a Christian gathering would either read the Scriptures or sing a hymn to God before departing from the *agapē* meal (*Apol.* 39.18).

The sheer volume of surviving Psalters, psalm commentaries, allusions to psalms, and references to David and his songbook attest to the centrality of the psalms in emerging Christian liturgies, and from the earliest period.[7] The biblical Odes, a collection of nine to fourteen songs drawn from biblical and apocryphal books that circulated separately from their biblical contexts, are more difficult to place. Still, they appear to have been sung as supplements to the Psalter early on, perhaps from the late second or early third century and perhaps in imitation of a pre-Christian Jewish context. Josephus, for example, mentions the Song of Moses

---

Host (Luke 2.14) in History and Culture," *NTS* 50 (2004): 147–66, esp. 148–54. The use of allusions to the Septuagint throughout these songs has led scholars to compare them to the Qumran *Hodayot* (thanksgiving songs) in particular. See Helmer Ringgren, "Luke's Use of the Old Testament," *HTR* 79 (1986): 227–35, esp. 229–32.

[5] On the christological hymns of the NT, see Jack T. Sanders, *The New Testament Christological Hymns: Their Historical Religious Background* (SNTSMS 15; Cambridge: Cambridge University Press, 1971).

[6] On the reception of these hymns in early Marian devotion, see Margot Fassler, "The First Marian Fest in Constantinople and Jerusalem: Chant Texts, Readings, and Homiletic Literature," in *The Study of Medieval Chant: Paths and Bridges, East and West: Essays in Honor of Kevin Levy* (ed. Peter Jeffrey; Suffolk: St. Edmundsbury Press, 1992), 25–87. On the Akathistos hymn, see Egon Wellesz, "The 'Akathistos': A Study in Byzantine Hymnography," *DOP* 9/10 (1956): 143–74.

[7] Christians are hardly unique in this regard. For further discussion, see the broad collection of essays in *L'hymne antique et son public* (ed. Yves Lehmann; Recherches sur les rhetoriques religieuses 7; Turnhout: Brepols, 2007); and Johannes Quasten, *Music and Worship in Pagan and Christian Antiquity* (trans. Boniface Ramsey; NPM Studies in Church Music and Liturgy; Washington, DC: National Association of Pastoral Musicians, 1983). Though the evidence is significantly later, it seems that some Jewish communities included a tradition of singing poems (*piyyutim*) after the reading of Scriptures and as part of the recitation of prayers, especially on the high holy days and as part of communal fasts. For discussion, see Leon J. Weinberger, *Jewish Hymnography: A Literary History* (Littman Library of Jewish Civilization; London: Littman, 1998). The earliest evidence for the *piyyutim* is late antique. See Laura Lieber, "Confessing from A to Z: Penitential Forms in Early Synagogue Poetry," in *Seeking the Favor of God*, vol. 3, *The Impact of Penitential Prayer beyond Second Temple Judaism* (ed. Mark J. Boda, Daniel K. Falk, and Rodney A. Werline; SBLEJL 23; Atlanta: Society of Biblical Literature, 2008), 102–5.

and the songs of David, presumably references to the first biblical Ode (the "Song of the Sea") and the Psalter.[8] In a Christian context, Melito of Sardis's *Peri Pascha* (lines 630–35) presumes that the Song of Moses was sung at the Easter vigil,[9] the *Didascalia Apostolorum* (7.1.87–92 and 7.2.80–88) comments on the Prayer of Manasseh at great length, and Hippolytus of Rome preached homilies both on the Song of the Three Boys (*Comm. Dan.* 2.30.7) and on the Song of Moses.[10] Eusebius of Caesarea refers to "Psalms and Odes written by faithful brothers from the beginning," and describes a great throng assembled to sing the martyrs of Palestine to victory as they marched to their deaths.[11] Thus, by the time a full complement of Odes was copied and bound within the great fifth-century majuscule Codex Alexandrinus (London, British Library, Royal MS 1.D.VIII; Rahlfs A; Greg.-Aland A 02), it is likely that various collections of these songs were already circulating, though Alexandrinus is our most ancient documentary witness to such a collection.[12]

---

[8] Josephus, *Ant.* 2.346: Μωυσῆς ᾠδὴν εἰς τὸν θεὸν ἐγκώμιόν τε καὶ τῆς εὐμενείας εὐχαριστίαν περιέχουσαν ἐν ἑξαμέτρῳ τόνῳ συντίθησιν, "Moses composed an ode to God expressing praise and also thanks for his favor, in hexameter verse"; and 7.305: Ἀπηλλαγμένος δ' ἤδη πολέμων ὁ Δαυίδης καὶ κινδύνων καὶ βαθείας ἀπολαύων τὸ λοιπὸν εἰρήνης ᾠδὰς εἰς τὸν θεὸν καὶ ὕμνους συνετάξατο μέτρου ποικίλου· τοὺς μὲν γὰρ τριμέτρους, τοὺς δὲ πενταμέτρους ἐποίησεν, "And David, having been set free by this time from military conflicts and dangers and enjoying a situation of deep peace, compiled songs and hymns to God of complex meter. For some he made trimeters, others pentameters." On the place of the biblical odes in pre-Christian Jewish practice, see James W. Watts, *Psalm and Story: Inset Hymns in Hebrew Narrative* (JSOTSup 139; Sheffield: JSOT Press, 1992); idem, "Biblical Psalms outside the Psalter," in *The Book of Psalms: Composition and Reception* (ed. Peter W. Flint and Patrick D. Miller Jr.; VTSup 99; Formation and Interpretation of Old Testament Literature 4; Leiden: Brill, 2005), 288–309; and Steven Weitzman, *Song and Story in Biblical Narrative: The History of a Literary Convention in Ancient Israel* (Indiana Studies in Biblical Literature; Bloomington: Indiana University Press, 1997). On Josephus's attempts to reconcile Jewish practices with Greek *comparanda*, including his discussion of Greek metric forms, see James L. Kugel, *The Idea of Biblical Poetry: Parallelism and Its History* (New Haven: Yale University Press, 1981), 127–29, 140–42.

[9] Melito, *Sur la pâque et fragments* (ed. Othmar Perler; SC 123; Paris: Cerf, 1966).

[10] Hippolytus, *Commentaire sur Daniel* (ed. Maurice Lefèvre; SC 14; Paris: Cerf, 1947); idem, *In canticum Mosis*, in *Hippolyt's kleinere exegetische und homiletische Schriften* (ed. Hans Achelis; GCS; Hippolytus Werke 1.2; Leipzig: Hinrichs, 1897), 83–84.

[11] *Hist. eccl.* 5.28.5: ψαλμοὶ δὲ ὅσοι καὶ ᾠδαὶ ἀδελφῶν ἀπ' ἀρχῆς ὑπὸ πιστῶν γραφεῖσαι τὸν λόγον τοῦ θεοῦ τὸν Χριστὸν ὑμνοῦσιν θεολογοῦντες, "And so many songs and odes, having been written by faithful brothers from the beginning, are sung about Christ, the word of God, speaking of his divinity"; *Hist. eccl.* 9.1.11: στίφη δ' οὖν πολυάνθρωπα κατὰ μέσας λεωφόρους καὶ ἀγορὰς ᾠδαῖς καὶ ψαλμοῖς τὸν θεὸν ἀνυμνοῦντα τὰ τῆς πορείας ἤνυεν, "Thus great throngs of people were following their journey along the roads and through the market places, singing praises to God with songs and odes."

[12] For further discussion, see Heinrich Schneider, "Die biblischen Oden im christlichen Altertum," *Bib* 30 (1949): 30–65; and James A. Miller, "Let Us Sing to the Lord: The Biblical Odes in Codex Alexandrinus" (Ph.D. diss., Marquette University, 2006), 27–33.

Once it is granted that the singing of hymns, including those preserved in biblical books, was a central component of ancient Christian worship, an important question is raised: How did the performance of these biblical texts as songs impact their transmission, not only within books of Odes but also within biblical manuscripts? As scholars of predominantly oral cultures have noted, oral works such as songs, chants, and jokes are fully realized only when performed, even when they also exist in written form.[13] Since the Odes are liturgical songs, sung in a culture that remained largely oral, they can be expected to have a particularly complex transmission history that can be linked, at least in part, to their oral mode: the audience and the singers would have had an impact on their performance, with the audience serving as both participant and judge of the fitness of their delivery; the occasion for their performance would also have been key—certain songs were to be sung at particular gatherings and found their "true home" only when sung at the right time and in the right place; as musical as well as literary pieces, the Odes would have carried with them expectations of how they should be sung, even when this information is omitted from written copies;[14] and, finally, the rhythm, meter, and sequence of stanzas could help to ensure the preservation of these songs as distinctive oral-literary events, with participants shaping their own singing practices around received rhetorical and liturgical formulae.[15] The oral and liturgical setting of an Ode was therefore just as likely to preserve its textual integrity as to undermine it.

A comment by the fourth-century pilgrim Egeria confirms these observations. As she put it when describing the Jerusalem liturgy for her sisters back home:

> What I admire and value most [about the Jerusalem liturgy] is that all the hymns and antiphons and readings they have, and all the prayers the bishop says are always relevant to the day which is being observed and to the place in which they are used. They never fail to be appropriate. (47.5)[16]

---

[13] Ruth Finnegan, *The Oral and Beyond: Doing Things with Words in Africa* (Chicago: University of Chicago Press, 2007), 78–85.

[14] On this point, see esp. Leo Treitler, *With Voice and Pen: Coming to Know Medieval Song and How It Was Made* (Oxford: Oxford University Press, 2003).

[15] See Robert C. Tannehill, "The Magnificat as Poem," *JBL* 93 (1974): 263–75. On rhyme, rhythm, and Greek singing, see John G. Landels, *Music in Ancient Greece and Rome* (London: Routledge, 1998), 110–29.

[16] Illud autem hic ante omnia ualde fit et ualde admirabile, ut semper tam ymni quam antiphonae et lectiones nec non etiam et orationes, quas dicet episcopus, tales pronunciationes habeant, ut et diei, qui celebratur, et loco, in quo agitur, aptae et conuenientes sint semper (Égerie, *Journal de voyage [Itinéraire]* [ed. and trans. Pierre Maraval; SC 296; Paris: Cerf, 1982], 314–16; Eng. trans. by John Wilkinson, *Egeria's Travels to the Holy Land: Newly Translated with Supporting Document and Notes* [rev. ed.; Jerusalem: Ariel; Warminster: Aris & Phillips, 1981], 146). Egeria's concern for the propriety of the song and the singers to the occasion mirrors non-Christian expressions of anxiety about the potential of singing to expose one to accusations of unseemly behavior. For further discussion, see Habinek, *World of Roman Song,* 199–219; and Donka D.

Though Egeria did not offer specific information about what was sung, she was appreciative of singers who knew what to sing, when to sing, and where particular songs should be sung. Participating in liturgy together, Egeria and the congregants in Jerusalem came to recognize themselves as Christians of the same faith who performed the right songs at the right time and could appreciate the performances they had witnessed.[17] To paraphrase Eusebius, Egeria and her companions performed their orthodoxy well—in this case, an orthodoxy demonstrated by orthopraxy—singing the ancient songs taught by the faithful brothers and sisters from the beginning.

The oral and liturgical character of the Odes therefore makes them a particularly valuable textual and historical source, though text critics and biblical scholars have tended to neglect them. As Leo Treitler observed in his studies of medieval Latin chant, oral media such as songs could achieve remarkable permanence even when written texts—the words to a chant or the tropes that accompanied them, for example—remained fluid.[18] Indeed, he has insisted, interpreters and editors are seriously disabled by the habit of juxtaposing written and unwritten forms of transmission and assuming too quickly that written texts tend toward fixity and oral toward fluidity. Oral and written modes are continuous, interrelated, and mutually generative.[19] When it comes to the text of the NT, a similar phenomenon can also be detected. Thus, as Larry Hurtado has argued, public reading of the NT writings had a double impact on the text: on the one hand, oral delivery could change texts, particularly as audiences harmonized what they were hearing to other, similar passages; on the other hand, public performance set limits on how much a writing could be changed, since audiences would have recognized and probably objected to certain alterations in texts they knew well.[20] A study of early documentary witnesses to the Odes confirms these observations.

Markus, "Performing the Book: The Recital of Epic in First-Century C.E. Rome," *Classical Antiquity* 19 (2000): 138–79.

[17] See Simon Frith, "Music and Identity," in *Questions of Cultural Identity* (ed. Stuart Hall and Paul du Gay; London: Sage, 1996), 108–27.

[18] Treitler, "Oral, Written, and Literate Process in the Music of the Middle Ages," in idem, *With Voice and Pen*, 230–51 (ch. 10); and, in the same volume, "The Early History of Music Writing in the West," 317–64 (ch. 13).

[19] Leo Treitler, "The 'Unwritten' and 'Written Transmission' of Medieval Chant and the Start-Up of Musical Notation," *Journal of Musicology* 10 (1992): 131–91. Also see John Spitzer, "'Oh! Susanna': Oral Transmission and Tune Transformation," *Journal of the American Musicological Society* 47 (1994): 90–136.

[20] Hurtado, "The New Testament in the Second Century: Text, Collection and Canon," in *Transmission and Reception: New Testament Text-Critical and Exegetical Studies* (ed. J. W. Childers and D. C. Parker; Piscataway, NJ: Gorgias, 2006), 13. Also see Harry Gamble, "Literacy, Liturgy, and the Shaping of the New Testament Canon," in *The Earliest Gospels: The Origins and Transmission*

II. The Textual and Paratextual Features of the Early Odes Manuscripts

This analysis of the early witnesses to the Odes proceeds in three steps: first, the Odes in Codex Alexandrinus are compared across their biblical and nonbiblical contexts, in their biblical books and within the Odes collection.[21] Slight differences between these songs in their diverse settings suggest that Alexandrinus's Odes (A^O) were copied from a distinct exemplar rather than excerpted from the biblical books when the manuscript was copied, further emphasizing the antiquity of the Odes. Next, the two sets of texts of Alexandrinus's Lukan Odes are considered, first as they appear in the Odes collection (A^O) appended to the Psalter (Odes 11–14) and then in the Gospel of Luke (A^L). This evaluation pays close attention to the possible impact of emerging liturgies on both sets of texts. Finally, the wider transmission of the Odes is surveyed by means of a comparison between the textual and paratextual features of these songs in Alexandrinus and in number of other significant early Odes manuscripts.[22]

---

of the Earliest Christian Gospels. The Contribution of the Chester Beatty Gospel Codex P^{45} (ed. Charles Horton; JSNTSup 258; London: T&T Clark, 2004), 27–39, esp. 37–38.

[21] The Prayer of Manasseh (Ode 8), which was clearly regarded as sacred by a number of Christians, is excluded from the comparison, since the apocryphal text is missing from the biblical books.

[22] Comparanda include:
- Codex Veronensis (Verona, Bibl. Cap. I 1; Rahlfs R) also known and the Verona Psalter, a Latin-Greek diglot with Greek written in Latin characters that was likely copied at the beginning of the seventh century (ca. 600). This volume includes the Psalter and Odes. (For further discussion, see Walter Berschin, "Griechisches in der Domschule von Verona," in *Scritture, Libri e Testi nelle aree provinciali di Bisanzio* [ed. Guglielmo Cavallo et al.; 2 vols.; Spoleto: Centro Italiano di Studi sull'Alto Medioevo, 1991], 1:226–28). We would like to thank the staff of the Centro Nazionale per lo Studio del Manoscritto of the Biblioteca Nazionale Centrale di Roma for their assistance in obtaining access to a microfilm of this manuscript.
- P. Vindob. K. 8706 (ed. pr. Sanz and Till; Rahlfs 2036; Greg.-Aland $\mathfrak{P}^{42}$), a sixth-century Greek-Coptic diglot that once contained sixteen Odes.
- Codex Turicensis (Zürich, Zentralbibl. RP1 [formerly C 84]; Rahlfs T) also known as the Zurich Psalter. Henry Swete describes it as a purple manuscript copied in the West, but from a Greek original, as evidenced by "occasional traces of the Greek στάσεις." The first five Odes and a part of the sixth have been lost. Gallican Latin was copied into the margins. For our transcriptions, we have depended on the edition of Constantin von Tischendorf, *Psalterium Turicense Purpureum* (Leipzig: Hinrichs, 1869), 208–23. As the recent comprehensive study of this manuscript by Edoardo Crisci, Christoph Eggenberger, Robert Fuchs, and Doris Oltrogge points out, this manuscript offers an important early example of the transformation of the Christian book from its simple, less professional early stages to the grander, more complex formats of the late antique and early Byzantine

The Odes in Codex Alexandrinus

In his now classic introduction to the text of the Septuagint, Henry Barclay Swete downplayed the differences between Alexandrinus's Odes and these same songs in their biblical contexts. He stated that "the deviations are not numerous" and claimed that the text appears "on the whole to belong to the same family as that of the body of the MS."[23] Swete's brief comments have been challenged, however, by more comprehensive studies, which have found numerous differences between the Odes and their biblical counterparts. Already in 1949, Heinrich Schneider, who has authored the most comprehensive studies of Odes traditions to date, suggested that Alexandrinus's Odes collection was copied from a separate and earlier exemplar, a suggestion that has now been extensively researched and defended by James A. Miller.[24] As Miller has decisively shown, Alexandrinus's collection of Odes was almost certainly copied from a distinct exemplar, and thus an Odes collection must have been circulating some time before the great majuscule was copied.

Miller defends this hypothesis on three grounds: (1) the numerous variants between the Odes and the biblical books, however slight, cannot be explained solely on the basis of scribal error and therefore must have originated in some other

---

periods ("Il Salterio Purpureo Zentralbibliothek Zürich, RP1," *Segno e Testo* 5 [2007]: 31–98). The grandeur of this edition suggests to Crisci that it may well have been copied in Constantinople before being taken to Rome sometime before the mid-eighth century (pp. 62–63).

- Vatican City, Bibl. Vat. Reg. Gr. 1 (Rahlfs 55), also known as the Leo Bible. This is the first volume of what was once a two-volume complete Bible with LXX and NT as well as a number of other items, including several miniatures and two dedicatory epigrams (one to the patron and a second to the Theotokos). The Odes are placed immediately following Psalms. (A full discussion of the Leo Bible has recently been published: Paul Canart, ed., *La Bible du Patrice Léon: Codex Reginensis Graecus 1. Commentaire codicologique, paléographique, philologique et artistique* [Studi e Testi 463; Vatican City: Biblioteca Apostolica Vaticana, 2011). The Odes appear on folios 559r–565v.

- Codex Diezianus (Berlin, Staatsbibl. Ms. Diez. B Sant 66) otherwise known as the Berlin Miscellany. This fascinating manuscript from the early Carolingian period (eighth century) includes a number of diverse works, perhaps collected as a study aid. The Song of Mary (Luke 1:46–55) is copied in Latin and Greek on folio 116 of the manuscript, with the Greek in Latin characters. (For a recent discussion, see Michael Gorman, "The Codex Diezianus from Verona," *RBén* 90 [2000]: 248–59).

[23] Swete, *An Introduction to the Text of the Old Testament in Greek* (Cambridge: Cambridge University Press, 1902), 254.

[24] Schneider published five essays on the Odes, as well as a full-length monograph on the Odes in Latin: "Die biblischen Oden im christlichen Altertum"; "Biblische Oden im syrohexaplarischen Psalter"; "Die biblischen Oden seit dem sechsten Jahrhundert"; "Die biblischen Oden in Jerusalem und Konstantinopel"; "Die biblischen Oden im Mittelalter," *Bib* 30 (1949): 28–65, 199–209, 239–72, 433–52, 479–500; and *Die altlateinischen biblischen Cantica* (Beuron: Beuroner Kunstverlag, 1938); Miller, "Biblical Odes."

source;²⁵ (2) differences occur even in the single instance when an Ode and the biblical book containing the Ode were copied by the same scribe, who must have employed more than one exemplar when copying the two books; and (3) the strange placements of the word διάψαλμα in Ode 6 (Hab 3:2–19) differs even from the placement of this same term in Alexandrinus's copy of Habakkuk. In terms of textual variants, the thirteen Miller labels as "compelling" are particularly striking.²⁶ To offer just a few examples, the Song of Moses (Exod 15:1–19) reads κύριος ἐπ' αὐτούς in the Odes but ἐπ' αὐτοὺς κύριος in Exodus (Exod 15:19); the Prayer of Moses (Deut 32:1–43) reads παύσω, μισοῦσιν, αὐτῷ, and ἐχθροῖς in the Odes but καταπαύσω, μισοῦσίν με, αὐτούς, and ἐχθροῖς αὐτοῦ in Deuteronomy (Deut 32:26, 41, 43); and, in the Lukan Odes, which will be discussed at greater length below, the Odes read μεγάλα and ἕως αἰῶνος whereas the Gospel reads μεγαλεῖα and εἰς τὸν αἰῶνα (Luke 1:49, 55).²⁷ These variants are not easily explained on the basis of simple transcription error but must have involved the presence of divergent textual traditions.

Differences between the A text's Ode 3 (1 Kgdms 2:1–10 = 1 Sam 2:1–10 MT) and this song in its biblical context are equally suggestive. Adopting the perspective of H. J. M. Milne and T. C. Skeat, Miller observes that a single scribe (scribe 2) copied all of the song-related material in the manuscript, including the Hypothesis of Psalms, the Periochae of Psalms, the Canons of Psalms, and the Book of Odes. By contrast, a different scribe (scribe 1) copied all of the biblical books from which the Odes were drawn, with the exception of 1 Kgdms 2:1–10, Hannah's Song.²⁸ Ode 3 therefore offers the unique example of a song transcribed by a single scribe both in the Odes and in its biblical context, yet even here there are important differences between the Ode and the biblical book. Miller lists fourteen points of variation in this song, characterizing all but one as "suggestive" of different sources for the Odes and their biblical counterparts. Thus, even when the same scribe copied both the Ode and the biblical book, the texts diverge, and in significant ways.

Appearances of the word διάψαλμα in Ode 6 (Hab 3:2–19) are also convincing. As Miller observes, the term διάψαλμα—which likely translates the Hebrew selâ—is lacking in vv. 3, 9, and 13 in the Ode but is present in these same verses within Habakkuk 3 (A^H). Yet διάψαλμα is included at the end of Ode 6:7 even though it is omitted at this point not only from the biblical text but from every other extant

---

²⁵ Miller found 100 points of textual divergence, 12 of which he labels "incidental," 14 as "uncertain," 74 as "suggestive," and 13 as "compelling."

²⁶ Miller, "Biblical Odes," 164.

²⁷ A full discussion of all thirteen variants, with an accompanying chart, can be found in ibid., 162–65.

²⁸ Ibid., 83–86. Cf. H. J. M. Milne and T. C. Skeat, *Scribes and Correctors of the Codex Sinaiticus* (London: British Museum, 1938), 93–95.

Greek manuscript of Habakkuk.[29] This is a curious situation, made even more curious by the careful attention to this term among contemporaneous Christian writers like Gregory of Nyssa, who devoted an entire chapter to the *dipsalmata* in his discussion of the inscriptions on the Psalms.[30] A focus of considerable speculation by a number of fourth- and fifth-century church fathers, the term was understood to refer to musical directions involving a pause, a modulation of voice, a change in instrumentation, a change of meter, rhythm, melody singers or even theme or, in Gregory's case, as a reminder to singers and readers that they should pause and thereby leave room for the further inspiration of the Holy Spirit. The differing placements of διάψαλμα in A^O and in A^H therefore suggest that Alexandrinus has transmitted two different versions of the same song, each with a different musical structure. Three compelling textual variants in Hab 3:6, 13, and 17 lend further support to this conclusion.[31]

Together this evidence confirms that Schneider and Miller are correct: scribe 2 of Codex Alexandrinus copied the Odes not from the exemplars employed when copying the biblical portions of the manuscript but from another exemplar, that is, from a previous collection of biblical Odes. If so, then one or more collections of Odes were already circulating by the time Alexandrinus was commissioned, a conclusion that receives further support from the (somewhat obscure) work *De psalmodie bono* of one Niceta(s) of Remesiana, an otherwise unknown hymn writer from the late fourth or early fifth century. Writing in a context very different from that of Alexandrinus, Nicetas knew of nine biblical Odes, which he discussed as part of his Psalms commentary as if they were part of a Psalms–Odes collection.[32]

---

[29] Miller, "Biblical Odes," 169–70.

[30] Gregory of Nyssa, *In inscriptiones Psalmorum*, Eng. trans. by Ronald E. Heine, *Gregory of Nyssa's Treatise on the Inscriptions of the Psalms: Introduction, Translation and Notes* (Oxford Early Christian Studies; Oxford: Clarendon, 1995). On Gregory, see Jørgen Raasted, "The 'laetantis adverbia' of Aurelian's Greek Informant," in *Aspects de la musique liturgique au Moyen Age: Actes des colloques de Royaumont de 1986, 1987 et 1988* (ed. Christian Meyer and Marcel Pérès; Collection "Rencontres à Royaumont"; Paris: Créaphis, 1991), 60–61. Also see Hilary of Poitiers, *Tractatus super Psalmos*, translated and discussed by Adam Kamesar, "Hilary of Poiters, Judea-Christianity, and the Origins of the LXX: A Translation of 'Tractatus super Psalmos' 2.2–3 with Introduction and Commentary," *VC* 59 (2005): 284–85; and Diodorus of Tarsus, *Commentary on Psalms* 3.5 (ed. J.-M. Olivier, *Diodori Tarsensis commentarii in psalmos*, vol. 1, *Commentarii in psalmos I-L* [CCSG 6; Turnhout: Brepols, 1980], 3–320).

[31] The variations are as follows (with A^O referring to the Book of Odes and A^H to Habakkuk):

v. 6: καὶ ἐτάκη ἔθνη A^O] καὶ διετάκη ἔθνη A^H

v. 13: ἐξήγειρας δεσμοὺς σοῦ A^O] ἐξήγειρας δεσμούς A^H

v. 17: ἐν τοῖς ἀμπέλοις A^O] ἐν ταῖς ἀμπέλοις A^H

[32] On the name Nicetas of Remesiana, see Carl P. E. Singer, "Nicetas and the Authorship of the *Te Deum*," in *Biblica et Apocrypha, Ascetica, Liturgica* [ed. Elizabeth A. Livingstone; StPatr 30; Leuven: Peeters, 1997), 325–31. "Nicetas's" works were edited by J.-P. Migne in vol. 68 of the *PL* (68:0371A–0375A). For further discussion, see Andrew E. Burn, *Niceta of Remesiana: His Life and*

Though his collection was not identical to that found in A, he too was dependent on some earlier source.

III. The Lukan Odes and the Text of the New Testament

Despite the importance of Alexandrinus as one of the earliest witnesses to the LXX text, Septuagint scholars have largely neglected the textual evidence of the Book of Odes, presumably because of the Christian setting of the collection.[33] A similar disregard by NT textual critics may also be noted, though of course there can be no pre-Christian *Urtext* behind the NT Odes. The Odes continue to be omitted from textual apparatuses, including the exhaustive volumes of the Gospel of Luke published by the International Greek New Testament Project (IGNTP).[34] Yet a comparison of Alexandrinus-Odes (A^O) to Alexandrinus-Luke (A^L), as presented below, further suggests that each book should be treated as a unique textual witness.[35] Indeed, there is a further inconsistency in the treatment of Odes in the IGNTP apparatus, as well as the current Nestle-Aland edition: the apparatuses of Luke (1:54–55; 2:29–32) do include the papyrus *P. Vindob. K.* 8706 under siglum

---

Works (Cambridge: Cambridge University Press, 1905). Nicetas's Odes included Exodus 15, Deuteronomy 32, 1 Samuel 2, Isa 26:9, Habakkuk 3, Jonah 2, Dan 3:57, and Luke 1:46. See Schneider, "Die biblischen Oden," 51; and Burn, *Nicetas of Remesiana*, xcv.

[33] Miller attributes this neglect to a mistaken "default hypothesis" that assumes that the texts of the Odes in their biblical and liturgical contexts have been copied from the same exemplar, making the evidence redundant ("Biblical Odes," 103 n. 8). Albert Pietersma offers a different point: if the aim is to recover the pre-Christian LXX Psalms, then the Odes, which clearly derive from a Christian setting, should not be published with them in text-critical editions ("The Present State of the Critical Text of the Greek Psalter," in *Der Septuaginta-Psalter und seine Tochterübersetzungen: Symposium in Göttingen 1997* [ed. Anneli Aejmelaeus and Udo Quast; Abhandlungen der Akademie der Wissenschaften in Göttingen, Philologisch-Historische Klasse 3/230; MSU 24; Göttingen: Vandenhoeck & Ruprecht, 2000], 27). While we agree that the Odes are not relevant to the recovery of the pre-Christian Psalter, this does not undermine their importance for those interested in the reception of LXX books by Christians. For a helpful discussion of this problem as it pertains to the Prayer of Manasseh, see James R. Davila, "Is the Prayer of Manasseh a Jewish Work?" in *Heavenly Tablets: Interpretation, Identity and Tradition in Ancient Judaism* (ed. Lynn LiDonnici and Andrea Lieber; JSJSup 119; Leiden: Brill, 2007), 75–86.

[34] *The New Testament in Greek*, vol. 3, *The Gospel according to St. Luke*, part 1, *Chapters 1–12*; part 2, *Chapters 13–24* (International Greek New Testament Project; Oxford: Oxford University Press, 1984, 1987).

[35] Since the Odes in Alexandrinus likely reflect a distinct textual tradition, which, of course, ultimately derives from the biblical textual tradition, their texts have important implications for NT textual criticism. Still, it cannot be excluded that these two distinct textual traditions reflect cross-fertilization, as scribes could have harmonized one text to another (in either direction).

𝔓⁴², though this is an Odes collection, not a copy of the Gospels. Kurt Aland and Barbara Aland classify 𝔓⁴², which they date to the seventh–eighth centuries, as belonging to category II, suggesting that this manuscript is a manuscript of special quality and importance for establishing the initial text.[36] Yet there are no deviations between this papyrus and the Majority Text in the few verses in Luke where the papyrus is extant. Moreover, Walter Till and Peter Sanz, the editors of the papyrus, observed that its Greek text is akin to the type of text in Codex Alexandrinus after comparing the text of the papyrus in the several extant Odes.[37] In sum, there is no reason why the earlier and complete NT portion of the Odes in Alexandrinus should not likewise be included in the Nestle-Aland apparatus, and under a proper siglum, especially since 𝔓⁴², a later manuscript that reflects the Majority Text, is included.[38]

A comparison of the two sets of text of Alexandrinus's Lukan Odes (Odes 11–14 [A^O]) and their counterpart in the Gospel of Luke [A^L] demonstrates the importance of A^O as an independent witness to the NT text. The sample size is extremely small and results must therefore remain tentative. Nevertheless, since the text of Alexandrinus-Odes attests to the state of these songs as they were being sung in the fifth century, and likely some time before that as well, they merit further scrutiny.

Given the rather limited scope of the data, the collations employ a method devised by Aland and Aland to examine the textual quality, transmission character, and nature of the readings of small papyri. Since the examined manuscript is not an early papyrus, however, but a fifth-century majuscule, the Alands' categories "free," "normal," or "strict" text are omitted. For the purpose of the analysis, texts in Codex Alexandrinus are compared to the hypothetically reconstructed initial text in NA²⁸, including all variation units also included in the NA²⁸ apparatus, supplemented with variation units where A differs from the printed text of Luke in either two sets of texts. There are eighteen variation-units in NA²⁸ for this stretch of text. Further, Alexandrinus's Lukan text has an additional deviation, which is included (1:76):

---

[36] Aland and Aland, *The Text of the New Testament: An Introduction to the Critical Editions and to the Theory and Practice of Modern Textual Criticism* (trans. Erroll F. Rhodes; 2nd ed.; Grand Rapids: Eerdmans, 1989), 98, 106.

[37] Till and Sanz, *Eine griechisch-koptische Odenhandschrift (Papyrus Copt. Vindob. K 8706)* (Monumenta Biblica et Ecclesiastica 5; Rome: Päpstliches Bibelinstitut, 1939), 26–28.

[38] See Stanley Porter, "Textual Criticism in the Light of Diverse Textual Evidence for the Greek New Testament: An Expanded Proposal," in *New Testament Manuscripts: Their Texts and Their World* (ed. Thomas J. Kraus and Tobias Nicklas; Texts and Editions for New Testament Study 2; Leiden: Brill, 2006), 305–37, esp. 330–35.

TABLE 1. THE TEXT OF ALEXANDRINUS-ODES (A^O)

Text	Variation units in NA²⁸	Additional variation units	Ratio of deviation from NA²⁸	Type of deviation	Harmonizations to the LXX	Harmonization to context
Luke 1:46b–55 (Ode 11); 2:29–32 (Ode 12); 1:68–79 (Ode 13); 2:14 (Ode 14)	18	1	11/19	4 Add. 7 Sub.	3–4	1–2

A^O has four additions of the definite article and, in one case, a pronoun (1:69[x2]; 1:70; 1:74 [+ pronoun]). There are seven substitutions, three of which involve a prepositional phrase in a formula or idiomatic expression (1:50; 1:55; 1:76); one is a substitution of a personal pronoun (1:77), one of a verb tense (1:78); and, finally, two substitutions of the case of a noun phrase (1:75; 2:14). Most of these deviations may be characterized as either stylistic improvements (1:69[x2]; 1:75), a different interpretation of the text (1:70), or harmonizations to either the LXX (1:50; 1:55; 1:74?; 1:76) or to the context (1:74?; 1:78). In this connection, two of the harmonizations are to the Psalms, the liturgical companion to the Book of Odes (1:50; 1:55). Moreover, three substitutions are arguably related to the liturgical *Sitz im Leben* of the text making the text more inclusive (1:77; 2:14) and/or easier to sing (1:78; 2:14). To give an idea of the textual affiliation, the agreements of A^O have been tabulated with some important witnesses representing various text-types:

```
C           15/18 (C is lacunose in Luke 2:14)
𝔐 (or pm)   15/19
A^L         14/19
ℵ           9/19
B           8/19
D           7/19
```

A^O differs from A^L in five readings (1:49; 1:50; 1:55; 1:76; 2:14), which supports the observation of Schneider and Miller that different exemplars were indeed used for the two sets of texts. Apparently, the text of A^O is generally rather close to the Majority Text and could be classified as Byzantine. In the four cases where A^O differs from the Majority Text (1:49; 1:50; 1:76; 1:77), the text shows no particular affiliation to any textual witness.

TABLE 2. THE TEXT OF ALEXANDRINUS-LUKE (A^L)

Text	Variation units in NA^{28}	Additional variation units	Ratio of deviation from NA^{28}	Type of deviation	Harmonizations to the LXX	Harmonization to context
Luke 1:46b–55 (Ode 11); 2:29–32 (Ode 12); 1:68–79 (Ode 13); 2:14 (Ode 14)	18	1	11/19	4 Add. 1 Om. 6 Sub.	2–3	1–2

𝔐 (or *pm*) 17/19
C 14/18 (C is lacunose in Luke 2:14)
A^O 14/19
ℵ 8/19
B 8/19
D 8/19

A^L shares the four additions of A^O (1:69[x2]; 1:70; 1:74 [+ pronoun]). Further, A^L has an omission of a conjunction (1:76). There are six substitutions, two of which involve a prepositional phrase in a formula or idiomatic expression (1:50; 1:76); one is a substitution of an adjective (1:49); one of a personal pronoun (1:77), one of a verb tense (1:78); and, finally, one substitution of the case of a noun phrase (1:75). These textual deviations represent either minor stylistic improvements or amplification (1:49; 1:69[x2]; 1:75; 1:76), or harmonizations to either the LXX (1:50; 1:74?; 1:76) or to the immediate context (1:74?; 1:78). In one case, the text has been made more inclusive, perhaps under liturgical influence (1:77), and in one case the text reflects a different interpretation which prompted an addition of an article (1:70).

As this survey of variation units and the orthographic variation in Alexandrinus demonstrates, the text of Alexandrinus-Odes was certainly copied from a different exemplar than Alexandrinus-Luke. It therefore is an independent witness to a number of important readings. While no new reading has been identified—suggesting, perhaps, that Alexandrinus's Lukan Odes had only recently been extracted from a copy of the Gospel and placed in a separate collection—Alexandrinus-Odes is nevertheless the only known majuscule to attest to the very rare reading ἀπὸ γενεὰς εἰς γενεάν in Luke 1:50, a harmonization to the phrase in the Psalter (LXX Pss 9:27; 76:9; 84:6). Moreover, Alexandrinus-Odes is an important witness to the reading ἐν ἀνθρώποις εὐδοκία ("good will toward people") in Luke 2:14, providing further support for the hypothesis that the final sigma in εὐδοκίας was dropped to make the song more amenable to liturgical use. Alexandrinus-Luke retains the more difficult reading ἐν ἀνθρώποις εὐδοκίας ("among those whom he favors"), but Alexandrinus-Odes preserves what Birger Olsson calls "the traditional, liturgical version," as does the *Apostolic Constitutions* (7.47.2, 8.13.48).[39] Nevertheless, whereas some of the readings likely reflect liturgical adaptation, this is not an exclusive feature of the Odes tradition, since all readings are found in the textual tradition of Luke as well, and the Gospel texts were of course also read in liturgy.[40] In spite of this very small sample, it is tempting to suggest that liturgically influenced changes are somewhat overrepresented in Alexandrinus-Odes, but this proposal remains tentative.[41]

The consistency of Alexandrinus-Odes with a Byzantine form of text in Luke may also attest to their liturgical character. By the time the Odes were collected and began to form a distinct textual tradition, the Byzantine text was also relatively fixed, a coincidence that accords well with the liturgical innovations of the fourth century, when Christian churches across the Roman world were reinventing their liturgies in light of imperial patronage, church construction, and the invention of a Roman-Christian identity. *P. Vindob. K.* 8706 offers further support for this hypothesis. As editors Till and Sanz note, the Odes tradition remained unaffected by the Egyptian (Alexandrian) text recension in the Greek-Coptic papyrus they examined, suggesting that their text was already fixed when it reached Egypt, although the selection of Odes remained varied. They also point to the absence of the collection from the major Alexandrian majuscules Vaticanus and Sinaiticus, concluding that the decision to include them—in a pandect Bible or appended to Psalters—appears to have been recent.[42]

---

[39] Olsson, "Canticle of the Heavenly Host," 157. Marcel Metzger, *Les constitutions apostoliques*, vol. 3, *Livres VII–VIII* (SC 336; Paris: Cerf, 1986). Text accessed via the TLG.

[40] For examples of possible liturgical adaptation in the NT, see Bruce M. Metzger, *A Textual Commentary on the Greek New Testament: A Companion Volume to the United Bible Societies' Greek New Testament (Fourth rev. ed.)* (2nd ed.; Stuttgart: Deutsche Bibelgesellschaft, 1994) on Matt 6:13, 15; 20:31; 28:20 (the addition of a liturgical "amen" applies to many NT books); Luke 11:2; 24:42; John 9:38–39; Rom 6:11; 7:25; 15:33; 16:20, 24; Heb 13:21; 1 Pet 5:14.

[41] See Olsson, "Canticle of the Heavenly Host," 157–59. The possibility of mutual influence between the two textual traditions should also be noted. Miller proposes from his study of the corrections in the Book of Odes and the corresponding canticles in the biblical books that, in some cases, the Odes were corrected to read like the biblical texts and vice versa ("Biblical Odes," 172–74). Thus, some correctors seemed to have noted the divergence between these sets of texts and sought, albeit in a limited way, to bring them into closer harmony. This means that readings that reflect liturgical adaptation may have originated in one of the traditions and later made their way into the other.

[42] Till and Sanz, *Eine griechisch-koptische Odenhandschrift*, 31.

Paratextual Features of the Transmission of the Odes

A close analysis of the Odes in Alexandrinus has shown that the Odes enjoyed a distinctive transmission history, circulating independently of their biblical contexts even while remaining rather stable at the level of their texts. A survey of other early witnesses, however, reveals another striking characteristic of these songs: their relative textual stability does not necessarily correspond to their paratextual features, which could be quite variable. The particular focus of this analysis has been on the Song of Mary, but it may be that these observations can be extended to include other well-known songs such as the Song of Moses (Exod 15:1–19), the Prayer of Moses (Deut 32:1–43), and the Song of the Three Boys (Dan 3:52–88). Quite familiar to the Christian communities that preserved them, these songs appear to have been resistant to textual change but also open to new uses and therefore subject to paratextual revisions in the copying process. The words of the songs mattered, but their placement within manuscripts seems to have been a secondary concern.

Perhaps the most obvious instance of paratextual fluidity when it comes to the Odes is their order, their distribution, and the titles they are given in early manuscript witnesses. The first three Odes—the Song of Moses (or the Song of the Sea, Exod 15:1–19), the Prayer of Moses (Deut 32:1–43), and the Song of Hannah (1 Kgdms 2:1–10)—regularly appear in positions 1, 2, and 3 in early Odes collections but after that diversity ensues (see table 3).

The titles of the Odes are similarly fluid, with the words "ode" (ᾠδή), "prayer" (προσευχή or εὐχή), and "song" (ὕμνος) used interchangeably. In some cases, the titles are quite short. In others, the introductory verse from the biblical passage serves as the title (see table 4).

The variation of order and distribution of the Odes in these manuscripts appears to reflect two competing schemes, which would continue to impact liturgical singing for some time: an older fourteen-ode scheme, reflected in Codex Alexandrinus, and a subsequent nine-ode scheme that eventually became established in Byzantine liturgical practice.[43] In other words, at the paratextual level, books of Odes remained exceptionally variable, particularly during the early Byzantine period, until finally settling into the nine-Ode pattern employed in Greek orthodox liturgies to this day.

When viewed at the level of the text, however, the Odes appear to have remained relatively consistent, at least as far as the Lukan text is concerned. Further examination of the ninth Ode (the Song of Mary, Luke 1:46–55)[44] shows that the relatively few textual variants that occur in the five most ancient Odes

---

[43] Schneider, "Die biblischen Oden seit dem sechsten Jahrhundert," 245–68.
[44] This is Ode 11 in Alexandrinus (A), Ode 7 in Codex Veronensis (R) and Codex Turicensis (T), Ode 12 in *P. Vindob. K.* 8706 and Ode 12 in the Leo Bible (55).

Table 3. The Order and Distribution of the Odes in Early Witnesses

Ode (Rahlfs's numbering)	Codex Alexandrinus (Rahlfs A, London, British Library Royal MS 1.D.VIII)	Codex Veronensis (Rahlfs R, Verona, Bibl. Cap. I)	Codex Turicensis (Rahlfs T, Zürich, Zentralbibl. RP 1)	P. Vindob. K. 8706 (Rahlfs 2036; p^{42} ed. pr. Sanz and Till)	Leo Bible (Rahlfs 55, Vatican City, Bibl. Vat. Reg. Gr. 1)
Exod 15:1–19 (1)	1	1	missing	1	1
Deut 32:1–43 (2)	2	2	missing	2	2
1 Kgdms 2:1–10 (3)	3	3	6	3	3
Isa 26:9–20 (5)	4	omitted	omitted	7	5
Jonah 2:3–10 (6)	5	5	missing	4	6
Hab 3:2–19 (4)	6	6	missing	missing	4
Isa 38:9–20 (11)	7	omitted	8	8	12
Pr. of Manasseh (12)	8	omitted	9	9	13
Dan 3:26–45 (7)	9	omitted	10	10	7
Dan 3:52–88 (8)	10	8	11 and 12	11	8
Luke 1:46–55 (9a)	11	7	7	12	9
Luke 2:29–32 (13)	12	omitted	14	13	11
Luke 1:68–79 (9b)	13	omitted	13	missing	10
Great Doxology (14)	14	omitted	15	missing	14
Isa 5:1–9 (10)	omitted	4	omitted	omitted	omitted
Isa 25:1–12 (omitted)	omitted	omitted	omitted	5	omitted
Isa 26:18 (omitted)	omitted	omitted	omitted	6	omitted

TABLE 4. THE TITLES OF THE ODES IN EARLY WITNESSES

Ode (Rahlfs's numbering)	Codex Alexandrinus (A)	Codex Veronensis (R)	Codex Turincensis (T)	P. Vindob. K. 8706 (2036; p[42])	Leo Bible (55)
Exod 15:1–19 (1)	ᾠδὴ Μωυσέως ἐν τῇ Ἐξόδῳ	omitted	missing	ᾠδὴ Μωυσέω[ς	ᾠδὴ Μωυσέως τῆς Ἐξόδου
Deut 32:1–43 (2)	ᾠδὴ Μωυσέως ἐν τῷ Δευτερονομίῳ	arxete ode deuteronomio	missing	missing	ᾠδὴ Μωυσέως ἐν τῷ Δευτερονομίῳ
1 Kgdms 2:1–10 (3)	προσευχὴ Ἄννας μητρὸς Σαμουήλ	proseuce annas	missing	[ᾠδὴ Ἄννας μρς] Σαμουέλ	προσευχὴ Ἄννης μητρὸς Σαμουήλ
Isa 26:9–20 (5)	προσευχὴ Ἠσαιοῦ	omitted	omitted	(see n. 47)	ᾠδὴ Ἠσαιοῦ
Jonah 2:3–10 (6)	προσευχὴ Ἰωνᾶ	proseuce iona	missing	πορσευχὴ Ἰωνᾶ ἔσω ἐν τῇ κοιλίᾳ τοῦ κήτους (Coptic only)	προσευχὴ Ἰωνᾶ τοῦ προφήτου
Hab 3:2–19 (4)	προσευχὴ Ἀμβακουμ	arxete ode ambacum	missing	missing	ᾠδὴ Ἀμβακουμ τοῦ προφήτου
Isa 38:(9)10–20 (11)	προσευχὴ Ἐζεκίου	omitted	προσευχὴ Ἐζεκίου τοῦ βασιλέως	προσευχὴ Ἐζεκίου βασιλέως Ἰουδαίας ἡνίκα ἐμαλακίσθη καὶ ἀνέστη ἐκ τῆς μαλακίας αὐτοῦ	προσευχὴ Ἐζεκίου
Pr. of Manasseh (12)	προσευχὴ Μανασσῆ	omitted	[προσευχὴ Μανασσῆ βασιλέως][45]	προσευχὴ Μανασσῆ υἱοῦ Ἐζεκίου	προσευχὴ Μανασσῆ
Dan 3:26–45 (7)	προσευχὴ Ἀζαρίου	omitted	[προσευχὴ Ἀζαρίου καὶ τῶν σὺν αὐτῷ ἐν μέσῳ τοῦ πυρός][46]	ὕμνος τῶν τριῶν παίδων	προσευχὴ τῶν τριῶν παίδων

[45] Hypothetical restoration based on the Coptic title.
[46] Hypothetical restoration based on the Coptic title.

TABLE 4 (cont.)

Ode (Rahlfs's numbering)	Codex Alexandrinus (A)	Codex Veronensis (R)	Codex Turincensis (T)	P. Vindob. K. 8706 (2036; p42)	Leo Bible (55)
Dan 3:52–88 (8)	ὕμνος τῶν πατέρων ἡμῶν	tote y tris os ex enos stomatos ymnoon ce edoxazon ce eulogun ton theon en te camin legontes (= Dan 3:51)	ὕμνος τῶν πατέρων ἡμῶν ἐν τῇ καμίνῳ	ὕμνος τῶν τριῶν παίδων	ᾠδὴ τῶν τριῶν παίδων Ἀνανία, Ἀζαρία Μισαήλ
Luke 1:46–55 (9a)	προσευχὴ Μαρίας τῆς θεοτόκου	proseuce marias	εὐχη Μαρίας ἐκ τοῦ εὐαγγελίου	Προσευχὴ Μαρίας τῆς θεοτόκου	προσευχὴ Μαρίας τῆς θεοτόκου ἐκ τοῦ κατὰ Λοῦκαν εὐαγγελίου
Luke 2:29–32 (13)	προσευχὴ Συμεῶνον	omitted	εὐχὴ Συμεῶνος ἐκ τοῦ εὐαγγελίου	προσευχὴ Συμεῶνος	προσευχὴ Συμεῶν ἐκ τοῦ κατὰ Λοῦκαν εὐαγγελίου
Luke 1:68–79 (9b)	προσευχὴ Ζαχαριοῦ	omitted	ᾠδὴ Ζαχαριοῦ ἐκ τοῦ εὐαγγελίου	missing	προσευχὴ Ζαχαριοῦ ἐκ τοῦ κατα Λοῦκαν εὐαγγελίου
Great Doxology (14)	ὕμνος ἑωθινός	omitted	ὕμνος ἑωθινός	missing	ὕμνος ἑωθινός
Isa 5:1–9 (10)	omitted	ode esaiu	omitted	omitted	omitted
Isa 25:1–12 (omitted)	omitted	omitted	omitted	ᾠδ[ή[47]	omitted
Isa 26:18 (omitted)	omitted	omitted	omitted	(see n. 47)	omitted

[47] Sanz and Till speculate that the songs from Isaiah included in the Vienna papyri may well have been subsumed under one title such as ᾠδαὶ Ἡσαίου or ᾠδαὶ τρεῖς Ἡσαίου (*Eine griechisch-koptische Odenhandschrift*, 24).

manuscripts are also consistent with the textual tradition of the Gospel of Luke. Indeed, the few comparatively unusual variation units—the omission of καί in 9:52 in the Verona Psalter (R) and the addition of αὐτοῦ in 9:54 in this same manuscript—are nevertheless attested in versional witnesses or, in the case of αὐτοῦ, in a late minuscule.[48] The Verona Psalter adds an ἀμήν at the close of the Ode of Habakkuk, the Song of Jonah, and the Song of Mary, though this is perhaps to be expected given the liturgical setting of these songs. In addition, the stichoigraphical arrangement of the Song of Mary across these manuscripts is also remarkably consistent: Alexandrinus-Odes (A), the Verona Psalter (R), *P. Vindob. K.* 8706 (2036/𝔓[42]), the Zurich Psalter (T), and the Leo Bible (55) retain similar sense lines, despite the differing contexts in which each was copied, as does Codex Diezianus, an especially curious miscellany manuscript from the early Carolingian period that places the Song of Mary among other, seemingly unconnected works. In other words, the text and the rhythmic structure of this song—its meter and arrangement into strophes—remained relatively stable across a range of diverse witnesses,[49] a coincidence that seems especially remarkable given that Alexandrinus was clearly copied in the Greek East, *P. Vindob K.* 8706 in late antique Egypt, the Leo Bible and (perhaps) the Zurich Psalter in early medieval Constantinople, and the rest of the manuscripts in the Latin West, though, as is now well known, it is rarely possible to assign text types to certain geographical areas.[50] Nevertheless, if the Song of Mary is any indication, the lyrics of these songs were significantly less variable than their order and arrangement (see table 5).

---

[48] This type of minor textual change can of course occur several times independently in a textual tradition.

[49] On the persistence of poetic structures, see Tannehill, "Magnificat as Poem." Tannehill is interested in the rhythmic structure of the Magnificat as a matter of literary interest. Still, as our study has shown, this rhythm was understood and carried forward by those who continued to sing this poem, even when Greek was no longer their first language.

[50] See Eldon Jay Epp, "Textual Clusters: Their Past and Future in New Testament Textual Criticism," in *The Text of the New Testament in Contemporary Research: Essays on the Status Questionis* (ed. Bart D. Ehrman and Michael W. Holmes; 2nd ed.; New Testament Texts, Studies, and Documents 42; Leiden: Brill, 2013), 556–58.

TABLE 5. STICHOI-GRAPHICAL ARRANGEMENT
OF THE SONG OF MARY

Codex Alexandrinus (A)	Codex Veronensis (R)[51]	Codex Turicensis (T)	P. Vindob. K. 8706 (2036; p[42])	Leo Bible (55)
Μεγαλύνει ἡ ψυχή μου τὸν κύριον,	Megalyni i psychi mu ton quirion	Μεγαλύνει ἡ ψυχή μου τὸν κύριον,	missing	Μεγαλύνει ἡ ψυχή μου τὸν κύριον,
καὶ ἠγαλλίασεν τὸ πνεῦμά μου ἐπὶ τῷ θεῷ τῷ σωτῆρί μου,	ce igalliasen to penuma mu epi to theo to sotiri mu	καὶ ἠγαλλίασεν τὸ πνεῦμά μου ἐπὶ τῷ θεῷ τῷ σωτῆρί μου,		καὶ ἠγαλλίασεν τὸ πνεῦμά μου ἐπὶ τῷ θεῷ τῷ σωτῆρί μου,
ὅτι ἐπέβλεψεν ἐπὶ τὴν ταπείνωσιν τῆς δούλης αὐτοῦ·	oti epeblepsen epi tin tapinosin tis dulis autu	ὅτι ἐπέβλεψεν ἐπὶ τὴν ταπείνωσιν τῆς δούλης αὐτοῦ·		ὅτι ἐπέβλεψεν ἐπὶ τὴν ταπείνωσιν τῆς δούλης αὐτοῦ·
ἰδοὺ γὰρ ἀπὸ τοῦ νῦν μακαριοῦσίν με πᾶσαι αἱ γενεαί,	idu car apo tu nyn macariusin me pas e genee	ἰδοὺ γὰρ ἀπὸ τοῦ νῦν μακαριοῦσίν με πᾶσαι αἱ γενεαί,		ἰδοὺ γὰρ ἀπὸ τοῦ νῦν μακαριοῦσίν με πᾶσαι αἱ γενεαί,
ὅτι ἐποίησέν μοι μεγάλα ὁ δυνατός,	oti epiisen my megalia o dynatos ce agion ton onamo autu	ὅτι ἐποίησέν μοι μεγαλεῖα ὁ δυνατός,		ὅτι ἐποίησέν μοι μεγάλα ὁ δυνατός,
καὶ ἅγιον τὸ ὄνομα αὐτοῦ,	ce to eleos autu	καὶ ἅγιον τὸ ὄνομα αὐτοῦ,		καὶ ἅγιον τὸ ὄνομα αὐτοῦ,
καὶ τὸ ἔλεος αὐτοῦ ἀπὸ γενεὰς εἰς γενεὰν τοῖς φοβουμένοις αὐτόν.	is genean ce genean tys fobumenys auton	καὶ τὸ ἔλεος αὐτοῦ εἰς γενεὰν καὶ γενεὰν τοῖς φοβουμένοις αὐτόν.		καὶ τὸ ἔλεος αὐτοῦ ἀπὸ γενεὰς εἰς γενεὰν τοῖς φοβουμένοις αὐτόν.

[51] Codex Diezianus offers an interesting comparison: Megalyni i psychi mu ton chirrion / che igalliasen to penuma mu / epi to theo / to sotiri mu /oti epeblepsen / epi tin tapinosin / tis dulis autu / idu gar apu to nun macariosin / me pas e genee / oti epiisen mi megalia o dynatos ghe agion ton onamo autu / che to eleos autu apo genean is genean / tis fobumenis auton/ epiisen cratos en brachioni autu diescorpisen yperifanus dyanias cardias auton / cathilen dynastas apo thronon ypsosen tapinos / pinontas eneplysen agathon che plutuntas exapestilen cenus/ antelabeto israel pedos autu mnisthine eleos / cathos elalysen pros tus patros imon to abraham ce to spermati autu eos eonos.

TABLE 5 (cont.)

Codex Alexandrinus (A)	Codex Veronensis (R)[51]	Codex Turicensis (T)	P. Vindob. K. 8706 (2036; p[42])	Leo Bible (55)
ἐποίησεν κράτος ἐν βραχίονι αὐτοῦ,	epiisen cratos en bracioni autu	ἐποίησεν κράτος ἐν βραχίονι αὐτοῦ,	missing	ἐποίησεν κράτος ἐν βραχίονι αὐτοῦ,
διεσκόρπισεν ὑπερηφάνους διανοίᾳ καρδίας αὐτῶν·	diescorpisen yperifanus dyanias cardias auton	διεσκόρπισεν ὑπερηφάνους διανοίᾳ καρδίας αὐτῶν·		διεσκόρπισεν ὑπερηφάνους διανοίας καρδίας αὐτῶν·
καθεῖλεν δυνάστας ἀπὸ θρόνων	cathilen dynastas apo thronon	καθεῖλεν δυνάστας ἀπὸ θρόνων		καθεῖλεν δυνάστας ἀπὸ θρόνων
καὶ ὕψωσεν ταπεινούς·	ypsosen tapinos	καὶ ὕψωσεν ταπεινούς·		καὶ ὕψωσεν ταπεινούς·
πεινῶντας ἐνέπλησεν ἀγαθῶν	pynontas eneplisen agathon	πεινῶντας ἐνέπλησεν ἀγαθῶν		πεινῶντας ἐνέπλησεν ἀγαθῶν
καὶ πλουτοῦντας ἐξαπέστειλεν κενούς.	ce plutuntas exapestilen cenos	καὶ πλουτοῦντας ἐξαπέστειλεν κενούς.		καὶ πλουτοῦντας ἐξαπέστειλεν κενούς.
ἀντελάβετο Ισραηλ παιδὸς αὐτοῦ μνησθῆναι ἐλέους,	antelabeto israel pedos autu mnesthine eleus autu	ἀντελάβετο Ισραηλ παιδὸς αὐτοῦ μνησθῆναι ἐλέους,	[αντελάβετο] Ισραηλ παιδὸ[ς α]ὐτοῦ [μνησθῆναι ἐλ]έους,	ἀντελάβετο Ισραηλ παιδὸς αὐτοῦ μνησθῆναι ἐλέους,
καθὼς ἐλάλησεν πρὸς τοὺς πατέρας ἡμῶν,	cathos elalisen pros tus pateras imon	καθὼς ἐλάλησεν πρὸς τοὺς πατέρας ἡμῶν,	καθὼς [ἐλάλησεν] πρὸς τ[οὺς πατέρας ἡμῶ]ν,	καθὼς ἐλάλησεν πρὸς τοὺς πατέρας ἡμῶν,
τῷ Αβρααμ καὶ τῷ σπέρματι αὐτοῦ ἕως αἰῶνος.	to abraham ce to spermati autu eos eonos amen	τῷ Αβρααμ καὶ τῷ σπέρματι αὐτοῦ ἕως αἰῶνος.	τῷ Αβρααμ καὶ τῷ σπέρματι αὐτοῦ εἰς τὸν αἰῶνα.	τῷ Αβρααμ καὶ τῷ σπέρματι αὐτοῦ ἕως αἰῶνος.

IV. Conclusion: Singing the Gospel

Textual variations that can be ascribed to "liturgical influence" are commonly treated as late, secondary accretions to what were once more pristine literary texts. When it comes to the biblical Odes, however, the issues of late versus early and variable versus stable may need to be revised. As oral performances, the Odes needed to be sung at the right times and places, in the right way, with the right rhythm, in the right language and with the right lyrics, a conclusion that is confirmed by the early documentary witnesses surveyed here. While it may have been possible to place these songs in a variety of diverse collections and to label them in any number of ways, liturgical singing helped to stabilize the song text even as paratextual features remained variable. Indeed, the commitment to a stable text, if not to a particular arrangement of texts, extended even beyond Greek-speaking contexts. Over time, these songs became so well known, so integral to Christian worship, that singers continued to sing them in Greek, even when Greek was no longer fully understood.[52] Thus, with the exception of Codex Alexandrinus, the Zürich Psalter, and the Leo Bible, all the earliest witnesses to the Greek text of the Odes were copied by scribes with limited Greek understanding who nevertheless preserved well-established and earlier forms of the Greek text.

This phenomenon is especially evident among the few fragmentary late antique copies of the Odes from Egypt. A number of ostraca with Greek Psalms, Odes and other liturgical texts were found at the Monastery of Epiphanius of Thebes, including a copy of the Song of the Three Boys (*P. Mon. Epiph.* 582, Rahlfs Ode 8) and a fragment of the Morning Hymn (*P. Mon. Epiph.* 607, Rahlfs Ode 14), both poorly written.[53] A fourth-century Greek copy of the Song of the Three Boys was preserved among the Coptic papyri edited in the Michigan collection, in this case

---

[52] The hymn of the Salii offers a helpful comparison. As Beard, North, and Price point out, by the time Augustus's name was inscribed in this hymn by the Roman senate, the words of this ancient hymn were "almost incomprehensible even to the priests themselves." The archaic and therefore less-than-comprehensible character of these lyrics lent status both to the hymn and to the priests who performed it, associating them with the (supposed) grandeur of early Rome. See Mary Beard, John North, and Simon Price, *The Religions of Rome*, vol. 1, *A History* (Cambridge: Cambridge University Press, 1998), 203–7 (quotation from 207).

[53] Walter Ewing Crum and H. G. Evelyn White, eds., *The Monastery of Epiphanius at Thebes*, Part 2 (New York: Metropolitan Museum of Art, 1926), 300 and 318. Also see Scott Bucking, "Scribes and Schoolmasters? On Contextualizing Coptic and Greek Ostraca Excavated at the Monastery of Epiphanius," *Journal of Coptic Studies* 9 (2007): 21–47. As Bucking shows, texts copied in Greek are nearly all hymns, including (by Trismegistos number): 62170 (Ode 8 – Song of the Three Boys), 65222 (trisagion), 65218 (trisagion), 65213 (trisagion with troparia and Psalm 95), 61459 (troparion with Matt 1:23), 65211 (troparion quoting Psalm 50 and Ode 8), and 65216, 65217, 65219, 65220, 65221 (troparia). Trismegistos no. 61312 is an exception that includes a gnomic anthology with Menander *Sententiae* and Prov 1:7.

copied out with a prayer written in Greek but by a Coptic scribe (*P. Mich.* Inv. 6427).[54] A seventh- or eighth-century copy of the Prayer of Isaiah (*P. Mich.* Inv. 1572, Rahlfs Ode 5) includes Arabic letters on the verso (unpublished) and was employed as an amulet.[55] Moreover, though copied in the East, the Zürich Psalter was brought to Rome quite early, at which point Gallican Latin notes were added by a Latin scribe,[56] and the Verona Psalter (R) is a Latin transliteration of the Odes that was later divided into separate quires, possibly so that Latin-trained priests could employ it as a Greek study-aid.[57] In other words, the Odes in Greek remained part of the lived religious tradition of both Coptic monks and Latin-speaking Christians, long after Alexandrinus was first copied and long after Greek had largely disappeared from daily use. Thus, despite the fluidity of their paratextual features and despite their liturgical importance—or, indeed, because of it—the Odes are a valuable textual witnesses with implications not only for the study of the Christian liturgy but also for the study of Christian texts. The biblical Odes provide a valuable window into the religious lives of Christian communities East and West and text critics should no longer overlook them.

[54] Edited by Martin Gronewald, "Ein liturgischer Papyrus: Gebet und Ode 8: P. Mich. Inv. 6427," *ZPE* 14 (1974): 193–200. Also see Helmut Satzinger, *Chronique d'Égypte* 46 (1971): 424–26, no. 2.

[55] Henry A. Sanders, "Isaiah XXVI, 9–10," in *Michigan Papyri* 3 (ed. John Garrett Winter; Ann Arbor: University of Michigan Press, 1936), 9.

[56] Crisci's most recent analysis of this manuscript suggests an Eastern rather than a Western origin, as earlier scholars had proposed ("Il Salterio Purpureo," 31–69, esp. 52–53). As Rahlfs also pointed out, contra Swete (*Introduction*, 142), the Latin marginal notes could have been added later and do not rule out an originally Eastern setting (*Psalmi cum Odis*, 39).

[57] E. A. Lowe, *Codices Latini Antiquiores*, vol. 4, *Italy: Perugia-Verona* (Oxford: Clarendon, 1947), 20, no. 472.

New Books from EERDMANS

DAVID REMEMBERED
Kingship and National Identity in Ancient Israel
JOSEPH BLENKINSOPP

"Joseph Blenkinsopp's treatment of the king of Israel who became the prototype for the Messiah is characteristically lucid and informed with intense historical and theological learning. ... An enthralling read." — John Barton

ISBN 978-0-8028-6958-6 • 231 pages • paperback • $26.00

DEUTERONOMY
A Commentary
JACK R. LUNDBOM

"The great merit of Lundbom's commentary is that it will make accessible to a broad scholarly readership theological themes that are essential for both Judaism and Christianity."
— Dominik Markl, SJ

ISBN 978-0-8028-2614-5 • 1064 pages • paperback • $80.00

THE DANCE BETWEEN GOD AND HUMANITY
Reading the Bible Today as the People of God
BRUCE K. WALTKE

"Well researched, incisive, and always instructive, Waltke's essays invite reading and rereading."
— V. Philips Long

ISBN 978-0-8028-6736-0 • 540 pages • paperback • $48.00

NOW IN PAPERBACK!
APOCALYPSE AGAINST EMPIRE
Theologies of Resistance in Early Judaism
ANATHEA E. PORTIER-YOUNG

"An excellent study of Judea during the Seleucid period. ... Portier-Young's in-depth look at apocalypses in relation to the Seleucid Empire and Judaism is a substantial work in the field of biblical studies." — *Review of Biblical Literature*

ISBN 978-0-8028-7083-4 • 486 pages • paperback • $35.00

At your bookstore,
or call 800-253-7521
www.eerdmans.com

WM. B. EERDMANS PUBLISHING CO.
2140 Oak Industrial Dr NE
Grand Rapids, MI 49505

The Blinding of Paul and the Power of God: Masculinity, Sight, and Self-Control in Acts 9

BRITTANY E. WILSON
bwilson@div.duke.edu
Duke Divinity School, Durham, NC 27708

Treatments on the Lukan Paul have traditionally taken his status as a "man" for granted, rarely assessing the central character of Luke's second volume in relation to ancient constructions of masculinity. Yet while Paul evinces some characteristically masculine traits, he is by no means the paragon of a "manly" man. This point is particularly evident in Acts 9 with Paul's conversion, or call to follow Jesus. Here Paul, while en route to Damascus, loses control of his bodily faculties as a result of his encounter with "the Lord," culminating in his loss of sight. For at least a number of Luke's hearers, Paul's divinely inflicted blindness would have arguably undermined his standing as a "manly" man, since blindness in the ancient world was viewed as particularly debilitating and, for a man who has that disability foisted upon him, emasculating. This article traces the story of Paul's encounter with "the Lord" Jesus and his resulting blindness in Acts 9, examining (1) Paul's loss of self-control, (2) the "unmanly" nature of blindness in the ancient world, and finally (3) Paul's restoration of sight and subsequent characterization. After journeying with Paul on his way to Damascus, I will maintain that Luke's first snapshot of his so-called hero Paul is anything but heroic and is, in fact, manifestly unmanly. When Paul loses his sight and self-control in Acts 9, he becomes subject to a God whose power is made complete in the persecuted person of Jesus, the crucified "Lord."

Despite Paul's status as one of the central male characters in the Acts of the Apostles, his status as a "man" often goes unmarked. Scholarship rarely situates the Lukan Paul in relation to constructions of masculinity in the Greco-Roman world, even though such constructions are increasingly becoming a topic of inquiry in the

An earlier version of this paper was presented at the Mid-Atlantic Region Society of Biblical Literature meeting held in New Brunswick, New Jersey, and led to my selection as a 2012 SBL Regional Scholar. I thank the participants of the Gospels/Acts section at the MAR-SBL, as well as the participants of the Duke New Testament and Judaic Studies Colloquium who heard a

field of NT studies.¹ The few works that do look at the Lukan Paul through a gender-critical lens, however, tend to dovetail with a popular trend in Acts scholarship that underlines Paul's apologetic role in the narrative as a whole.² According to this typical interpretative bent, Luke parades Paul as a "hero" of the faith in an effort to legitimate Paul in the eyes of his elite audience. Paul, so the argument often goes, navigates the landscape of Acts in the guise of an able philosopher and rhetorician, displaying the cardinal virtues of the Hellenistic world, especially the virtue of self-control. Before his conversion, or call on the road to Damascus, Paul was out of control, but after his conversion, he in fact epitomizes self-control.³

Works on the Lukan Paul and gender, few though they may be, take up this emphasis on Paul as a powerful speaker and a man of self-mastery.⁴ Such works

---

later draft of this paper. I am also grateful to Beverly Gaventa, Ross Wagner, Jacqueline Lapsley, Cavan Concannon, Jason Sturdevant, and the anonymous *JBL* reviewers for their insightful comments and suggestions.

[1] For a brief summary of masculinity studies in the field of NT studies, see Stephen D. Moore, "'O Man, Who Art Thou…?': Masculinity Studies and New Testament Studies," in *New Testament Masculinities* (ed. Stephen D. Moore and Janice Capel Anderson; SemeiaSt 45; Atlanta: Society of Biblical Literature, 2003), 1–22.

[2] For those who favor an *apologia pro Paulo*, see esp. Robert L. Brawley, "Paul in Acts: Lucan Apology and Conciliation," in *Luke-Acts: New Perspectives from the Society of Biblical Literature Seminar* (ed. Charles H. Talbert; New York: Crossroad, 1984), 129–47; Abraham J. Malherbe, "'Not in a Corner': Early Christian Apologetic in Acts 26:26," *SecCent* 5 (1986): 197–208; John T. Carroll, "Literary and Social Dimensions of Luke's Apology for Paul," in *SBL 1988 Seminar Papers* (SBLSP 27; Atlanta: Scholars Press, 1988), 106–18; John Clayton Lentz Jr., *Luke's Portrait of Paul* (SNTSMS 77; Cambridge: Cambridge University Press, 1993); James A. Kelhoffer, "The Gradual Disclosure of Paul's Violence against Christians in the Acts of the Apostles as an Apology for the Standing of the Lukan Paul," *BR* 54 (2009): 25–35.

[3] Debate still arises over whether Saul's experience in Acts 9 constitutes a conversion or a call. This debate largely stems from Krister Stendahl's famous essay "Call Rather Than Conversion," in idem, *Paul among Jews and Gentiles and Other Essays* (London: SCM, 1977), 7–23. For a survey of this debate, see Larry W. Hurtado "Convert, Apostate, or Apostle to the Nations: The 'Conversion' of Paul in Recent Scholarship," *SR* 22 (1995): 23–54.

[4] While no work treats the Lukan Paul's relation to gender in any sustained fashion, a few studies do treat Paul tangentially. See Abraham Smith, "'Full of Spirit and Wisdom': Luke's Portrait of Stephen (Acts 6:1–8:1a) as a Man of Self-Mastery," in *Asceticism and the New Testament* (ed. Leif E. Vaage and Vincent L. Wimbush; New York: Routledge, 1999), 101–4; Mary Rose D'Angelo, "The ANHP Question in Luke-Acts: Imperial Masculinity and the Deployment of Women in the Early Second Century," in *A Feminist Companion to Luke* (ed. Amy-Jill Levine with Mariane Blickenstaff; Feminist Companion to the New Testament and Early Christian Writings 3; London: Sheffield Academic Press, 2002), 56–58; D'Angelo, "'Knowing How to Preside over His Own Household': Imperial Masculinity and Christian Asceticism in the Pastorals, *Hermas*, and Luke-Acts," in Moore and Anderson, *New Testament Masculinities*, 284–93; Todd Penner and Caroline Vander Stichele, "Gendering Violence: Patterns of Power and Constructs of Masculinity in the Acts of the Apostles," in *A Feminist Companion to the Acts of the Apostles* (ed. Amy-Jill Levine with Mariane Blickenstaff; Feminist Companion to the New Testament and Early Christian

highlight that public speaking and control of one's body were important masculine traits in the ancient world, and they portray Paul as an especially potent "manly man" who perpetuates imperial virtues of masculinity and reinscribes male control among followers of "the Way."[5] Paul, so some claim, functions as a powerful apologetic in Luke-Acts, for he persuades men of high standing like himself that following a crucified "Lord" (κύριος) is actually manly.

To be sure, such arguments have validity on several fronts. In the ancient world, public speaking and self-control were important markers of masculinity, and Paul exhibits both of these qualities after his encounter with Jesus on the Damascus road.[6] Paul speaks quite frequently in a variety of public forums ranging from the Areopagus in Athens (17:22) to the audience hall in Caesarea (25:23). He also addresses his speeches to other men (13:16; 14:15; 17:22; 22:1; 23:1, 6; 27:21, 25; 28:17) in the vein of his predecessors Peter and Stephen (2:14, 22; 3:12; 7:2) and frequently follows rhetorical practices that were popular among elite males.[7] Paul also conveys more self-control after his Damascus road encounter in the sense that he no longer performs excessive acts of violence against followers of Jesus (8:3; 9:1–2, 13–14; 22:4–5; 26:9–11) and often remains calm in crisis situations in contrast to those around him (e.g., 27:17–36). He even discusses "self-control" (ἐγκράτεια) with the Roman procurator Felix (24:25) and counters the charge that he is "out of his mind" (μαίνομαι, 26:24) with the response that he speaks words of "reason" (σωφροσύνη, 26:25).[8] Furthermore, as a prominent male leader, Paul reinforces the overall impression throughout Acts that men play a more vital role in the leadership of the early church than women.

Yet while Paul—or Saul, as he is consistently called until Acts 13:9—evinces some characteristically masculine traits, he is by no means the epitome of a "manly," self-controlled man according to ancient elite standards. Saul's failure to fit the

---

Writings 9; Edinburgh: T&T Clark, 2004), 203–8; Penner and Vander Stichele, "Script(ur)ing Gender in Acts: The Past and Present Power of *Imperium*," in *Mapping Gender in Ancient Religious Discourses* (ed. Todd Penner and Caroline Vander Stichele; Atlanta: Society of Biblical Literature, 2007), 247–66; Colleen M. Conway, *Behold the Man: Jesus and Greco-Roman Masculinity* (New York: Oxford University Press, 2008), esp. 127–42; Bonnie J. Flessen, *An Exemplary Man: Cornelius and Characterization in Acts 10* (Eugene, OR: Pickwick, 2011), esp. 32–35.

[5] See esp. Penner and Vander Stichele, "Gendering Violence," 208.

[6] For an overview of public speaking and corporeal control as key markers of Greco-Roman masculinity, see Maud W. Gleason, "Elite Male Identity in the Roman Empire," in *Life, Death, and Entertainment in the Roman Empire* (ed. D. S. Potter and D. J. Mattingly; Ann Arbor: University of Michigan Press, 1999), 67–84.

[7] See, e.g., Fred Veltman, "The Defense Speeches of Paul in Acts," in *Perspectives on Luke-Acts* (ed. Charles H. Talbert; Danville, VA: Association of Baptist Professors of Religion, 1978), 243–56; Derek Hogan, "Paul's Defense: A Comparison of the Forensic Speeches in Acts, *Callirhoe*, and *Leucippe and Clitophon*," *PRSt* 29 (2002): 73–87.

[8] On Paul's "virtue" of self-control in this passage and the larger narrative of Acts, see Lentz, *Luke's Portrait of Paul*, 62–104.

profile of a "manly" man is particularly evident when he is blinded on the road to Damascus in Acts 9. In this defining event for his later characterization, Saul encounters "the Lord" in a contest of power and as a result loses control of his bodily faculties, including his ability to see. To an elite hearer, Saul's God-inflicted blindness would have arguably undermined his standing as a "manly" man, since blindness was typically viewed as debilitating and, for a man who had that disability foisted upon him, emasculating. In our first in-depth glimpse of Saul, then, we find that this central male character loses two important markers of "manliness" in the ancient world: (1) self-control and, more specifically, (2) sight.

To illuminate this twofold "loss" of manliness, this article traces the story of Saul's encounter with Jesus and Saul's resulting blindness. After first exploring Saul's blinding in Acts 9, I turn to the intersections of masculinity and sight in the Greco-Roman world. Here I devote extended attention to these intersections, since the gendered ramifications of blindness and sight in ancient discourse remain largely unexplored. Third and finally, I discuss Saul's restoration of sight and how his encounter with the power of God shapes his character as a follower of "the Way."

After journeying with Saul on the road to Damascus, we will see that Luke's first snapshot of his so-called hero Saul is anything but heroic but is, in fact, manifestly unmanly. As a result of his "unmanning" on the Damascus road, Saul is rendered powerless and recognizes that ultimate power resides with the God of Israel, who has acted in Jesus. According to Luke, Saul's loss of sight and self-control launches his newfound status as a man subject to God's Son, the one whom he has been persecuting (9:5). Like Saul, followers of "the Way" do not subscribe to elite understandings of power and masculinity, for their identity is found in a persecuted, crucified messiah.

I. The Blinding of Saul in Acts 9

To ancient elite hearers, Saul's blinding would very likely have amounted to his "unmanning," since "manly" men were expected to maintain self-control, or control over themselves and others. As Michel Foucault and many since have demonstrated, manly men were to exercise self-control and to safeguard the boundaries of their bodies from outside invasion or penetration.[9] Maintaining self-control and

---

[9] See esp. Foucault, *The History of Sexuality*, vol. 2, *The Use of Pleasure* (trans. Robert Hurley; New York: Pantheon, 1985), esp. 63–77; Jonathan Walters, "Invading the Roman Body: Manliness and Impenetrability in Roman Thought," in *Roman Sexualities* (ed. Judith P. Hallett and Marilyn B. Skinner; Princeton: Princeton University Press, 1999), 29–46; David Fredrick, "Mapping Penetrability in Late Republican and Early Imperial Rome," in *The Roman Gaze: Vision, Power, and the Body* (ed. David Fredrick; Arethusa Books; Baltimore: Johns Hopkins University Press, 2002), 236–64.

bodily boundaries distinguished "true" men from all those marked as non-men, including effeminate men, women, the conquered, "barbarians," and slaves.[10] The "rules" of ancient masculinity dictate that a man is "manly" when he exerts control over himself and others, but "unmanly" when he loses self-control or falls under the control of others.

In Acts 9, Saul's own loss of self-control occurs as a result of an encounter with the "Lord" (κύριος), an encounter that leaves him powerless and reliant on others. Even though Saul begins his journey to Damascus by breathing threats and murder against the "disciples of the Lord" (9:1), he ends up being accosted by "the Lord" before he reaches his destination (vv. 4–6). Luke concludes this confrontation by focusing on Saul's three-day duration of blindness and abstention from eating and drinking (v. 9). Before switching scenes to the disciple Ananias and Saul's reliance on him (vv. 10–19), Luke leaves Saul in Damascus decimated, lacking basic bodily necessities such as food and drink.[11] Saul begins his journey to Damascus actively seeking to imprison members of "the Way" (vv. 1–2), yet he ends passively waiting in Damascus, sightless, weak, and dependent on others.

Luke sets up this human–divine encounter in a manner that pits Saul against Jesus in a contest of power. While Luke applies the epithet κύριος to both the God of Israel and Jesus throughout Luke-Acts with purposeful ambiguity,[12] he quickly specifies that Saul encounters Jesus on his way to Damascus (v. 5; see also v. 17). Just as Saul is singled out earlier in 7:58–8:3 for his zealous persecution of the church, so is he singled out—by Jesus no less!—throughout 9:1–9. Saul's plans for further persecutions (9:1–2) are abruptly interrupted, however, for as he draws near Damascus, "suddenly" (ἐξαίφνης) a light from heaven shines around him (v. 3). Saul is the target of this heavenly light, for the light shines around "him" (αὐτόν) alone (v. 3). Saul is also the only one to fall to the ground (v. 4), which is made all the more ignominious since his traveling companions are still standing (v. 7).[13] In Jewish Scripture, manifestations of light often signify a theophany (e.g., Isa 60:19), and

---

[10] Dio Chrysostom, for example, writes that a man who could not control himself was not capable of controlling others nor suitable to control an empire (*3 Regn.* 34–35). See also Craig A. Williams, *Roman Homosexuality: Ideologies of Masculinity in Classical Antiquity* (Ideologies of Desire; New York: Oxford University Press, 1999), esp. 132–42.

[11] Interpreters often claim that Saul's lack of food and drink reflects penance or prebaptismal fasting. Beverly Roberts Gaventa, however, is correct that Luke does not describe this three-day period as penance and that evidence elsewhere in Luke-Acts (see Luke 4:2; 7:33; Acts 23:12) does not support either of these conclusions (*The Acts of the Apostles* [ANTC; Nashville: Abingdon, 2003], 150). Instead, Saul's lack of food and drink (coupled with his lack of sight) highlights his passivity. This parallels his earlier passivity in Acts 7:58 and likewise hints that his passivity will be followed by activity: except this time Saul will proclaim—not persecute—"the Way."

[12] See, e.g., C. Kavin Rowe, *Early Narrative Christology: The Lord in the Gospel of Luke* (BZNW 139; Berlin: de Gruyter, 2006).

[13] Compare these details to Saul's later account of his call in Acts 26:13–14. Here the light shines around Saul and his companions, and they "all" fall to the ground. See discussion below.

earlier in Luke's Gospel, such manifestations of light are applied to both God and Jesus (Luke 2:9, 32). The heavenly light, then, is not a "natural" phenomenon but points to "the Lord's" very presence and, in this case, a presence that causes Saul to lose control of his body.

Through this theophany—or Christophany—Jesus continues to single out Saul by speaking to him. Jesus opens his address to Saul by twice repeating his name, confronting him with the double vocative: "Saul, Saul" (v. 4).[14] Jesus then twice repeats that Saul is persecuting him (vv. 4–5) and connects this persecution to his identity: "I am [ἐγώ εἰμι] Jesus, whom you are persecuting" (v. 5). Saul persecutes "the church" (8:3) and the "disciples of the Lord" (9:1), but Jesus identifies this persecution as an attack upon himself. Saul is in effect fighting against God, something that the Jewish leader Gamaliel warns against earlier in 5:34–39 when he cautions that, if the disciples' plan is from God and not of human origin, the Jewish council may be "fighting against God" (θεομάχοι, v. 39). As Gamaliel, Saul's former instructor (22:3), ironically predicts, Saul does not have the power to overthrow Jesus' disciples. God's power instead overthrows Paul's plan of persecution (cf. 5:38–39). In this one-on-one contest of power, Jesus clearly comes out on top, for the light (and presumably voice) comes from heaven (ἐκ τοῦ οὐρανοῦ, v. 3) and Saul falls to the earth (ἐπὶ τὴν γῆν, v. 4). Saul, the single most persistent persecutor of Jesus, is literally brought down.

In this contest of power, Saul experiences a loss of bodily control, culminating in his loss of sight. Despite Jesus' command for Saul to stand up (ἀνάστηθι, v. 6), Saul is able to stand only with assistance, suggested by Luke's usage of the passive verb: "Saul was raised [ἠγέρθη] from the earth" (v. 8).[15] Saul then discovers that he is not able to see: "but when his eyes were opened, he saw nothing [ἀνεῳγμένων δὲ τῶν ὀφθαλμῶν αὐτοῦ οὐδὲν ἔβλεπεν]" (v. 8). After Saul is assisted to his feet, he may also receive assistance in opening his eyes since the participle ἀνεῳγμένων can function as either a middle or a passive.[16] Regardless, Saul finds that he sees "nothing" (οὐδέν). Saul's inability to see means that he can complete his journey to

---

[14] For Luke's use of a double vocative as a form of rebuke or correction, see Luke 10:41; 13:34; 22:31; cf. 6:46.

[15] The aorist passive ἠγέρθη may also convey a middle (intransitive) sense (see, e.g., Luke 11:8; 13:25). However, rendering ἠγέρθη as a passive ("he was raised") provides a sharper contrast with the detail that Saul raises himself up (ἀναστάς) after his recovery in 9:18.

[16] A passive reading of ἀνεῳγμένων is preferable, given Saul's reversal from being an active subject to a passive one in vv. 1–9. Note that after Saul encounters Jesus, Saul is associated with a plethora of passive or passive/middle verbs (ἀνάστηθι, v. 6; λαληθήσεται, v. 6; ἠγέρθη, v. 8; ἀνεῳγμένων, v. 8) and an absence of action (being led around, v. 8; not seeing, vv. 8, 9; not eating nor drinking, v. 9). See Dennis Hamm, "Paul's Blindness and Its Healing: Clues to Symbolic Intent (Acts 9, 22 and 26)," *Bib* 71 (1990): 64–65; Daniel Marguerat, *The First Christian Historian: Writing the "Acts of the Apostles"* (trans. Ken McKinney, Gregory J. Laughery, and Richard Bauckham; SNTSMS 121; Cambridge: Cambridge University Press, 2002), 191–92.

Damascus only with assistance (v. 8), and his blindness continues while he is in Damascus for a total of three days (v. 9). Despite this demarcation of time, Saul's restoration of sight does not occur for another nine verses, and his inability to see during this interim is specifically recalled in vv. 12 and 17.[17] Throughout this period of Saul's blindness, narrative tension hinges on whether Saul will have his sight restored and simultaneously whether he will fully "see" Jesus.

Luke also depicts Saul's blindness as a punitive miracle. Some commentators attempt to elide Saul's punishment, pointing to the "light" (φῶς) as a naturalistic explanation for Saul's blinding.[18] Yet this light, as we saw earlier, is anything but "naturalistic" since it points to God's presence. Saul's encounter with Jesus is the source of his blindness, and this divinely instigated punishment can be overcome only by a divinely instigated healing, which God performs through the disciple Ananias (vv. 10–19). When Saul is finally healed, the detail that "something like scales [ὡς λεπίδες] fell from his eyes" (v. 18) cements the impression that Saul's blindness is the result of divine infliction. Scalelike objects, after all, are outside obstructions that do not naturally appear from gazing too long at a light. Saul's blindness, then, is foisted upon him from an outside divine source; he is a man who loses his sight due to the intervention of Jesus.

Luke continues to dwell on Saul's loss of control by depicting his resulting dependence on others. This dependence includes most immediately the men who are traveling with him. Directly after his blinding, Saul is at the mercy of his traveling companions and has to be led into the city, a leading that is emphasized twice: "leading by the hand, they led him into Damascus" (χειραγωγοῦντες δὲ αὐτὸν εἰσήγαγον εἰς Δαμασκόν, v. 8). The detail of being led by the hand underlines Saul's lack of control, as evidenced by the use of this image elsewhere in Acts and other ancient texts. In Acts, Luke incorporates this image a total of four times: twice in reference to Saul's blinding (9:8; 22:11), once in reference to the magician Bar-Jesus's blinding (13:11), and once in reference to Saul's nephew (23:19), who remains unnamed but is thrice identified as a "young man" (νεανίας, 23:17; νεανίσκος, 23:18, 22).[19] In this latter instance, the nameless young man is led to the Roman tribune Claudius Lysias (23:17, 18), and Claudius himself takes the young man aside by the hand (v. 19). Here Claudius's hand-holding gesture itself testifies to the age and

---

[17] Compare this again to the abbreviated accounts of Saul's conversion in Acts 22:6–16 and 26:12–18.

[18] See, e.g., Ernst Haenchen, *The Acts of the Apostles: A Commentary* (trans. Bernard Noble et al.; Philadelphia: Westminster, 1971), 323.

[19] In Acts 7:58, Saul is initially introduced as a "young man" (νεανίσκος), but he has presumably attained full "manhood" by the time he encounters Jesus in 9:1–9, since Ananias protests in 9:13 that he has heard from many people about "this man" (τοῦ ἀνδρὸς τούτου). It is clear that some time passes between 8:3 and 9:1, although definite time markers are absent. After 7:58, Saul is consistently identified as a "man" (ἀνήρ) in Acts: 9:13; 21:11; 22:3; 23:27, 30; 24:5; 25:5, 14, 17.

power differential between Claudius and the youth, reinforcing for the hearer that Claudius, as the government official acting on behalf of Rome, is the one who is (at least ostensibly) in control.

Luke's incorporation of this hand-holding gesture in reference to the blind and a youth, or not-yet man, is consonant with other texts in the ancient world that likewise make these associations. Greek, Roman, Jewish, and Christian texts all associate this gesture with those who are dependent on others due to age (usually old age), disability, or some other marker that disqualified a person from attaining "manly" prowess.[20] In Luke's Gospel, Jesus himself connects the image of being "led by the hand" to both blindness and dependence when he asks, "Can a blind person guide [ὁδηγεῖν] a blind person? Will they not both fall into a pit?" (6:39; cf. Matt 15:14). In Luke's narrative and beyond, the image of guiding a person by the hand signals their reliance on others and lack of control. Since "manly" men are supposed to be in control of both themselves and others, such dependence is by definition unmanly.

Saul's dependence continues in Damascus, for the disciple Ananias acts as a mediator for Saul and the one on whom Saul's restoration of sight depends.[21] After Ananias abruptly makes his appearance (v. 10), Jesus commands him to heal Saul (vv. 11–12) and, despite Ananias's objections (vv. 13–14), to reveal the role that Saul will play in God's divine plan (vv. 15–16). Yet, although Jesus addresses Ananias, we never witness Jesus directly addressing Saul. Despite Jesus' earlier assurance that once Saul arrives in Damascus, "it will be told to you what it is necessary for you to do" (v. 6), Saul does not actually "do" anything to regain his sight. Instead, Saul discovers in a vision that a man named Ananias will heal him (vv. 11–12). What is more, Luke also relates this detail indirectly: we only know of this vision because Jesus tells Ananias in a vision (vv. 10–12). Saul thus becomes a passive recipient of healing and a doubly indirect object of sight in that we only see him through Ananias's own vision. Saul is not simply dependent on Ananias for his sight; he has also become the object of sight itself.

Overall, Saul's encounter with Jesus on the road to Damascus leaves him passive, powerless, and dependent on others. In Acts 9, Saul is a man who loses power, sight, and self-control and in the process recognizes the greater power of God. Saul's loss of sight is especially noteworthy since sight, as we shall now see, was considered the most powerful and the most masculine of all the senses in the ancient world. I begin with a wide-lens view by surveying Greek and Roman constructions of sight and then narrow my field of vision to Jewish and early Christian

---

[20] See, e.g., Euripides, *Phoen.* 834–48, 1530–50; Lucian, *Nigr.* 34; Seneca, *Oed.* 300; Sophocles, *Ant.* 988–90, 1087; Deut 27:18; Isa 42:16; Tob 11:16; Mark 8:23; Rom 2:19–20; Philo, *Somn.* 2.102, 161; *Spec.* 4.70. On the liminal status of male youths and disabled men with respect to masculinity, see Walters, "Invading the Roman Body," 33–35.

[21] Saul also apparently relies on the character Judas, since he is staying at his house (9:11, 17).

(including Lukan) representations. When read in light of these ancient intersections, we will find that Saul's loss of sight severely undermines his standing as a "manly" man.

II. Masculinity and Sight in the Greco-Roman World

Sight played a critical role in constructions of Greco-Roman masculinity. This point is made all the more clear by Foucault, among others, who highlights how vision, or "the gaze," functions as an instrument and symbol of power.[22] Indeed, a common theme in twentieth- and twenty-first-century philosophy concerns "ocularcentrism," or the tendency in Western thought to valorize vision as the most powerful and masculine sense.[23] Feminists and cultural theorists further demonstrate how "the politics of sight" often encode men as the subject of the gaze and women as the object.[24] Although scholars debate the degree of continuity between ancient and modern modes of "seeing," it is evident that sight and power are often linked in the ancient world.[25] The Latin linguist Varro, for instance, aptly illustrates this widespread association of sight with power when he writes, "I see from sight, that is, from *vis*, 'force,' since it is the strongest of the five senses."[26] The eye itself was also viewed as powerful, with ancient theories envisioning the eye as an active agent rather than a passive recipient.[27] According to the popular theory known as

---

[22] Foucault famously discusses the intimate relationship between power and sight in his book *Surveiller et punir: Naissance de la prison* (Bibliothèque des histoires; Paris: Gallimard, 1975; Eng. trans., 1995). Other theorists who discuss "the gaze" include Luce Irigaray, Jacques Lacan, Emmanuel Levinas, and Jean-François Lyotard. For an exploration of this philosophical trend with respect to ancient Rome, see the essays in Fredrick, *Roman Gaze*.

[23] For an overview of Western ocularcentrism and its critics, see Martin Jay, *Downcast Eyes: The Denigration of Vision in Twentieth-Century French Thought* (Berkeley: University of California Press, 1993).

[24] For an application of these theoretical concerns to the ancient world, see *Pornography and Representation in Greece and Rome* (ed. Amy Richlin; Oxford: Oxford University Press, 1992). See also Jennifer Glancy, "Text Appeal: Visual Pleasure and Biblical Studies," *Semeia* 82 (1998): 63–78.

[25] Foucault, for example, classifies premodern modes of seeing as "spectacle" and modern modes as "surveillance." On the debate regarding continuity between different visual traditions, see David Fredrick, "Introduction," in idem, *Roman Gaze*, 1–30. On the association of sight with power, see esp. Cindy Benton, "Split Vision: The Politics of the Gaze in Seneca's *Troades*," in Fredrick, *Roman Gaze*, 31–56.

[26] Varro, *De lingua latina* 6.80; trans. Fredrick, "Introduction," in idem, *Roman Gaze*, 1. While the derivation of the verb *video* ("I see") from the word *vis* ("force," "violence") is incorrect, Varro's association of sight with power is telling.

[27] For an outline of ancient vision theories, see Dale C. Allison, "The Eye Is the Lamp of the Body (Matthew 6:22–23 = Luke 11:34–36)," *NTS* 33 (1987): 61–83; Hans Dieter Betz, "Matthew vi.22f and Ancient Greek Theories of Vision," in *Text and Interpretation: Studies in the New*

"extramission," the eye actively emits rays of light toward the object of sight rather than passively receiving light rays as in modern optics. The eye also had the power to inflict harm, as seen in widespread beliefs concerning the "evil eye" and the proliferation of countervailing apotropaic remedies.[28] From Plato and Aristotle onward, sight is typically considered the most important of all the senses, and numerous texts stress the power of sight and assume that men are the ones who exercise this power.[29]

However, since not all males were considered "true" men in antiquity, only those with considerable power, such as the emperor or other elites, correspondingly had powerful gazes.[30] Yet Greek and Roman authors emphasize how, even among elite males, the eyes (as well as the ability of those eyes to see) reveal a man's manliness or lack thereof. In the "scientific" discipline known as physiognomy, which discerns a person's inner character on the basis of their outward traits, the eye held a place of prominence as the most important "sign" in discerning a man's masculinity.[31] The Greek rhetorician Polemo, for instance, expounds at length on how the eye betrays characteristics ranging from courage to effeminacy in his handbook on physiognomy.[32] Other elite males such as Quintilian apply these principles while declaiming and survey their opponent's eyes for signs of weakness or effeminacy.[33] Many considered the eye to "reflect the man" more than any other physical feature, for the eye was "the gateway to the soul."[34]

Given the prominence of sight in Greek and Roman texts, it should come as no surprise that blindness or other sight impairments often equated to the absence

---

Testament Presented to Matthew Black (ed. Ernest Best and R. McL. Wilson; Cambridge: Cambridge University Press, 1979), 43–56.

[28] Apotropaic remedies against the "evil eye" often include phalluses in the form of amulets. For examples of the "evil eye," see, e.g., Pliny the Elder, *Nat.* 7.2.16–18; Philo, *Flacc.* 29; Wis 4:12; Sir 14:8–10; 31:13; Mark 7:22. John H. Elliot has written extensively on the topic of the "evil eye" (see esp. "The Evil Eye and the Sermon on the Mount: Contours of a Pervasive Belief in Social Scientific Perspective," *BibInt* 2 [1994]: 51–84).

[29] See Plato, *Tim.* 45b–47e; Aristotle, *Sens.* 437a–439a.

[30] See, e.g., Epictetus, *Diatr.* 4.1.145; Seneca, *Ira* 3.19.1; Tacitus, *Agr.* 45.1–2.

[31] For the classic text on ancient physiognomy, see Elizabeth C. Evans, *Physiognomics in the Ancient World* (Transactions of the American Philosophical Society n.s. 59.5; Philadelphia: American Philosophical Society, 1969). See also *Seeing the Face, Seeing the Soul: Polemon's Physiognomy from Classical Antiquity to Medieval Islam* (ed. Simon Swain; New York: Oxford University Press, 2007).

[32] See Polemo, *Physiogn.* 1 passim. See also Adamantius, *Physiogn.* A4–A23, B1, B36, B44–B60; *Anon. Lat.* 20–43, 81, 91–133; Aristotle, *[Physiogn.]* 3, 6. (All citations and translations are in Swain, *Seeing the Face.*)

[33] See, e.g., Cicero, *De or.* 3.221–23; *Leg.* 1.26–27; Quintilian, *Inst.* 11.3.75–76.

[34] Adamantius, *Physiogn.* A4. See also Pliny, *Nat.* 11.54.145–46. On the relationship between eyesight and character in the ancient world, see Chad Hartsock, *Sight and Blindness in Luke-Acts: The Use of Physical Features in Characterization* (Biblical Interpretation Series 94; Leiden: Brill, 2008), esp. 58–60.

of power, such as ignorance and helplessness.[35] When it comes to the punishment of blindness itself, this bodily invasion was often employed in instances of sexual violations and associated with emasculation.[36] A common trope throughout Greek and Roman myth, for example, involves men being blinded for seeing a goddess naked.[37] A famous example involves the prophet Tiresias, who is blinded for accidentally glimpsing Athena as she bathed (Callimachus, *Hymn.* 5). In other accounts of his blinding, Hera takes away Tiresias's sight for divulging that women enjoy sex more than men, although Zeus grants him the gift of prophecy in compensation.[38] Another common theme in Greek and Roman texts involves women planning to avenge themselves against men by gouging out their eyes.[39] Even the act of blinding itself often involves *piercing* the pupils. In the case of Oedipus, for instance, he self-inflicts his blindness by piercing his eyes with the pins of his mother's (and wife's) brooches.[40] Oedipus's self-blinding in effect mimics his own incestuous bodily penetration, except instead of penetrating his mother, he uses his mother's brooches to penetrate himself.

Blindness with respect to sexual transgressions, however, falls within a larger pattern of blindness involving transgressions of the natural and social order, especially boundaries between the human and divine.[41] When these boundaries become blurred, the punishment of blindness is often a result. Indeed, blindness was the most frequent punishment inflicted by the gods in Greek and Roman literature.[42] An example that appears in numerous artistic representations involves the lyre player Thamyris, whom the Muses blind for boasting that his musical

---

[35] For a discussion of the theme of blindness as ignorance, helplessness, and punishment in the Greco-Roman world, see Eleftheria A. Bernidaki-Aldous, *Blindness in a Culture of Light: Especially the Case of Oedipus at Colonus of Sophocles* (American University Studies Series 17, Classical Languages and Literature 8; New York: P. Lang, 1990), 11–131; Hartsock, *Sight and Blindness in Luke-Acts*, 60–81. For a comprehensive compilation of blindness in Greek and Roman sources, see Albert Esser, *Das Antlitz der Blindheit in der Antike: Die kulturellen und medizin-historischen Ausstrahlungen des Blindenproblems in den antiken Quellen* (Janus Supplements 4; Leiden: Brill, 1961).

[36] See Gerard Devereux, "The Self-Blinding of Oidipous in Sophokles: *Oidipous Tyrannos*," *JHS* 93 (1973): 36–49; R. G. A. Buxton, "Blindness and Limits: Sophokles and the Logic of Myth," *JHS* 100 (1980): 22–37.

[37] See Buxton, "Blindness and Limits," esp. 30–35.

[38] Apollodorus, *Bibl.* 3.6.7; Ovid, *Metam.* 3.316–40.

[39] E.g., Apollodorus, *Bibl.* 2.8.1; Apuleius, *Metam.* 8.12–13; Chariton, *Chaer.* 6.5; Ovid, *Metam.* 6.615–19; 13.533–575; Pausanius, *Descr.* 2.20.2; Terence, *Eun.* 645, 740.

[40] See Sophocles, *Oed. tyr.* 1265–1275; Devereux, "Self-Blinding of Oidipous," esp. 48–49.

[41] Buxton, "Blindness and Limits," 22–37; Bernidaki-Aldous, *Blindness in a Culture of Light*, 57–93.

[42] See Buxton, "Blindness and Limits," esp. 30–35; Bernidaki-Aldous, *Blindness in a Culture of Light*, 57–93; Nicholas Vlahogiannis, "Disabling Bodies," in *Changing Bodies, Changing Meanings: Studies on the Human Body in Antiquity* (ed. Dominic Montserrat; London: Routledge, 1998), 13–36, esp. 29–32.

accomplishments surpassed their own.[43] Thamyris dares to challenge the power of the gods, and he is blinded as a result. In like manner, Zeus blinds the king Lycurgus for his persecution of Dionysus (Homer, *Il.* 6.130–40), and Philip of Macedon loses an eye because he saw his wife in bed with the god Amon (Plutarch, *Alex.* 3.1–2). When such men transgress the boundary between the human and divine, they are "put back in their place," so to speak, through the act of blinding. With this demonstration of power, the transgressor is rendered relatively powerless and reminded of his place in the cosmic hierarchy.

Of course, blindness is not always portrayed as a negative, powerless condition. Prophecy and poetry, for example, are linked to blindness. Tiresias epitomizes the blind prophet who can "truly see," and Homer represents the quintessentially blind poet.[44] Even when men are punished with blindness, this "deficiency" is often balanced by extraordinary traits.[45] As noted earlier, Hera blinds Tiresias, but Zeus grants him the gift of prophecy. Supernatural abilities coincide with disabilities, divinely instigated or otherwise, and sometimes divinely instigated disabilities such as blinding are only temporary if the blinded party makes amends.[46] What is more, representations of blindness in both written and material culture do not necessarily correspond to the lived experience of blind people in the ancient world. A large percentage of the population probably had vision impairments of some kind, and many may have conceived of blindness in ways that were more empowering than our extant evidence suggests.[47]

All the same, our available Greek and Roman sources overwhelmingly depict blindness as an undesirable, unmanly condition. Even with the example of the iconic blind prophet, prophetic prowess does not necessarily overcome the gendered liminality of blindness. Tiresias, for instance, hardly qualifies as a "manly"

---

[43] E.g., Homer, *Il.* 2.590–600; Pausanius, *Descr.* 4.33.7; Robert Garland, *The Eye of the Beholder: Deformity and Disability in the Graeco-Roman World* (Ithaca, NY: Cornell University Press, 1995; 2nd ed., London: Bristol Classical, 2010), 112.

[44] Other blind prophets and poets include, *inter alios*, Euenius (Herodotus, *Hist.* 9.93–94), Phineus (Apollodorus, 1.9.21), Phormion (Pausanias, *Descr.* 7.5.7–8), Ophioneus (Pausanius, *Descr.* 4.12.10, 13.3), and Stesichoros (Plato, *Phaedr.* 243). Dio Chrysostom (*Or.* 36.10–11) even records that blindness is a prerequisite for all poets, a blindness that is "contracted" from Homer.

[45] On the paradox of blindness and insight, see Bernidaki-Aldous, *Blindness in a Culture of Light*, passim.

[46] Stesichorus, for example, regains his eyesight after making amends to Helen (Plato, *Phaedr.* 243). Blindness is also a temporary, contingent condition for Antylus (Plutarch, *Mor.* 310A), Ilus (Plutarch, *Mor.* 309F), and Phormion (Pausanias, *Descr.* 7.5.7–8).

[47] On the ubiquity of sight impairments and the incongruity between representation and reality with respect to these impairments, see Martha L. Rose, *The Staff of Oedipus: Transforming Disability in Ancient Greece* (Corporealities; Ann Arbor: University of Michigan Press, 2003), 79–94; Dominik Opatmy, "The Figure of a Blind Man in the Light of the Papyrological Evidence," *Bib* 91 (2010): 583–94.

man, given his well-known status as a successive hermaphrodite.[48] Blindness also tends to be gendered in that men, rather than women, are the ones who are punished with blindness.[49] Men are the ones who exercise the power of sight, and men are the ones who correspondingly have this power taken away. When this occurs, they are effectively "feminized," for they are descending to the level of women, who do not exercise the right to "gaze" in the first place.

Constructions of sight and blindness in Jewish and early Christian literature are consonant with the above constructions in the larger Greco-Roman world.[50] Like their Greek and Roman contemporaries, Jewish and Christian authors do not always depict blindness as a negative feature.[51] Overall, however, sight indicates power in Jewish and Christian texts, and blindness indicates powerlessness, as well as ignorance and bad judgment.[52] Blindness also tends to be gendered in Jewish and Christian texts in that men are typically the ones who lose their ability to see. As Rebecca Raphael argues, in Genesis, for example, physical disability manifests itself along gendered lines: males are blind (Isaac and Jacob) and females are barren (Sarah and Rachel).[53]

As in Greek and Roman texts, Jewish texts also specifically connect eyes and their ability to see to a man's character and "manliness." Moses, for example, is one of God's ideal male representatives and never loses his "seeing" power. Unlike Isaac

---

[48] Tiresias's gender liminality is connected to both sight and sex: he becomes a woman after seeing two snakes copulating, and he is turned back into a man when he sees the same snakes copulating again (Apollodorus, *Bibl.* 3.6.7; Ovid, *Metam.* 3.316–40). See Luc Brisson, *Sexual Ambivalence: Androgyny and Hermaphroditism in Graeco-Roman Antiquity* (trans. Janet Lloyd; Berkeley: University of California Press, 2002), 115–45.

[49] It is telling, for example, that Ovid lists a number of characters afflicted with blindness, all of whom are men (*Ib.* 259–74).

[50] For a comprehensive discussion of blindness in Jewish and early Christian texts, see Felix N. W. Just, "From Tobit to Bartimaeus, from Qumran to Siloam: The Social Role of Blind People and Attitudes Toward the Blind in New Testament Times" (Ph.D. diss., Yale University, 1998), esp. 71–238. For a catalogue of references to blindness in Jewish sources, see Lynn Holden, *Forms of Deformity* (JSOTSup 131; Sheffield: JSOT Press, 1991), 122–41.

[51] For example, the blind prophet Ahijah possesses divine insight in spite of—or perhaps because of—his blindness (1 Kgs 14:1–18), and the blind beggar Bartimaeus actively pursues Jesus in a way that many of his "sighted" followers do not (Mark 10:46–52). See also instances where God and humans are advocates for the blind (e.g., Lev 19:14; Deut 27:18; Job 29:15; Isa 42:16; Ps 146:8).

[52] On sight, see, e.g., Philo, *Abr.* 149–50; *T. Reu.* 2.1–9; Rev 1:14. On blindness, see, e.g., Exod 23:8; Deut 16:19; 2 Sam 5:6; Isa 6:9–10; 42:18–20; 56:10; 59:10; Zeph 1:17; Matt 15:14; 23:16–17, 19, 24; Luke 6:39; John 9:39–41; Rom 2:19–20; 2 Cor 4:4; 2 Pet 1:9; 1 John 2:8–11; Rev 3:17; Philo, *Cher.* 58–59; *Ebr.* 155–56.

[53] See Raphael, *Biblical Corpora: Representations of Disability in Hebrew Biblical Literature* (Library of Hebrew Bible/Old Testament Studies 445; London: T&T Clark International, 2008), esp. 54–81. See also Jer 31:8, where the blind and the lame are associated with women.

or Eli, who have "dim" or "fading" eyesight that parallels their own fading acumen (Gen 27:1; 1 Sam 3:2; 4:15), Moses remains a sighted, active man even in his old age (Deut 34:7). Legal texts also point to the connection between sight and the model male, a connection that falls within a larger tendency to exalt physical wholeness, or "perfection."[54] Vision and masculinity are even more explicitly wed in the story of Tobit, who memorably becomes blind due to bird droppings and as a result loses manly control as well as spiritual insight. When Tobit loses his eyesight, a reversal of the patriarchal family occurs: all of his kindred pity him, his nephew Ahikar becomes his caregiver, and his wife Anna must earn money in his stead (2:9–14). The once wealthy man Tobit is reduced to relying on others, including his wife, and this inversion of gender relations causes Tobit so much grief that he prays for death (3:6; see also 5:10). As a man known for his acts of charity, Tobit must now depend on the charity of others, and he only regains his wealth, piety, and ability to command his family when he regains his ability to see (esp. 11:7–12:5; 14:1–2).

Blindness in Jewish texts also functions as a punishment for men who violate sexual protocols and exemplify other character "flaws." Two angels blind the men of Sodom for their attempted rape (Gen 19:11), and the Philistines blind the lusty Samson after Delilah subdues his insurmountable strength by having his hair cut (Judg 16:21, 28). With Samson, the Philistines specifically gouge out his eyes when he is in his weakened state and then subject his body to further humiliations (16:19–27).[55] Indeed, eye gouging was a common wartime practice (along with other forms of bodily mutilation) in both the ancient Near East and the Greco-Roman world.[56] This practice—along with blinding in general—visually marks the body as being under the power of another and signifies a person's place in the domination–subordination schema.

---

[54] See Lev 21:18, 20; Deut 28:28–29; cf. Lev 22:22; 2 Sam 5:8; Mal 1:8; Thomas Hentrich, "Masculinity and Disability in the Bible," in *This Abled Body: Rethinking Disabilities in Biblical Studies* (ed. Hector Avalos, Sarah J. Melcher, and Jeremy Schipper; SemeiaSt 55; Atlanta: Society of Biblical Literature, 2007), 73–87. Among the Dead Sea Scrolls, see 1QM 7:4–6; 1QS^a 2:3–11; 4QMMT B 49–54; 11Q19 45:12–14; CD 15:15–18. See also Saul M. Olyan, *Disability in the Hebrew Bible: Interpreting Mental and Physical Differences* (Cambridge: Cambridge University Press, 2008), 101–18.

[55] For a discussion of Samson's gender instability, see Ela Lazarewicz-Wyrzkowska, "Samson: Masculinity Lost (And Regained?)," in *Men and Masculinity in the Hebrew Bible and Beyond* (ed. Ovidiu Creangă; Bible in the Modern World 33; Sheffield: Sheffield Phoenix, 2010), 171–88.

[56] See Num 16:14; 1 Sam [10:27]; 11:2; 2 Kgs 25:7; Jer 39:7; 52:11; 4 Macc 5:30; 18:21; cf. Exod 21:23–26; Lev 24:19–20; Deut 19:21; Ezek 12:10–13; T. M. Lemos, "Shame and Mutilation of Enemies in the Hebrew Bible," *JBL* 125 (2006): 225–41; Olyan, *Disability in the Hebrew Bible*, 38–45; Maud W. Gleason, "Mutilated Messengers: Body Language in Josephus," in *Being Greek under Rome: Cultural Identity, the Second Sophistic, and the Development of Empire* (ed. Simon Goldhill; Cambridge: Cambridge University Press, 2001), 50–85.

Jewish texts also specifically refer to God employing the punishment of blindness. In Isaiah, an important text for the Gospel authors, a common theme includes God (or God's servants) figuratively blinding Israel (e.g., Isa 6:9–10; 29:10) and in turn offering sight (e.g., Isa 29:18; 35:5–6; 42:6–7).[57] God also more explicitly "blinds" a number of men due to their disobedience. Deuteronomy 28:28–29, for example, maintains that God inflicts blindness (and additional physical vulnerability) on those who fail to follow the Law.[58] In such accounts, blinding points to a power differential and highlights a favorite theme found throughout Jewish Scripture: namely, the all-powerful nature of the God of Israel.[59] God can both blind (e.g., Exod 4:11) and restore sight (e.g., Ps 146:8), and both of these acts demonstrate God's power.

In early Christian texts, sight, though not as explicitly wed to masculinity as in Greek, Roman, or Jewish texts, still plays an especially prominent role.[60] Sight is powerful and even dangerous, to the extent that Jesus says it is better for a man to tear out his eye than to look at a woman with lust (Matt 5:27–29; cf. Mark 9:47; Matt 18:9).[61] Sight also reflects a man's character. Jesus maintains that the eye is the "lamp of the body" (Matt 6:22–23; Luke 11:34–36) and that a "speck" or "log" in the eye reveals sin (Matt 7:3–5; Luke 6:41–42).[62] Blindness, on the other hand, functions as a metaphor for spiritual ignorance or rejection of the gospel. All of the Gospel authors, for example, connect Isaiah's commission to "shut eyes" (Isa 6:9–10) in relation to Jesus' message and its reception, and Jesus' ministry itself captures the

---

[57] See Robert P. Carroll, "Blindsight and the Vision Thing: Blindness and Insight in the Book of Isaiah," in *Writing and Reading the Scroll of Isaiah: Studies in an Interpretive Tradition* (ed. Craig C. Broyles and Craig A. Evans; 2 vols.; VTSup 70; Formation and Interpretation of Old Testament Literature 1–2; Leiden: Brill, 1997), 1:79–93; Raphael, *Biblical Corpora*, 119–30.

[58] See also 2 Kgs 6:17–18; *3 Bar.* 3:8; *L.A.B.* 27:10; *L.A.E. (Apoc.)* 8:2; *(Vita)* 34:1–2; cf. *T. Sol.* 12:2; *Vis. Ezra* 40. Such blindings relate to a larger pattern of men suffering physical impairments after encountering the divine. See, e.g., Gen 32:24–32; Isa 6:5–7; Dan 8:27; 10:15–17; Luke 1:19–22; Apuleius, *Metam.* 11.14.

[59] Olyan, among others, also highlights how disability points to the power of God (*Disability in the Hebrew Bible*, 9).

[60] Sight plays an important role also in later Christian texts. In Christian martyr accounts, for example, the language of vision and spectacle is paramount. See Elizabeth A. Castelli, *Visions and Voyeurism: Holy Women and the Politics of Sight in Early Christianity* (ed. Christopher Ocker; Protocol of the Colloquy of the Center for Hermeneutical Studies n.s. 2; Berkeley: Center for Hermeneutical Studies, 1995). See also Blake Leyerle, "John Chrysostom on the Gaze," *JECS* 1 (1993): 159–74.

[61] On the power of vision, spectacle, and "the gaze" in the book of Revelation, see Christopher A. Frilingos, *Spectacles of Empire: Monsters, Martyrs, and the Book of Revelation* (Divinations; Philadelphia: University of Pennsylvania Press, 2004).

[62] See Hartsock, *Sight and Blindness*, 143–46. On the eye revealing effeminacy, see, e.g., Clement of Alexandria, *Paed.* 3.11.

Isaianic theme of bringing sight to the blind.⁶³ Unnamed blind men are frequently depicted as being objects of Jesus' healing, and "the blind" as a group often appear alongside marginalized groups such as the lame and the poor.⁶⁴

The author of Luke-Acts in particular weaves sight and blindness throughout his two-volume work. Jesus begins his ministry in the Gospel of Luke by announcing that he will bring "recovery of sight to the blind" (Luke 4:18; cf. Isa 58:6; 61:1–2), and Paul's final words in the book of Acts reference Israel's blindness (Acts 28:26–27; cf. Isa 6:9–10).⁶⁵ Jesus himself has a powerful gaze (e.g., Luke 22:61), yet he also becomes the object of sight during the "spectacle" (θεωρίαν) of the crucifixion (23:48). Sight likewise plays an important role on the road to Emmaus, for the disciples' eyes are kept from recognizing the resurrected Jesus until he breaks bread in their presence (24:16, 31). Sight imagery pervades Acts as well, with visions occurring throughout the narrative, and with Paul, Peter, and John exercising their own powerful gaze.⁶⁶ Indeed, "witnessing," or "testifying," is one of the central themes in Acts, and "seeing" often serves as a necessary prerequisite (e.g., 1:8, 21–22).

In concert with this emphasis on the power of sight, Luke also couches blindness in terms of helplessness and punishment more than the other Gospel authors do. Luke, for example, presents the blind beggar that Jesus heals outside of Jericho as being more helpless than his Markan counterpart (Mark 10:46–52//Luke 18:35–43). Unlike blind Bartimaeus in Mark, the blind beggar in Luke is nameless, shows less initiative, is more reliant on others, and has to be led to Jesus.⁶⁷ Luke also includes a number of punitive miracles in his narrative, two of which include the blinding of Paul in Acts 9 and the blinding of Bar-Jesus in Acts 13.⁶⁸ In the blinding

---

⁶³ See Craig A. Evans, *To See and Not Perceive: Isaiah 6.9–10 in Early Jewish and Christian Interpretation* (JSOTSup 64; Sheffield: Sheffield Academic Press, 1989).

⁶⁴ On blind men as the objects of Jesus' healing, see Mark 8:22–26; 10:46–52; Matt 9:27–31; 12:22; 15:30–31; 20:29–34; Luke 18:35–43; John 9:1–41. On "the blind" appearing alongside other marginalized groups, see, e.g., Matt 11:5; 15:30–31; Luke 4:18; 7:22; 14:13, 21; John 5:3; S. John Roth, *The Blind, the Lame, and the Poor: Character Types in Luke-Acts* (JSNTSup 144; Sheffield: Sheffield Academic Press, 1997).

⁶⁵ See also R. Alan Culpepper, "Seeing the Kingdom of God: The Metaphor of Sight in the Gospel of Luke," *CurTM* 21 (1994): 434–43; Dennis Hamm, "Sight to the Blind: Vision as Metaphor in Luke," *Bib* 67 (1986): 63–72; Stephen D. Moore, *Mark and Luke in Poststructuralist Perspectives: Jesus Begins to Write* (New Haven: Yale University Press, 1992), 111–44; Nils Aksel Røsæg, "The Blinding of Paul: Observations to a Theme," *SEÅ* 71 (2006): 159–85.

⁶⁶ For visions in Acts, see 2:17; 7:55–56; 9:10–16; 10:3–11:18; 12:9; 16:9–10; 18:9–10; 26:19. For the powerful gaze of Peter, John, and Paul, see 3:4; 11:6; 13:9; 14:9; 23:1.

⁶⁷ Mary Ann Beavis, "From the Margin to the Way: A Feminist Reading of the Story of Bartimaeus," *JFSR* 14 (1998): 19–39; Hartsock, *Sight and Blindness*, 182–84. Cf. Matt 9:27–31; 20:29–34.

⁶⁸ In addition to Paul (Acts 9:1–19a) and Bar-Jesus (Acts 13:4–12), see Zechariah (Luke 1:19–22), Ananias and Sapphira (Acts 5:1–11), Herod (Acts 12:20–23), and the sons of Sceva (Acts 19:11–20).

of Bar-Jesus, which has many parallels to Paul's own blinding, the false prophet Bar-Jesus leaves the scene groping about in the darkness (13:11). This detail in particular alludes to God's curse of blindness in Deut 28:28–29, a text that also comes into play with Luke's second retelling of Paul's blinding in Acts 22.[69] With these depictions, Luke mimics larger cultural conceptions of blindness as a debilitating, powerless condition. At the same time, he applies these conceptions to Paul himself, an ostensible "hero" of the faith, to help craft a picture of Paul that does not easily align with elite conceptions of masculinity. Indeed, Luke reveals that Paul gains the ability to "see" only when he loses his ability to see with his eyes.[70]

In sum, sight signifies power (with its correlate, blindness, signifying powerlessness) across Greek, Roman, Jewish, and early Christian discourse. Elite Greek and Roman authors in particular connect sight to masculinity and underscore the feminizing gender liminality of blindness. When a man is specifically punished with blindness, he not only becomes reliant on others, but he loses the most powerful and "masculine" of all the senses. His lack of power in relation to the one who blinded him (human or divine) is literally inscribed in his body. Men stripped of their power to see fail to protect the boundaries of their body and to exercise their assumed right "to gaze." In short, they lose their standing as "manly" men. While early Christian authors do not link sight to masculinity as explicitly as Greek, Roman, and even Jewish authors do, it is evident that they are familiar with the wider associations of sight with power, the latter of which was virtually synonymous with manliness in the ancient world.

In our first detailed picture of Saul, then, Luke presents a man whose claims to "manliness" are suspect (especially according to elite norms) since the "Lord" blinds him in a contest of power. Saul's loss of sight positions him outside the realm of the sighted, impenetrable, self-controlled male who exerts his power over himself and others.[71] Instead, Jesus is the one who exerts power over Saul by blinding him. When viewed in light of ancient vision theories, Jesus impedes Saul's eyes from emitting rays by covering his eyes with scalelike objects, turning his eyes from active to passive agents. By rendering Saul and his eyes passive, Luke demonstrates that Saul's ostensible power pales in comparison with God's ultimate power. By

---

[69] In Acts 22:6, Paul specifically mentions that he is blinded at "noon" (μεσημβρία), and Deut 28:28–29 reads: "you shall grope about at noon [μεσημβρίας] as blind people grope in darkness." See also Isa 42:16; 59:10.

[70] For a discussion of how the power of God is paradoxically made complete in "inability," see Simon Horne, "'Those Who Are Blind See': Some New Testament Uses of Impairment, Inability, and Paradox," in *Human Disability and the Service of God: Reassessing Religious Practice* (ed. Nancy L. Eiesland and Don E. Saliers; Nashville: Abingdon, 1998), 88–102.

[71] Hence, blindness as emasculation does not apply, for example, to the philosopher Democritus, who allegedly blinded himself in order to gain better spiritual insight (Aulus Gellius, *Noct. att.* 10.17). Since Democritus exercises control over his own body with this act and does not fall under the control of others, his self-inflicted blindness may have even been considered "manly." See also Seneca, *Ben.* 3.17.2; *Ep.* 9.4, 122.4.

impeding Saul's ability to see, Luke shows the futility of fighting against this God. Indeed, by blinding Saul, Luke effectively emasculates Saul, thus dissociating Saul from elite understandings of what it takes to "be a man."

III. The Power of God in Acts 9 and Beyond

To be sure, Saul's blindness is a temporary situation. After Ananias lays his hands on Saul and speaks to him, Saul immediately regains his sight (vv. 18–19). Saul once was associated with a plethora of passive verbs; now he is an active subject. Earlier he fell and had to be assisted to his feet (vv. 4, 8); now he stands on his own (v. 18). For three days Saul neither ate nor drank (v. 9); now he eats and is subsequently strengthened (ἐνίσχυσεν, v. 19). Saul once was blind, but now he can see.

Yet Saul's recovery after his blinding does not amount to a newfound manliness or mastery of control.[72] Instead, Luke is quick to show that Saul remains dependent on others and that he regains strength—soon followed by speaking prowess—in service to Jesus, his former foe. After receiving his sight via Ananias, Saul is instantly baptized (v. 18), an act that inaugurates him into Jesus' service and that Saul must likewise receive via a mediator. After Saul is strengthened, he is with the disciples in Damascus, and he "immediately" (εὐθέως) proclaims in the synagogues that Jesus is "the Son of God" (vv. 19–20). In the following verse Saul goes from gaining strength to proclaiming Jesus, showing that his public speech is subject to the one whom he once persecuted (see also vv. 21–30). Directly after his conversion, Saul also depends on the disciples and his "brothers" to help him escape two separate attempts on his life (vv. 23–25, 29–30). He must even rely on Barnabas to plead his case before the apostles on account of suspicions among the disciples themselves (vv. 26–27). In the immediate aftermath of Saul's unmanly encounter, Luke depicts him as a man dependent on others, persecuted on behalf of the one he once persecuted, and subject to "the Son of God" whom he now proclaims.

Throughout the rest of Acts, Saul—referred to mainly now as Paul—remains a man who is subject to the one he formerly persecuted and literally "bound" (via incarceration) to God's divine plan (see esp. 21:10–11). Paul is also "bound" to the Holy Spirit (e.g., 20:22), and he does not act unless the Spirit directs him (e.g., 16:6–10). Luke even describes Paul as a "slave" of God (16:17; 20:19), a designation that positions Paul at the opposite end of the spectrum from "manly men."[73]

---

[72] For a fuller discussion of Paul's correspondence (and lack thereof) to ancient articulations of "manliness," see Brittany E. Wilson, *Unmanly Men: Refigurations of Masculinity in Luke-Acts* (Oxford University Press, forthcoming).

[73] See Walters, "Invading the Roman Body," 29–43; Williams, *Roman Homosexuality*, 30–38.

According to Luke, Paul does not "control" his actions, for his actions must now coincide with God's course of action.

What is more, Luke repeatedly emphasizes that Paul does not exercise control over his own body. For one, Paul does not always master his emotions, or "passions," after his conversion. Paul may no longer perform excessive acts of violence, but he at times betrays anger (15:39; 16:18; 17:16) and even grief (20:19, 31).[74] According to many ancient authors, especially those with Stoic leanings, "manly" men were to control their emotions and avoid emotional displays, given the association of the "passions" with women, effeminate men, and other "non-men."[75] Thus, even as a follower of "the Way," Paul does not strictly adhere to widespread articulations of manly self-control.

More importantly, Paul's body becomes vulnerable to persecution after his encounter on the Damascus road. Paul is not the master of his own body, for Paul, the former persecutor, is now the persecuted. In his vision to Ananias, Jesus foretells the divine necessity (δεῖ) of Paul's suffering (9:16), and his words are fulfilled in short order.[76] Paul experiences persecution almost immediately after his conversion (9:23–25, 29–30), and this persecution continues throughout the remainder of Acts. Paul is pelted with stones (14:19), stripped naked (16:22), beaten and whipped (16:22–23; 21:32), incarcerated (16:24–40; 21:33–28:31), and presumably killed while imprisoned in Rome (20:22–25; 21:13).[77] As someone who undergoes persecution, incarceration, and a slow march to his implied death, Paul knows that his body is no longer simply his own.

The story of Paul's blinding is our first in-depth look at this central character and sets the stage for his ensuing depiction in Acts. Although his blindness is temporary, Paul is not the same after his unmanly encounter in Acts 9. Paul's blinding is so integral to his identity as a follower of Jesus that Luke recounts this story three separate times. After the narrator's account in Acts 9, Paul twice repeats his conversion story, during both his first defense speech (22:6–16) and his final defense speech (26:12–18). As Beverly Roberts Gaventa notes, "Because Luke does tell of

---

[74] See also 14:14; 20:37; 21:13. To be sure, Paul's most obvious displays of "passion" relate to his pre-conversion acts of persecution (see 8:3; 9:1–2, 13–14; 22:4–5; 26:9–11). Yet Luke's main point appears to be that Paul shifts from being a person who perpetuates violence to one who endures violence.

[75] See, e.g., Marcus Aurelius, *Med.* 11.18; Cicero, *Tusc.* 2.50; Dio Chrysostom, *3 Regn.* 34–35; Pliny, *Ep.* 4.2, 7; Plutarch, *Mor.* 452F–464D; Seneca, *Ep.* 99; *Ira* 1.20.3. On the varied accounts of the passions in the Greco-Roman world, see *Passions and Moral Progress in Greco-Roman Thought* (ed. John T. Fitzgerald; New York: Routledge, 2007).

[76] On δεῖ conveying divine necessity, see the frequently cited article by Charles H. Cosgrove ("The Divine ΔΕΙ in Luke-Acts," *NovT* 26 [1984]: 168–90).

[77] On the indignity and emasculation of being physically beaten in particular, see Jennifer A. Glancy, *Corporal Knowledge: Early Christian Bodies* (Oxford: Oxford University Press, 2010), 24–47.

Paul's conversion three times, and at three significant points in the narrative, it appears that Luke understands the conversion to be definitive or constitutive of Paul."[78] To be fair, Paul—despite the defining nature of his out-of-control conversion—does increasingly recover a modicum of control in the latter two accounts. At the same time, Luke also increasingly emphasizes God's power in each of these accounts.[79] In like manner, Paul exercises a powerful gaze after his conversion (13:9; 14:9; 23:1), but this gaze functions to further God's—not Paul's—purposes (e.g., 13:12; 14:15–17; 23:1, 6). From beginning to end, Luke consistently directs his hearers to the power of God and characterizes Paul himself as God's "overthrown enemy" in service to this larger theme.[80]

Despite the claims of many commentators, then, it is not so much the case that Paul moves from being out of control (pre-conversion) to exemplifying self-control (post-conversion).[81] Instead, Paul moves from exerting control over other people's bodies (pre-conversion) to having others exert control over his body (post-conversion). In other words, Paul goes from exercising power to recognizing the "Lord's" power via a divine encounter in which he completely loses power and self-control. Overall, self-control per se is not a virtue Luke applauds, for Luke is more interested in humans recognizing that God is ultimately in control. According to Luke, faithful followers do not exert power or cultivate self-control for their own purposes, but act under the auspices of the all-powerful God of Israel who has acted in Jesus.[82] Faithful followers are "slaves" of God (Luke 1:38; Acts 2:18; 4:29; 16:17; 20:19), and the master they serve is not the masculine ideal of self-mastery. For Luke, dependence—not self-control—is the necessary disposition of discipleship.

IV. Conclusion

In sum, Paul's blinding on the road to Damascus ushers in his characterization as a "slave" and persecuted follower of Jesus. Paul may gain relative power after his

---

[78] Gaventa, "What Ever Happened to Those Prophesying Daughters?" in Levine, *Feminist Companion to the Acts of the Apostles*, 57.

[79] See Marguerat, *First Christian Historian*, 179–204.

[80] See Beverly Roberts Gaventa, "The Overthrown Enemy: Luke's Portrait of Paul," in *SBL 1985 Seminar Papers* (SBLSP 24; Atlanta: Scholars Press, 1985), 439–49.

[81] E.g., Lentz, *Luke's Portrait of Paul*, passim.

[82] See Susan R. Garrett, "'Lest the Light in You Be Darkness': Luke 11:33–36 and the Question of Commitment," *JBL* 110 (1991): 93–105; Beverly Roberts Gaventa, "Initiatives Divine and Human in the Lukan Story World," in *The Holy Spirit and Christian Origins: Essays in Honor of James D. G. Dunn* (ed. Graham N. Stanton, Bruce W. Longenecker, and Stephen C. Barton; Grand Rapids: Eerdmans, 2004), 79–89.

conversion and display some characteristically "manly" traits, but his identity is primarily rooted in following the persecuted "Lord" and not in the ideals of elite masculinity. After his programmatic conversion to "the Way," Paul becomes subject to his former foe, Jesus of Nazareth, and his body—like Jesus' own body—becomes vulnerable to persecution and penetration. In Acts 9, Paul's "unmanning" initiates his status as a man who obeys Jesus and who models this obedience for other believers. By losing his "seeing" power, Paul is able to "see" God's power. Indeed, by losing his sight and self-control, Paul is able to follow a God whose power is made complete in the persecuted person of Jesus, the crucified κύριος.

NEW *from* EERDMANS

JESUS RESEARCH
New Methodologies and Perceptions
The Second Princeton-Prague Symposium on Jesus Research
James H. Charlesworth, editor
with **Brian Rhea** and **Petr Pokorný**

With contributions from forty internationally respected Jewish and Christian scholars, this volume explores nearly every facet of contemporary Jesus research — from eyewitness criteria to the reliability of memory, from archaeology to psychobiography, from oral traditions to literary sources.
ISBN 978-0-8028-6728-5 · 1087 pages
paperback · $70.00

THE UNRELENTING GOD
God's Action in Scripture
Essays in Honor of Beverly Roberts Gaventa
David J. Downs and
Matthew L. Skinner, editors

Sixteen accomplished scholars engage in theologically informed interpretation of Scripture, exploring how various biblical writers describe God's unrelenting commitment to and activity in the world.
ISBN 978-0-8028-6767-4 · 339 pages
paperback · $45.00

JOHN, JESUS, AND THE RENEWAL OF ISRAEL
Richard Horsley and **Tom Thatcher**

"Two skilled scholars here provide a brilliant and creative synthesis of literary and social-historical-political approaches. . . . Their holistic approach to the Fourth Gospel is innovative, well-informed, and informative."   — CRAIG S. KEENER
ISBN 978-0-8028-6872-5 · 207 pages
paperback · $20.00

BORN OF A VIRGIN?
Reconceiving Jesus in the Bible, Tradition, and Theology
Andrew T. Lincoln

"A groundbreaking book that arrives like a breath of fresh air and allows us to see the familiar with new eyes. . . . Lincoln's excellent, clear, and comprehensive treatment is sure to be considered the volume to turn to on this topic for many years to come."
— JAMES MCGRATH
ISBN 978-0-8028-6925-8 · 334 pages
paperback · $35.00

At your bookstore, or call 800-253-7521
www.eerdmans.com

WM. B. EERDMANS
PUBLISHING CO.
2140 Oak Industrial Drive NE
Grand Rapids, MI 49505

JBL 133, no. 2 (2014): 389–397

Three New Coptic Papyrus Fragments of 2 Timothy and Titus (*P.Mich.* inv. 3535b)

BRICE C. JONES
brice.jones@concordia.ca
Concordia University, Montreal, QC H4B 1R6, Canada

This article publishes for the first time the extant remains of a Sahidic Coptic papyrus codex containing portions of 2 Timothy 1–4 and Titus 1. The papyri are currently housed in the Univeristy of Michigan Papyrology Collection. Overlooked for nearly a century, these new papyri extend the manuscript evidence for the Sahidic text of these Deutero-Pauline epistles. The edition includes a transcription, paleographical analysis, commentary, as well as images of the fragment.

I. The Fragments

The University of Michigan Papyrology Collection contains numerous Coptic biblical manuscripts that have been published over the years, not least of which is the famous Middle-Egyptian Fayyumic codex of the Gospel of John (*P.Mich.* inv. 3521).[1] There are, however, a number of Coptic fragments at Michigan that have never been published or identified. Just recently, for example, I published *P.Mich.* inv. 546, a Sahidic parchment fragment of the Gospel of Luke, and *P.Mich.* inv. 547, some early Christian fragments with Gospel excerpts written in Fayyumic.[2] The collection thus continues to reveal its contents. In March 2013, I examined three Coptic papyrus fragments from the Michigan collection and securely identified all

---

[1] Elinor M. Husselman, ed., *The Gospel of John in Fayumic Coptic (P. Mich. Inv. 3521)* (Kelsey Museum of Archaeology Studies 2; Ann Arbor: University of Michigan Press, 1962). For a list of corrections to Husselman's edition in addition to those documented by Hans-Martin Schenke, see Brice C. Jones, "P.Mich. inv. 3521," *BASP* 49 (2013): 299–300. An inventory of Coptic biblical manuscripts in the Michigan collection was prepared by multiple contributors in William H. Worrell, ed., *Coptic Texts in the University of Michigan Collection* (Ann Arbor: University of Michigan Press, 1942).

[2] On *P.Mich.* inv. 546, see Brice C. Jones, "A New Sahidic Fragment of the Gospel of Luke from the Michigan Collection," *NovT* 56 (2014): 198–204. On *P.Mich.* inv. 547, see idem, "Two Unidentified Christian Fragments in the Michigan Collection," *ZPE* 186 (2013): 121–23.

389

three fragments as copies of 2 Timothy 1–4 and Titus 1. In this article, I publish for the first time all three fragments, which are assigned the Michigan inventory number 3535b.[3]

The papyri published here were purchased from the well-known Cairo dealer Maurice Nahman in 1925 and came to the University of Michigan in October 1926 as a gift of Oscar Webber and Richard H. Webber of Detroit. The archaeological provenance of the papyri is unknown. There are several different Coptic manuscripts in the Michigan collection under the inventory number "3535," all purchased from Nahman in 1925 and likely brought together due to the similar language of composition (Coptic). Inventory 3535a (michigan.apis.2003) is a small papyrus fragment of Gal 5:11–6:1, which was published by Gerald M. Browne in 1979.[4] Inventory 3535c (michigan.apis.8868) is a larger unpublished documentary papyrus fragment. Inventory 3535d (michigan.apis.4639) is a small, unidentified scrap of parchment that may be from an amulet. Inventory 3535e (michigan.apis.8869) is a small, unpublished papyrus fragment of a documentary nature. Our papyri have the inventory number 3535b and are codicologically unrelated to the other manuscript fragments bearing the inventory number "3535." The Galatians papyrus (3535a) is written in a different hand and dialect than inventory 3535b and thus was presumably not part of the same codex as our Deutero-Pauline fragments.

Fragment 1 is broken on all sides except the bottom, where the lower margin has been preserved. It measures 4.7 x 10.7 cm and contains twelve partial lines of text on both the recto and verso. Fragment 2, which measures 3 x 14 cm, also preserves only the lower margin, and contains seventeen partial lines on the recto and eighteen partial lines on the verso. Fragment 3, measuring 2.3 x 5.5 cm, is broken on all sides and contains seven partial lines of text on the recto and eight partial lines on the verso. The contents of the fragments are conveniently listed in the following table according to recto (R) and verso (V):

Fragment 1	Fragment 2	Fragment 3
R: 2 Tim 2:26–3:3	R: 2 Tim 1:18–2:6	R: 2 Tim 4:18–20
V: 2 Tim 2:14–18	V: 2 Tim 1:6–11	V: Titus 1:7–9

The fragments are written in the same hand, and so we are dealing with a multitext codex, likely comprised of (at least) the *corpus Paulinum*. In terms of sequence, frg. 2 would have come first in the codex, followed by frgs. 1 and 3. All three papyri

---

[3] For permission to publish the fragments here, I thank Prof. Arthur Verhoogt, Acting Archivist of the University of Michigan Papyrology Collection. Images have been digitally reproduced with the permission of the Papyrus Collection, Graduate Library, University of Michigan.

[4] Browne, *Michigan Coptic Texts* (Papyrologica Castroctaviana, Studia et textus 7; Rome: Pontificio Istituto Biblico, 1979), 6.

belong to separate folios, and, as the contents demonstrate, there are gaps of text between them. The average number of letters per line (the reconstructed text considered) is around twenty-two to twenty-four. Based on these calculations, we may conclude that the number of lines missing between the last word of frg. 1V and the beginning of the extant portion of frg. 1R is approximately twenty-eight lines. Since the lower margin of frg. 1 is preserved, we may therefore add the approximate number of missing lines (ca. twenty-eight) with those extant (twelve) to get a total of approximately forty lines per page. These calculations demonstrate that the codex of which our fragments were once a part was medium to large in size and written in a single column.

The script may be characterized as biblical majuscule or unimodular (i.e., uniform in dimension and shape), upright and roughly bilinear. The curved back of ϭ is heavily extended upward and to the right to such a degree that it hovers over two or more subsequent letters (cf. frg. 1R line 5 and frg. 2V line 5). Otherwise, the hand is largely undecorated, except for light finials on the tips of some letters (e.g., ⲗ, ⲩ, ⲡ). The thickness of strokes is virtually uniform; horizontal strokes are at times only slightly thinner than the vertical strokes. The scribe is inconsistent in his or her use of "single-letter" or "connective" supralinear strokes for consonants in the sonorant class (i.e., ⲃ, ⲗ, ⲙ, ⲛ, ⲣ).[5] The trema (or diaeresis) is written over the letter ⲓ (see frg. 1R line 7), and logical punctuation is present occasionally in the form of a middle dot (e.g., frg. 1R line 10). The scribe has added accidentally omitted text interlinearly in frg. 1R line 4 (ϩ) and frg. 1V line 10 (ⲙⲛ̄ ⲫⲓⲗⲏⲧⲟⲥ).

In view of the difficulties in dating Coptic manuscripts, I have followed others in not assigning a specific date.[6] Most coptologists will agree with Christian Askeland's lament that "the most intimidating and crucial desideratum for Coptic literature is the development of an objective science of Coptic manuscript dating."[7] We can note that the dialect is classical Sahidic, which was standardized in the periods prior to the Arab conquest of ca. 640 C.E. Professor Karlheinz Schüssler has brought to my attention the many similarities in handwriting between our 3535b

---

[5] On the distinction between "single-letter" and "connective" systems of supralineation, see Bentley Layton, *A Coptic Grammar: With Chrestomathy and Glossary. Sahidic Dialect* (3rd rev. ed.; Porta Linguarum Orientalium n.s. 20; Wiesbaden: Harrassowitz, 2011), §38 (31–32).

[6] On the difficulties in dating Coptic manuscripts, see Bentley Layton, "Towards a New Coptic Palaeography," in *Acts of the Second International Congress of Coptic Studies, Roma 22–26 September 1980* (ed. Tito Orlandi and Frederik Wisse; Rome: CIM, 1985), 149–58. The standard manual of Coptic paleography remains that of Viktor Stegemann, *Koptische Paläographie: 25 Tafeln zur Veranschaulichung der Schreibstile koptischer Schriftdenkmäler auf Papyrus, Pergament und Papier für die Zeit des III.–XIV. Jahrhunderts. Mit einem Versuch einer Stilgeschichte der koptischen Schrift* (2 vols.; Quellen und Studien zur Geschichte und Kultur des Altertums und des Mittelalters C/1; Heidelberg: Bilabel, 1936).

[7] Askeland, "The Coptic Versions of the New Testament," in *The Text of the New Testament in Contemporary Research: Essays on the Status Quaestionis* (ed. Bart D. Ehrman and Michael W. Holmes; 2nd ed.; New Testament Tools, Studies, and Documents 42; Leiden: Brill, 2013), 219.

and *P.Mich.* inv. 3992, another Sahidic papyrus codex housed in Michigan.[8] According to Elinor M. Husselman, 3992 "was written perhaps as early as the third century A.D. and certainly not later than the fourth."[9] Paul E. Kahle placed it in the fourth century, and most of the literature supports this date.[10] While I think that we should be cautious of assigning a rigid date for *any* Coptic manuscript, the similarities in script between our papyri and 3992 and the general consensus regarding the dating of the latter suggest that our codex may have been written sometime between the fourth and sixth centuries.

The correspondence between the text of our Coptic papyri and the Greek NT is close. There is only one significant variation unit where our text is extant that may be noted here. In 2 Tim 2:18 some manuscripts (א F G 048 33 *pc*) omit the definite article in the phrase τὴν ἀνάστασιν ("the resurrection"). The editors of the 25th edition of Nestle-Aland's *Novum Testamentum Graece* left the article τήν out of the printed text but subsequent editions retain it. The editorial committee of the UBS Greek NT gave it a "C" rating and enclosed it within brackets "in order to indicate that א F G 048 33 Cyril may correctly represent the original in omitting the word."[11] In frg. 1V, line 11, our text follows the majority of manuscripts in reading the definite article (ⲧⲁⲛⲁⲥⲧⲁⲥⲓⲥ).

II. Text

For convenience, restorations of lacunae and word division are based on the edition of Herbert Thompson (unless otherwise noted), which is based on a famous codex in the Chester Beatty collection (Ms. A; Copt.Ms. 813; Schmitz/Mink sa 4; Schüssler sa 505) that contains the complete text of the Pauline and Deutero-Pauline epistles.[12] Punctuation, tremeta, and supralinear strokes have been reproduced as they appear in the papyri with the exception that connective supralinear

---

[8] The complete codex originally contained John, an unknown text, 1 Corinthians, Titus, Psalms, and Isaiah. *P.Mich.* inv. 3992 is still unpublished, even though it is regularly cited and described in the literature. See, e.g., Bruce M. Metzger, *The Early Versions of the New Testament: Their Origin, Transmission and Limitations* (Oxford: Oxford University Press, 1977), 111; Simon J. Gathercole, "The Titles of the Gospels in the Earliest New Testament Manuscripts," *ZNW* 104 (2013): 61. See also the comments in the APIS catalogue at http://quod.lib.umich.edu/a/apis/x-16134.

[9] Husselman, "The Collection of Papyri," in Worrell, *Coptic Texts in the University of Michigan Collection*, 5.

[10] Kahle, *Bala'izah: Coptic Texts from Deir el-Bala'izah in Upper Egypt* (2 vols.; London: Oxford University Press, 1954), 1:270.

[11] Bruce M. Metzger, *A Textual Commentary on the Greek New Testament* (2nd ed.; Stuttgart: Deutsche Bibelgesellschaft, 1994), 579–80.

[12] Herbert Thompson, *The Coptic Version of the Acts of the Apostles and the Pauline Epistles in the Sahidic Dialect* (Cambridge: University Press, 1932).

strokes have been positioned over the letter of the most likely intended syllabic consonant. The transcript has been arranged according to the sequence of fragment numbers (recto first), not according to the sequence of text. We have also compared our transcript with the edition of George W. Horner, which is cited in the commentary below at relevant points of discussion.[13]

Fragment 1, recto: 2 Timothy 2:26–3:3

1	[ⲁⲩⲱ ⲛ̄ⲥⲉⲛ]ⲏⲫⲉ ⲉⲃ[ⲟⲗ ϩⲛ̄ ⲧϭⲟⲣϭⲥ̄ ⲙ̄-]	2 Tim 2:26
	[ⲡⲇⲓⲁⲃ]ⲟⲗⲟⲥ ⲉⲩϭⲏⲡ [ⲉⲃⲟⲗ ϩⲓⲧⲟⲟⲧϥ̄]	
	[ⲉⲡⲟⲩ]ⲱϣ ⲙ̄ⲡⲉⲧⲙ̄ⲙⲁ[ⲩ. ⲉⲓⲙⲉ ⲇⲉ]	2 Tim 3:1
	[ⲉⲡⲁⲓ ϫ]ⲉ `ϩ´ⲛ̄ⲑⲁⲏ ⲛ̄ⲛⲉϩ[ⲟⲟⲩ ⲥⲉⲛ-]	
5	[ⲁϣⲱⲡⲉ] ⲛ̄ϭⲓϩⲉⲛⲟⲩⲟⲉⲓϣ [ⲉⲩⲛⲁϣⲧ̄.]	
	[ⲛ̄ⲣⲱⲙⲉ ⲅ]ⲁⲣ ⲛⲁϣⲱⲡⲉ ⲙ̄[ⲙⲁⲓⲡⲉⲩ-]	2 Tim 3:2
	[ⲙ̄ⲧⲟⲛ ⲙ̄ⲙ]ⲁⲓϩⲟⲙⲛ̄ⲧ ⲃ̄ⲃⲁ[ⲃⲉⲣⲱⲙⲉ ⲛ̄-]	
	[ϫⲁⲥⲓϩⲏⲧ ⲛ̄]ϫⲁⲧⲟⲩⲁ ⲛ̄ⲥⲉ[ⲥⲱⲧⲙ̄ ⲁⲛ]	
	[ⲛ̄ⲥⲁⲛⲉⲩⲉⲓ]ⲟⲧⲉ ⲛ̄ⲛⲁⲧϣⲡ̄[ϩⲙⲟⲧ ⲉⲩ-]	
10	[ϫⲁϩⲙ̄ ⲛ̄ⲣⲉ]ϥⲙⲓϣⲉ· ⲛ̄ⲟⲩⲁ[ϩⲓⲏⲧ ⲛ̄ⲇⲓⲁ-]	2 Tim 3:3
	[ⲃⲟⲗⲟⲥ ⲛ̄ⲁ]ⲧⲁⲙⲁϩⲧⲉ ⲥ̣[ⲉⲟ ⲁⲛ ⲛ̄ϩ-]	
	[ⲙⲉⲣⲟⲥ ⲉⲩ]ⲙⲟⲥⲧⲉ ⲙ̄ⲡⲉ[ⲧⲛⲁⲛⲟⲩϥ]	

Fragment 1, verso: 2 Timothy 2:14–18

1	[ⲛ̄ⲛⲉⲧⲥⲱⲧⲙ̄ ϭ]ⲉⲡⲏ [ⲧⲁϩⲟⲕ ⲉⲣⲁⲧⲕ̄]	2 Tim 2:14, 15
	[ⲛ̄ⲟⲩⲥⲱⲧ]ⲡ̄ ⲙ̄ⲡⲛⲟⲩⲧⲉ [ⲛ̄ⲟⲩⲉⲣⲅⲁⲧ-]	
	[ⲏⲥ ⲉⲙⲉϥ]ϫⲓϣⲓⲡⲉ ⲉϥϣ[ⲱⲱⲧ ⲙ̄ⲡ-]	
	[ϣⲁϫⲉ ⲛ̄ⲧ]ⲙⲉ· ⲛⲓϣⲙⲏ ⲇ[ⲉ ⲉⲧϣⲟ-]	2 Tim 2:16
5	[ⲩⲉⲓⲧ ⲁⲩⲱ] ⲉⲧⲃⲏⲧ ⲙ̄ⲡ[ⲣⲟⲩⲱϣ]	
	[ⲉϥⲓ ϩⲁⲣⲟ]ⲟⲩ· ⲛⲁⲥⲉⲃⲏ[ⲥ ⲅⲁⲣ ⲛⲁ-]	
	[ⲡⲣⲟⲕⲟⲡⲧ]ⲉ ⲉⲡⲉϩⲟⲩ ⲁ[ⲩⲱ ⲡⲉⲩ]	2 Tim 2:17
	[ϣⲁϫⲉ ⲛⲁ]ⲣⲟⲩⲁⲙⲟⲙⲉ ⲛ̄[ⲑⲉ ⲛⲟⲩⲅⲁⲅ-]	
	[ⲅⲣⲁⲓⲛⲁ ⲛ]ⲁⲓ̈ ⲉⲩⲉⲃⲟⲗ ⲛ̄ϩ[ⲏⲧⲟⲩ ⲡⲉ ϩⲩ-]	
10	[ⲙⲉⲛⲁⲓⲟ]ⲥ· `ⲙⲛ̄ⲫⲓⲗⲏⲧⲟⲥ´ ⲛⲁⲓ̈ ⲉⲛⲧⲁⲩⲣ̄[ϩⲁⲉ ⲉⲧⲙⲉ]	2 Tim 2:18
	[ⲉⲩϫⲱ] ⲙ̄ⲙⲟⲥ ϫⲉ ⲁⲧ[ⲁⲛⲁⲥⲧⲁⲥⲓⲥ]	
	[ⲟⲩⲱ ⲉⲥϣⲱ]ⲡⲉ ⲉⲩϣⲟⲣϣⲣ̄ [ⲛ̄ⲧⲡⲓⲥⲧⲓⲥ]	

---

[13] Horner, *The Coptic Version of the New Testament in the Southern Dialect Otherwise Called Sahidic and Thebaic*, vol. 5 (Oxford: Clarendon, 1920).

Fragment 2, recto: 2 Timothy 1:18–2:6

1	[..]	
	[ⲡϫⲟⲉⲓⲥ ϩⲙ̄ⲡⲉϩ]ⲟⲟⲩ ⲉⲧ[ⲙ̄ⲙⲁⲩ ⲁⲩⲱ]	2 Tim 1:18
	[ⲛⲉⲛⲧⲁϥⲁⲁⲩ ⲛ]ⲁⲓ̈ ⲧⲏⲣ[ⲟⲩ ϩⲛ̄ⲉⲫⲉ-]	
	[ⲥⲟⲥ ⲕⲥⲟⲟⲩⲛ ⲙ̄]ⲙⲟⲟⲩ ⲛ̄[ϩⲟⲩⲟ.]	
5	[ⲛ̄ⲧⲟⲕ ϭⲉ ⲡⲁϣⲏ]ⲣⲉ ϭⲙ̄ϭ[ⲟⲙ ϩⲙ̄ⲡⲉ-]	2 Tim 2:1
	[ϩⲙⲟⲧ ⲉⲧϩⲙ̄ⲡⲉ]ⲭⲥ̄ ⲓ̄ⲥ̄ ⲁⲩ[ⲱ ⲛⲉⲛⲧⲁⲕⲥⲟ-]	2 Tim 2:2
	[ⲧⲙⲟⲩ ⲛ̄ⲧⲟⲟⲧ] ϩⲓⲧⲛ̄ϩⲁ[ϩ ⲙ̄ⲙⲛ̄ⲧⲣⲉ ⲛⲁⲓ̈]	
	[ⲕⲁⲁⲩ ⲉϩⲣⲁⲓ̈] [[ϩ]]ⲛ̄ϩⲙ̄ⲡ[ⲓⲥⲧⲟⲥ ⲛ̄-]	
	[ⲣⲱⲙⲉ ⲛⲁⲓ̈ ⲉⲩⲛ]ⲁϣϭⲙ̄ϭ[ⲟⲙ ⲉⲧⲥ-]	
10	[ⲁⲃⲉϩⲉⲛⲕⲟⲟⲩⲉ] ϣⲡ̄ϩⲓⲥⲉ [ϩⲱⲥ ⲙⲁ-]	2 Tim 2:3
	[ⲧⲟⲓ̈ ⲉⲛⲁⲛⲟⲩϥ] ⲛ̄ⲧⲉⲡⲉⲭ[ⲥ̄ ⲓ̄ⲥ̄ ⲙⲉ-]	
	[ⲣⲉⲗⲁⲁⲩ ⲉϥⲟ] ⲙ̄ⲙⲁⲧⲟⲓ̈ [ⲧⲁϩϥ̄ ⲙⲛ̄]	2 Tim 2:4
	[ⲛⲉϩⲃⲏⲩⲉ ⲙ̄ⲡ]ⲃⲓⲟⲥ ϫⲉ ⲉ[ϥⲉⲁⲣⲉⲥⲕⲉ]	
	[ⲙ̄ⲡⲉⲛⲧⲁϥⲁⲁϥ] ⲙ̄ⲙⲁⲧⲟ[ⲓ̈ ⲉϣⲱⲡⲉ]	
15	[ⲇⲉ ⲟⲛ ⲉⲣϣ]ⲁⲛⲟⲩⲁ ⲣ̄[ϣⲟⲉⲓϫ ⲙⲉ-]	2 Tim 2:5
	[ϥϫⲓⲕⲗⲟⲙ ⲉⲓ]ⲙⲏⲧⲓ ⲛ̄ϥ[ⲙⲓϣⲉ ⲕⲁ-]	
	[ⲗⲱⲥ ⲡⲟⲩⲟⲉⲓⲉ] ⲉⲧϩⲟⲥⲉ [ⲛ̄ⲧⲟϥ ⲉϣⲁϥ-]	2 Tim 2:6

Fragment 2, verso: 2 Timothy 1:6–11

1	[ⲧⲣⲉⲕⲉⲓ]ⲣⲉ ⲙ̄[ⲡⲙⲉⲉⲩⲉ ⲉⲧⲣⲉⲕⲧⲟⲩ-]	
	[ⲣⲟⲧ ⲙ̄]ⲡⲉ[ϩ]ⲙⲟ[ⲧ ⲙ̄ⲡⲛⲟⲩⲧⲉ ϩⲛ̄ⲧⲕ̄]	2 Tim 1:6
	[ϩⲓⲧⲙ̄ⲡ]ⲧⲁⲗⲟ [ⲛ̄ⲛⲁϭⲓϫ ⲛ̄ⲧⲁⲡⲛⲟⲩⲧⲉ]	2 Tim 1:7
	[ⲅⲁⲣ ϯ ⲛ]ⲁⲛ ⲁⲛ [ⲛ̄ⲟⲩⲡ̄ⲛ̄ⲁ̄ ⲙ̄ⲙⲛ̄ⲧϭⲱⲃ]	
5	[ⲁⲗⲗⲁ] ⲛ̄ϭⲟⲙ ϩ[ⲓⲁⲅⲁⲡⲏ ϩⲓⲙⲛ̄ⲧ-]	
	[ⲣⲙ̄ⲛ̄ϩ]ⲏⲧ ⲙ̄ⲡ[ⲣ̄ϣⲓⲡⲉ ϭⲉ ⲛ̄ⲧⲙⲛ̄ⲧⲙⲛ̄-]	2 Tim 1:8
	[ⲧⲣⲉ ⲙ̄]ⲡⲉⲛϫⲟⲉ[ⲓⲥ ⲟⲩⲇⲉ ⲛⲁⲓ̈ ⲡⲉⲧⲙⲏⲣ ⲛ̄ⲧⲁϥ]	
	[ⲁⲗⲗ]ⲁ ϣⲡ̄ϩⲓ[ⲥⲉ ⲙⲛ̄ⲡⲉⲩⲁⲅⲅⲉⲗⲓⲟⲛ ⲕⲁⲧⲁ-]	
	[ⲧϭⲟⲙ] ⲙ̄ⲡⲛⲟⲩ[ⲧⲉ ⲡⲁⲓ̈ ⲉⲛⲧⲁϥⲧⲁⲛϩⲟⲛ ⲁⲩⲱ]	2 Tim 1:9
10	[ⲁϥⲧ]ⲁϩⲙⲛ̄ ϩ[ⲛ̄ⲟⲩⲧⲱϩⲙ̄ ⲉϥⲟⲩⲁⲁⲃ ⲉⲛⲕⲁⲧⲁ-]	
	[ⲛⲉ]ⲛϩⲃⲏⲩⲉ [ⲁⲛ ⲁⲗⲗⲁ ⲕⲁⲧⲁⲡⲉϥⲧⲱϣ ⲙ̄-]	
	[ⲙⲓⲛ] ⲙ̄ⲙⲟϥ ⲙⲛ̄[ⲧⲉϥⲭⲁⲣⲓⲥ ⲉⲛⲧⲁϥⲧⲁⲁⲥ]	
	[ⲛⲁⲛ ϩ]ⲙ̄ⲡⲉⲭⲥ̄ ⲓ̄ⲥ̄ [ϩⲁⲑⲏ ⲛ̄ⲛⲉⲩⲟⲉⲓϣ ⲛ̄ϣⲁ-]	
	[ⲉⲛ]ⲉϩ ⲉⲁⲥⲟⲩⲱ[ⲛϩ̄ ⲇⲉ ⲉⲃⲟⲗ ⲧⲉⲛⲟⲩ ϩⲓ-]	2 Tim 1:10
15	[ⲧⲙⲡⲟ]ⲩⲱⲛϩ̄ [ⲉⲃⲟⲗ ⲙ̄ⲡⲉⲛⲥⲱⲧⲏⲣ ⲡⲉⲭⲥ̄ ⲓ̄ⲥ̄]	
	[ⲉⲁ]ϥⲟⲩⲟⲥϥ̄ [ⲙⲉⲛ ⲙ̄ⲡⲙⲟⲩ ⲁϥⲟⲩⲱⲛϩ̄]	
	[ⲇⲉ] ⲉⲃⲟⲗ ⲙ̄[ⲡⲱⲛϩ̄ ⲙⲛ̄ⲧⲙⲛ̄ⲧⲁⲧⲧⲁⲕⲟ]	
	[ϩⲓⲧⲙ̄ⲡ]ⲉⲩⲁⲅⲅⲉⲗⲓ[ⲟⲛ ⲡⲁⲓ ⲉⲛⲧⲁⲩⲕⲁⲁⲧ-]	2 Tim 1:11

Fragment 3, recto: 2 Timothy 4:18–20

1	[ϥⲛⲁⲧⲟⲩϫⲟⲓ̈ ⲉ]ϩⲟⲩ[ⲛ ⲉⲧⲉϥⲙⲛ̄ⲧⲉⲣⲟ	2 Tim 4:18
	ⲉⲧϩⲛ̄ⲧⲡⲉ ⲡ]ⲁⲓ̈ ⲡⲉ[ⲟⲟⲩ ⲛⲁϥ ϣⲁⲉⲛⲉϩ]	
	[ⲛ̄ⲉⲛⲉϩ ϩⲁⲙ]ⲏⲛ· ϣ[ⲓⲛⲉ ⲉⲡⲣⲓⲥⲕⲁ ⲙⲛ̄-]	2 Tim 4:19
	[ⲁⲕⲩⲗⲁ ⲙⲛ̄]ⲁⲡⲏⲓ̈ [ⲛ̄ⲟⲛⲏⲥⲓⲫⲟⲣⲟⲥ]	
5	[ⲁⲉⲣⲁⲥⲧⲟⲥ ϭ]ⲱ ϩⲛ̄[ⲕⲟⲣⲓⲛⲑⲟⲥ ⲁⲓ̈ⲕⲁ-]	2 Tim 4:20
	[ⲧⲣⲟⲫⲓⲙⲟⲥ] ⲇⲉ [ϩⲛ̄ⲙⲓⲗⲏⲧⲟⲥ ⲉϥϣⲱ-]	
	[..]	

Fragment 3, verso: Titus 1:7–9

1	[ⲉⲛⲟⲩⲛⲟϣϥ̄ ⲁⲛ ⲡ]ⲉ [ⲉⲛⲟⲩ-]	Titus 1:7
	[ⲙⲁⲓ̈ϩⲏⲩ ⲛ̄ϣⲗⲟϥ] ⲁⲛ [ⲡⲉ ⲁⲗⲗⲁ]	Titus 1:8
	[ⲉϥⲟ ⲙ̄ⲙⲁⲓ̈ϣⲙ̄]ⲟ ⲙ̄ⲙⲁ[ⲓ̈ⲡⲉⲧⲛⲁⲛⲟⲩϥ]	
	[ⲛ̄ϩⲁⲕ ⲛ̄ⲇⲓⲕⲁⲓⲟⲥ] ⲉϥⲟⲩⲁ[ⲁⲃ ⲛⲉⲅⲕⲣⲁ-]	
5	[ⲧⲏⲥ ⲉϥϭⲟⲗϫ̄ ⲙ̄ⲡ]ϣⲁϫⲉ [ⲉⲧⲛ̄ϩⲟⲧ ⲕⲁ-]	Titus 1:9
	[ⲧⲁⲧⲉⲥⲃⲱ ϫⲉⲕⲁ]ⲥ ⲉϥⲉϣ[ϭⲙ̄ϭⲟⲙ]	
	[ⲉⲥⲟⲡⲥ̄ϩⲛ̄ⲧⲉⲥⲃ]ⲱ ⲉⲧⲟⲩ[ⲟϫ ⲁⲩⲱ]	
	[·]	

III. COMMENTARY

Fragment 1, Recto

7 ⲃⲃⲁ[ⲃⲉⲣⲱⲙⲉ: The assimilation of syllabic ⲛ̄ to the following consonant (here ⲃ) is common. According to Bentley Layton, "In some early manuscripts, morphs spelled ⲛ̄- are often replaced by the variants ⲃ̄-, ⲗ̄, ⲡ̄ when followed by non-syllabic ⲃ, ⲗ, ⲣ respectively."[14]

8 ⲛ̄ⲥⲉ[ⲥⲱⲧⲙ̄: The editions of both Thompson and Horner read ⲉⲛⲥⲉⲥⲱⲧⲙ̄.

9 ⲛ̄ⲛⲁⲧϣⲡ̄[ϩⲙⲟⲧ: The editions of both Thompson and Horner read ⲛ̄ⲁⲧϣⲡ̄[ϩⲙⲟⲧ. The additional *nu* is a common variant doubling of the morph ⲛ̄-, especially before vowels.[15]

11 ⲥ̣[ⲉⲟ: The back of the *sigma* is clear before the break, which means the scribe did not include the initial *nu*, which is read in the edition of Thompson. Horner's edition lacks the word completely, which at this point reads ⲛ̄ⲁⲧⲁⲙⲁϩⲧⲉ ⲛ̄[ⲁⲛ]ⲏⲙⲉⲣⲟⲥ.

12 ⲙ̄ⲡⲉ[ⲧⲛⲁⲛⲟⲩϥ: The editions of Thompson and Horner read ⲙ̄ⲡⲡⲉⲧⲛⲁⲛⲟⲩϥ (Horner: ⲙ̄ⲡⲡⲉⲧⲛⲁⲛⲟ[ⲩϥ]), with the additional *pi*.

---

[14] Layton, *Coptic Grammar*, §21b (21).
[15] See ibid., §22b (21).

Fragment 1, Verso

2–3 [ⲛ̄ⲟⲩⲉⲣⲅⲁⲧ | ⲛⲥ ⲉⲙⲉϥ]ϫⲓϣⲓⲡⲉ: We have restored the lacuna with Thompson's text. The manuscripts consulted by Horner are fragmentary at this point, so that his text at 2 Tim 2:15 reads ϭⲉⲡⲏ ⲉⲧⲁϩⲟⲕ ⲉⲣⲁⲧⲕ̄ ⲛ̄ⲟⲩⲥⲱⲧⲛ̄ ⲙ̄ⲡⲛⲟⲩⲧⲉ [ⲉⲕ]ϣⲱⲧ ⲉⲃⲟⲗ ⲙ̄ⲡϣⲁϫⲉ ⲛ̄ⲧⲙⲉ.

10 ⲉⲛⲧⲁⲩⲣ̄[ϩⲁⲉ: The sentence converter ⲉⲛⲧ as read here is found in Horner's edition with the common orthographic alternative as ⲛ̄ⲧ.

12 ⲉⲥϣⲱ]ⲡⲉ: The papyrus lacks the following ⲁⲩⲱ that is read in both Thompson's and Horner's editions. Here, the Greek καί stands behind ⲁⲩⲱ, but this does not necessarily mean that the *Vorlage* of the Coptic translator did not contain this word. Elina Perttilä has demonstrated that asyndeton is very common in Coptic texts, and that "to read the Greek behind the Coptic text is in the case of conjunctions mostly impossible."[16]

Fragment 2, Recto

8 [[ϩ]]ⲛ̄ϩⲙ̄ⲡ[ⲓⲥⲧⲟⲥ: The scribe initially wrote ϩⲛ̄ ϩⲙ̄ⲡⲓⲥⲧⲟⲥ but canceled the initial *horeh* with a cross-stroke, thereby producing the reading ⲛ̄ϩⲙ̄ⲡ[ⲓⲥⲧⲟⲥ, a mistake for the correct ⲛ̄ϩⲉⲛⲡⲓⲥⲧⲟⲥ (read in both Thompson and Horner).

---

[16] Elina Perttilä, "How to Read the Greek Text behind the Sahidic Coptic," in *Scripture in Transition: Essays on Septuagint, Hebrew Bible, and Dead Sea Scrolls in Honor of Raija Sollamo* (ed. Anssi Voitila and Jutta Jokiranta; JSJSup 126; Leiden: Brill, 2008), 376. Layton states that, with main clauses in the past tense, "asyndeton expresses closer linkage than ⲁⲩⲱ, ⲇⲉ, ⲙⲛ̄ⲛ̄ⲥⲱ-ⲥ, or other conjunctions" (*Coptic Grammar*, §237 [183]).

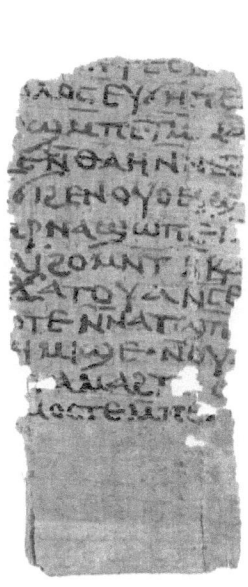

P.Mich. inv. 3535b – Recto

P.Mich. inv. 3535b – Verso

scholarship that matters

Uncovering Early Christianity

Seeing the Lord's Glory
Kyriocentric Visions and the Dilemma of Early Christology
CHRISTOPHER BARINA KAISER
9781451470345 384 pp pbk $49

A Theory of Character in New Testament Narrative
CORNELIS BENNEMA
9781451472219 240 pp pbk $39

Jesus and Temple
Textual and Archaeological Explorations
JAMES H. CHARLESWORTH
9781451480368 248 pp pbk $39

Irony in the Matthean Passion Narrative
INHEE C. BERG
9781451470338 192 pp pbk $39

Teaching All Nations
Interrogating the Matthean Great Commission
MITZI J. SMITH and
JAYACHITRA LALITHA, editors
9781451470499 240 pp pbk $49

Idols of Nations
Biblical Myth at the Origins of Capitalism
ROLAND BOER and
CHRISTINA PETTERSON
9781451465440 208 pp pbk $29

The Nonviolent Messiah
Jesus, Q, and the Enochic Tradition
SIMON J. JOSEPH
9781451472196 240 pp pbk $39

Future of the Prophetic
Israel's Ancient Wisdom Re-presented
MARC H. ELLIS
9781451470109 336 pp pbk $39

Available wherever books are sold or
800-328-4648
fortresspress.com

Rethinking the Origins of the Nag Hammadi Codices

NICOLA DENZEY LEWIS
ndenzey@brown.edu
Brown University, Providence, RI 02912

JUSTINE ARIEL BLOUNT
justineariel@icloud.com
1383 Pacific Street, Brooklyn, NY 11216

The famous find-story behind the Nag Hammadi codices, discovered in Egypt in 1945, has been one of the most cherished narratives in our field. Yet a close examination of its details reveals inconsistencies, ambiguities, implicitly colonialist attitudes, and assumptions that call for a thorough reevaluation. This article explores the problematic moments in the find-story narrative and challenges the suggestions of James M. Robinson and others that the Nag Hammadi codices were intentionally buried for posterity, perhaps by Pachomian monks, in the wake of Athanasius's thirty-ninth *Festal Letter*. We consider, rather, that the Nag Hammadi codices may have derived from private Greco-Egyptian citizens in late antiquity who commissioned the texts for personal use, depositing them as grave goods following a practice well attested in Egypt.

The Nag Hammadi codices, discovered in 1945, have perhaps the most compelling find-story of any ancient Egyptian book cache. When Mohamed Ali al-Samman, both the hero and the antihero of this story, discovers that his brother has found a jar while digging for fertilizer, he immediately takes control of the operation. Taking the jar into his hands, the moment is tense. Should he open it? He is a cautious, superstitious man, clearly pious and afraid of *jinni*; yet he also loves gold, and as in those old Arabian nights tales, his curiosity gets the better of him and he smashes the jar, only to find—is it gold?!—pieces of golden papyrus, flying through the air. Little does Mohamed Ali know, when he takes them home and tosses them into the little barn attached to his mother's home, that he has discovered thirteen books of more than fifty "lost Gospels" representing a Gnostic library of heretical documents, carefully secreted away in the increasingly theologically oppressive atmosphere of late-fourth-century Egypt.[1]

But what if this famous story, which has become the canonical genesis for scholars of Gnosticism, is merely a fiction? Even the earliest and most direct versions of the story reveal unsettling inconsistencies. Elements are unstable, and the key witness, Mohamed Ali, himself recants and changes his account.[2] While we may speculate on the reasons for these inconsistencies, it becomes difficult to believe Mohamed Ali at all, not to mention the orientalizing fantasy of his encounter with a papyrus-filled jar somewhere in the geese-grazing territories of Chenoboskion. Indeed, two prominent Coptologists, Rodolphe Kasser and Martin Krause, long ago went on record to distance themselves from the "official"—that is, much publicized and disseminated—find-story.[3]

We begin by reexamining different accounts of the find-story, noting the central instability of its narrative. We take this starting point because it matters whether this story is true: from it, scholars of Gnosticism have built up fifty years of work based on the assumption that back in the late fourth century, the codices were secreted away together in a jar in order to preserve them for "posterity." We argue here that this was unlikely to have been the intention of those who buried the codices. Rather than parts of a Pachomian library that had been intentionally hidden by monks to avoid persecution by the emerging Alexandrian orthodoxy, we suggest that the Nag Hammadi codices could just as plausibly have been private productions commissioned by late ancient Egyptian Christians with antiquarian interests. The books were later deposited in graves, following a late antique modification of a custom known in Egypt for hundreds of years. Furthermore, we

---

[1] The details here come from Marvin Meyer's version of the story, which he credits to James M. Robinson in a chapter called "Fertilizer, Blood Vengeance, and Codices" in his book *The Gnostic Discoveries: The Impact of the Nag Hammadi Library* (San Francisco: HarperSanFrancisco, 2005), 13–32.

[2] See James M. Robinson, "The Discovery of the Nag Hammadi Codices," *BA* 42 (1979): 208–13.

[3] *The Facsimile Edition of the Nag Hammadi Codices*, vol. 1, *Introduction* (Published under the auspices of the Department of Antiquities of the Arab Republic of Egypt. In conjuction with the United Nations Education, Scientific and Cultural Organization; Leiden: Brill, 1972), 3 n. 1 offers a lengthy disclaimer: "Kasser and Krause and others who were involved do not consider as assured anything more than the core of the story (the general location and approximate date of the discovery), the rest not having for them more than the value of stories and fables that one can collect in popular Egyptian circles thirty years after an event whose exceptional significance the protagonists could not at the time understand. R.K. and M.K." An English publication that also casts suspicions on the find-story is C. Wilfred Griggs, *Early Egyptian Christianity: From Its Origins to 451 C.E.* (Brill Scholars' List; Leiden: Brill, 2000), 217: "The doubts and concerns expressed by this author are similar to those held by Rodolphe Kasser and Martin Krause." Very recently, the veracity of the find-story has also been raised by Mark Goodacre, "How Reliable Is the Story of the Nag Hammadi Discovery?" *JSNT* 35 (2013): 303–22. We thank Mark Goodacre for making this article available prior to its publication, and for our discussions on the topic.

contend that their eventual placement in graves may not have been coincidental; the arrangement of certain volumes reflects eschatological as well as antiquarian interests, meaning that at least some volumes may have been intentionally crafted as funerary deposits, Christian "Books of the Dead" that only made sense in the context of late antique Egypt.

I. Find-Stories and Suspicions

A full thirty years after the initial appearance of the Nag Hammadi codices on the Cairo antiquities market, James M. Robinson traveled to Egypt to survey the area and to see if he might track down the person who initially made the discovery.[4] Robinson's efforts yielded a vastly entertaining account of the codices' discovery and brief sojourn in a "modern" Upper Egyptian village; riveting details included the burning of an unspecified number of papyrus leaves by Mohamed Ali's mother (horrors! how could they not have known their value?) and his family's acts of murder and cannibalism. In this modern, Western recounting of 1940s *fellaheen* life, we have not come far from W. Robertson Smith's 1889 *Religion of the Semites* (where the "birth" of Judaism comes from a primordial act of sacrifice and collective consumption of a tribe's totem animal in the desert),[5] a text much beloved by Freud, who transmuted Smith's postulated sacrifice and consumption of the totem animal into a communal act of parricide in his *Totem and Taboo* (1913).[6] Like Smith's account of primordial religion and Freud's revisioning of it with an Oedipal cast, the Nag Hammadi find-story is one more appropriate for fantastic literature, with parts surely lost in translation, other parts surely fabricated.[7]

---

[4] Robinson, head of the UNESCO-funded project to generate critical editions and translations of the Nag Hammadi codices, published numerous accounts of the find-story: see James M. Robinson, "From the Cliff to Cairo: The Study of the Discoverers and Middlemen of the Nag Hammadi Codices," in *Colloque international sur les textes de Nag Hammadi (Québec, 22–25 août 1978)* (ed. Bernard Barc; Bibliothèque copte de Nag Hammadi, "Etudes" 1; Québec: Les presses de l'Université Laval, 1981), 21–58; idem, "The Coptic Gnostic Library Today," *NTS* 14 (1968): 356–401; and idem, "Discovery of the Nag Hammadi Codices," 206–24.

[5] Smith, *Lectures on the Religion of the Semites: First Series, Fundamental Institutions* (London: A. & C. Black, 1889); 2nd ed. [posthumous], edited by J. S. Black (1894), repr., New York: Meridian, 1956; 3rd ed., introduced by S. A. Cook (1927); later edition with introduction by James Muilenburg (New York: Ktav 1969).

[6] Freud, *Totem und Tabu: Einige Übereinstimmungen im Seelenleben der Wilden und der Neurotiker* (Leipzig: H. Heller, 1913); published in English as *Totem and Taboo: Some Points of Agreement between the Mental Lives of Savages and Neurotics* (trans. James Strachey; New York: Norton, 1952).

[7] The sole scholar to have manifestly criticized the overtly colonialist and orientalizing aspects of the Nag Hammadi find-story is Maia Kotrosits, "Romance and Danger at Nag Hammadi," *Bible and Critical Theory* 8 (2012): 39–52.

When we press at its contours, this famous and oft-recounted find-story of the Nag Hammadi codices becomes vexing because of its revisionist nature. It turns out, to begin with, to have been rather late in coming; the very first account of the codices' discovery came from the French scholar Jean Doresse, who, five years after the appearance of the codices in Cairo, traveled to the hamlet of Hamra Dum, close to Nag Hammadi and the actual location of the codices' provenance.[8] Local villagers directed him to the southern part of an ancient cemetery at Qasr es-Sayyad. It was there, in the cemetery, that some had found the codices, secreted in a jar. Doresse writes,

> Was it in one of these tombs that the papyri were found? Certainly, one cannot, even if one searches very far around, see any other place—any ruin or sepulcher —from which they could have come. The peasants who accompanied us ... showed us a row of shapeless cavities. Not long since, they said, some peasants of Hamra-Dûm and of Dabba, in search of manure, found here a great *zir*—which means jar—filled with leaves of papyrus; and these were bound like books. The vase was broken and nothing remains of it; the manuscripts were taken to Cairo and no one knows what then became of them. As to the exact location of the find, opinion differed by some few dozen yards, but everyone was sure that it was just about here. And from the ground itself we shall learn nothing more; it yields nothing but broken bones, fragments of cloth without interest and some potsherds.[9]

When Robinson returned to Hamra Dum twenty-five years later to pick up the trail, his persistence yielded more satisfying results. He came up with names and a more specific (and in fact, quite different) find-spot: Mohamed Ali al-Samman was out that day in December of 1945 on the Gebel al-Tarif, looking for *sabakh*, a natural fertilizer. He dug, according to Robinson, along a talus—a slope of debris along the cliff face and just beyond the area of Nile cultivation. There he found the jar. So let us start here with this puzzling detail. If the jar were embedded in alluvial soil at the base of a cliff, it is highly unlikely that a papyrus codex would have survived for sixteen centuries of Nile inundations and shifting soil at the base of the cliffs. And yet, if the jar had actually been found up higher, inside a cave along the Gebel al-Tarif, this is hardly the place to dig for *sabakh*. In fact, it is even debatable whether the base of the Gebel al-Tarif would have produced this *sabakh*, as the areas of cultivation around the Nile end abruptly and turn very quickly to desert, where nothing exists but sand. Whatever Mohamed Ali was doing that day, it is safe to say

---

[8] Doresse visited Upper Egypt three times in the lead-up to his 1950 investigations—in 1947, 1948, and 1949. See Jean Doresse, "Sur les traces des papyrus gnostiques: Recherches à Chenoboskion," *Bulletin de l'Académie royale de Belgique, Classe des Lettres,* 5th series 36 (1950): 432–39.

[9] Doresse, *The Secret Books of the Egyptian Gnostics: An Introduction to the Gnostic Coptic Manuscripts Discovered at Chenoboskion* (trans. Philip Mairet; New York: Viking, 1960), 133.

that he was not digging for fertilizer. It is entirely reasonable to suspect that he was searching for illegal antiquities: tomb robbing. The jar—one of the only details on which Doresse and Robinson agree—is equally mysterious; as the NT scholar Mark Goodacre noted recently, it grows in size from 20 cm to 3–4 ft in height, depending on who is telling the story.[10] At any rate, the jar no longer exists.[11]

A quick cross-referencing of various versions of the story reveals many such shifting details. In one account, a "party" of *sabakh* gatherers find the jar at the foot of a cliff sheltered by a large boulder.[12] The number in this party appears to change; sometimes it is Mohamed Ali and his brother Khalifah Ali and/or another brother Abu al-Magid;[13] sometimes Mohamed Ali is alone;[14] sometimes more are present.[15] Sometimes Mohamed Ali finds the jar; sometimes it is Abu al-Magid. Bart Ehrman retains the detail that Abu al-Magid (unnamed in his account) digs and finds a skeleton first, then a "large earthenware jar";[16] curiously, most modern versions of the story omit the detail of the corpse found alongside.[17] However, if we are searching for a "smoking gun" to prove that the Nag Hammadi codices were deposited

---

[10] Goodacre, "How Reliable Is the Story of the Nag Hammadi Discovery?" 305–6. According to Robinson ("Discovery," 214), the jar was 60 cm tall, with an opening of some 20 cm. He includes Ali's discovery of the jar on p. 212.

[11] Robinson reports that, although the jar was smashed, Mohamed Ali's brother, Khalifah Ali, kept the small bowl that he says sealed the mouth of the jar, affixed with bitumen (Robinson, "Discovery," 218). A photograph of it remains in Claremont's archives. It is a fairly standard piece of fourth- or fifth-century pottery of the sort that litters the Thebaid, fully intact, and we remain skeptical that the artifact in Khalifah's possession once sealed the jar.

[12] J. W. B. Barns, G. M. Browne, and J. C. Shelton, eds., *Nag Hammadi Codices: Greek and Coptic Papyri from the Cartonnage of the Covers* (Coptic Gnostic Library; NHS 16; Leiden: Brill, 1981), 1.

[13] Mohamed Ali and one brother: James M. Robinson, *The Nag Hammadi Library in English* (New York: Harper & Row, 1977), 21.

[14] See, for instance, the Border Television documentary produced in 1987 entitled *The Gnostics*, in which Gilles Quispel interviews Mohamed Ali, who reports that he was all alone when he found the jar, later returning alone to break it open, and finally returning with six others. "So I took it to the ministry over here and he told me, well we really don't need it." The antecedent of "it" is unclear. *The Gnostics* was written by Tobias Churton and produced and directed by Stephen Segaller. It was aired on UK's Channel 4 in November 1987. For a "transcript" of the interview (which, strangely, varies from the videotape version), see Tobias Churton, *The Gnostics* (New York: Barns & Noble, 1999), 9.

[15] Bart Ehrman (*Lost Christianities: The Battles for Scripture and the Faiths We Never Knew* [Oxford: Oxford University Press, 1995], 52) says that seven people were present, following Robinson ("Discovery," 213), which lists three brothers and four camel drivers. *The Facsimile Edition* (p. 5) lists eight camel drivers. Robinson ("From the Cliff to Cairo," 37) mentions that ten people were present (three brothers and seven camel drivers).

[16] Ehrman, *Lost Christianities*, 52.

[17] The skeleton is mentioned in Barns et al., *Nag Hammadi Codices*, 2, where it is dismissed as "modern."

with a burial, here indeed is one, with Mohamed Ali's insistence that the jar was next to a corpse with oddly elongated fingers and teeth.[18]

The "afterlife" story of the codices' discovery, trapped as they were in a sort of fugue state that was neither the protective dry soils of Egypt nor a proper museum conservatorship, points to a Western collector's mentality that perdured in the field of Egyptian archaeology. The reported incident of Mohamed Ali's mother tossing some of the ancient papyrus folios into the fire proved to Western minds that peasants—native Egyptians—could not be trusted with their own antiquities; only enlightened Europeans knew their true value. The story has a remarkable parallel in Constantin von Tischendorf's "rescuing" of the Codex Sinaiticus from St. Catherine's Monastery in Sinai in 1845. Tischendorf reports that the monks charged with caring for the precious manuscript tossed papyri leaves into the fire for warmth.[19] The message was clear: native Egyptians could not be trusted to care for their own antiquities, which required "rescuing" by scholars and collectors in the West. A similar colonialist meme emerges in the story circulated at the end of the nineteenth century concerning the Cureton manuscript, a fifth-century biblical manuscript discovered by Western travelers in a monastery in Nitria: apparently William Cureton found ancient papyrus folios being used as coverings for the monk's butter jars.[20] Concerning the Scottish explorer Agnes Lewis's 1892 discovery of a precious Syriac NT manuscript at St. Catherine's in Sinai, the rumor also emerged that it was (mis)used to cover butter dishes at the monastery, although Lewis herself notes that in fact the manuscript there was safely under lock and key.[21]

But let us return to the Nag Hammadi find-story. Its details—particularly salacious moments such as the blood vengeance scene and the ostensible tossing of the codices into the fire—dissemble; they deflect our attention from key questions: What were these texts doing together? Who could have put them there? What was the relationship of the books to the corpse lying nearby?[22] Egypt has a rich

---

[18] Robinson, "Discovery," 213. Robinson writes that Mohamed Ali's brother denied the existence of a corpse, which makes some sense: Mohamed Ali's insistence that the jar and corpse were found together on what looked like a "bed of charcoal" certainly looks like grave robbing. Either the assemblage had been sitting out in the open at the base of a cliff when the brothers found it, or they were exploring a burial cave. They could not have dug down to the level of a jar buried in rubble and also noted what material it (and the skeleton) were sitting on unless they carried out some fairly sophisticated archaeological investigation to reach the ground level of the jar.

[19] David C. Parker, *Codex Sinaiticus: The Story of the World's Oldest Bible* (London: British Library, 2010), 128–31.

[20] "The Current," 1, no. 1 (Dec. 22, 1883): 348.

[21] Adina Hoffman and Peter Cole, *Sacred Trash: The Lost and Found World of the Cairo Geniza* (New York: Schocken, 2011), 5.

[22] The corpse is a troubling detail, since tomb robbing has always been a serious problem in Egypt; see Pascal Vernus, *Affairs and Scandals in Ancient Egypt* (Ithaca, NY: Cornell University Press, 2003). In addition, the likelihood of the body being identified as Christian would have

history of books and corpses found together, and indeed all our other so-called Gnostic manuscripts—the Berlin Codex, the Askew Codex, and the Codex Tchacos—came from, or most probably came from, burial sites. Yet, for the Nag Hammadi codices, it is asserted that they were hidden for posterity by Pachomian monks, the result of Athanasius's *Festal Letter* of 367.[23] This story is repeated again and again, as if it were not scholarly conjecture but rather a "believed" fact of early Christian history: as if it were hand in hand with the Donatist controversy, for instance, with letters, trials, and creeds to go alongside it. There are no letters or trials for our "controversy," and so we must rely on what we can safely piece together from Pachomian monastic resources. The role of these monks and the presumed monastic *Sitz im Leben* for these texts deserve more attention.

II. The Nag Hammadi Codices and Monasticism: Rethinking the Links

Jean Doresse's initial suggestion that what had been discovered near Nag Hammadi was a secret library of Egyptian Sethian Gnostics was fairly quickly abandoned. Torgny Säve-Söderbergh suggested an intriguing alternative: perhaps the Nag Hammadi "library" constituted a heresiological compilation of primary "Gnostic" sources from which heresiologists could draw their ammunition.[24] By

---

caused additional problems in the environs of Nag Hammadi, where tensions between Copts and Muslims historically run high.

[23] See Robinson, *Nag Hammadi Library in English*, 19; idem, in *Facsimile Edition of the Nag Hammadi Codices*, 12:20; Meyer, *Gnostic Discoveries*, 30; Elaine Pagels, *The Gnostic Gospels* (New York: Random House, 1979), 120–21; Charles Hedrick, "Gnostic Proclivities in the Greek Life of Pachomius and the *Sitz im Leben* of the Nag Hammadi Library," *NovT* 22 (1980): 93. The notion of the texts buried "for posterity" trickles down into popular literature: see, e.g., Lewis Keizer, *The Kabbalistic Words of Jesus in the Gospel of Thomas* (Kindle Book; Amazon Digital Services, 2009), 17; Jeffrey J. Kripal, *The Serpent's Gift: Gnostic Reflections on the Study of Religion* (Chicago: University of Chicago Press, 2006), xi (Kripal also mentions the detail of the skeleton: "was the skeleton a monk?"); Louis A. Ruprecht Jr., *This Tragic Gospel: How John Corrupted the Heart of Christianity* (New York: Jossey-Bass, 2008), 132: Kenneth C. Davis, *Don't Know Much about the Bible: Everything You Need To Know about the Good Book But Never Learned* (San Francisco: Harper, 1999), 344.

[24] Torgny Säve-Söderbergh, "Gnostic and Canonical Gospel Traditions (with Special Reference to the Gospel of Thomas)," in *Le origini dello gnosticismo: Colloquio di Messina 13–18 Aprile 1966. Testi e discussioni* (ed. Ugo Bianchi; SHR 12; Leiden: Brill, 1970), 552–53; and, more developed, idem, "Holy Scriptures or Apologetic Documentations? The *Sitz im Leben* of the Nag Hammadi Library," in *Les Textes de Nag Hammadi: Colloque du Centre d'histoire des religions, Strasbourg, 23–25 octobre 1974* (ed. Jacques-É. Ménard; NHS 7; Leiden: Brill, 1975), 9–17. Here Säve-Söderbergh argues persuasively that Pachomians had no reason to house the Nag Hammadi documents based on what we know about Pachomian attitudes toward heresy; therefore, if in fact Pachomians kept them, they must have been kept out of circulation and thus "to study them in

far the most popular theory, however, is that the codices found their home in a monastic setting, perhaps that of Pachomian monks whose sense of the orthodox/heretical divide may have been less well entrenched than elsewhere in Egypt or than it came to be after the middle of the fourth century.[25] The Pachomian theory emerges as early as Robinson's 1975 *Preliminary Report* on the excavation, which in fact establishes it as self-evident truth:

> ... since it is hardly conceivable that there would have been more than one orthodox monastic organization simultaneously operating in the same place, we should be justified in concluding, *even without further evidence*, that the Nag Hammadi material came from a Pachomian monastery.[26]

The arguments for the Nag Hammadi codices having been housed in, if not created by and for, a Pachomian monastery are founded on two main circumstantial facts. The first is simply physical proximity of the find-spot to known Pachomian centers: Pabau was 8 km away; Tabennesi, 12 km; and Chenoboskion, 9 km.[27] At the same time, the physical environs of Hamra Dum and El Bousa and the tomb caves of the Gebel al-Tarif are better suited to the life of anchorites than coenobites.[28] They are also far closer; the grave site of the Sixth Dynasty Pharaoh Thauti is a mere 750 m

---

order to be able to refute them" (p. 12). If, however, the purpose of the Nag Hammadi codices were to serve as a compendium of heretical works, their arrangement in codices—including duplications of individual writings and organization across established sectarian lines—makes little sense; see Williams, *Rethinking Gnosticism*, 247.

[25] See, notably, F. Wisse, "The Nag Hammadi Library and the Heresiologists," *VC* 25 (1971): 220–21; see also his "Language Mysticism in the Nag Hammadi Texts and in Early Coptic Monasticism, I: Cryptography," *Enchoria* 9 (1979): 101–19. Compare James E. Goehring, "New Frontiers in Pachomian Studies," in idem, *Ascetics, Society, and the Desert: Studies in Early Egyptian Monasticism* (SAC; Harrisburg, Pa.: Trinity Press International, 1999), 185–86; and idem, "Some Reflections on the Nag Hammadi Codices and the Study of Early Egyptian Monasticism," *Meddelanden fran Collegium Patristicum Lundense* 25 (2011): 61–70. In a later article, Wisse appears to reverse his view somewhat, claiming that the books were in the hands of a variety of individuals: F. Wisse, "Gnosticism and Early Monasticism in Egypt," in *Gnosis: Festschrift für Hans Jonas* (ed. Barbara Aland; Göttingen: Vandenhoeck & Ruprecht, 1978), 438. A different, "closed stacks" theory is that the texts came from a Pachomian monastery where they were gathered for posterity but kept away from the monks; see Clemens Scholten, "Die Nag-Hammadi-Texte als Buchbesitz," *JAC* 31 (1988): 145–49.

[26] Robinson, *Preliminary Report on the Excavation*, 12–13 (emphasis added). See further Goehring, who, while admitting that the evidence for the Pachomian provenance of the Nag Hammadi codices is "purely circumstantial," nevertheless feels that the amount of evidence is mounting (*Ascetics, Society, and the Desert*, 180). For more on the excavation, see Bastiaan Van Elderen, "The Nag Hammadi Excavation," *BA* 42 (1979): 225–31.

[27] So W. C. van Unnik, *Evangelien aus dem Nilsand* (Frankfurt: Scheffler, 1960); Robinson's estimations in *The Nag Hammadi Library in English* (p. 21) are slightly different (Pbow, 5.3 km and Chenoboskion, 8.7 km).

[28] So Hedrick, "Gnostic Proclivities," 78.

from the jar's ostensible find-spot[29] and the tombs of two more Sixth Dynasty pharaohs, Pepi I and II (2332–2184 B.C.E.) perched just above the talus where the jar was ostensibly uncovered.[30] Indeed, anchorites came to inhabit these burial caves, which were still decorated with painted red crosses and inscribed lines from the psalms in Coptic.[31] They prayed in them; they also were buried in them.

The second piece of circumstantial evidence for a Pachomian provenance is the cartonnage of the codices. The first to have made this claim, papyrologist John W. B. Barns, died suddenly before all the cartonnage was fully analyzed. The team of papyrologists assigned to complete the task concluded, against Barns, that they could not think of a satisfactory single source for the wide range of documents contained in the cartonnage other than a "town rubbish heap."[32] The conclusion of the team was unequivocal: there is no evidence that the codices were created in a Pachomian monastery.[33] Despite all the evidence to the contrary, the connections between the Nag Hammadi codices and Pachomian monasticism are still virtually assumed by a wide range of scholars, no doubt because of the surety with which an early generation of Nag Hammadi scholars asserted them in the first place.

III. THE CURIOUS CASE OF THE DISHNA PAPERS

The Nag Hammadi codices were not the only set of late antique Egyptian writings discovered in Upper Egypt. The Dishna papers, also known as the Bodmer papyri after their purchase by the Swiss banker Martin Bodmer, appear to have been found in 1952 (seven years after the Nag Hammadi discovery) in the Thebaid 7.5 miles from Nag Hammadi and a mere 5 km from the major Pachomian site of Pbow.[34] Now dispersed from Barcelona to Oslo with a substantial number in

---

[29] *Facsimile Edition*, 15:5; see also Robinson, "Discovery," 212.
[30] Robinson, *Nag Hammadi Library in English*, 21.
[31] Ibid., 22.
[32] Barns et al., *Nag Hammadi Codices*, 11.
[33] Ibid., 2. See also Ewa Wipszycka, "The Nag Hammadi Library and the Monks: A Papyrologist's Point of View," *JJP* 30 (2000): 179–91, who similarly demolishes the Pachomian provenance theory. More agnostic is Goehring in his unpublished paper "Some Reflections on the Nag Hammadi Codices and the Study of Early Egyptian Monasticism"; he maintains the same cautious refusal to reject the Pachomian theory in virtually all his publications. See Goehring, "The Provenance of the Nag Hammadi Codices Once More," in *Ascetica, Gnostica, Liturgica, Orientalia: Papers Presented at the Thirteenth International Conference on Patristic Studies Held in Oxford 1999* (ed. M. F. Miles and E. J. Yarnold; StPatr 35; Leuven: Peeters, 2001), 234–53; and idem, "Monastic Diversity and Ideological Boundaries in Fourth-Century Christian Egypt," *JECS* 5 (1997): 61–84.

[34] The original circumstances of the find are hazy, since the seller of the hoard did not want to reveal his sources; thus, indeed, the story of the provenance of the Dishna papers seems to us to be as potentially suspicious as that of the Nag Hammadi codices. At any rate, they are curiously

Dublin at the Chester Beatty library, the original cache consisted of nine Greek papyrus rolls, twenty-two papyrus codices, and seven parchment documents, dating from approximately 100 to 699 C.E. The languages of the hoard show that its audience was multilingual, moving not just between Greek and Coptic but also between Greek and Latin. All told, we have in the Dishna papers an astonishing range of materials: nine classical texts, including parts of Homer plus its *scholia*, Menander, Achilles Tatius, Thucydides, and Cicero,[35] twelve papyri with writings from the Hebrew Bible; six with writings from the NT; three that include both. We also find a few apocryphal and pseudepigraphical texts, plus a great deal of liturgical and homiletic material.

Robinson, fascinated with the points of contact between the Nag Hammadi codices and the Dishna papers—both were found in jars in the same vicinity—hypothesized that the Dishna papers were buried for safekeeping following the imposition of Chalcedonian orthodoxy.[36] In effect, the case of the Dishna papers appeared to raise the likelihood that Pachomian monks, around 387 C.E., had engaged in a dramatic purge of their libraries, at the same time ridding themselves of their clearly heretical Nag Hammadi books.

And yet we should not make the mistake of assuming that the two book caches had the same audiences or were deposited for the same reason. Regardless of whether the Dishna papers were from the first Pachomian library at Pbow, they are far different from the Nag Hammadi codices in content. For example, the Sahidic Coptic Crosby-Shøyen Codex (ca. 250 C.E.) consists of fifty-two leaves written in a large bold Coptic uncial and contains three biblical texts (Jonah, 2 Macc 5:27–7:41, 1 Peter) plus two other texts for liturgical use: Melito of Sardis's *Peri Pascha* and an unidentified paschal sermon.[37] Another codex, now disassembled and scattered to various modern libraries, once contained the *Nativity of Mary*, apocryphal correspondence between Paul and the Corinthians, the eleventh *Ode of Solomon*, Jude, Melito's *Homily on the Passion*, a fragment of a liturgical hymn, the *Apology of Phileas*, Pss 33:2–34:16 from the LXX, and 1–2 Peter.[38] The Dishna papers and the

---

parallel. Furthermore, both accounts trace back to the research of Robinson. On the Dishna find, see James M. Robinson, *The Pachomian Monastic Library at the Chester Beatty Library and the Bibliothèque Bodmer* (Institute for Antiquity and Christianity Occasional Papers 19; Claremont, CA: Institute for Antiquity and Christianity, 1990).

[35] On Dishna's classical sources, see Harry Y. Gamble, *Books and Readers in the Early Church: A History of Early Christian Texts* (New Haven: Yale University Press, 1995), 173; Juan Gil, *Hadrianvs: P. Monts. Roca III*, 29 (Orientalia Montserratensia; Montserrat: Publicacions de l'Abadia de Montserrat y CSIC, 2010).

[36] Robinson, *Pachomian Monastic Library*, 28.

[37] R. Pintaudi, "Proprietà imperiali e tasse in un papiro della Collezione Schoyen," *ZPE* 130 (2000): 197–200; James E. Goehring, *The Crosby-Schøyen Codex MS 193 in the Schøyen Collection* (CSCO 521, Subsidia 85; Louvain: Peeters, 1990).

[38] Tommy Wasserman, "Papyrus 72 and the *Bodmer Miscellaneous Codex*," *NTS* 51 (2005): 140.

Nag Hammadi codices share no common texts. We will return presently to the significance of this point.

The assignation of a Pachomian provenance to the Nag Hammadi collection lies in part with its similarity to the Dishna papers. Yet this argument is largely circumstantial, based on (1) the physical proximity of the Dishna papers to the Nag Hammadi codices, on the one hand, and of both to Pbow, on the other; and (2) the circumstances of their deposition.[39] Papyrologists have argued, however, that the Dishna papers were apparently hidden in a jar during the Arabic conquest—long after Athanasius's *Festal Letter*. But we can also note some significant differences in the contents of the two collections. There are no overlaps across the collections; thus even the canons of apocryphal or pseudepigraphic writings on which the two sets of scribes drew appear to have been significantly different, with the Dishna collection being much closer to what we might tentatively call a "standard" list of apocrypha set apart from canonical writings but nevertheless in wide circulation. To put this differently, there are among the Dishna papers no so-called Gnostic writings. This is indeed remarkable, if one considers that a few of the Nag Hammadi writings do in fact appear in other ancient codices. The *Apocryphon of John*, in different recensions, can be found in Codices II, III, and IV but is also in the Berlin Codex (BG 8502). The *Sophia of Jesus Christ* is in the Berlin Codex as well as in Codex III; we also have this text in a complete Greek copy from Oxyrhynchus, *P.Oxy.* 8.1081.[40] The *Gospel of Thomas* of Codex II also appears in Greek fragments discovered at Oxyrhynchus. If, then, the Dishna hoard is a highly eclectic collection from a Pachomian library, the fact that it shares not a single tractate with the Nag Hammadi is curious. Conversely, the Nag Hammadi codices contain not a single fragment of Scripture or any monastic correspondence. In short, while the two collections appear to have shared a general provenance (and this is speculative rather than factual), this is all that the two collections share, and this ultimately reveals little about whether the Nag Hammadi library was truly Pachomian.

It should be said, finally, that not all scholars accept the Pachomian provenance of the Dishna papers. The case against it includes the high number of documentary and school texts preserved, including exercises in grammar, lexicography, and mathematics in three different languages including several dialects of Coptic.[41] There is also a Greek–Latin lexicon for deciphering Paul's letters.[42] Raffaella Cribiore argues that the collection derived from a "Christian school of advanced learning,"[43]

---

[39] The case for the equation of the two is made by Goehring, "Monastic Diversity and Ideological Boundaries," 81–82.

[40] Cornelia Römer, "Manichaeism and Gnosticism in the Papyri." in *The Oxford Handbook of Papyrology* (ed. Roger S. Bagnall; Oxford: Oxford University Press, 2009), 631.

[41] Gil, *Hadrianvs*, 29.

[42] Wasserman, "Papyrus 72," 139.

[43] Cribiore, *Gymnastics of the Mind: Greek Education in Hellenistic and Roman Egypt* (Princeton: Princeton University Press, 2001), 200 and n. 74. See, too, A. Blanchard, "Sur le milieu

perhaps even as examples of *paideia*, which experienced a revival in the second century and remained popular among elites until the sixth century.

In summary, the evidence for a Pachomian provenance for the Nag Hammadi codices is entirely lacking, as is any solid basis for their monastic setting. We are forced to concur with Stephen Emmel, who some time ago commented, "I—like many others—am not convinced that the Nag Hammadi Codices, as particular books, as artifacts, are the direct products of a monastic milieu."[44] Emmel follows the conclusions of Alexandr L. Khosroyev, who, through an intensive study of linguistic and codicological data, demolished the "Pachomian monastic milieu" theory in a 1995 volume that has not had the impact that it should have.[45]

IV. Athanasius and the Burying of Books: Dispelling a Myth

The theory that the Nag Hammadi codices found their way out of their Pachomian setting in the wake of Athanasius's thirty-ninth *Festal Letter* (367 C.E.) has also recently been revealed to be unfounded. As David Brakke has convincingly argued, the heretical writings with which Athanasius was concerned were not "Gnostic" but Arian and Meletian.[46] The idea that the letter in any way effected the removal of the Nag Hammadi codices from a Pachomian library is merely scholarly conjecture too often taken as fact. If we admit that the Pachomian, or even generally monastic, context for the codices is entirely absent, then Athanasius's letter becomes irrelevant. We are still left with a final *Sitz im Leben* for which we do have clear evidence: the tomb sites of the Gebel al-Tarif. If the codices were not likely to have

---

d'origine du papyrus Bodmer de Ménandre," *ChrEg* 66 (1991): 211–20; J.-L. Fournet, "Une éthiopée de Caïn dans le codex des Visions de la Fondation Bodmer," *ZPE* 92 (1992): 253–66; R. Kasser, "Status quaestionis 1988 sulla presunta origine dei cosidetti Papiri Bodmer," *Aegyptus* 68 (1988): 191–94. Some would retort that obviously not all Pachomians were unlettered; see Elizabeth Ann Clark, *Reading Renunciation: Asceticism and Scripture in Early Christianity* (Princeton: Princeton University Press, 1999), 54; it is certainly possible that monks took their book collections with them into the monastery.

[44] Emmel, "The Coptic Gnostic Texts as Witnesses to the Production and Transmission of Gnostic (and Other) Traditions," in *Das Thomasevangelium: Entstehung, Rezeption, Theologie* (ed. Jörg Frey, Enno Edzard Popkes, and Jens Schröter; BZNW 157; Berlin: de Gruyter, 2008), 36.

[45] Khosroyev, *Die Bibliothek von Nag Hammadi: Einige Probleme des Christentums in Ägypten während der ersten Jahrhunderte* (Arbeiten zum spätantiken und koptischen Ägypten 7; Altenberge: Oros, 1995), esp. ch. 4, "Zur Frage nach dem vermutlichen Besitzer der Bibliothek." See, similarly, idem, "Bemerkungen über die vermutlichen Besitzer der Nag-Hammadi-Texte," in *Divitiae Aegypti: Koptologische und verwandte Studien zu Ehren von Martin Krause* (ed. Cäcilia Fluck et al.; Wiesbaden: Reichert, 1995), 200–205.

[46] Brakke, "Canon Formation and Social Conflict in Fourth-Century Egypt: Athanasius of Alexandria's Thirty-Ninth Festal Letter," *HTR* 87 (1994): 395–419.

been buried by Pachomian monks for safekeeping, it is safe to say that the site of Gebel al-Tarif does not represent an extension of Pachomian monastic life and that Athanasius's letter was meant to address an entirely different phenomenon.

Brakke has examined the social contexts in which Athanasius wrote the thirty-ninth *Festal Letter*, pointing out that "teachers and Meletians" posed the greatest threat to Athanasius's authority as bishop and therefore were the target of many of his letters.[47] Brakke points out that "study circles," an important feature of Alexandrian life since arguably the second century B.C.E., represented the source of fundamental anxieties confronted by early Christian bishops like Athanasius because to follow a charismatic teacher both undermined the emerging ecclesiastical authority and was dangerously like following Christ—or, the wrong Christ.[48] Indeed, Athanasius's thirty-ninth *Letter* is tremendously important to the formation of early Christianity for all of the reasons Brakke outlines, but if we are to read this letter as a warning against so-called heretics who read apocryphal literature (as the narrative of the fate of the Nag Hammadi codices is interpreted), the attack is rather innocuous. In fact, a close reading of the letter reveals an almost bureaucratic tone, as if Athanasius is sighing in the subtext, saying: "Must we go over this?"

Compare, for instance, Athanasius's list of canonical texts in the thirty-ninth letter to *Letter 40, To Adelphius*, where he fights tooth and nail against Arianism and for his own orthodox Christology: "Where has this evil of theirs erupted from?" and "We do not worship a creature. Never!"[49] These Arian "heretics" he calls "enemies of Christ ... urged on by their father the devil."[50] This is the standard polemic for which Athanasius is known and that is markedly missing in *Letter* 39. In this letter, those who do not read the Scriptures according to the list are merely called "heretics and ... simple folk."[51] Here our argument is not much different from Brakke's. Athanasius was concerned with Arianism and the threats that such a belief posed to both his view of Christology and his right to authority. And regardless of whether the community for which the *Letter* was written accepted this authority, it is safe to say that those who did not—the Arians, Meletians, and other unnamed "heretics"—paid little attention to a list of canonical books.

Yet this is not the final point of our argument. We have attempted to remove the Nag Hammadi codices from a Pachomian monastic origin and place them in the hands of an Egyptian who commissioned them for private use. Once these texts are removed from the ecclesiastical struggles against "heresy," they belong to a little explored history of fourth-century Egypt. For even if Athanasius's letter is meant to define a canon, what can be said of the Nag Hammadi codices if we venture to

---

[47] Ibid., 398.
[48] Ibid., 398–99.
[49] Khaled Anatolios, *Athanasius* (Early Church Fathers; New York: Routledge, 2004), 236.
[50] Ibid., 236.
[51] David Brakke, *Athanasius and the Politics of Asceticism* (Oxford Early Christian Studies; Oxford: Oxford University Press, 1995), 330.

say that they were *not* being read in a monastic setting? Like the Theban Magical Library, they exist beyond the reach of the episcopate. One of the purposes of this article is to suggest, or recall, that fourth-century Egypt was not a landscape dominated by ecclesiastical struggles. While such conflicts certainly played a major role in the formation of Egyptian Christianity, we argue that a significant portion of the Egyptian population was not concerned with these struggles. The reason they dominate the literature of fourth-century Egypt is because voices such as that of Athanasius are dynamic ones that live on in the orthodox world. So dynamic is his voice, in fact, that we often forget that he was banished five times during his career, his ecclesiastical authority called into question by many in spite of his victory over Arian theology. And so, while Athanasius remains a posthumous authority, his writings only reflect the politics of fourth-century Egyptian Christianity in proportion to his turbulent career. The archaeological record, not surprisingly, does not reveal the strict oppressiveness that scholars read into the literature of the era but instead reveals a fruitful desert of newly commissioned books of all natures: pagan, Christian, monastic, liturgical, classical, and magical.

V. Books and Tombs

The Gebel el-Tarif, where the Nag Hammadi codices were discovered, was not a monastic site; it was (and had been for millennia) a vast ancient burial ground. In the fourth century, numerous caves and rock-cut tombs were still in use for burials. Twenty meters south of the Nag Hammadi find-spot, in Cave T1, excavators found bones and pottery remains; in T114, eight hundred meters away, excavators found a burial shroud that yielded a ^{14}C date of the fifth century C.E.[52] Robinson himself concludes, "at least the talus was used as a burial site at the time in question."[53] Even Doresse's earlier, unelaborated account of the find-spot places it in a cemetery, although in that case the cemetery was not a series of caves but a flatter plain.[54] Although Doresse believed the cemetery to have been pagan and thus earlier than the codices, there is some evidence that it was still in use by late antique Christians.

The concrete link between the Nag Hammadi codices and late antique graves has largely, if mystifyingly, been replaced by the unfounded assumption that monks intentionally *hid* the books for posterity. Is it not more likely that someone put them in a grave as a funerary deposit? One scholar to have proposed the tomb theory was the esteemed Coptologist Martin Krause, who, in an article from 1978, commented,

---

[52] Robinson, "Discovery," 213.
[53] Ibid.
[54] Doresse, *Secret Books*, 58.

Das Auffinden der Bibliothek in einem Grabe spricht für eine, und zwar wohl reiche, Einzelperson als Besitzer.... Es ist ein auch in christlicher Zeit noch nachweisbarer altägyptischer Brauch, dem Toten heilige Bücher ins Grab beizugeben.[55]

Krause maintained—and we present a similar thesis here—that a private individual with eclectic and esoteric interests commissioned the collection, which was buried with him at the time of his death.[56]

If indeed the jar containing the Nag Hammadi codices came from a burial cave rather than a ruinated monastic library, it would be in good company. The Berlin Codex, which contains the *Gospel of Mary*, the *Apocryphon of John*, the *Sophia of Jesus Christ*, and the *Acts of Peter*, appeared on the antiquities market in 1896. Although the dealer claimed that the book had been found in a wall niche, the text's first editor, Carl Schmidt, assumed it had been taken from one of Akhmim's cemeteries.[57] The Codex Tchacos, which contains (among other so-called Gnostic texts) the *Gospel of Judas*, was discovered near El-Minya, in a family tomb by Gebel Qarara. At this late antique Christian burial site, the Codex Tchacos was only one of the books found in a limestone box that tomb robbers unearthed; the three others do not survive intact, having been divided up by antiquities dealers. However, we know that one of these was a fourth- or fifth-century papyrus codex containing a Greek version of Exodus.[58] The second, dating from the same period, was a Coptic translation of Paul's letters; the third, interestingly, was a Greek mathematical text called the Metrodological Tractate.[59] "If nothing else," comments April DeConick, their burial together

> points to their privileged place in the life of an early Christian living in ancient Egypt, a Christian who seems to have had esoteric leanings. This ancient person buried with these books had no difficulty during his or her lifetime studying canonical favorites like Paul and Exodus alongside the Gnostic *Gospel of Judas*. As for the mathematical treatise, its burial along with these others should not be that surprising given that both the Hermetics and Gnostics studied mathematical theorems in order to understand and map their universe.[60]

---

[55] Krause, "Die Texte von Nag Hammadi" in Aland, *Gnosis: Festschrift für Hans Jonas*, 243. Armand Veilleux cautiously seconds the idea ("Monasticism and Gnosis in Egypt," in *The Roots of Egyptian Christianity* [ed. Birger A. Pearson and James E. Goehring; SAC; Philadelphia: Fortress, 1986], 278–83.

[56] Krause, "Die Texte von Nag Hammadi," 242–43.

[57] Schmidt, *Die alten Petrusakten im Zusammenhang der apokryphen Apostelliteratur nebst einem neuentdeckten Fragment untersucht* (TU n.F. 9/1; Leipzig: Hinrichs, 1903), 2.

[58] The Greek papyrus now exists in pieces in private collections at the Schøyen Collection, Yale's Beinecke Library, and Ashland Theological Seminary.

[59] Heavily illustrated, the codex was bisected, with half being purchased by Lloyd Cotsen and donated to Princeton University, and half to an anonymous private collector.

[60] DeConick, *The Thirteenth Apostle: What the Gospel of Judas Really Says* (New York: Continuum, 2009), 64–65.

Thus, in the history of late antique Egyptian books, we have some intriguing commonalities between the Nag Hammadi codices and the El-Minya find: a Christian tomb site, a durable container, and a cache of books. In the case of the El-Minya find, we are clearly dealing with a private commission or collection of books, not a monastic library.

There are other cases of manuscripts found in burial sites in late antique Egypt. The parchment Codex Panopolitanus, which contained a full Greek version of *1 Enoch*'s Book of the Watchers, fragments of an *Apocalypse of Peter*, and the *Gospel of Peter*, was excavated by a French archaeological team in the winter of 1886–87; it was found in an eighth-century Christian grave in Akhmim.[61] Interestingly, as in the case of the Codex Tchacos, the Codex Panopolitanus was found along with a mathematical treatise.[62] Among non-Christian texts, the fourth-century Theban Magical Library—composed of both scrolls and codices—was, like the Nag Hammadi codices, discovered by *fellaheen* under suspicious circumstances, almost certainly tomb robbing in the Thebaid.[63]

Our hypothesis here that the Nag Hammadi codices were intentionally deposited in a grave or graves rather than buried for "posterity"—the latter practice, in contrast to the former, not attested in Egypt—raises an inevitable question: what was the rationale for burying a book in a grave? Put simply, as a grave good, a book was a luxury item that marked the prestige of the grave owner.[64] It is helpful, perhaps, to think (as Emmel does) of the codices as *artifacts* rather than as books, where the primary importance is the social meaning of the object rather than its contents.[65] In this way of thinking, there is no need to connect the content of a book with the practice of depositing it with a corpse. This explains why a mathematical book would be deposited in a grave with the Codex Tchacos and the Codex Panopolitanus; it also helps us to make sense of other book finds from Egyptian graves. For example, W. M. Flinders Petrie reported having found a copy of the second book of the *Iliad*, in Greek, on a papyrus roll tucked under the head of an elite

---

[61] Isaac H. Hall, "The Newly Discovered Apocryphal Gospel of Peter," *Biblical World* 1, no. 2 (1893): 88.

[62] George W. E. Nickelsburg, "Two Enochic Manuscripts: Unstudied Evidence for Egyptian Christianity," in *Of Scribes and Scrolls: Studies on the Hebrew Bible, Intertestamental Judaism, and Christian Origins presented to John Strugnell* (ed. Harold W. Attridge, John J. Collins, and Thomas H. Tobin; College Theology Society Resources in Religion 5; Lanham, MD: University Press of America, 1990), 251–60, esp. 254.

[63] For more on the Theban Magical Library, see Jacco Dieleman, *Priests, Tongues, and Rites: The London-Leiden Magical Manuscripts and Translation in Egyptian Ritual* (Religions in the Graeco-Roman World 153; Leiden: Brill, 2005); and also Roger Bagnall, *Early Christian Books in Egypt* (Princeton: Princeton University Press, 2009). Both Dieleman and Bagnall note the interesting parallels between the Theban Magical Library and the Nag Hammadi codices.

[64] AnneMarie Luijendijk, "Sacred Scriptures as Trash: Biblical Papyri from Oxyrhynchus," *VC* 64 (2010): 232 n. 50.

[65] Emmel, "Coptic Gnostic Texts," 32.

woman in a grave at Hawara in the Fayyum.[66] The papyrus dates to the fifth century C.E. and was both well copied and well preserved. The practice of placing the roll at the head of a corpse in a sense continued the Ptolemaic practice of placing brief "Documents for Breathing"—the Greco-Egyptian form of earlier "Books of the Dead" written in Demotic, hieratic, and Greek—at the top of a mummy's head at burial.[67]

However, because of Egypt's rich history of funerary texts, there remains the possibility that there was intended to be a connection between individual books' contents and their function as grave deposits. The speculation that archaeologists had discovered a Christian "Book of the Dead" had already been made in the case of Codex Panopolitanus, with its apocalyptic, "heavenly journey" writings.[68] The Nag Hammadi codices are particularly interesting to consider from this perspective, for a few reasons. First, they are an apparently deliberate collection of documents that are overwhelmingly concerned with cosmology and eschatology. They contain no "secular" writings, no Scripture, no correspondence, and precious little homiletical, ethical, or paraenetic material, with the exception of (for example) the *Gospel of Truth* in Codex I and what remains (very little) of the *Interpretation of Knowledge* in Codex XI. Still, even these works are very far in tone and spirit from, let us say, Melito's sermons and homilies, which we find in papyrus copies from late antique Egypt. Therefore, the Nag Hammadi collection as a whole is far from a random one, but seems to specialize in obscure cosmologically and eschatologically focused treatises with a liturgical dimension.[69]

---

[66] Petrie, *Hawara, Biahmu, and Arsinoe with Thirty Plates* (London: Field & Tuer, 1889), 24–28.

[67] Werner Forman and Steven Quirke, *Hieroglyphs and the Afterlife in Ancient Egypt* (Norman: University of Oklahoma Press, 1996). These documents Quirke likens to "passports" held by the deceased to give them free access into the next world; they contained a sort of declaration by Thoth that the traveler was to be allowed to pass through the stomach of Nut through the circuit of the otherworld. A standard line went, "O guardians of the Underworld, let me come and go." The last secure date for a "Document for Breathing" included with a burial is late first to early second century C.E., from the family grave of Soter, a governor of Thebes.

[68] For the site report, see Klaus P. Kuhlmann, *Materialien zur Archäologie und Geschichte des Raumes von Achmim* (Sonderschrift, Deutsches Archäologisches Institut, Abteilung Kairo 11; Mainz: von Zabern, 1983), 53, 62. The codex was published by U. Bouriant, "Fragments grecs de Livre d'Enoch," in *Mémoires publiés par les membres de la Mission archéologique française au Caire* 9.1 (Paris: Leroux, 1892), 91–147, esp. 93–94. For additional manuscript information, plates, and the *editio princeps* of both the *Gospel of Peter* and the *Apocalypse of Peter*, see A. Lods, "L'evangile et L'apocalypse de Pierre: Le texte grec du livre d'Énoch," in *Mémoires publiés par les membres de la Mission archéologique française au Caire* 9.3 (Paris: Leroux, 1893), 217–35 and plates 1–34. For the Christian "Book of the Dead" claim, see Nickelsburg, "Two Enochic Manuscripts," 254.

[69] Some may argue that the existence of the *Apocryphon of John* in four different copies argues against the obscurity of that text at least; the *Gospel of Thomas* is also present in multiple versions. See, however, the observations of Larry Hurtado, "The Greek Fragments of the *Gospel of Thomas* as Artefacts: Papyrological Observations on Papyrus Oxyrhynchus 1, Papyrus

VI. A New Context: Exploring the Possibilities

Who, in late antique Egypt, might have been particularly interested in commissioning an eschatologically oriented collection of texts to deposit in a burial? There exists a range of possible suspects, from the Melitians to the class of monks Jerome called the *remnuoth* (*Ep.* 22.34).[70] Robinson has speculated that perhaps the codices belonged to a monk or monks who began in the Pachomian monastery but then moved out to an eremitic life.[71] In support of this theory, Robinson cites the case of Hierakas of Leontopolis, a fourth-century monk of the Delta who was both a scribe and a biblical exegete. He was also a radical encratite—so radical, in fact, that he was declared a heretic for his views.[72] The example of Hierakas, so far from the Thebaid, reminds us only that the lines between coenobitic monks, anchorites, and private citizens were fluid in the fourth century.

Our intuition is that the Nag Hammadi codices belonged to private (i.e., nonmonastic) individuals who commissioned them for their own purposes. Whether the scriptoria that composed them were monastic or not we cannot tell, but private scriptoria certainly existed in the fourth century.[73] The "private individual" model requires that we break with our tendency to interpret the landscape of late antique Egypt as purely populated by monks, a perception largely influenced by Derwas J. Chitty's highly influential *The Desert a City*.[74] These individuals may or may not have been Christians; if it was correct in any sense to call them "Gnostic," they certainly did not ascribe to any sectarian Gnostic school.[75]

Oxyrhynchus 654 and Papyrus Oxyrhynchus 655," in Frey et al., *Das Thomasevangelium*, 23, on the total number of copies of Christian texts from late ancient Egypt.

[70] Veilleux first suggested the Nag Hammadi documents might have held special appeal for Melitians ("Monasticism and Gnosis in Egypt," 10). See also Brakke, "Canon Formation," 249: "while the nature of the apocryphal books accepted and used by the Melitians seems different from the texts found in the Nag Hammadi codices, the undecided nature of the canon evidenced in the debate suggests a period in which one can well imagine individual ascetics and ascetic groups involved in the sort of textual exploration that led to an interest in such texts."

[71] Robinson suggests this (*Nag Hammadi Library in English*, 18).

[72] Robinson, *Nag Hammadi Library in English*, 18; Wisse, "Gnosticism and Early Monasticism," 438–40.

[73] Although Pachomians had scriptoria and copied texts, the evidence is later than the fourth century. There is no evidence for fourth-century Pachomian scriptoria. For the earliest references, see Palladius, *Lausiac History* 32.12 (where working in the *kalligreiphon* is one form of Pachomian monastic labor) and John Cassian, *Institutes* 4.12 (which details how a Pachomian monk must stop writing immediately if called by a superior). We thank David Brakke for the references.

[74] Chitty, *The Desert a City: An Introduction to the Study of Egyptian and Palestinian Monasticism under the Christian Empire* (1966; repr., Crestwood, NY: St. Vladimir's Seminary Press, 1995).

[75] See the loosely affiliated Christian fellowships discussed by E. Wipszycka, "Les confréries

That the Nag Hammadi codices were commissioned by private individuals was the hypothesis of Krause, but also of Khosroyev, who systematically and painstakingly demolished the theory of Pachomian provenance and argued instead that the codices had been commissioned by urban intellectuals among whom they were copied and exchanged.[76] These intellectuals operated outside the reach of the developing orthodox Christianity and represented the religious complexity of their day, like their contemporary Zosimus of Panopolis or those who read and circulated the Theban Magical Papyri. Indeed, the concept of *paideia* once again comes to mind. If elite education meant to instruct even Christian theologians, like Basil the Great, in the reading of classical Greek mythology, it is not difficult to suggest that some Egyptian elites were interested in the cosmological and eschatological writings of the Neoplatonic era, during which *paideia* experienced a revival, thus necessarily including the so-called Gnostic writings of the second century in their learning in the fourth century.

Emmel has also cautiously agreed with Khosroyev's analysis, although he sees no reason to locate the Nag Hammadi codices in Egypt's major urban centers as products of life in the city. He posits, instead,

> bilingual "Hellenized" Egyptians who grew up and remained in the largely Greek-speaking metropoleis of the Nile Valley, where they were in communication with like-minded members of the same "class" or "group" who shared an interest in this sort of esoteric and in some sense also erudite literature."[77]

In a different article, Emmel suggests that to understand the codices in their context, we need to "reconstruct the reading experience of whoever owned each of the Codices," taking into full consideration the culture of Upper Egypt from the third to the eighth centuries and developing a "theory of Coptic reading and Coptic readers."[78] But Emmel raises a vital question: why are the Nag Hammadi Codices in Coptic (and often poor Coptic, at that)? Rejecting the idea that they could have been translated from Greek to Coptic for the benefit of those who could not read Greek (the tractates are unintelligible without an advanced knowledge of Greek language and culture), he proposes an intriguing hypothesis:

> I think we have to do with the products of a kind of Egypt-wide network (more or less informal) of educated, primarily Greek-speaking ... philosophically and esoteric-mystically like-minded people, for whom Egypt represented (even if

---

dans la vie religieuse de l'Égypte chrétienne," in *Proceedings of the Twelfth International Congress of Papyrology* (Toronto: A. M. Hakkert, 1970), 511–25.

[76] This is the central argument of Khosroyev, *Die Bibliothek von Nag Hammadi*.

[77] Emmel, "Coptic Gnostic Texts," 36.

[78] Emmel, "Religious Tradition, Textual Transmission, and the Nag Hammadi Codices," in *The Nag Hammadi Library after Fifty Years: Proceedings of the 1995 Society of Biblical Literature Commemoration* (ed. John D. Turner and Anne McGuire; Nag Hammadi and Manichaean Studies 44; Leiden: Brill, 1997), 34–43.

only somewhat vaguely) a tradition of wisdom and knowledge to be revered and perpetuated ... it is easy to imagine a kind of rush to create a new "esoteric-mystical Egyptian wisdom literature"—being "Egyptian" above all by virtue of being in Coptic rather than in Greek (even if the Coptic was sometimes barely comprehensible.[79]

If Emmel is right, then it seems that Egyptian, rather than Greek, would be the "natural" language for these new Christian Books of the Dead. Even though the content of the writings betrayed Greek thought, the language connected those who commissioned such volumes with an archaic practice of leaving guides for the afterlife in Egyptian graves. In fact, seen in this light, the sometimes poor Coptic, the mishmash of writings (Valentinian and Sethian; Christian and non-Christian), and the theological inconsistencies that vex modern scholars were likely to have been of no concern whatsoever to a fourth-century elite who planned out in advance a "real, Egyptian" burial.

It is worth asking, in conclusion, what difference it makes if the Nag Hammadi find-story was, indeed, a scholarly fiction. To begin, we might do well to recognize its many colonialist, orientalizing elements as relics of a bygone era in Egyptian archaeology. The narrative is a fine one for classroom telling, but it works less and less effectively as we become more sensitized to our own Western prejudices and assumptions. Egyptian peasants do not fear *jinni* in bottles or rip out each other's hearts and eat them on the spot—and shame on us for believing, even for a moment, that they do.

To those whose work has been in uncovering the second-century contexts of the various tractates contained in the Nag Hammadi codices, it may not matter at all whether the books derived from a grave or were secreted away by monks. On the other hand, the attention to the second-century, posited Greek "originals" of these writings has steered us down a path that virtually ignores the vital context of the writings in the only form in which they have survived, as if this real, fourth-century setting means nothing and only our reconstructed and imagined Greek "originals" have anything to teach us about the development of Christianity. To be suspicious of the find-story and the assumed Pachomian provenance is to allow these late antique codices to belong to a uniquely Egyptian archaeological context, placing them in a funerary tradition that began in the dynastic era and endured, arguably, well into the Muslim era. To think of the Nag Hammadi codices as fourth-century artifacts that may have been intentionally created, in some instances, as grave goods radically changes the way we think about late antique Egyptian Christianity, where studies have been divided between those who study monasticism and those who study documentary papyri. Yet what of the vibrant cultural life of the late antique Roman era, the systems of learning that fostered an interest in these second-century heritages, be they pagan or Christian, Roman or Egyptian? If we

---

[79] Emmel, "Coptic Gnostic Texts," 48.

group the Nag Hammadi codices with other similar products—namely, the Tchacos, Bruce, and Askew codices—we have a rather large corpus of late antique Egyptian books that stand in a class of their own and demand from us not only contextualization but also a deeper understanding of the diversity of the fourth-century Roman world.

Reevaluating the true provenance of the Nag Hammadi codices also means that we need to change the way we think about so-called Gnostic texts as being theologically marginal writings that really only had one century of good use before they became dangerous curiosities that some theologically suspect monks felt compelled to hide. Contextualizing the Nag Hammadi codices in the grave of a private citizen removes them from the background drama of fourth-century ecclesiastical politics. It has been difficult for scholars of Gnosticism to avoid the temptation to connect the Nag Hammadi codices with dominant figures such as Athanasius or movements such as Pachomian monasticism; however, such a connection situates our field of study conveniently within the narrative that Athanasius himself propagated: a community of unified Christians, loyal to their bishops, all together fighting groups of renegade monks and teachers who commission heretical texts and then, like demons, disappear into the night. Could there be any other way to understand the landscape of late antique Egypt? Yes, of course.

Our job has been to draw threads of connection, however tenuous, between one historical figure or moment and another. But if we sever these silken threads and admit to what we simply do not know about late antique Egypt, the true reason that someone saw fit painstakingly to copy the Nag Hammadi codices and carefully to preserve them becomes a compelling mystery we might begin to consider with a fresh set of eyes.

Introductory Texts

The Bible
An Introduction
Second Edition, with Course Pack
JERRY L. SUMNEY

Neither polemical nor apologetic, Sumney presents clear answers to the most basic questions about the Bible's content, history, and methods of understanding. Course Pack includes *A Study Companion to the Bible*.

9781451483635 pbk
Textbook 464 pp
Study Companion 160 pp
$59 for both

A Short Introduction to the Hebrew Bible
Second edition
JOHN J. COLLINS

A widely adopted marvel of conciseness and erudition, now with even more student-friendly features, including charts, maps, photographs, chapter summaries, illuminating vignettes, and bibliographies.

9781451472943
336 pp pbk $45.00

Introduction to the Hebrew Bible
Second Edition, with Course Pack
JOHN J. COLLINS

A reliable, highly praised text presenting the current state of historical, archaeological, and literary understanding of the biblical text, and engaging the student in questions of significance and interpretation for the contemporary world. Course Pack includes *A Study Companion*.

9781451483642 pbk
Textbook 640 pp
Study Companion 160 pp
$75 for both

Available wherever books are sold or
800-328-4648
fortresspress.com

Introducing the
JBL Forum,
an Occasional Exchange

As the flagship journal of the Society of Biblical Literature, *JBL* aims to reflect the breadth and depth of our field. For this reason, it has a broad scope ranging from the issues and approaches that have been staples for many decades to those that continue to emerge as a result of growing international participation in the SBL as well as encounters with other disciplines and with new theoretical perspectives. In this issue, *JBL* introduces an occasional series that will highlight approaches, points of view, and even definitions of "biblical scholarship" that may be outside the usual purview of many of our readers. The format may vary from time to time but will always include an exchange of ideas on the matter at hand. SBL members are invited to join in the discussion on our website: http://www.sbl-site.org/publications/journals_jbl_Login.aspx.

With this series, we hope not only to inform our readers but, more important, to spark conversation and thereby to enhance the journal's contribution to the primary mission of the SBL: to foster biblical scholarship.

I welcome your thoughts and comments, as well as suggestions for future forum topics. Just send them along to me at jbleditor@gmail.com.

Adele Reinhartz
General Editor, *Journal of Biblical Literature*

Mind the Gap: Modern and Postmodern in Biblical Studies

RONALD HENDEL
hendel@berkeley.edu
University of California, Berkeley, CA 94570

This article is a critical engagement with the theoretical entailments of postmodernism and the implications for a more sophisticated historical-critical method. Topics include the distinction between strong and weak versions of postmodernism, the conceptual and ethical problems of the strong version in biblical scholarship, and the relationship between the modern history of biblical studies and the Enlightenment project (in dialogue with recent postmodern scholarship). A rapprochement between a viable postmodernism and an enlightened modernism is desirable, despite entrenched ideologies and institutional constraints.

> Like any self-respecting logic, historical criticism has its contradictions.
> —Marc Bloch, *The Historian's Craft*

In recent years there have appeared two well-articulated invitations to biblical scholars to engage the issue of postmodernism in biblical studies. One is a *JBL* article by George Aichele, Peter Miscall, and Richard Walsh, "An Elephant in the Room: Historical-Critical and Postmodern Interpretations of the Bible,"[1] and the other a short monograph by Stephen D. Moore and Yvonne Sherwood, *The Invention of the Biblical Scholar: A Critical Manifesto*.[2] The former is an invitation to dialogue,[3] and the latter is an ambitious proposal for a "second wave" of theory-inflected biblical scholarship that will be more philosophically aware than the first. Both of these are thoughtful and in some ways courageous works and are worth serious deliberation by historical-critical biblical scholars.

My thanks to Steve Weitzman and double thanks to Yvonne Sherwood for astute comments on a previous draft, particularly where we cordially disagree.

[1] *JBL* 128 (2009): 383–404.
[2] Minneapolis: Fortress, 2011.
[3] See my preliminary response, "Talking Postmodernism," in *The Bible and Interpretation* (www.bibleinterp.com/opeds/hen358011.shtml).

I have already implicated myself in this discussion by criticizing the disparagement of reason by "some postmodernists,"[4] leading to some animadversions. For this reason, I feel obliged to enter into it more fully. As Aichele et al. aptly comment, these are "embattled camps" in the field of biblical studies, which tend to communicate mostly by mutual derision. In light of this dismal past, the opening of an open and irenic dialogue is entirely for the good.

I begin by exploring the diversity of postmodern theory and will argue for a distinction between strong and weak versions of postmodernism. By the strong version, I mean the position associated with the French masters of postmodernism (Michel Foucault, Jacques Derrida, and others), which develops the Nietzschean critique of rationality and humanism into a vigorous critique of all epistemological claims. The weak version accepts aspects of this critique but also maintains the practical reality of reason and human agency. The strong version is, I will argue, theoretically and practically untenable, whereas the weak version is justifiable and warranted. Moreover, the weak version is indistinguishable from an enlightened modernism. Second, I will argue that strong postmodernism in biblical studies poses an ethical problem regarding the relative values of truthfulness and social consequences. Third, I will address the history of biblical studies and its relationship to the Enlightenment project, in dialogue with Moore and Sherwood.

Through these steps I propose to "mind the gap" between modernism and postmodernism—I will be mindful of it, but I will also critique it.[5] I will argue (a) that this gap is an unstable and, in some respects, illusory binary opposition, and (b) that this perceived gap should be acknowledged, but also disrupted and reconfigured.

I. Postmodernism: Strong and Weak Versions

There are many conceptual problems in postmodern theory and practice, both within and without biblical studies. First, there is a problem of definition; many who claim to practice postmodernism do not clarify how they understand this term. The absence of definitions is not entirely surprising, given that postmodernism as such eschews fixed essences and meanings. Postmodernism identifies itself as something other than, or as a metacriticism of, modernist discourse, which it often characterizes as mired in the illusions of metaphysics and other "logocentric" disorders. Prominent postmodernists—including Derrida, Foucault, Jacques Lacan, and, in America, Judith Butler—tend to disavow the term "postmodernism" because it is so heterogeneous. This disavowal is, in a sense, a

---

[4] Hendel, "Farewell to SBL: Faith and Reason in Biblical Studies," *BAR* 36 (2010): 74.
[5] See further Moore and Sherwood's critique of what they call the first wave of theory in biblical scholarship (*Invention of the Biblical Scholar*, 31–41, 84–100).

distinctive postmodern gesture. I will use the term "postmodernism," for lack of a better term, acknowledging that it is a family of practices and that not every member of the family agrees (or gets along) with other family members.

Other problems with postmodernism lie primarily in the consequences of its critique of modernism. In my attempt to untangle some of these problems, I will draw on the sympathetic critiques by Seyla Benhabib and Thomas McCarthy, both associated with the Frankfurt School of critical theory,[6] and the not-so-sympathetic critiques by Luc Ferry and Alan Renaut, political philosophers who studied with the Parisian masters of postmodernism.[7] My approach is also indebted to the (neo-Nietzschean) genealogical critique of postmodernism by Bernard Williams.[8]

Benhabib observes, "If there is one commitment which unites postmodernists from Foucault to Derrida to Lyotard it is the critique of western rationality as seen from the perspective of the margins."[9] This postmodern critique is itself descended from the Enlightenment critique of reason, particularly as carried out in Immanuel Kant's three voluminous *Critiques* (of Pure Reason, Practical Reason, and Judgment). Most postmodernists tend to reduce the diversity of rational practices (e.g., Kant's three kinds) to an undifferentiated "western rationality." Despite this collapse of distinctions, the problems identified are real and significant.

Benhabib describes succinctly the "metaphysical illusions" that are the foci of the postmodern critique of Western rationality: "These are the illusions of a self-transparent and self-grounding reason, the illusion of a disembedded and disembodied subject, and the illusion of having found an Archimedean standpoint, situated beyond historical and cultural contingency."[10] Benhabib immediately adds, "These have long ceased to convince." She observes that postmodern critique of these "illusions" is already well established in modernist scholarship. The combined legacy of Friedrich Nietzsche, Karl Marx, Émile Durkheim, Max Weber, Sigmund Freud, Ludwig Wittgenstein—and many others—have demonstrated that reason is "impure" in many respects.[11] That is to say, the critiques are valid, but they

---

[6] Benhabib, *Situating the Self: Gender, Community and Postmodernism in Contemporary Ethics* (New York: Routledge, 1992); eadem, "Democracy and Difference: Reflections on the Metapolitics of Lyotard and Derrida," *Journal of Political Philosophy* 2 (1994): 1–23; McCarthy, *Ideals and Illusions: On Reconstruction and Deconstruction in Contemporary Critical Theory* (Cambridge, MA: MIT Press, 1991).

[7] Ferry and Renaut, *French Philosophy of the Sixties: An Essay on Antihumanism* (trans. Mary H. S. Cattani; Amherst: University of Massachusetts Press, 1990); eidem, eds., *Why We Are Not Nietzscheans* (Chicago: University of Chicago Press, 1997).

[8] Williams, *Truth and Truthfulness: An Essay in Genealogy* (Princeton: Princeton University Press, 2002).

[9] Benhabib, *Situating the Self*, 14.

[10] Ibid., 4.

[11] See McCarthy on "the intrinsic 'impurity' of what we call 'reason'—its embeddedness in culture and society, its entanglement with power and interest, the historical variability of its

are not postmodern as such. Nonetheless, they are the founding principles (if one may use such language) of postmodernism.

The main problem concerns the consequences that postmodernists draw from these (valid) critiques. As Benhabib points out, these critiques can give rise to different conceptual options. She usefully distinguishes two main versions of postmodernism, which differ in the consequences they draw. These two ideal types (which are often hybridized in practice) may be characterized as strong and weak versions of postmodernism.[12]

A pervasive problem of the strong version is what McCarthy calls its "all or nothing" or "either/or" stance.[13] This tendency arguably derives from the desire of the French postmodern theorists to radicalize the critiques of Western philosophy developed by Nietzsche and Martin Heidegger.[14] This radicalization, however, often leads to untenable philosophical and political consequences.

I will briefly outline the strong and weak versions in regard to the metaphysical illusions described by Benhabib.

1. "The illusions of a self-transparent and self-grounding reason." Strong postmodernism holds that the "impurity" of reason entails that it is wholly an ideological projection of power. According to Foucault,

> The historical analysis of this rancorous will to knowledge reveals that all knowledge rests upon injustice (that there is no right, not even in the act of knowing, to truth or a foundation for truth) and that the instinct for knowledge is malicious (something murderous, opposed to the happiness of mankind).[15]

This is a good example of an all-or-nothing stance: because there are no transcendental grounds for our rational practices, "all knowledge rests upon injustice." This overstates the case. While it is clear that many "regimes of truth" (Foucault's term) rest on varying kinds and degrees of injustice and violence, this condition does not justify the claim that *all* knowledge "rests upon injustice." This radicalization of Nietzsche's critique of reason and the effects of his primordial "will to power" pushes the critique beyond the plausible. Knowledge is not always the same thing as injustice, as Foucault knew quite well.

Some kinds of reason are indeed dominating, like Foucault's all-seeing coercive Panopticon, but others are not so dominating, and it is arguable that some are

---

categories and criteria, the embodied, sensuous, and practically engaged character of its bearers" (*Ideals and Illusions*, 43–44).

[12] Benhabib, *Situating the Self*, 213–25. These labels are somewhat ironic, since the strong version is analytically weak, and the weak is the stronger version.

[13] McCarthy, *Ideals and Illusions*, 55, 75, 111.

[14] Ferry and Renaut, *French Philosophy*, 68–121 (Foucault's radicalization of Nietzsche), 122–52 (Derrida's radicalization of Heidegger).

[15] Foucault, "Nietzsche, Genealogy, History," in *The Foucault Reader* (ed. Paul Rabinow; New York: Pantheon, 1984), 95.

not at all. Legislative reason and the rationality of political propaganda do not have the same procedures and consequences as solving a mathematical equation, doing textual criticism, or even teaching a course in biblical studies. (Although admittedly I police my students' essays with respect to the truth regime of critical scholarship!) One must make distinctions among rational forms, rather than lump them together in a totalizing manner.

Furthermore, Foucault's argument seems to disavow the conditions of its own possibility. As Jürgen Habermas argues, "reason can be convicted of being authoritarian in nature only by having recourse to its own tools."[16] If one grants that there are forms of rationality intrinsic to linguistic communication, then one can hardly use language to advance a rational argument for grounding *all* forms of knowledge solely on injustice.

The weak version of postmodernism accepts that reason is impure—it is embedded in culture and society, entangled with power and interest, embodied, sensuous, and practically engaged. The practices of reason cannot be eliminated simply because they—admittedly—have no transcendental foundation. On the contrary, the practices of reason are native to our everyday practices—linguistic, empirical, cognitive, ethical, and instrumental. Everyday rationality is fallible and corrigible, but we cannot do without it.

Wilfrid Sellars, an analytical philosopher, diagnosed this condition decades ago: "empirical knowledge, like its sophisticated extension, science, is rational, not because it has a *foundation* but because it is a self-correcting enterprise which can put *any* claim in jeopardy, though not *all* at once."[17] Reason is intrinsic to our everyday empirical knowledge, and our more specialized rational practices are merely extensions of everyday reason. Moreover, reason is intrinsic to language itself—that is why we have epistemic modality in our verbal system, to specify the degrees of our epistemological certainty about things and events in the present, future, and past. The critique of reason must be a "naturalized epistemology," that is, a critique from within our rational practices.[18] The critical task is to describe its conditions and limits while we are reasoning, since there is no outside foundation from which to conduct a critique. Reason is a "self-correcting enterprise," which means we are capable of learning, and even of learning to reason better. We can critique and modify our arguments and truth claims. But we can criticize and improve our rational practices only piecemeal, from within, one plank at a time. This is a modest goal, which has no end, no utopian "arrival" at the house of an "other" reason. As Benhabib writes, "reason is the contingent achievement of

---

[16] Habermas, *The Philosophical Discourse of Modernity: Twelve Lectures* (Studies in Contemporary German Social Thought; Cambridge, MA: MIT Press, 1987), 185.

[17] Sellars, *Empiricism and the Philosophy of Mind*, with an introduction by Richard Rorty (1956; repr., Cambridge, MA: Harvard University Press, 1997), 79.

[18] Willard Van Orman Quine, *Word and Object* (Cambridge, MA: MIT Press, 1960), 3–5 and passim.

linguistically socialized, finite and embodied creatures."[19] That is all we get, and it is enough.

2. "The illusion of a disembedded and disembodied subject." Since there is no "pure" or "transcendental" subject, strong postmodernists argue that there is no "subject" at all. The "subject" is wholly a cultural and linguistic artifact, an effect of the grammatical "I." This was famously proclaimed by Foucault as the "end" or "erasure" of humanity, and seconded in Derrida's essay, "The Ends of Man."[20] This position is an extension and radicalization of Heidegger's "deconstruction" (*Abbau*) of the metaphysics of subjectivity and humanism.[21] As Derrida writes, with his customary verbal play, "C'est la fin de l'homme fini" (It is the end of finite man).[22]

However, the "death of the subject" in strong postmodernism has both theoretical and practical flaws. McCarthy points to one layer of contradiction in Foucault's argument, which again seems to be a "performative contradiction" (Habermas's term):

> If the self-reflecting subject is nothing but the effect of power relations under the pressure of observation, judgment, control, and discipline, how are we to understand the reflection that takes the form of genealogy? Whence the free-play in our reflective capacities that is a condition of possibility for constructing these subversive histories?[23]

Similarly, Ferry and Renaut criticize Derrida's deconstruction of the subject:

> It is always a subject who decides to vanish as a subject.... The author of the nonbook is as much an author as that of the most traditional book, with the same strengths and weaknesses. In spite of Derrida's statement, "These texts were assembled otherwise," the nonbook remains the product of an intention, with all the consciousness, will, and reflection that implies.[24]

Is it not a logical contradiction for a famous professor to claim in a lecture that there is no such thing as the "subject" of discourse? One can say that the "subject" is complicated (as Freud illustrated). But to say that it is nothing at all is another instance of an unwarranted all-or-nothing stance.

Benhabib articulates the consequences for the feminist project of emancipation, and by extension for other projects of emancipation (liberty, equality, free speech, etc.).

---

[19] Benhabib, *Situating the Self*, 6.
[20] Foucault, *The Order of Things: An Archaeology of the Human Sciences* (New York: Random House, 1970), 386–87; Derrida, "The Ends of Man," in idem, *Margins of Philosophy* (Chicago: University of Chicago Press, 1982), 109–36.
[21] Ferry and Renaut, *French Philosophy*, xxiii–xxiv, 122–52.
[22] Derrida, "Ends of Man," 121.
[23] McCarthy, *Ideals and Illusions*, 59.
[24] Ferry and Renaut, *French Philosophy*, 148.

> The strong version of the Death of the Subject thesis is not compatible with the goals of feminism. Surely, a subjectivity that would not be structured by language, by narrative and by the symbolic codes of narrative available in a culture is unthinkable.... We can concede all that, but nevertheless we must still argue that we are not merely extensions of our histories, that vis à vis our own stories we are in the position of author and character at once.... I want to ask how in fact the very project of female emancipation would be thinkable without such a regulative ideal of enhancing the agency, autonomy and selfhood of women.[25]

In other words—and this is an important point—the emancipatory goals of feminism and modern democracy are literally unthinkable without granting agency, autonomy, and selfhood to human beings. In this respect, the "death of the subject" logically entails a quiescent and disengaged politics. However, in practice, many postmodernists are passionately engaged in emancipatory projects. Benhabib aptly criticizes this inner contradiction:

> [In practice] postmodernism presupposes a super-liberalism, more pluralistic, more tolerant, more open to the right of difference and otherness.... What is baffling though is the lightheartedness with which postmodernists simply assume or posit those hyper-universalist and superliberal values of diversity, heterogeneity, eccentricity and otherness. In doing so they rely on the very norms of the autonomy of subjects and the rationality of democratic procedures which otherwise they seem to so blithely dismiss. What concept of reason, which vision of autonomy allows us to retain these values?... To this question postmodernists have no answer.[26]

This disconnect between radical theory and liberal practice is a deep flaw in the strong postmodern view of the "death of the subject."

The weak version of postmodernism accepts that every "subject" is embedded and embodied, but this version holds that we exercise the capacities of agency and subjectivity in our everyday lives. As Benhabib states, "we are in the position of author and character at once."

Supplementing Foucault's project of analyzing the dominating techniques of power, Michel de Certeau investigates the tactics by which people evade, negotiate, and subvert these structures:

> If it is true that the grid of "discipline" is everywhere becoming clearer and more extensive, it is all the more urgent to discover how an entire society [and the individual—RH] resists being reduced to it, what popular procedures (also "miniscule" and quotidian) manipulate the mechanisms of discipline and conform to them only in order to evade them.[27]

---

[25] Benhabib, *Situating the Self*, 214.
[26] Ibid., 16.
[27] Certeau, *The Practice of Everyday Life* (Berkeley: University of California Press, 1984), xiv.

What Certeau describes as the "tactics" of everyday life provides a way to open up to discussion "this elusive yet fundamental *subject.*"[28] In this way, Certeau's postmodern scholarship reinstates the "subject" in a sophisticated discussion that takes the postmodern critique of the subject seriously but that resists its reductive logic. In this respect, Certeau makes a compelling argument for a weak version of postmodernism.

3. "The illusion of having found an Archimedean standpoint, situated beyond historical and cultural contingency." This problem is complementary to the first two discussed above. Just as reason and the self are always situated, so there is no transcendental historical standpoint outside of our everyday situations, no "view from nowhere." For the strong postmodernist, the absence of a transcendental foundation for critical discourse has dire consequences. In its all-or-nothing stance, the absence of an Archimedean standpoint entails the endless and agonistic struggle of local perspectives. As Benhabib writes,

> like Dostoevsky and Nietzsche before them, postmodernists seem to say that "God is dead; everything is allowed." In their case the phrase would be "Transcendental guarantees of truth are dead; in the agonal struggle of language games there is no commensurability; there are no criteria of truth transcending local discourse, but only the endless struggle of local narratives vying with one another for legitimation."[29]

She is referring to Jean-François Lyotard's influential characterization of postmodernism in *The Postmodern Condition*:

> I define *postmodern* as incredulity toward metanarratives.... To the obsolescence of the metanarrative apparatus of legitimation corresponds, most notably, the crisis of metaphysical philosophy and of the university institution which in the past relied on it.[30]

Since there are no believable "metanarratives," that is, plausible transcendental accounts for legitimating knowledge, there remain only "little narratives" (*petits récits*) which are local and incommensurate.[31] There is no possibility of genuine discussion across these little narratives, only an endless "agonistics" of language. Lyotard writes, "to speak is to fight, in the sense of playing, and speech acts fall within the domain of a general agonistics."[32] Since there is no hope for consensus,

---

[28] Ibid., xi (emphasis added).
[29] Benhabib, *Situating the Self*, 209.
[30] Lyotard, *The Postmodern Condition: A Report on Knowledge* (Minneapolis: University of Minnesota Press, 1984), xxiv.
[31] Ibid., 60.
[32] Ibid., 10.

which is "an outmoded and suspect value," all that one can hope for is a "temporary contract" among local narratives.[33]

Benhabib criticizes this position as "the prison house of perspectives."[34] She observes that its "premise of the absolute heterogeneity and incommensurability of regimens and discourses is never argued for; it is simply posited."[35] This position, which is sometimes called hard perspectivalism, is philosophically untenable. Benhabib avers that there is a more acceptable response to the critique of transcendental foundations:

> the demise of rationalistic and transcendental philosophies from Descartes to Kant and Husserl does not signify the end of but yet another "transformation" of the philosophical project.... It is the emergence of a fallibilistic and procedural concept of rationality and the normative options allowed by this in ethics and politics.[36]

As analytical philosophers have argued, the very idea of a "foundation" for knowledge is a conceptual mistake, perhaps a piece of linguistic enchantment. Sellars maintains:

> *Above all*, the picture [of a foundation] is misleading because of its static character. One seems forced to choose between the picture of an elephant which rests on a tortoise (What supports the tortoise?) and the picture of a great Hegelian serpent of knowledge with its tail in its mouth (Where does it begin?). Neither will do.[37]

Without transcendent foundations, with no Archimedean point beyond history and culture, we are left with the corrigible but self-correcting practices of reason, which we can critique only within our practices. There is no static "outside" on which to stand. But why should this be a dire problem? Gödel's theorem demonstrates that mathematics does not have a self-consistent foundation.[38] Yet mathematicians still do math, and some do it exceedingly well. An analogous situation applies to inquiry in other forms of critical scholarship. The illusion of foundationalism has resolvable consequences for weak postmodernists and enlightened modernists—we accept the fallibility and corrigibility of critical scholarly discourse. We do not need the dream of perfect knowledge—which in any case may well be a secularized form of divine revelation.

Nietzsche, who clarified the idea of perspectival (nonfoundationalist)

---

[33] Ibid., 66.

[34] Benhabib, "The Liberal Imagination and the Four Dogmas of Multiculturalism," *Yale Journal of Criticism* 12 (1999): 409.

[35] Benhabib, "Democracy and Difference," 7 n. 17.

[36] Benhabib, *Situating the Self*, 210.

[37] Sellars, *Empiricism and the Philosophy of Mind*, 78–79.

[38] See, e.g., Willard Van Orman Quine, "Gödel's Theorem," in idem, *Quiddities: An Intermittently Philosophical Dictionary* (Cambridge, MA: Belknap Press of Harvard University Press, 1987), 82–86.

knowledge, also showed how to contend with and partially overcome it.[39] He described this critical practice as "philology"; for Nietzsche, this means "the art of reading well—of reading facts without falsifying them by interpretation, without losing caution, patience, delicacy, in the desire to understand."[40] While granting that knowledge is necessarily perspectival, Nietzsche argued that the art of philology provides an adequate concept of things, which one can—tentatively and seriously—call "objectivity":

> "Objectivity"—understood not as "contemplation without interest" (which is a nonsensical absurdity), but as the ability to have one's For and Against *under control* and to engage and disengage them, so that one knows how to employ a *variety* of perspectives and affective interpretations in the service of knowledge.... There is *only* a perspective seeing, *only* a perspective "knowing"; and the *more* affects we allow to speak about a thing, the *more* eyes, different eyes we can use to observe a thing, the more complete will our "concept" of this thing, our "objectivity," be.[41]

This task can also be described as "learning to see":

> Learning to *see*—accustoming the eye to calmness, to patience, to letting things come up to it; postponing judgment, learning to go around and grasp each individual case from all sides.... Learning to *see*, as I understand it, is almost what, unphilosophically speaking, is called a strong will: the essential feature is precisely *not* to "will"—to *be able* to suspend decision.[42]

By "learning to see" with "*more* eyes, different eyes" we can negotiate our intrinsic perspectivalism and achieve warranted knowledge.

Nietzsche, who called himself an "old philologist," elucidates our philological task. This task is compatible with weak postmodernism and enlightened modernism (of which he is one of the patrons). Weak postmodernism is not limited to conventional philology (as in Hebrew or Greek philology), but neither does it exclude it. Rather, it amalgamates the traditional skills of philology (which Nietzsche described as "a goldsmith's art"[43]) with the conditions of possibility for literary, historical, and philosophical inquiry. Nietzsche's analysis provides an exemplary model for critical scholarship.

---

[39] In the following I am indebted to Christoph Cox, *Nietzsche: Naturalism and Interpretation* (Berkeley: University of California Press, 1999).

[40] Nietzsche, *The Antichrist*, 52, in *The Portable Nietzsche* (ed. and trans. Walter Kaufmann; New York: Viking, 1968), 635. Elsewhere Nietzsche maintains that there are no uninterpreted facts (in modern parlance, all facts are theory laden; here he seems to refer to second-order interpretation that is intellectually mendacious or lazy; see Cox, *Nietzsche*, 164 n. 115.

[41] Nietzsche, *Genealogy of Morals* 3.12; trans. Cox, *Nietzsche*, 111–12.

[42] Nietzsche, *Twilight of the Idols*, "What the Germans Lack" §6; trans. Kaufmann, *Portable Nietzsche*, 511.

[43] Nietzsche, *Daybreak: Thoughts on the Prejudices of Morality*, preface §5 (trans. R. J. Hollingdale; Texts in German Philosophy; Cambridge: Cambridge University Press, 1982), 5.

II. Truth or Consequences

The collectively authored volume *The Postmodern Bible* is an influential example of strong postmodernism in biblical studies. The introduction states the authors' goals:

> by sweeping away secure notions of meaning, by radically calling into question the apparently stable foundations of meaning on which traditional interpretation is situated … postmodern readings demonstrate that traditional interpretations are themselves enactments of domination or, in simpler terms, power plays.[44]

This is the strong version of postmodernism in its all-or-nothing stance. Since "the apparently stable foundations of meaning" are illusory, scholarly interpretations are merely "power plays." Conventional scholarship consists of "enactments of domination." Presumably this condition also applies to the scholarship in *The Postmodern Bible*. However, the authors suggest that their project escapes this mode of domination because their subjectivity disappears in the "theoretical collapse of the subject-object dichotomy."[45] This is an appeal to the "death of the subject" discussed above.

An example of a local and politically engaged reading of Exodus raises an ethical problem for strong postmodernism in biblical studies. According to *The Postmodern Bible*, the critical mode called "ideological criticism" or "resistance reading" involves the following questions:

> Does the text or a particular reading of the text liberate? Does the reading bring about positive social change? Does the reading expose injustices of race, class, neo-colonialism, gender, and sexuality? Who is represented? Who is excluded?… We have taken the position in this chapter and throughout our volume that because there is no nonideological reading of the Bible, there is no reading of the Bible that is not political or that does not have political consequences.[46]

The goal for a strong postmodern ideological criticism of the Bible is to have political consequences. This is not problematic in itself, since we all want to change the world; the problem arises when this is the only goal. In strong postmodernism, all interpretation is only political. The felicity of any reading of the Bible is, therefore, measured by its political aims and consequences. This is another instance of the all-or-nothing stance of strong postmodernism: in the absence of transcendental foundations, only politics remains.

---

[44] The Bible and Culture Collective, *The Postmodern Bible* (ed. Elizabeth A. Castelli, Stephen D. Moore, Gary A. Phillips, and Regina M. Schwartz; New Haven: Yale University Press, 1995), 2–3. This Foucauldian point is reiterated later: "Interpretation is an expression of power, the result of violence exercised upon the text in the act of reading, which is always an act of appropriation, a taking possession" (p. 131).

[45] Ibid., 51.

[46] Ibid., 303.

What happens when the political value of a "resistance reading" conflicts with the evidence? Do desirable social consequences trump the philological imperative of "reading facts without falsifying them" (Nietzsche's phrase)? To put this quandary another way: Can a strong postmodernist or an ideological critic make a justifiable decision to prefer truth over consequences? If all scholarly interpretations are "enactments of domination," then perhaps a commitment to truthfulness becomes a minor or dispensable value in critical scholarship.

And yet our everyday practices (including our use of language and our scholarship) have the expectation of truthfulness built into them. That is why we are shocked when a scientist creates false data or a when a historian plagiarizes someone else's writings. We do not require transcendental foundations in order to be truthful or to value truthfulness.

But consider the implications of the following "resistance reading," summarized as an exemplary case in *The Postmodern Bible*:

> Charles Copher seeks to recover the African presence in the Exodus narrative. Of the main characters—Moses, Zipporah, Aaron, and Miriam—Copher argues that "the issue was hardly one of black color, for all of them were black." He bases his argument on several factors: "the three definitions of black/Negro; scholarly opinion that views Moses' family as of Nubian origin; and the existence of Cushites in Asia as well as in Africa." The implications of this reading are far-reaching, for it forces into the foreground consideration of the ideological character of white Eurocentric (and sometimes white supremist [sic]) exegesis against which it stands in stark contrast.[47]

The political implications of this reading may indeed be "far-reaching" in its stark contrast with white Eurocentric and white supremacist exegesis. The authors do not unpack the political implications of this contrast, but the upshot is relatively clear: this reading highlights the racism of white Eurocentric biblical scholarship.

Now, while I am opposed to white supremacist exegesis of the Bible (or of anything else), I would argue that Copher's claim that Moses and his family were black Africans is unwarranted. The "factors" on which Copher bases his confident conclusion that "all of them were black" are philologically and historically unfounded.[48] It would be just as untenable to claim that Moses and his family were white Aryans or Hasidic Jews.[49]

---

[47] Ibid., 290, citing Charles B. Copher, "The Black Presence in the Old Testament," in *Stony the Road We Trod: African American Biblical Interpretation* (ed. Cain Hope Felder; Minneapolis: Fortress, 1991), 146–64.

[48] For example, the ethnonym *kûš* ("Cush" = Nubia/Ethiopia) occurs in Gen 10:8 as the name of Nimrod's father. While this is unexpected, it does not provide warrant for any historical conclusions about Nubians in Mesopotamia. E. A. Speiser plausibly suggested that this instance may refer to the Kassites (Akkadian *kaššu*), whose ethnonym has fallen together with Cush (*Genesis: Introduction, Translation, and Notes* [AB 1; Garden City, NY: Doubleday, 1964], 72).

[49] Cf. the claim of some German scholars in the late nineteenth and early twentieth

This point has been made convincingly by Michael Joseph Brown.[50] Regarding Copher's reasons for confidently inferring that Moses and his family were black, he states, rather delicately, "this argument is far from historically convincing."[51] He concludes that "serious questions of method and proof (independent or otherwise) lie behind any such attempt to make historically valid ethnic claims."[52] Brown supports the political effects of African American biblical scholarship, but he does not condone poor scholarship.

Why, then, do the authors of *The Postmodern Bible* present and endorse this instance of "resistance reading"? Perhaps they did not realize that Copher's argument, which they accurately summarize, is untruthful. Otherwise, it seems that the value of promoting a local "resistance narrative" that putatively exposes white Eurocentric racism (even where it is not operating) trumps the value of truthful scholarship.

The strong version of postmodernism necessarily faces an ethical dilemma. If there is no transcendental foundation for truth claims, is anything permitted? If all scholarship is an assertion of domination, then should we not choose to dominate on behalf of the marginalized and dispossessed? Should we not prefer consequences to truth? This position is epistemologically and morally untenable. Truthfulness is a category internal to all human communication, including our class lectures and scholarly publications. Why should we bear false witness about the Bible to African Americans—or anyone else? Because we think their collective dignity is enhanced by teaching pseudo-scholarship? Is their marginalization lessened by promoting lies about the past? There are plenty of powerful truths about the African and African American past—why not promote these truths instead?[53]

Certeau describes the writing of history as a "heterology," a writing about the Other. This implies an ethical obligation and responsibility to the absent dead whose history we write: "The other is the phantasm of historiography, the object that it seeks, honors, and buries."[54] We dishonor the dead when we provide them with false "scriptural tombs." There are also other Others for our scholarship. We have an ethical obligation to our students, to our readers, and to other scholars. All of these others deserve our respect. Only by being truthful do we deserve theirs.

---

centuries that Jesus was a white Aryan; see Susannah Heschel, *The Aryan Jesus: Christian Theologians and the Bible in Nazi Germany* (Princeton: Princeton University Press, 2008).

[50] Brown, *Blackening of the Bible: The Aims of African American Biblical Scholarship* (African American Religious Thought and Life; Harrisburg, PA: Trinity Press International, 2004), 31.

[51] Ibid., 32.

[52] Ibid., 34.

[53] See, e.g., Allen Dwight Callahan, *The Talking Book: African Americans and the Bible* (New Haven: Yale University Press, 2006).

[54] Michel de Certeau, *The Writing of History* (New York: Columbia University Press, 1988), 2.

III. Biblical Studies and the Enlightenment Project

Having disentangled the positions of the strong and weak versions of postmodernism, and having criticized aspects of the former in biblical studies, I turn to a perspicuous example of the latter. In their monograph *The Invention of the Biblical Scholar: A Critical Manifesto*,[55] Stephen Moore and Yvonne Sherwood construct a postmodern genealogy of our academic discipline. I agree that an inquiry into the invention of our disciplinary practices—including their unspoken aims and anxieties—is an important step toward reforming them.

The book begins with a lament that Theory (viz., poststructuralist/postmodern theory) has not had much purchase in biblical studies. They aptly quip that "'Theory's Empire' in biblical studies is approximately the size of Tobago or the Falkland Islands. This is the underwhelming reality."[56] After registering their disappointment, they state their own goals:

> [Our aim] is not to launch yet another ad campaign to sell Theory to biblical scholars.... Our intent, rather, is diagnostic and analytic. We want to look at what happened, and what has failed to happen, and what might yet happen in biblical studies under the heading of "Theory." ... Contending that Theory's most important contribution is the self-reflexive and metacritical moves it makes possible, our reflection on Theory's reception in biblical studies is intended to defamiliarize the histories and peculiarities of our own disciplinary space.[57]

This is a laudable and impressive aim, and the authors make good on it. They provide a genealogy of "the biblical scholar" from the Enlightenment to the present, concentrating not on the progressive accumulation of "assured results" but on the epistemic shifts that made various moves in biblical scholarship possible. This is a broadly Foucauldian enterprise, which they execute with aplomb. I will argue, however, that they were insufficiently Foucauldian in their approach, and that there are some notable (and remediable) exclusions in their genealogy. I propose that a focus on issues of power and knowledge will improve this genealogy and broaden its critical scope.

Sherwood and Moore begin their historical genealogy of "the biblical scholar" with what Jonathan Sheehan calls the invention of the "Cultural Bible."[58] This new concept of the Bible, created primarily by German scholars in the eighteenth century, was a response to the crisis in the theological authority of the Bible. Sheehan writes,

---

[55] See n. 2 above.
[56] Moore and Sherwood, *Invention of the Biblical Scholar*, 9.
[57] Ibid., 15.
[58] Sheehan, *The Enlightenment Bible: Translation, Scholarship, Culture* (Princeton: Princeton University Press, 2005).

If the answer to the question: "Why should I read the Bible?" was, before 1700, overwhelmingly "because it reveals the means to your salvation," by the middle of the eighteenth century, Protestant answers began to proliferate, jostle, and compete with the standard one. In a sense, the Enlightenment Bible was this series of alternative answers.[59]

As Sherwood and Moore remark, through the new concept of the Cultural Bible, "Biblical scholarship was established as the space in which this task of extending and sustaining the relevance of the Bible—now positioned under a Damoclean sword of potential irrelevance for the first time in its history—would take place."[60]

They add that the invention of the Cultural Bible entailed a further crisis, in which the *morality* of the Bible came to be seen as a problem. Philosophers and savants such as Bayle and Kant subjected the Bible to moral critique, often focusing on the immoralities of the patriarchs, the mass killing of Canaanites by Joshua's armies, and Abraham's aborted sacrifice of Isaac. They argue that the historical and textual critique was subordinated to the moral critique: "In early Enlightenment biblical critique, the fragmented nature of the biblical text is articulated as a subset of the critique of the Bible as all-too-human in the sense of immoral, sinful, and fallen."[61]

They grant, however, that the moral critique was often part of a larger strategy of rehabilitating the "core" morality of the Bible. For these critics (such as Kant and Shaftesbury), "the subhuman(e), violent, and intolerant nature of parts of the Bible ... [is] set up in contrast to the intrinsic morality of the true Bible."[62] The ethical critique burned away the dross, so that the "core" of the Cultural Bible was morally fit. In this respect, I would suggest, the moral critique was entirely consistent with the Enlightenment project of refashioning biblical authority. The bits of immorality could be explained away as primitive relics, or simply as "Jewish" immorality.

According to Sherwood and Moore's genealogy, the imperative of moral critique was deliberately "forgotten" by biblical scholars of the nineteenth and twentieth centuries, for whom historical issues came to be seen as central. The focus on historical problems allowed scholars to avoid the dilemmas (and potential heresy) implicit in moral critique:

> After the eighteenth century, the investigation of biblical morality was quietly dropped from the job description of the biblical scholar. This was because the moral questions put to the Bible by the early rationalists were deemed to be irresolvable and socially corrosive, whereas historical questions were (or so it was imagined) resolvable and less incendiary.[63]

---

[59] Ibid., xii–xiii.
[60] Moore and Sherwood, *Invention of the Biblical Scholar*, 47–48.
[61] Ibid., 52.
[62] Ibid., 54.
[63] Ibid., 59–60.

The disciplinary focus on historical questions, therefore, silenced the moral critique of the Bible. Consequently "debates over historicity became convoluted, fraught, and obsessive in biblical studies—and remain so to this day."[64] Only with the recent rise of Theory have nonhistorical topics—including literary criticism and moral critique—become thinkable once again.

This is an elegant explanation for the obsession of biblical scholarship with issues of history and for its resistance to attempts—by the Theory-inflected—to swerve away from historical concerns and to subject the Bible to ethical critique. It is, in my view, a brilliant explanation. Historical and philological inquiries often serve as a refuge for biblical scholars who wish to avoid more vexing or corrosive inquiries. We all know people who became technicians of the text due to their theological commitments. It is arguable that the field as a whole suffers from this fear, enabling its practitioners to avoid deeper, less controllable forms of intellectual inquiry.

Sherwood and Moore argue that postmodern scholarship provides a way to revive the task of moral critique of the Bible, thereby, in a sense, returning to this early modern intellectual space:

> the early modern strategy of holding the Bible accountable to an ethical standard that is in some sense beyond or outside the Bible has resurfaced after centuries of hiatus. Ethical criticism is once again an active element of biblical scholarship; and so while biblical scholarship has seemingly drifted far from its early Enlightenment moorings, in another sense it has simply returned to port.[65]

By means of this historical genealogy, in which the postmodern revives the moral mission of early modern scholars, the authors achieve many of their goals. They succeed in denaturalizing our practices of historical scholarship, of making us reconsider their rationale and motivations, and also in integrating postmodern scholarship into the genealogy. This is an impressive achievement. However, I believe that some aspects of the genealogy need further historical refinement, the result of which may reorient some of these points.

My main criticism of this genealogy of the biblical scholar is that is too idealist in orientation and insufficiently political. It is too much a "history of ideas" and not enough a Foucauldian genealogy of the cultural strategies of power/knowledge. I propose to insert some politics into the genealogy. The crisis of biblical authority to which the Cultural Bible was a response was also a crisis of political authority. As Sheehan notes, the skepticism toward the Bible was accompanied by skepticism toward the authority of kings and priests.[66] The intellectual motor for both forms of skepticism was a movement of philosophers and heretics that Jonathan Israel calls the Radical Enlightenment. Its goals were decisively political:

---

[64] Ibid., 61.
[65] Ibid., 69.
[66] Sheehan, *Enlightenment Bible*, xi.

Radical Enlightenment is a set of basic principles that can be summed up concisely as: democracy; racial and sexual equality; individual liberty of lifestyle; full freedom of thought, expression, and the press; eradication of religious authority from the legislative process and education; and full separation of church and state.[67]

The most brilliant, controversial, and consequential figure of the Radical Enlightenment was Baruch Spinoza, whose *Theological-Political Treatise* (1670) scandalized all of Europe and became an underground best-seller. In this book, Spinoza laid out the major arguments of the Radical Enlightenment. He also invented the modern method of historical-critical biblical scholarship. These two tasks were deeply interrelated. Spinoza was, and remains, a very controversial figure in the field of biblical studies, for it was the afterlife of his ideas (in the context of religious and political conflicts) that caused the modern crisis of biblical authority.

Spinoza, in other words, is the patriarch of the genealogy of the modern biblical scholar. The reception of his work created the rupture in the episteme. Sherwood and Moore's genealogy begins after Spinoza, but everyone after him was reacting to his work and creating new waves in its wake, including Bayle, Kant, Gotthold Ephraim Lessing, Johann Gottfried Herder, and everyone else. Spinoza's intellectual project—and its later adventures—created the conditions for the invention of modern biblical studies.

Modern biblical scholarship was therefore complicit in radical politics at its birth. Spinoza's aim in constructing the historical-critical method of biblical scholarship was precisely to undermine the theological-political authority of the Bible, which was the basis for the governmental power of kings, princes, and clergy. In his argument for freedom of speech (which he called freedom to philosophize), liberty, equality, and inalienable natural rights, he knew that the biblical foundation of the power of kings was the major obstacle. As he writes in his preface,

> It may indeed be the highest secret of monarchical government and utterly essential to it, to keep men deceived, and to disguise the fear that sways them with the specious name of religion, so that they will fight for their servitude as if they were fighting for their own deliverance, and will not think it humiliating but supremely glorious to spill their blood and sacrifice their lives for the glorification of a single man. But in a free republic, on the other hand, nothing that can be devised or attempted will be less successful. For it is completely contrary to the common liberty to shackle the free judgment of the individual with prejudices or constraints of any kind.... This is the core thesis that I have set out to demonstrate in this treatise.[68]

---

[67] Israel, *A Revolution of the Mind: Radical Enlightenment and the Intellectual Origins of Modern Democracy* (Princeton: Princeton University Press, 2010), vii–viii.

[68] Benedict de Spinoza, *Theological-Political Treatise* (ed. Jonathan Israel; trans. Michael Silverthorne and Jonathan Israel; Cambridge Texts in the History of Philosophy; Cambridge: Cambridge University Press, 2007; Latin original 1670), 6–7 (§§7–8).

Spinoza's critique of the Bible—particularly his critique of prophecy, miracles, and Mosaic authorship—serves to undermine the theological authority of the Bible's doctrines. His invention of the historical-critical method—and, it is arguable, his invention of the modern concept of history—serves to historicize and defamiliarize the Bible, making it a new book, written by ancient authors and rooted in the culture of ancient Israel. Hence, he argues, the Bible's laws are not timeless but are historically situated in a particular time and place and are therefore not binding or mandatory for the present. From his history of the Bible, Spinoza is able to marshal evidence for an argument *against* the divine right of kings and priests.

In Spinoza's revolutionary concept of the Bible, the book now provides arguments *for* a democratic polity that respects freedom of speech and inalienable human rights. This is a philosophical tour de force that set into motion many radical aims that, in the centuries since, have become naturalized as part of the modern worldview. The invention of modern biblical criticism and its historical-critical method was basic to the Radical Enlightenment's invention of modernity.

The controversial ideas of the Radical Enlightenment generated two major responses, the Moderate Enlightenment and the Counter-Enlightenment. The Moderate Enlightenment, whose luminaries includes John Locke, David Hume, and Voltaire, sought in various ways to accommodate the reformist aims of the Radical Enlightenment with the stability of a monarchic, aristocratic, and Christian society. Hence, for example, the radical enlighteners Spinoza and Bayle argued that the principles of liberty and tolerance extend to all people as a natural right, regardless of their philosophy, religion, gender, race, or lifestyle. In contrast, Locke's principles of liberty and tolerance have theological limits: civil rights belong only to those who believe in divine revelation. Atheists were deliberately excluded, as were those of "libertine" lifestyle. Slaves had freedom of religion, but nothing else.[69]

In sum, the intellectual disputes of the early Enlightenment always had political aims and involved a clash of principles among the radical fringe, the moderate mainstream, and the conservative opposition. As Israel writes,

> The rivalry between moderate mainstream and radical fringe was always as much an integral part of the drama as that between the moderate Enlightenment and conservative opposition. In this triangular battle of ideas what was ultimately at stake was what kind of belief-system should prevail in Europe's politics, social order, and institutions, as well as in high culture and, no less, in popular attitudes.[70]

In biblical studies, the revolution begun by Spinoza and continued by Bayle and the radical deists was countered by the ameliorating aims of the moderate

---

[69] Jonathan I. Israel, *The Enlightenment Contested: Philosophy, Modernity, and the Emancipation of Man, 1670–1752* (Oxford: Oxford University Press, 2006), 135–63.

[70] Jonathan I. Israel, *Radical Enlightenment: Philosophy and the Making of Modernity, 1650–1750* (Oxford: Oxford University Press, 2001), 11.

mainstream, including the historical-critical studies of Richard Simon, the biblical researches of Locke, Kant, and Herder, and the blossoming of professional biblical scholarship in Germany in the work of Johann David Michaelis, Johann Gottfried Eichhorn, and others.[71] These scholars and philosophers adapted the concepts and methods of Spinoza's historical-critical method to the making of the Cultural Bible, whose historical, literary, and moral authority became independent from systematic theology but remained religiously conservative.

The new guild of professional biblical scholars, who pursued Simon's ameliorating combination of piety and historical-critical method, were located in theology faculties. The interest of these institutions—their "regime of truth"—was served by silencing the radical theological-political critiques of Spinoza, Bayle, and the radical deists. There were no Spinozists in the ranks of the *theologische Fakultät*, no radical fringe. The policed boundaries of the guild made this unthinkable. Spinoza's historical-critical method had been domesticated to the interests of the church by the moderate mainstream.

The Cultural Bible was accommodated to the interests of the Moderate Enlightenment, for which historical truth became a counterpart to doctrinal truth. The new authority of historical writing is illuminated by Certeau's concept of "the scriptural economy": as scriptural authority diminished, new forms of writing—especially historical writing—colonized its epistemological space. As Certeau writes, "History has become our myth."[72] This condition is not confined to biblical studies but is scattered across the "scriptural" space of modernity.

In the moderate guild of biblical scholars, theological concerns were never far from the surface. To this day, as Sherwood and Moore note, scholarly articles and monographs often end with a coda of faith—a nod to Christian doctrines of salvation. The theological truth-regime of church-run institutions ensures that this is so. The political issues and moral criticisms raised by the radicals had faded into oblivion. Whereas, in a very tangible sense, the program of the Radical Enlightenment has largely prevailed in modern politics, the Moderate Enlightenment still rules the roost in biblical studies.

In some nations the institutional locus of biblical studies has spread beyond theological faculties. Departments of Near Eastern Studies, Religious Studies, and other hybrids provide a potentially less restrictive epistemological space for biblical scholarship. But the stable epistemology of the moderate mainstream suits the biographies of most biblical scholars, whose intellectual horizons were shaped in theological institutions. Scholars trained or located in humanities faculties may put theory in the space elsewhere reserved for theology, or wrestle with the writings of Roland Barthes rather than Karl Barth. But in biblical studies, the political and

---

[71] Sheehan, *Enlightenment Bible*, 87–217; see also Michael C. Legaspi, *The Death of Scripture and the Rise of Biblical Studies* (Oxford Studies in Historical Theology; Oxford: Oxford University Press, 2010), 3–26.

[72] Certeau, *Writing of History*, 45.

intellectual gap between the Radical and the Moderate Enlightenment is still palpable. Our discipline, as Sherwood and Moore observe, is still enmeshed in the discourse of the Enlightenment Bible, but the situation is more complex than they envision. The inclusions and exclusions of our disciplinary space—of what is thinkable as biblical scholarship—are still mired in the theological-political rifts of enlightened modernism (including its offshoot, postmodernism), mainstream moderation, and conservative reaction.

IV. Conclusions: Toward a Future Philology

I have entered into the discussion of modernism and postmodernism in biblical studies by several steps. I have argued that biblical scholarship has much to gain by the theoretical critique engaged by postmodern scholars. I have distinguished between strong and weak versions of postmodernism and have observed the conceptual, practical, and ethical flaws of the former. I argue that the weak version of postmodernism does not suffer from these flaws, and that it is compatible with (or indistinguishable from) an enlightened modernism. In this respect I agree with Moore's observation that much postmodern biblical scholarship is "better viewed as a case of positivistic biblical scholarship awakening from its 'dogmatic slumber' (Kant's term for his own awakening) to a still more enlightened modernity."[73] Awakening from dogmatic slumber is, I submit, an entirely good thing for biblical studies. But this does not mean that the historical-critical method will fade away; rather it means that this method criticizes itself, which it should have done all along (and indeed has done, in fits and starts).[74]

I have agreed with many of the arguments in the critical manifesto by Moore and Sherwood, although I have supplemented their impressive genealogy of the biblical scholar with further historical details and emphases. I concur that "a discipline's myth of origins powerfully predetermines its practice,"[75] and I encourage others to engage in this genealogical project, which explores the deep structures and dialectics of knowledge, power, and agency in our discipline. This is a Foucauldian strategy, although I have followed Certeau by inserting "agency" into its epistemic field.

I have argued that Nietzsche, who saw himself as "an old philologist," is in some respects a figure who can bridge the gap between modern and postmodern. Strong postmodernists read him selectively (this is not a major criticism—one can

---

[73] Stephen D. Moore, "The 'Post-'Age Stamp: Biblical Studies and the Postmodernism Debate," *JAAR* 57 (1989): 547.
[74] E.g., F. W. Dobbs-Allsopp, "Rethinking Historical Criticism," *BibInt* 7 (1999): 235–71; E. A. Knauf, "From History to Interpretation," in *The Fabric of History: Text, Artifact and Israel's Past* (ed. Diana Vikander Edelman; JSOTSup 127; Sheffield: JSOT Press, 1991), 26–64.
[75] Moore and Sherwood, *Invention of the Biblical Scholar*, 131.

hardly do otherwise). In my selections, I demonstrate that Nietzsche's concept of philology aptly describes how the critical scholar can gain knowledge, and even a measure of objectivity, by "the incomparable art of reading well."[76] While, as he writes, there is "*only* a perspective 'knowing,'"—that is, our reason and subjectivity are situated, embodied, and embedded—yet we can achieve warranted knowledge. "The *more* affects we allow to speak about a thing, the *more* eyes, different eyes we can use to observe a thing, the more complete will our 'concept' of this thing, our 'objectivity,' be."[77] The art of philology, in Nietzsche's sense, requires intellectual integrity, conscience, and humility. It is a difficult art, whose yield is sometimes difficult or corrosive. It is the gift of critical scholarship—yet it can also be *Gift* ("poison") to entrenched concepts and practices. Genuine philology, in this sense, does not always suit the accommodationist desires of the Moderate Enlightenment; sometimes it has radical implications. But, I submit, a genuine critical biblical scholarship demands no less.

There are two more concluding points I wish to make in dialogue with Moore and Sherwood. First, their concept of Theory has some strong exclusions. They are interested in the poststructuralist theories that swept through literature departments in the 1980s and '90s. But why should Theory exclude so much theory? What about theories from classics, anthropology, history, and (Anglo-American) philosophy? Surely innovative theoretical models from these fields are germane for a sophisticated biblical scholarship. In addition to French postmodern theory, let us read Mary Douglas with the ritual texts of Leviticus, Bernard Williams with narratives of shame and honor, Maurice Halbwachs with the cultural memories of the Pentateuch and prophets, Carlo Ginzburg with texts of witchcraft and heresy, and so on. I don't think Sherwood and Moore would disagree with this, but it needs to be stated clearly. The broad expanse of critical academic scholarship is our domain, not just the fashions of English departments.

My last point concerns the persistence of hard perspectivalism in the identity politics of much postmodern biblical scholarship. Moore and Sherwood write:

> Contemporary moral critique of the Bible is largely conducted in the name of certain marked identities.... We hear and must hear the voices of those who have been damaged by a Bible that has repeatedly lent itself to racist, sexist, homophobic, colonizing, and other dehumanizing agendas. Such battles stage a clash of identities that, under the aegis of tolerance, demand a hearing in the public and academic spheres.[78]

I respectfully demur. While I am opposed to all of these dehumanizing agendas, I don't think critical scholarship must give special preference to "the voices of those who have been damaged by [the] Bible." This is arguably the domain of pastoral

---

[76] Nietzsche, *Antichrist*, 59; trans. Kaufmann, *Portable Nietzsche*, 650.
[77] Nietzsche, *Genealogy of Morals* 3.12.
[78] Moore and Sherwood, *Invention of the Biblical Scholar*, 74.

theology. More importantly, there is some fuzzy thinking here. The Bible doesn't have agency; people have agency. No one has "been damaged" by a book (unless, of course, someone threw it at them), and a book hasn't "lent itself" to anything (note the use of passive and middle voices, and abstract nouns as subjects and objects). It is people who have harmed other people by interpreting the Bible and mobilizing their interpretations in various ways. The problem of the "death of the subject" in strong postmodernism too often yields a silencing of human agency and, correspondingly, a fuzzy (and ahistorical) victimology. Moreover, I don't think that Sherwood and Moore would disagree, since they gesture toward rehabilitating "universal notions ... which, by definition, are the very antithesis of the ethnic, the cultural, and the local."[79]

Let us study how people have used the Bible to promote dehumanizing and humanizing agendas. This task—the reception and uses of the Bible—clearly belongs to the field of critical biblical scholarship. Let's tone down the agonistics of local narratives (or, more colloquially, "the airing of grievances") and study the complex and often sordid history of the Bible's life and afterlife in Western culture. We don't need to limit ourselves to the historical horizons of ancient Israel. The disciplinary scope of critical biblical scholarship should include all cultural discourses involving the Bible—what we might describe as the scriptural economy from the Iron Age to today.[80] This project will revitalize biblical scholarship and, perhaps, bridge the gap that currently afflicts the field. As Anthony Grafton writes, "What characterizes modernity—so more than one philosopher has argued—is its state of perpetual revolution."[81] A little revolution now and then is good thing for critical biblical scholarship.

---

[79] Ibid., 121.

[80] See my recent attempt, *The Book of Genesis: A Biography* (Princeton: Princeton University Press, 2013).

[81] Grafton, *Bring Out Your Dead: The Past as Revelation* (Cambridge, MA: Harvard University Press, 2002), 249.

Watch the Target: A Post-Postmodernist Response to Ronald Hendel

STEPHEN D. MOORE
smoore@drew.edu
The Theological School, Drew University, Madison, NJ 07940

What and when was postmodernism, and why is the postmodernism debate now pushing up shoots in the pages of *JBL* decades after it has wilted, withered, and all but vanished in the fields in which it first flourished? Yvonne Sherwood and I are grateful to Ronald Hendel for featuring our jointly authored book, *The Invention of the Biblical Scholar*, so prominently in his "Mind the Gap: Modern and Postmodern in Biblical Studies"—grateful but also puzzled, since the book marks our own distance from postmodernism.

First, our gratitude. Hendel deftly pencils the figure of Spinoza into our Foucauldian sketch of early modern biblical scholarship. Hendel argues compellingly that Spinoza's absence from our sketch is a notable lacuna and missed opportunity. His intriguing analysis of Spinoza's significance and his recourse to the concept of the Radical Enlightenment to contextualize it suggest how our redescription of biblical-scholarly origins might have begun farther back.

We are less convinced, however, that Hendel's introduction of Spinoza significantly alters our sketch, turning a "genealogy of the biblical scholar ... that is too idealist in orientation" into a more "political" one.[1] "Political" is a thoroughly mystified term in contemporary academic discourse, as Sherwood and I argue in our book.[2] To claim that term for one's interpretation while engaging in the language game of one's discipline is a strategic move that automatically elevates one to the moral high ground—however remote that language game might be from

---

[1] Ronald Hendel, "Mind the Gap: Modern and Postmodern in Biblical Studies," *JBL* 133 (2014): 437.

[2] Stephen D. Moore and Yvonne Sherwood, *The Invention of the Biblical Scholar: A Critical Manifesto* (Minneapolis: Fortress, 2011), 89–91; cf. 86–88, 116–22.

the extra-academic world, one in which the "political" is now, paradoxically, the virtual antonym of the virtuous.³ We'll see you and raise you, Professor Hendel.

Now, our puzzlement at our prominence in Hendel's article. Our book does not represent itself as a postmodern intervention in biblical studies. On the contrary, our stance toward biblical postmodernism was one of critical distance: "Our argument in this book is that contemporary biblical scholarship, including even those developments within it that most readily invite the label 'postmodern(ist),' is still fundamentally predetermined and contained by the Enlightenment *épistémè*, and far more that is generally realized."⁴ And we had even more unkind things to say about biblical postmodernism:

> Theory, in the form of a banalized and sloganized postmodernism, was translated into biblical studies as an exhortation to overhaul and refuel the aged methodological engine of the discipline. Theory in this perhaps inevitably narrowed form extended, rather than challenged, the fundamental project of the Enlightenment Bible—however much anti-Enlightenment polemic might feature in biblical postmodernist rhetoric.⁵

We also complained: "The revelation that knowledge of the object (in this case, the biblical text) can only ever be mediated by the subject, and hence objectivity by subjectivity, was trumpeted as a postmodern epiphany in work that was frequently oblivious to how such issues had been hotly-debated ones for philosophy when biblical scholarship was still in its infancy."⁶ And so on.⁷ We were not unaware that our own earlier, postmodernism-besotted selves were spread-eagled on the targets at which we were taking aim.⁸ It is not so much that we were renouncing the postmodernism of our early careers as observing its myopic limitations with the benefit of hindsight. With apologies to the Bard, we had come neither to bury biblical postmodernism nor to praise it. Our entire book was premised on the conviction that it was now high time for a critical look back at the ways in which "theory," generally of the anti-foundationalist type, has been appropriated in biblical studies—"postmodernism" being the term of convenience for that appropriation—and to consider how and why it might be appropriated differently.

Our critical distance on postmodernism is entirely erased in Hendel's account of our project. Our book is a "perspicuous example" of "weak postmodernism" (the good kind, in his mind).⁹ It "construct[s] a postmodern genealogy of our academic

---

³ Ibid., 89.
⁴ Ibid., 48; cf. xi.
⁵ Ibid., 85; cf. 86, 91, 130.
⁶ Ibid., xii; cf. 102, 99–100, 115.
⁷ See also ibid., 90, 123.
⁸ See esp. ibid., 126 n. 104.
⁹ Hendel, "Mind the Gap," 435.

discipline."[10] This is in keeping with Hendel's employment of the term(s) "postmodern(ism)" in his article as a whole. He repeatedly applies "postmodernist" to a congeries of influential thinkers who themselves do not identify with the term. Hendel himself is not unaware of this: "Prominent postmodernists—including Derrida, Foucault, Jacques Lacan, and, in America, Judith Butler—tend to disavow the term 'postmodernism' because it is so heterogeneous. This disavowal is, in a sense, a distinctive postmodern gesture."[11] One could quibble at length with this statement. If Lacan ever had anything to say about postmodernism, it does not seem to have survived; and one has to sift very exhaustively through Derrida's voluminous writings, and even more exhaustively through Foucault's, to find even passing remarks on postmodernism—remarks that amount less to a strategic disavowal than a casual shrug.[12]

It is only Butler who disavows the term "postmodernism" for its heterogeneity. She does so in a 1992 essay that Hendel may know but does not cite. What Butler has to say about the heterogeneity of what is routinely stuffed into the postmodern pigeonhole is worth quoting, at least in part: "A number of positions are ascribed to postmodernism…: discourse is all there is, as if discourse were some kind of monistic stuff out of which all things are composed; the subject is dead, I can never say 'I' again; there is no reality, only representations."[13] These (caricatured) positions correspond roughly to Hendel's "strong" postmodernism. Butler continues:

> These characterizations are variously imputed to postmodernism or poststructuralism, which are conflated with each other and sometimes conflated with deconstruction, and sometimes understood as an indiscriminate assemblage of French feminism, deconstruction, Lacanian psychoanalysis, Foucaultian analysis, Rorty's conversationalism and cultural studies.… It may come as a surprise to some … to learn that Lacanian psychoanalysis in France positions itself officially against poststructuralism, that Kristeva denounces postmodernism, that Foucaultians rarely relate to Derrideans …

and so on.[14] In other words, the term "postmodernism" plasters over significant differences. It is a term of homogenization, of oversimplification. It is a polemical

---

[10] Ibid.

[11] Ibid., 423–24.

[12] For example, Derrida's passing reference to a conference "on 'Postmodernism and Religion'—two things which are foreign to me" (in Catherine Malabou and Jacques Derrida, *Counterpath: Traveling with Jacques Derrida* [trans. David Wills; Cultural Memory in the Present; Stanford, CA: Stanford University Press, 2004], 95).

[13] Judith Butler, "Contingent Foundations: Feminism and the Question of 'Postmodernism,'" in *Feminists Theorize the Political* (ed. Judith Butler and Joan W. Scott; New York: Routledge, 1992), 4.

[14] Ibid.

term, on the one hand, a crudely constructed target against which to loose one's arrows. It is a rallying cry, on the other hand, or a banner under which to march.

Or it *was* a banner and rallying cry, at any rate. Increasingly since the 1990s, biblical scholars, younger scholars especially, who happen to be fluent in the languages of theory, have ceased to appropriate the term "postmodernism" for their projects. This is apparent whether one peruses their dissertations or published work, or whether one haunts the theory ghettos of the SBL at the annual meeting. Postmodernism is not what it used to be, even in biblical studies. As a concept, it has been leaking energy for quite some time.

This renders Hendel's article mysterious to me. All through its first half I found myself wondering, who or what *in biblical studies* is he critiquing? With the beginning of the section titled "Truth or Consequences," it appeared as though the veil was about to be lifted, as Hendel turned to postmodernism in biblical studies.[15] The principal specimen text of biblical postmodernism, for Hendel (indeed, the only example he discusses other than *The Invention of the Biblical Scholar*), is *The Postmodern Bible* (henceforth, *PMB*). Hendel labels as "strong postmodernism" *PMB*'s assertion that biblical interpretation is always necessarily ideological and political.[16] The sole example, however, of biblical exegesis that Hendel highlights from *PMB* is its summary of Charles Copher's argument for a black African presence in the exodus narrative.[17] Hendel characterizes Copher's argument as pseudo-scholarship, and wonders why the authors of *PMB* "endorse this instance of 'resistance reading.'"[18]

My interest in this example, however, lies elsewhere. It is striking to me that Copher's exegetical argument is the only concrete instance of biblical interpretation that Hendel considers in his article on biblical postmodernism. Yet it is an argument that does not present itself as postmodern nor does it rely, however remotely, on the brand of French theory that Hendel is critiquing in his article. The "strong postmodernism," for Hendel, rather resides in the possibility that the *PMB* authors were allowing "a local 'resistance narrative'" to "[trump] the value of truthful scholarship."[19] But Copher's argument is adduced by the authors simply as an illustration of the thesis that scholarship on the exodus narrative has been marred by a "politics of omission" (Clarice Martin's term). That thesis in turn is presented as an important aspect of *Stony the Road We Trod*, the seminal example of African

---

[15] Hendel, "Mind the Gap," 432–34.

[16] Ibid., 430; The Bible and Culture Collective, *The Postmodern Bible* (ed. Elizabeth A. Castelli, Stephen D. Moore, Gary A. Phillips, and Regina M. Schwartz; New Haven: Yale University Press, 1995), 303.

[17] Hendel, "Mind the Gap," 433, which quotes *PMB*, 290, which in turn quotes Charles Copher, "The Black Presence in the Old Testament," in *Stony the Road We Trod: African American Biblical Interpretation* (ed. Cain Hope Felder; Minneapolis: Fortress, 1991), 156.

[18] Hendel, "Mind the Gap," 434.

[19] Ibid.

American biblical hermeneutics, to which Copher (and Martin) contributed. That volume is the first item considered in *PMB*'s subsection on African American Biblical Hermeneutics, which itself occurs in a section titled "Decolonizing Exodus and Conquest." These humdrum contextual considerations make Hendel's rhetoric on "bear[ing] false witness about the Bible to African Americans" and "dishonor[ing] the dead [by] provid[ing] them with false 'scriptural tombs'" seem overblown.[20]

Hendel does provoke us to ask, however, why Charles Copher has been dragged into *PMB* in the first place (before being dragged subsequently into this exchange about *PMB*).[21] And Copher is not alone. *PMB*'s chapter on "Ideological Criticism" features an odd-bedfellows cast of politically minded biblical interpreters, none of whom describes his or her project or approach as postmodern, such as Robert Allen Warrior, Norman Gottwald, Renita Weems, Marc Ellis, Ched Myers, and Fernando Belo. Furthermore, "Ideological Criticism" is not a preliminary or early chapter of *PMB* but, rather, its climactic chapter. To this extent, *PMB* performs the same operation that Hendel does, although for different reasons. Like Hendel, *PMB* promiscuously affixes the postmodern sticker to scholars who do not apply it to themselves, and, were their attention to be drawn to it, would likely peel it off.

In retrospect, *PMB* might be said to have been the consummate expression of a "big tent" postmodernism in biblical studies. The fuel that drove *PMB* was uncompromising opposition to historical criticism. Consequently for *PMB*, biblical "postmodernism" was the generic name for criticism that was non–historical-critical.[22] This epitomized a larger phenomenon. As Sherwood and I phrase it in our book, "the wagon train setting off into the sunset of Theory" in the closing decades of the twentieth century "was packed with self-proclaimed dissidents, discontents, refugees, and asylum seekers from the totalitarian state of historical criticism, demanding the right to do something, anything, else...."[23] The overdetermined term "(literary) theory"—and even more the term "postmodernism"—came to stand in some circles for that anything, and everything, else. But the dichotomization of theory and historiography signified by the name "postmodernism" also served to ensure from the outset that the latter's impact on biblical studies would be minimal, given the immense historiographical investments of the discipline.[24]

---

[20] Ibid.

[21] I have a personal investment in this question and the reflections it prompts, as I was one of the ten members of The Bible and Culture Collective that authored *PMB*, and one of its four editors. I do not regret my part in this project or have anything but respect for my colleagues in it. The passage of time, however, has opened perspectives on certain aspects of the volume that were invisible to me at the time of writing.

[22] Most especially, *PMB*'s "postmodernism" was the name for criticism that was ethical or political (e.g., *PMB*, 10–15).

[23] Moore and Sherwood, *Invention of the Biblical Scholar*, 41.

[24] It also served to ensure that tirades against "postmodernist" theory would be few and far between in biblical studies (ibid.)—that of Professor Hendel being the first in quite some time.

Ironically, meanwhile, "even as the wagon train of Theorists was trundling out of historical-critical territory in biblical studies" on its journey of discovery, literary and cultural critics were busy rediscovering history in such forms as colonial discourse analysis (later to be relabeled "postcolonial theory") and New Historicism. These developments, especially the former, would eventually be imported into biblical studies, although not through *PMB*.[25]

PMB's methodological Manichaeism was predicated not on the conviction that historical criticism was destined to disappear[26] but rather on the more modest assumption that historical criticism's disciplinary influence would diminish significantly, would be ever more deeply eroded by the tide now washing over it, "postmodernism" being the term of convenience for that tide. That has not happened, however, which is one reason why postmodernism has ceased in biblical studies to serve as a rallying point, a rallying cry, or a banner under which to march—again rendering Hendel's intervention oddly belated.

Another complication, likewise absent from Hendel's account, is that postmodernism in biblical studies, and also in theology, has split asunder. Through the 1980s and into the 1990s, postmodernism in the theological disciplines was firmly associated with hypersecular sensibilities.[27] In biblical studies, such sensibilities yielded not just *The Postmodern Bible* but also *What Is Postmodern Biblical Criticism?*; *Handbook of Postmodern Biblical Interpretation*; *Postmodern Interpretations of the Bible*; and, completing the circle, *The Postmodern Bible Reader*.[28] Beginning in earnest in the 1990s, meanwhile, academic evangelicals, theologians in particular, were appropriating postmodernism for confessional purposes.[29] At present, the term "postmodern" is far more likely to be found in the title of a work of the latter

---

(The last such attack of note occurred in John J. Collins, *The Bible after Babel: Historical Criticism in a Postmodern Age* [Grand Rapids: Eerdmans, 2005]; see esp. 11–17.) Such theory "has had too little impact, all told, to merit much attention—while the confrontation between historical 'minimalism' and 'maximalism' is frequently the occasion for sell-out duels with pistols at dawn" (Moore and Sherwood, *Invention of the Biblical Scholar*, 41).

[25] Postcolonial studies as such receives no discussion in *PMB*. New Historicism receives two paragraphs (*PMB*, 146).

[26] As the authors make clear (*PMB*, 12).

[27] Mark C. Taylor's *Erring: A Postmodern A/theology* (Chicago: University of Chicago Press, 1984) early set the tone.

[28] See A. K. M. Adam, *What Is Postmodern Biblical Criticism?* (GBS; Minneapolis: Fortress, 2005); *Handbook of Postmodern Biblical Interpretation* (ed. A. K. M. Adam; St. Louis: Chalice, 2000); *Postmodern Interpretations of the Bible: A Reader* (ed. A. K. M. Adam; St. Louis: Chalice, 2001); and *The Postmodern Bible Reader* (ed. David Jobling, Tina Pippin, and Ronald Schleifer; Oxford: Blackwell, 2001). In effect, the latter *Reader* was published as a companion to *PMB*.

[29] See, e.g., *The Challenge of Postmodernism: An Evangelical Engagement* (ed. David S. Dockery; Wheaton, IL: Victor Books, 1995); Brian D. Ingraffia, *Postmodern Theory and Biblical Theology: Vanquishing God's Shadow* (Cambridge: Cambridge University Press, 1996); Millard J. Erickson, *Postmodernizing the Faith: Evangelical Responses to the Challenge of Postmodernism* (Grand Rapids: Baker, 1998). In biblical studies, A. K. M. Adam has bridged the two trajectories,

kind[30] than in the title of a work that unreservedly embraces the French poststructuralism that Hendel critiques in his article. Theory-immersed works[31] in biblical studies, especially, that explicitly bill themselves as "postmodern" are a dying species. This reflects a perception among the authors of such works that the term has outlived its usefulness, that its energies have shifted elsewhere, or simply drained away.

In literary and cultural studies, meanwhile, postmodernism has been on its deathbed for quite some time.[32] It lost its virtue before its vitality, and as early as 1984, when Fredric Jameson argued in an influential essay that would grow into an even more influential book that postmodernism is best construed as the culture of late capitalism.[33] Yet even Jameson's frequently dystopian *Postmodernism, or, The Cultural Logic of Late Capitalism* was not devoid of utopian hope. The very phrase "late capitalism" bespoke a neo-Marxist optimism.[34] But the hour is now even later, and capitalism, despite some nasty shocks to its system, is still quite well, thank you for asking. The challenge for the academic project that Jeffrey Nealon dubs "post-postmodernism" would be that of constructing a theoretical and analytical vocabulary to dialogue meaningfully and incisively on "cultural production in the present moment, where capitalism seems nowhere near the point of its exhaustion."[35] Correspondingly, the more modest post-postmodern challenge in biblical studies, which would also be a post-*Postmodern Bible* challenge, would be that of reappropriating critical and cultural theory anew in an era when unreconstructed historical criticism—now almost as late as capitalism—likewise seems nowhere near the point of its exhaustion. As much as anything, that was what Yvonne Sherwood and I were attempting to do in our modest manifesto.[36]

---

especially in his *Faithful Interpretation: Reading the Bible in a Postmodern World* (Minneapolis: Fortress, 2006), which is more confessional than his *What Is Postmodern Biblical Criticism?*

[30] Works by now too numerous to list, at least in theology, but epitomized by the seven volumes that, to date, have appeared in Baker Academic's The Church and Postmodern Culture series, beginning with James K. A. Smith, *Who's Afraid of Postmodernism? Taking Derrida, Lyotard, and Foucault to Church* (Grand Rapids: Baker Academic, 2006). For an analogous work in biblical studies, see Richard Bauckham, *Bible and Mission: Christian Witness in a Postmodern World* (Grand Rapids: Baker Academic, 2003).

[31] Understanding "theory" here in the admittedly circumscribed sense of poststructuralist or poststructuralist-derived theory (see Hendel, "Mind the Gap," 442).

[32] See Jeffrey T. Nealon, *Post-Postmodernism, or, The Cultural Logic of Just-in-Time Capitalism* (Stanford, CA: Stanford University Press, 2012), x. As he notes, titles of the "What Was Postmodernism?" variety have been in vogue since the 1990s.

[33] Jameson, "Postmodernism, or, The Cultural Logic of Late Capitalism," *New Left Review* 146 (1984): 59–92; idem, *Postmodernism, or, The Cultural Logic of Late Capitalism* (Postcontemporary Interventions; Durham, NC: Duke University Press, 1991).

[34] As Nealon observes (*Post-Postmodernism*, 15).

[35] Ibid.

[36] See esp. Moore and Sherwood, *Invention of the Biblical Scholar*, 115–31.

Response to Ron Hendel

PETER MISCALL
docmiscall@aol.com
2685 S. Dayton Way #182, Denver, CO 80231

GEORGE AICHELE
gcaichele@gmail.com
2248 Shannon Drive, Adrian, MI 49221

RICHARD WALSH
rwalsh@methodist.edu
Methodist University, Fayetteville, NC 28301

A "scientific" interpretation of the world ... might therefore still be one of the *most stupid* of all possible interpretations of the world, meaning that it would be one of the poorest in meaning.... We cannot reject the possibility that *it* [the world] *may include infinite interpretations.*[1]

Ron Hendel's article, "Mind the Gap: Modern and Postmodern in Biblical Studies," is a response to our coauthored *JBL* article "An Elephant in the Room: Historical-Critical and Postmodern Interpretations of the Bible," as well as to the book by Stephen D. Moore and Yvonne Sherwood, *The Invention of the Biblical Scholar: A Critical Manifesto*. In addition, Hendel discusses *The Postmodern Bible*.[2] The article is a thoughtful attempt to further the conversation that we called for in our article and for that we are grateful. We are happy to find points of agreement with Hendel.

---

[1] Friedrich Nietzsche, *The Gay Science: With a Prelude in Rhymes and an Appendix of Songs* (trans. Walter Kaufmann; New York: Vintage, 1974), 335–36, §§373–74 (emphases in original). Nietzsche also describes "science" as "the will to truth" (see ibid., 280–83, §344).

[2] Hendel, "Mind the Gap: Modern and Postmodern in Biblical Studies," *JBL* 133 (2014): 422–43; George Aichele, Peter Miscall, and Richard Walsh, "An Elephant in the Room: Historical-Critical and Postmodern Interpretations of the Bible," *JBL* 128 (2009): 383–404; Moore and Sherwood, *The Invention of the Biblical Scholar: A Critical Manifesto* (Minneapolis: Fortress, 2011); Bible and Culture Collective, *The Postmodern Bible* (ed. Elizabeth A. Castelli, Stephen D. Moore, Gary A. Phillips, and Regina M. Schwartz; New Haven: Yale University Press, 1995); both Moore and George Aichele were among the ten members of the Bible and Culture Collective.

However, he attempts to extend the conversation and to "bridge" the gap between modern and postmodern biblical studies by making a distinction between strong and weak forms of postmodernism.[3] His distinction recognizes varied meanings of the word "postmodernism," a matter we acknowledged in "An Elephant."[4] We rarely use the term ourselves, except as a catch-all for a variety of approaches that are suspicious of "the modern" or "modernism." As Hendel does, we use "postmodernism" to acknowledge (an often squabbling) family of practices. For us this diversity is not a problem. Rather, it is a matter to celebrate.

In contrast, Hendel finds this diversity a "minor" problem inherent in postmodernism's tendency to eschew fixed meaning. Then the minor problem escalates into the issue of how much diversity is acceptable in biblical studies. The impetus seems to be to rule out unacceptable diversity. This trajectory differs markedly from our own.

Further, Hendel leaves postmodernism's bewildering diversity behind and begins to assert more commonality in postmodernism than we would. After acknowledging that his discussion of postmodernism is indebted to the works of Seyla Benhabib, Thomas McCarthy, and others, Hendel cites Benhabib, "If there is one commitment which unites postmodernists from Foucault to Derrida to Lyotard it is the critique of western rationality from the perspective of the margins."[5] Hendel unpacks this "commitment" and orders his article using three categories offered by Benhabib: (1) the illusion of a self-transparent and self-grounding reason; (2) the illusion of a disembedded and disembodied subject; and (3) the illusion of an Archimedean standpoint, situated beyond historical and cultural contingency. This describes three French philosophers as though they embody postmodernism, but there are many differences in the works of these three. These thinkers and other postmodernists do critique Western rationality, but from this it does not follow that they reject the power of reason, and one would have a hard time making a case that any of them does.

Hendel depicts strong postmodernism as marked by radicalism, by "all or nothing" and "either/or" statements. He cites Foucault's article "Nietzsche, Genealogy, Knowledge":

> The historical analysis of this rancorous will to knowledge reveals that all knowledge rests upon injustice (that there is no right, not even in the act of

---

[3] Much of the conversation after "Elephant in the Room" did little more than defend the opposed fortifications of modernist and postmodernist camps. The exceptions are those, like Hendel, who have tried to find some agreed middle ground. For another example, see William John Lyons, who rephrases historical criticism as a "reception history" that would include forms of postmodern criticism ("Hope for a Troubled Discipline: Contributions to New Testament Studies from Reception History," *JSNT* 33 [2010]: 217–20).

[4] Aichele et al., "Elephant in the Room," 385.

[5] We wrote this response to an earlier draft of Hendel's article, so we limit our quotations of him, for the most part, to his quotations of others.

knowing, to truth or a foundation for truth) and that the instinct for knowledge is malicious (something murderous, opposed to the happiness of mankind).[6]

For Hendel, this example typifies all-or-nothing postmodernism, which he constructs as rejecting all rational practices. However, Foucault's words do not seek to dispense with the "will to knowledge," but to assert that it is not benevolent. Foucault's essay describes the power inherent in the uses of reason, and it criticizes the ideal (suggested by Hendel) of any rational methodology as a gradual accumulation of "self-correcting" truths.

Hendel's weak postmodernism acknowledges reason's cultural embeddedness, entanglements with power and interest, and embodied, practical nature. We agree. But then he asserts that reason is self-correcting and that it advances "one plank at a time."[7] Here we can agree only with the "(strong) postmodern proviso" that the one plank, once put in place, can always shift or break. For Foucault and for us there is no guarantee that the paradigm will not shift and knowledge once attained will not be challenged and altered or even rejected at some future point. And if there is no final or absolute right to truth, then all knowledge does rest on injustice. After all, if reason is entangled with power, as Hendel says, how could it be anything but unjust? This does not assert that there are no differences in types of knowledge and degrees of certitude, but it is a necessary reminder that no act of knowing, no truth, is ever fully free of a charge of injustice.

As he contrasts strong and weak postmodernisms, Hendel decries the self-contradiction of a critique of Western rationality that is carried out within the very structures of that rationality; of philosophers who declare the subject dead but only as subjects; and of a claim that there are only local perspectives, when that can only be known from the perspective of a general reason. But for philosophers such as Michel Foucault, Jacques Derrida, or Jean-François Lyotard, a central predicament is their awareness that at every stage their projects are carried out within the frameworks that they are critiquing or deconstructing. They explicitly recognize the self-contradictions and aporias that haunt their writings.

In our earlier article, we noted the parasitical relation of postmodernism to modernism:

> Thus, postmodernism is not something "other" than modernism, as though they were two distinct historical eras or philosophical movements. Postmodernism cannot exist apart from modernism. Nevertheless, postmodernism does not uncritically accept the modern myth or its inclusions and exclusions. As noted previously, the basic mode of postmodernism is that of suspicion, and this includes, indeed it foregrounds, critical self-suspicion. It resists the desire

---

[6] Foucault, "Nitezsche, Genealogy, History," in *Language, Counter-Memory, Practice* (trans. Donald F. Bouchard and Sherry Simon; Ithaca, NY: Cornell University Press, 1977), 163; Hendel, "Mind the Gap," 425.

[7] Hendel, "Mind the Gap," 426.

for mythic metanarratives and prefers instead a multiplicity of partial, little narratives.[8]

A parasite exists next to or within its host.[9] Indeed, as Lyotard claims (and as we quoted him in our essay), the postmodern "would be that which, *in the modern*, puts forward the unpresentable in presentation itself."[10] Hendel cites Lyotard's book but ignores this clear definition of the postmodern.

Discussing Benhabib's third category, the illusion of an Archimedean standpoint,[11] Hendel comments that the postmodern absence of a transcendental foundation has the dire consequence of the endless conflict between local perspectives. He cites Lyotard to bolster the point:

> I define *postmodern* as incredulity toward metanarratives.... To the obsolescence of the metanarrative apparatus of legitimation corresponds, most notably, the crisis of metaphysical philosophy and of the university institution which in the past relied on it.[12]

For Hendel, the demise of metanarratives leaves the postmodernists with no ground in "general reason" for conversation; therefore, "to speak is to fight, in the sense of playing, and speech acts fall within the domain of a general agonistics."[13]

Here we and Hendel clearly disagree. While we acknowledge (above) our preference for "partial, little narratives" and our resistance to "the desire for mythic metanarratives," we do not agree that this leaves no room for the use of reason. It troubles us that Hendel, in his focus on struggle, sets aside Lyotard's immediate qualification of "fight" with the phrase, "*in the sense of playing.*" Indeed, Lyotard refers repeatedly to game theory in his book. Play is of crucial importance to us, as we said, "Postmodernism uncovers unlimited semiosis, an endless play of intertextual signification.... This is a disturbing thought to modernist critics, for whom postmodern *jouissance* is too playful."[14] Would we and Hendel be in more agreement if we focused on scholarly agons as *playful*?

In this analysis of little, local narratives and endless struggle, Hendel also

---

[8] Aichele et al., "Elephant in the Room," 397–98.

[9] See Michel Serres, *The Parasite* (trans. Lawrence R. Schehr; Baltimore: Johns Hopkins University Press, 1982).

[10] Lyotard, *The Postmodern Condition: A Report on Knowledge* (trans. Geoff Bennington and Brian Massumi; Minneapolis: University of Minnesota Press, 1984), 81 (emphasis added).

[11] Hendel's second category, the illusion of a disembodied subject, leads him to the radical claims of "the death of the subject" by philosophers such as Foucault and Derrida. We devoted only two sentences to this massive topic in our article: "Postmodernism dismantles the modern concept of the individual, treating the self as yet another narrative. As Foucault and others have shown, it is modernity that creates the individual self and our knowledge of the self" ("Elephant in the Room," 398–99). The topic has little to do with the thesis of our article.

[12] Lyotard, *Postmodern Condition*, xxiv.

[13] Ibid., 10, cited by Hendel, "Mind the Gap," 429.

[14] Aichele et al., "Elephant in the Room," 399.

weaves a concern with, using Benhabib's phrase (and parodying Fredric Jameson), "the prison house of perspectives," which he terms "hard perspectivalism."[15] For us this topic demands a study far beyond the bounds of Hendel's article or our response. Nevertheless, we note that, as part of his development of weak postmodernism, Hendel echoes his previous call for patient, rational work that will lead piecemeal to more, better warranted knowledge.

Before turning to Moore's and Sherwood's work,[16] Hendel proposes to look at the varieties of postmodernism in biblical studies, but in fact he discusses only one work, *The Postmodern Bible*—which he sees as an example of strong postmodernism—and then only one example from it. In an article entitled "The Black Presence in the Old Testament," Charles Copher claims that Moses, Zipporah, Aaron, and Miriam were all black.[17] The claim is challenged by Michael Joseph Brown in his monograph *Blackening the Bible: The Aims of African American Biblical Scholarship*, who dismisses Copher's argument as unconvincing.[18] Hendel is interested not in Copher's claim but in the fact that the authors of *The Postmodern Bible* endorse the claim, even though it has been seriously challenged, as an example of resistance or ideological reading.

The example of Copher is cited in the chapter on ideological reading, one of seven interpretive approaches exemplified in *The Postmodern Bible,* and the example is one of several in the chapter. Hendel asks whether the authors are incompetent scholars and did not do their homework on the status of Copher's claims. He opts for an even more damning conclusion that the authors deliberately endorsed the "nonsense" in order to promote a local narrative resisting white European racism. In fact, he suggests that strong postmodernism, because it lacks transcendental foundations, necessarily leads to a preference for consequences over truths.

For the sake of argument, let us grant that Copher's claim has no solid textual or historical support, as Brown maintains. The claim must be challenged not by an appeal to some transcendental foundation, which Hendel admits does not exist, but by patient, "one plank at a time" literary and historical argument and evidence. Further, one "bad example" does not nullify the whole book or postmodern approaches more generally. In fact, to dismiss postmodernist approaches on the basis of one bad example smacks of all-or-nothing thinking.

Hendel is critiquing the strong postmodernism of *The Postmodern Bible* and

---

[15] Hendel, "Mind the Gap," 430, citing Benhabib, "The Liberal Imagination and the Four Dogmas of Multiculturalism," *Yale Journal of Criticism* 12 (1999): 409; see also Jameson, *The Prison-House of Language* (Princeton: Princeton University Press, 1972).

[16] Since Moore will also be responding to Hendel's remarks, we make no attempt to respond to his critique of Moore and Sherwood's book.

[17] Copher, "The Black Presence in the Old Testament," in *Stony the Road We Trod: African American Biblical Interpretation* (ed. Cain Hope Felder; Minneapolis: Fortress, 1991), 146–64.

[18] Brown, *Blackening of the Bible: The Aims of African American Biblical Scholarship* (African American Religious Thought and Life; Harrisburg, PA: Trinity Press International, 2004).

its all-or-nothing stance: interpretations are all "power plays" and "enactments of domination,"[19] and we would respond as we did previously. This does not deny the many differences in the status of interpretive claims, but it does emphasize that the most unobjectionable interpretation can still be looked at through the lens of power and domination, especially when that interpretation is presented as "true."

We agree with Hendel that we have an obligation to tell the truth as we see it, and not to "doctor" it in ways that we would prefer. It is more important for people to see biblical texts as flawed human products than it is to "rescue" them for some ideological purpose. We too deplore anyone who would make these texts more politically correct, but we also recall that liberal activists are not the only ones to succumb to such temptations. How many historians have arranged their interpretation of a text to suit theological or political expediency? (In some respects, this is precisely Foucault's point.) The scholar also has an obligation to own up to her own preconceptions and biases, as well as the consequences of her judgments. As scholars we should acknowledge the inescapable limitations on our understanding and admit that other understandings are also possible.

This brings us back to what is a major sticking point between us and Hendel, the attitude toward diversity in interpretation. We are trying to create a space for more acceptance of diversity in biblical studies. In our original article, we stressed postmodernism's diversity and rejection of "final interpretations":

> Other readings are always possible, and often invited. Postmodernism does not reject the need for rigor in the analysis of actual texts, but it does call for the acknowledgment of one's approach, including its underlying assumptions and its goals and limitations.[20]

Thus, where Hendel wants to build up certain results piecemeal, we would prefer, like Nietzsche, to dismantle our assumptions one at a time, or, at least, to consider their intellectual and political consequences. Even the most assured results—however rational or "scientific"—are subject to further questioning (see the epigraph to this response).

While we applaud Hendel's attempt to further the conversation, we would like to focus the conversation on an acceptance of diversity, built on postmodern rejection of final interpretations and recognition of the need to lay out one's approach and assumptions honestly and patiently. We do not wish to focus the conversation on large-scale theoretical issues of postmodernism, but we do not think that Hendel's distinction between strong and weak postmodernism adequately accounts for the gap between modernists and postmodernists. Hendel's weak postmodernism is practically identical to modernism—that is, the ideology that drives historical criticism of the Bible (and has done so for two hundred years or more). This seems to

---

[19] Hendel, "Mind the Gap," 432, quoting *Postmodern Bible*, 131.
[20] Aichele et al., "Elephant in the Room," 384.

rename all historical-critical scholars as weak postmodernists and, more importantly, to dismiss most postmodernists as radical and illogical (both of which seem more important descriptions in Hendel's analysis than "strong"). If that is the case, it would then follow that there is little point in further discussion.

We are not denying the need for evidence and argument in interpretation; we are not supporting an everything-goes approach. We also recognize that interpretive claims, whether small scale or large scale, have a wide range of relationships to biblical texts. One plausible interpretation can be distinguished from another in terms of the amount and strength of both evidence and argument. And all of these interpretations with their evidence and arguments are open to challenge even at the most theoretical levels. We agree with Hendel that we can critique and modify our arguments and truths.[21]

To be sure, a particular study using a "postmodern" method, for example, narrative, ideological, or feminist criticism, can still be modernist in its claims to a final account, an assured and agreed on interpretation. This is unfortunate, in our view. We are concerned with methods and practitioners who celebrate diversity within and between approaches and do not seek to control or contain scholarship with a metanarrative or an overarching method. Practitioners of a given strategy may themselves have quite different concepts of what counts within that strategy. Evidence or "facts" and argument are theory laden; they may have little or no meaning or weight outside of a given approach. And, to go back to Lyotard, there is no metanarrative, no grand, overarching method, to unite the different interpretive strategies or to decide that one is better than another or that one is best of all. We all have partial, little methods, and as scholars, as readers and interpreters, we will propose a wide variety of readings and then, in a hopefully playful agonistics, we will fight over them, rework them, and argue for their "truth" over against the views of others.

By now it should be apparent that we are speaking only of postmodernism with no distinction between strong and weak varieties, and we distinguish postmodernism and modernism while noting the parasitical relationship that the former has with the latter. Postmodernism exists at once with, within, and against modernism. Postmodernism is not upset by paradox; indeed, it thrives on paradox. It is reason that tells me that reason is always limited, ideologically bound, based on fallible knowledge—but that is all the reason that I have. Further, "I" say that "I" think or do various things, but that does not keep "me" from being an assemblage,

---

[21] Our position is not unlike that expressed recently by James G. Crossley: "This may well lead to scholarship of the sort some of us hate, love, are indifferent towards, think ridiculous, and so on, but such is the price of free thinking and freedom of speech" ("Essay: An Immodest Proposal for Biblical Studies," *Relegere: Studies in Religion and Reception* 2 [2012]: 176), available online at http://www.relegere.org/index.php/relegere/article/viewFile/515/473 (accessed September 8, 2012).

a fiction. This does not keep my freedom and creativity from being useful ways to think and speak. Finally, truth is always my truth (the truth of a fiction!), a local, little truth, no matter how universal I may say that it is—and so is every truth. To recognize that I see only part of the picture does not require or imply that I see the whole picture, or even that there *be* a whole picture. Indeed, I can only learn other truths by making them my truth. Even if we find some commonality between our various truths, we can never know that with any certainty.

Although Hendel for his part makes no statement of or systematic attempt to defend any historical-critical theory, to judge from his words such a theory is indistinguishable from weak postmodernism (and thus does not require separate treatment): reason as self-critical, the integral self retained as freedom/agency, and optimistic ("soft"?) perspectivalism. Furthermore, Hendel thinks that no transcendental standpoint is possible, that we are always limited by perspective, as are our truths. We call this postmodernism. Perhaps "the gap" between us is not so wide after all? In any case, we thank Professor Hendel for his thoughtful response to our essay, and, despite our disagreements with him, we regard his statement as a valuable contribution to a conversation among biblical scholars such as we have called for.

Invaluable Resources from Authors You Trust

From Crisis to Christ:
A Contextual Introduction to the New Testament
9781426751042   August 19, 2014 $39.99

Why Salvation?
Reframing New
Testament Theology
9781426756993
$29.99

The Abingdon
Introduction to the Bible:
Understanding Jewish
and Christian Scriptures
9781426751073
$39.99

The New Testament:
Methods and Meanings
9781426741906
$39.99

The Dead Sea Scrolls
9780687494491
$29.99

Abingdon Press
AbingdonPress.com | 800.251.3320

Visit
AbingdonAcademic.com to learn more
and request an exam copy today.

NEW FROM B&H ACADEMIC

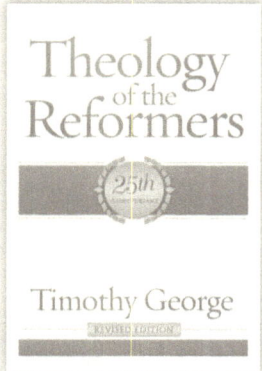

Theology of the Reformers
Revised Edition by Timothy George

"Timothy George's *Theology of the Reformers* is a masterpiece of penetrating theological analysis and lucid historical narrative. This classic study of sixteenth-century Protestant theology (with a new chapter devoted to William Tyndale) deserves to be rediscovered by a new generation of Reformation scholars and students."

—SCOTT MANETSCH, Professor of Church History and Christian Thought, Trinity Evangelical Divinity School

9780805401950, 432 pgs, PB, $29.99

Preaching the Farewell Discourse
L. Scott Kellum

"A beautiful medley of hermeneutical, exegetical, and homiletical insight. For the preacher preparing sermons on the Farewell Discourse (John 13:31–17:26), this volume will prove invaluable."

—ROBERT L. PLUMMER, professor of New Testament Interpretation, The Southern Baptist Theological Seminary

9781433673764, 368 pgs, PB, $29.99

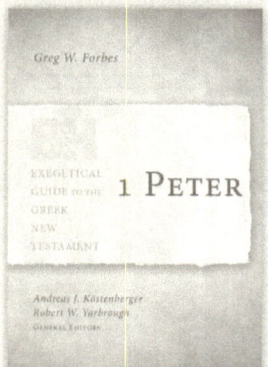

1 Peter EGGNT
Greg W. Forbes

"Forbes leads readers through the text and enables them to navigate their way safely around the various textual, semantic, syntactical, and lexical chasms. The high standard of the EGGNT has been set even higher."

—MICHAEL F. BIRD, Ridley Melbourne College of Mission and Ministry

9781433676024, 232 pgs, PB, $24.99

BECAUSE TRUTH MATTERS
BHAcademic.com

The most comprehensive volume ever produced in defense of the Gospels and Acts.

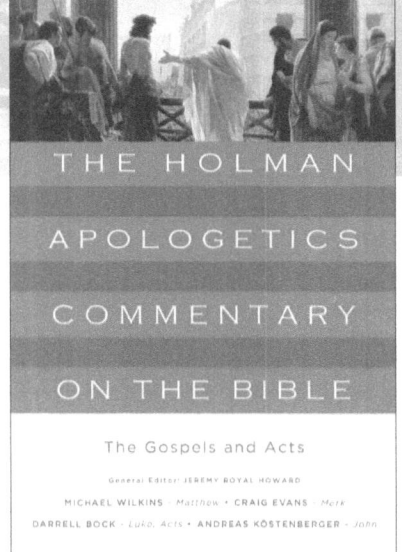

Jeremy Royal Howard
General Editor

Michael J. Wilkins
Matthew

Craig A. Evans
Mark

Darrell L. Bock
Luke, Acts

Andreas J. Köstenberger
John

The primary purpose of the *Holman Apologetics Commentary on the Bible* is to equip readers to defend the reliability of Scripture and the historic evangelical understanding of its teachings. It is designed for use by general readers, though scholars will find it a probing and welcome resource as well. A secondary purpose is to encourage awareness and discussion of Bible difficulties that are not commonly mentioned from the pulpit or even the seminary lectern.

Now available at your favorite bookstore.

BHPublishingGroup.com

New from Mohr Siebeck

Eberhard Bons
Textkritik und Textgeschichte
Studien zur Septuaginta und zum hebräischen Alten Testament
2014. 270 pages (est.) (FAT).
ISBN 978-3-16-150966-7 cloth (May)
eBook

Laurie Brink
Soldiers in Luke-Acts
Engaging, Contradicting and Transcending the Stereotypes
2014. XII, 222 pages (WUNT II/362).
ISBN 978-3-16-153163-7 sewn paper
eBook

Paul J. Brown
Bodily Resurrection and Ethics in 1 Cor 15
Connecting Faith and Morality in the Context of Greco-Roman Mythology
2014. XV, 312 pages (WUNT II/360).
ISBN 978-3-16-153038-8 sewn paper
eBook

John J. Collins
Scriptures and Sectarianism
Essays on the Dead Sea Scrolls
2014. 350 pages (est.) (WUNT).
ISBN 978-3-16-153210-8 cloth (May)
eBook

John Granger Cook
Crucifixion in the Mediterranean World
2014. 500 pages (est.) (WUNT).
ISBN 978-3-16-153124-8 cloth (April)
eBook

Werner Eck
Judäa – Syria Palästina
Die Auseinandersetzung einer Provinz mit römischer Politik und Kultur
2014. 340 pages (est.) (TSAJ).
ISBN 978-3-16-153026-5 cloth (April)
eBook

Benjamin A. Edsall
Paul's Witness to Formative Early Christian Instruction
2014. 310 pages (est.) (WUNT II).
ISBN 978-3-16-153048-7 sewn paper (April)
eBook

Reinhard Feldmeier
Der Höchste
Hellenistische Religionsgeschichte und biblischer Gottesglaube
2014. 520 pages (est.) (WUNT).
ISBN 978-3-16-152718-0 cloth (May)
eBook

Ferdinand Christian Baur und die Geschichte des frühen Christentums
Hrsg. v. Martin Bauspieß, Christof Landmesser u. David Lincicum
2014. 400 pages (est.) (WUNT).
ISBN 978-3-16-150809-7 cloth (May)
eBook

Gösta Gabriel
***enūma eliš* – Weg zu einer globalen Weltordnung**
Pragmatik, Struktur und Semantik des »Lieds auf Marduk«
2014. 500 pages (est.) (ORA 12).
ISBN 978-3-16-152872-9 cloth (May)

Konrad Hammann
Hermann Gunkel – Eine Biographie
2014. XII, 439 pages.
ISBN 978-3-16-150446-4 cloth

Mohr Siebeck
Tübingen
info@mohr.de
www.mohr.de

Information on Mohr Siebeck eBooks:
www.mohr.de/ebooks

New from Mohr Siebeck

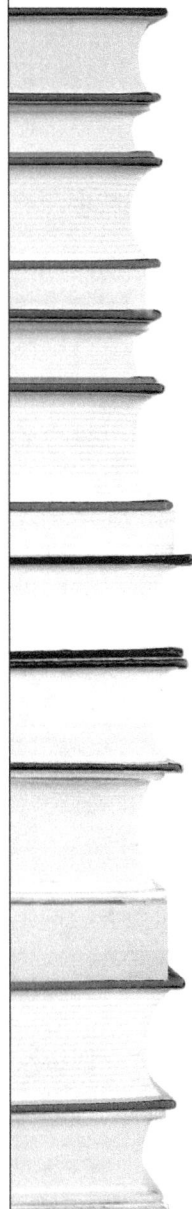

Meghan Henning
Educating Early Christians through the Rhetoric of Hell
»Weeping and Gnashing of Teeth« as *Paideia* in Matthew and the Early Church
2014. 420 pages (est.) (WUNT II).
ISBN 978-3-16-152963-4
sewn paper (May)
eBook

Jesus, Paulus und die Texte von Qumran
Hrsg. v. Jörg Frey u. Enno Edzard Popkes
2014. 440 pages (est.) (WUNT II).
ISBN 978-3-16-153212-2
sewn paper (April)
eBook

Literature or Liturgy?
Early Christian Hymns and Prayers in their Literary and Liturgical Context in Antiquity
Ed. by Clemens Leonhard and Hermut Löhr
2014. 230 pages (est.) (WUNT II).
ISBN 978-3-16-153218-4
sewn paper (April)
eBook

Reconsidering the Relationship between Biblical and Systematic Theology in the New Testament
Essays by Theologians and New Testament Scholars
Ed. by Benjamin E. Reynolds, Brian Lugioyo and Kevin J. Vanhoozer
2014. 380 pages (est.) (WUNT II).
ISBN 978-3-16-152719-7
sewn paper (April)
eBook

Heinz-Dieter Neef
Die Prüfung Abrahams
Eine exegetisch-theologische Studie zu Gen 22,1–19
2., rev. ed. 2014. XI, 160 pages.
ISBN 978-3-16-153099-9 sewn paper

Justin Jeffcoat Schedtler
A Heavenly Chorus
The Dramatic Function of Revelation's Hymns
2014. 370 pages (est.) (WUNT II).
ISBN 978-3-16-153126-2 sewn paper (May)
eBook

Die Septuaginta – Text, Wirkung, Rezeption
4. Internationale Fachtagung veranstaltet von Septuaginta Deutsch (LXX.D), Wuppertal 19.–22. Juli 2012
Hrsg. v. Wolfgang Kraus u. Siegfried Kreuzer in Verb. m. Martin Meiser u. Marcus Sigismund
2014. 900 pages (est.) (WUNT).
ISBN 978-3-16-152653-4 cloth (April)
eBook

Samson Uytanlet
Luke-Acts and Jewish Historiography
A Study on the Theology, Literature, and Ideology of Luke-Acts
2014. 340 pages (est.) (WUNT II).
ISBN 978-3-16-153090-6
sewn paper (May)
eBook

Mohr Siebeck
Tübingen
info@mohr.de
www.mohr.de

Information on Mohr Siebeck eBooks:
www.mohr.de/ebooks

top scholarship made available by
BAYLOR UNIVERSITY PRESS

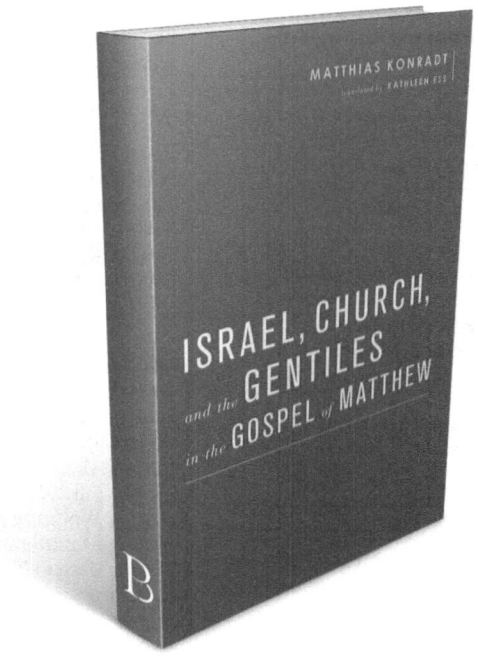

by MATTHIAS KONRADT

"…a new foundation for all future work on the crucial topic of Israel and the Church in Matthew's Gospel."

—DALE C. ALLISON, JR.,
Richard J. Dearborn Professor of New Testament,
Princeton Theological Seminary

B
baylorpress.com

www.ingramcontent.com/pod-product-compliance
Lightning Source LLC
Chambersburg PA
CBHW021402290426
44108CB00010B/346